Penguin Education

KU-514-564

Third World
Employment
Problems and Strategy

Edited by Richard Jolly, Emanuel de Kadt, Hans Singer
and Fiona Wilson

Penguin Modern Economics Readings

General Editor

B. J. McCormick

Advisory Board

K. J. W. Alexander
R. W. Clower
G. R. Fisher
P. Robson
J. Spraos
H. Townsend

Michael Maddle

Third World Employment
Problems and Strategy
Problems and Strategy

Selected Readings

Edited by Richard Jolly, Emanuel de Kadt,
Hans Singer and Fiona Wilson

Penguin Education

Penguin Education
A Division of Penguin Books Ltd,
Harmondsworth, Middlesex, England
Penguin Books Inc, 7110 Ambassador Road,
Baltimore, Md 21207, USA
Penguin Books Australia Ltd,
Ringwood, Victoria, Australia

First published 1973
This selection copyright © Richard Jolly, Emanuel de Kadt, Hans Singer,
Fiona Wilson, 1973
Introduction and notes copyright © Richard Jolly, Emanuel de Kadt, Hans Singer,
Fiona Wilson, 1973
Copyright acknowledgement for items in this volume
will be found on page 448

Made and printed in Great Britain by
Cox & Wyman Ltd, London, Reading and Fakenham
Set in Monotype Times

This book is sold subject to the condition that
it shall not, by way of trade or otherwise, be lent,
re-sold, hired out, or otherwise circulated without
the publisher's prior consent in any form of
binding or cover other than that in which it is
published and without a similar condition
including this condition being imposed on the
subsequent purchaser

Contents

Introduction

Unemployment is increasingly emerging as the most striking symptom of inadequate development in most countries of the Third World. In many countries, open unemployment in the urban areas now affects 15–25 per cent of the labour force and often much higher percentages of persons aged fifteen to twenty-four. Even larger fractions of the labour force, urban as well as rural, are underemployed – in the sense of lacking the resources and opportunities for increasing their incomes to levels comparable to those of persons with urban jobs in the modern sector (or even to levels comparable to what could generally be achieved throughout the country).

The proportions affected by these employment problems often far exceed the rates of unemployment in the industrialized countries at the worst periods of the depression in the 1930s. But in the Third World today, the problem is chronic, not cyclical. A general upturn in world trade might help but would not fundamentally solve the underlying imbalances. Moreover, because growing unemployment in the developing countries occurs at a time of comparative and sustained prosperity in the developed countries, the contrasts between the rich and poor nations of the world are more sharply revealed. To the extent that this has increased consciousness of the need for fundamental reform within the world economy, the widening gap may have been beneficial. Nevertheless, the reluctance of the rich countries to make more than marginal concessions has in many areas led to a growing polarization of attitudes and interests.

The problem of employment in the Third World is in reality a range of related problems, some more serious, some less serious, most extending well beyond the groups directly affected by open unemployment. The danger of judging the employment situation in the Third World by concepts and measures of unemployment derived from the rich countries is increasingly recognized. Readings in Part One of this volume identify the different dimensions of the employment problem found in most developing countries, in particular;

1. The shortage of work opportunities.
2. The underemployment and underutilization of labour in addition to open unemployment.
3. Attitudes and job expectations, particularly amongst the young and educated, which are often sharply at variance with the work available and with the jobs of priority for accelerating national development.

By most of these measures the proportion of the labour force severely affected by 'employment problems' greatly exceeds the percentage openly unemployed.

Closely related to the problems of employment is the question of income distribution, both in the sense of the share of income which different groups of the population receive and in terms of the proportion of the whole population living on or below the margins of real poverty. Some have argued that the problem of poverty is so central that any separate concern with employment problems is misleading. Although this view seems too extreme to accept in its entirety, there is no doubt in our minds that adequate analysis of the employment problem must keep the connections with incomes and income distribution clearly in focus at every stage of the analysis.

A major feature of unemployment in the Third World is its concentration among the young and educated. In almost all the twenty or so Third World countries for which data exist, the rate of open unemployment among persons aged fifteen to twenty-four is double or more the rate among the labour force as a whole (Turnham and Jaeger, 1971).

These proportions are the reverse of those of unemployment in the industrialized countries in the 1930s which was concentrated among older and mature workers and relatively light among the very young. In part, this concentration of unemployment among the younger age groups reflects the disproportionate numbers of younger persons within the whole population, in turn the result of the rapid rates of population growth and labour force over the last two decades. Yet the high proportion of young persons among the unemployed also reflects the rapid expansion of education, which each year encourages larger numbers of school leavers to aspire to urban wage earning jobs far in excess of the number of openings available – leading thousands of young persons into a demoralizing delay before they are able to adjust to the realities of the job market either to take what is going in the way of a wage earning job or to make what they can of self-employment. But whatever the causes of the concentration of unemployment among the younger age groups its significance for future economic development, as well as for political and social stability, is enormous, since persons under twenty-five often comprise a high proportion of the literate and most go-ahead sections of the total population.

In a social sense, however, unemployment in many developing countries, even in the urban areas, is less serious a personal problem than in industrial societies where most of the labour force is now largely dependent on wage-earning income, and where traditional family structures have been almost entirely replaced by the nuclear family. In many areas of the Third World, those seeking an urban job can still rely on relatives for food and shelter or for a chance to return to the family farm if their urban ambitions are frustrated. Moreover, the very meaning of seeking work – on which the statistics of open unemployment depend – to some extent reflects attitudes and ambitions for a *particular type* of working life, often in a wage-earning white-collar job, rather than the total *lack* of an alternative source of income or economic activity.

There are also major differences between the causes of unemployment in the Third World and in the industrialized countries. In industrialized countries, a major cause of underutilization of labour is deficiency of aggregate demand – leading in turn to inadequate job opportunities and involuntary idleness for a section of the labour force able, qualified and willing to work. In the developing countries, there is a range of employment problems, not one, and a wide range of causes, inadequate demand, deficiencies of supply, mismatching between employment opportunities and individual expectations and abilities, inadequate institutions and market distortions, both inside the country and internationally. Such factors also operate, of course, in the developed countries, but in the less developed countries debilitating disease, worm infestation, inadequacies of skills and knowledge, misplaced attitudes and incentives, lack of land, tools and other necessary inputs are often the *prime* causes of underutilization of labour, of underemployment and of low incomes. Even when aggregate demand is deficient, the causes for this can often be traced back to structural distortions in the domestic or world economy or in relations between the two.

There are other structural weaknesses on the supply side, particularly in the rural areas, which should be mentioned. Gross inequalities in land ownership exist in many developing countries to such an extreme that many families have insufficient to provide adequate work or income, given their poor access to capital and lack of knowledge of current technologies. At the same time, large land-holdings are often underutilized. And more generally, inequities in the terms of trade, in the availability of transport and in other relationships with the urban areas and the world abroad are such as to deprive the typical peasant of many opportunities for using his energies and talents to best advantage.

In summary, we may emphasize three major conclusions about the nature of the employment problem in the Third World. First, it has a number of dimensions, many affecting much larger proportions of the labour force than did open unemployment in the industrialized countries in the worst phases of the Great Depression. Second, the causes of the employment problem are very broad, much more than simply inadequate demand. Indeed, as the readings of this volume will indicate, to trace through the various causes rapidly leads to an analysis which involves the whole socio-economic structure and touches on almost every element of development strategy. Finally, although the circumstances of the employed and the unemployed may differ less sharply in the developing countries than in industrialized countries the human circumstances of increasing numbers of *both* the unemployed and the employed in terms of poverty and growing frustration are increasingly serious – and increasingly seen to differ sharply from general conditions in the richer countries (though the richer countries, too, have marginal groups living on the edge of real poverty). There is an urgent need for action both by major changes in domestic policy and in terms of relationships between the rich and poor countries of the world.

Three economic models of unemployment

In the last two decades the literature of economics has approached the problem of employment in developing countries in two ways: by constructing formal models and by empirical analysis. The formal models have essentially been of three types: (a) models concerned with the transfer of labour from rural to urban areas or from the subsistence to the modern sector, (b) models focused on the growth of output and employment, and (c) models concerned with factor price disequilibrium particularly in relation to the employment of labour in relation to some quantity of capital, land and other resources. Empirical analyses have been more eclectic in approach, analysing whatever variables the investigator thought to be important with whatever data and tools of analysis he had at hand. There was, of course, some sort of model underlying this more factual analysis but such models were usually partial and not explicit.

How adequate are the formal economic models as a starting point for analysing the current situation?

Probably the most well known of the employment models is that of Arthur Lewis (1954, 1958), later refined, possibly over-formalized by Fei and Ranis (1964). In the Lewis–Fei–Ranis model, the underdeveloped economy comprises two sectors – the agricultural, subsistence sector characterized by surplus labour, and an industrial, modern sector into which labour from the subsistence sector is gradually transferred. The focus of the model is both on the process of transfer and on the growth of employment in the modern sector. Both transfer and labour absorption in the modern sector take place at a rate which is given by the rate of capital accumulation in industry which in turn is given by the excess of profits over wages, on the assumption that 'capitalists' re-invest the entire surplus. The level of wages in the industrial sector in the original Lewis model is assumed constant, fixed as a proportion of the subsistence level of wages in the traditional sector. As the transfer of labour proceeds, unemployment (or underemployment) in the rural sector would be reduced as employment in the modern industrial sector increases.

Already we may note, with the benefit of hindsight, two key assumptions of the model which seem sharply at variance with the situation in most developing economies. First, the model assumes surplus labour in the rural areas, full employment in the urban. Contemporary research suggests that in many developing countries almost exactly the opposite is true: considerable open unemployment exists in the urban areas but almost no *general* surplus labour in the rural. (Seasonal surpluses of rural labour are widespread and some surplus labour may exist in countries where rural population–land ratios are extremely high or land ownership extremely unequal.) Second, the Lewis model assumes constant real wages, until the point where surplus labour in the rural areas disappears. The typical situation in developing countries has been for urban real wages to rise considerably, both absolutely and relative to rural living standards, even in the presence of open unemployment.

Such criticisms should however not disguise the fundamental contribution of this model in emphasizing two major elements in the problem: the differences between the rural and urban sectors and the enormous significance of the transfer of labour between them.

These two elements have recently been developed along new lines by Todaro (Reading 8), in a model which formalizes the individual decision to migrate as a function of the *expected* gains from migration. Expected gains are measured by the *difference* in real incomes between rural and urban work and the *probability* of a new migrant obtaining an urban job.[1] Though simple, this model marks an important advance on the mechanism of labour transfer in the earlier Lewis model, which was essentially assumed to take place only to the extent that new jobs were created, with only a marginal difference between rural and urban incomes (sufficient to offset the real and psychic costs of urban life and overcome any frictional reluctance to move). In formal terms, the Lewis mechanism of labour transfer can be seen as an extreme case, (no difference in real incomes, 100 per cent probability of finding a job) of the more general Todaro model.

Although one can criticize the Todaro model of labour transfer for assuming a too simple and exclusively economic motivation for migration, its great strength lies in this simplicity and in incorporating in a form easily quantified a major driving force of migration, even if it is not the only driving force.

1. To be fair, particularly to a number of anthropologists, it should be made clear that Todaro was by no means the first to posit this relationship. His contribution was primarily in expressing the relationship in algebraic terms and in exploring its broader economic implications.

The second type of employment model is a variant of a basic Harrod–Domar model,[2] with attention focused on the growth of employment rather than of output. This is the model (implicitly or explicitly) most commonly used both in planning the rate of economic growth required to absorb the forthcoming additions to the labour force and in calculating the size of the unemployment gap if such growth is not achieved. Employment growth is related to output either by assuming constant labour–output coefficients or by incorporating productivity assumptions in which the output–labour coefficient increases often steadily and usually exogenously over time. The growth of employment is then essentially a function of the level and change in productivity, the rate of savings and the capital–output ratio.

The growth of the labour force in such models is usually a function of the growth of population, though often calculated with reference to the age structure of the population on the assumption of constant or changing age-specific participation rates. Unemployment is then the gap between the projected labour force supply and the demand given by the projected number of job opportunities.

Perhaps the two greatest weaknesses of this approach often embodied in actual projections are the exogenous treatment of productivity and the assumption of a fixed capital–output ratio. As with the original Harrod–Domar model, assumptions of fixed coefficients almost inevitably create a knife-edge equilibrium path, in which either the unemployment gap steadily widens or, if investment demand sustains a very rapid growth of production, increasing labour shortages give rise to rapid inflation. In principle, such crude assumptions are not necessary and reflect weaknesses of empirical knowledge about more sophisticated relationships rather than the inability of the basic model to incorporate them.

In terms of relevance for analysing developing country problems, a major weakness of the Harrod–Domar approach is its failure to distinguish between the different sectors of a fragmented economy or to be concerned with the transfer of labour between them. It is perhaps better seen as a more complete model of the growth of modern sector employment within the framework of a Lewis type model. Indeed, just as the Lewis mechanism of labour transfer can be seen as a limiting case of the Todaro model, so the Lewis mechanism of capital accumulation and job expansion can be seen to be a special case of accumulation in a simple Harrod–Domar model (assuming a closed economy, no savings from wages, 100 per cent savings by capitalists from profits, all savings invested, a constant capital–labour ratio and decreasing returns).

These criticisms must not lead one to ignore the important insights which

2. Selections from the original presentations and a brilliant introductory essay can be found in Sen (ed.) (1970).

the Harrod–Domar model and its subsequent developments have offered. The model has been generalized both to take account of a number of productive sectors in an economy (very important for employment analysis because of differing labour–output and labour–capital ratios between the different sectors) and to allow for the external influences upon an open economy. These extensions of the original model are not merely at the level of theoretical treatment but have been carried through into operational, computerized models of many economies throughout the Third World.

The third approach in the analysis of unemployment in developing countries has emphasized the results of factor price disequilibrium for resource use and allocation, particularly of employment. Often, this analysis of unemployment has been partial, concentrating on disequilibrium of the factor prices directly related to the operations of the labour market, implicitly assuming that the rest of the economy operates on neo-classical assumptions but without analysing all the implications. Many analysts have made use of this approach but perhaps the most significant are Eckaus in his classic article (1955), and Blaug, Layard and Woodhall (1969) in their recent analysis of educated unemployment in India.[3] Eckaus analyses the effects of factor price disequilibrium with different production functions, showing how in the static case either factor price disequilibrium or limited possibilities for efficiently substituting labour for capital or both, could cause the labour market to fail to clear itself and result in open unemployment.

Blaug, Layard and Woodhall set up a simple dynamic adjustment model, introducing dynamic shifts over time in the demand and supply curves for labour, but simplifying the analysis by concentrating on changes in wages rather than relative factor prices and on educated employment, rather than on unemployment in general. Whereas Eckaus explores the reasons why equilibrium in the labour market may *never* be achieved, Blaug's dynamic analysis shows that even when market forces are tending towards equilibrium, they may operate *too slowly* to eliminate some initial amount of unemployment before dynamic shifts in supply and demand create yet another situation of disequilibrium.

A synthesis

Although it would be possible to continue the detailed criticisms of particular assumptions made in each of the above approaches, it may be more helpful to emphasize the way each of these three approaches contains important elements in a more general framework for analysing the problem. The Lewis–Fei–Ranis approach emphasizes the need to distinguish at least two sectors in the dual economy and to be concerned with the transfer of labour between them. The Todaro model provides a starting point for a

3. A summary of their argument is given in Blaug (Reading 18).

quantitative analysis of this transfer. The Harrod–Domar approach and its subsequent extensions identify important elements for analysing the growth of employment in the modern sector of the economy, if less adequately in the traditional sector. The Eckaus–Blaug approach draws direct attention to the process of adjustment or maladjustment within the labour markets, in relation both to the conditions of production and to relative factor prices. At least at this general level, the particular points on which each author focuses attention all appear to be necessary and complementary parts of a fuller analysis rather than alternatives.

Nevertheless, many of the particular assumptions of the individual models are in conflict and, more fundamentally, the mechanisms of adjustment within each can be extremely different. The Lewis–Fei–Ranis model achieves full employment in time by the transfer of labour from the traditional to the modern sector which follows automatically from self-sustaining growth within the modern sector. The Blaug–Layard–Woodhall model achieves full employment, or at least moves towards the reduction of unemployment, by a reduction in wages set in motion by competition in the labour market. In contrast, the Harrod–Domar model and the Eckaus approach embody the possibility of situations in which adjustment may not be automatic and, in some cases, in which the elimination of unemployment may not be possible. For them, it all depends on the nature of the production functions and the extent to which factor prices and technology are flexible. Their basic models can be extended along varying lines dependent on the particular assumptions which best seem to fit the actual situation.

These underlying mechanisms of adjustment are significant because they lead to very different implications regarding the need for institutional change and government intervention as well as for future prospects. Thus two models (Lewis–Fei–Ranis and Blaug) tend to lead to a more optimistic future prediction in which, after a lag, longer or shorter, unemployment cures itself. The other two models (Harrod–Domar and Eckaus) draw attention to the possibility of underlying conditions which would lead to perpetual unemployment, if not to ever-widening gaps between the forthcoming supply of job seekers and the number of job opportunities created by the economy.

The empirical approach

Rather than continue with further comments on the models, let us now approach the problem from the other side. What are the items which empirical analysts and practitioners have identified as the main causes accounting for different parts of the employment problem as it has been studied in developing countries in different parts of the world? To approach the problem this way is admittedly to run the risk of reaching partial conclusions about causation, but this risk is offset by the benefits of relevance.

In what follows we do no more than touch upon some of the factors brought out in more detail in the readings of this volume. A preliminary survey may however be useful as a guide to what is to come, as an indication of the broad range of factors involved and as a way of underlining those factors of dominating importance.

The first point which emerges strongly from the empirical studies is the important differences which exist in the experience of the employment problem and the interpretation of its causes between different countries and even between different regions and districts within countries. In Ceylon, unemployment among secondary school leavers and university graduates is the dominant part of the problem (dominant, at least in political terms) and urban–rural differences are small. In India, rural open unemployment is much less important than seasonal underemployment. In Colombia the highly unequal system of land tenure has deprived a large proportion of the rural population of sufficient land for adequate work or income and left some of them totally landless. In most African countries there is still no landless class, but often inadequate transport, capital, knowledge, institutional channels and incentives to stimulate full employment and adequate income. Moreover, as noted earlier and developed further in the readings of Part One of this volume, unemployment, underemployment and the other dimensions of employment problems often involve aspects of employment beyond those treated in the basic models. (Almost all the models have omitted explicit consideration of income distribution, let alone specific consideration of incomes of the poorest section of the labour force. And most models draw a sharp dichotomy between employment and unemployment in contrast to empirical work which stresses the importance of a mid zone of low income but still productive employment in the 'informal sector'.)

In spite of such differences in the nature and incidence of employment problems a number of the causes identified are common to many of the empirical analyses. Most studies stress in one way or another the difficulty of reaching full employment created by the rapid rate at which the labour force has been growing. As the readings in Part Two indicate, total population, urban population and the educated population, have each been expanding in most developing countries at unprecedented rates – unprecedented whether by earlier experience within the developing countries or by the standards of the now industrialized countries in their early stages of development. It is not unusual for the population to be growing by 2·5–3·5 per cent per annum, the urban labour force by 6–12 per cent per annum, the stock of educated persons (say with secondary education or above) by 10–15 per cent per annum. Even in a labour market which was fairly flexible and competitive, such rates of growth, mostly far in excess of the growth of output, would raise severe problems of dynamic adjustment. If the growth of work opportunities cannot keep up, it is inevitable that unemployment will arise.

Yet these are merely the measurable elements in the rapid expansion of supply. Less easily measured are the rates at which job aspirations and expectations have been rising in the last decade, in part the result of expanding education but also the consequence of the tremendous spread and influence of mass communications and the automatic quickening of political change. The promises of politicians on the road to Independence in many countries coincided with the spread of individual aspirations for a new job in the wage-earning economy.

The significance of aspirations (and other factors affecting the characteristics of supply, such as education, training, nutrition, etc.) is that they crucially affect the job expectations of the labour force and not merely its aggregate growth. Since part of the employment problem is due to mismatching of work opportunities and expectations, it is important to get to grips with the structural imbalance between demand and supply as well as with disparities in their aggregate rates of growth.

On the demand side, the empirical analysis of job opportunities reveals the tremendous importance of economic structure. Although hinted at in dualistic models of the economy, reality runs far beyond a simple division between a traditional and modern sector. Developing economies display a variety of forms in their crucial structural characteristics: in the nature of their dependence on exports, in the type of land tenure, in the size and characteristics of the government and service sector, of agriculture and industry and the extent of foreign control. All these can directly affect the extent of unemployment and the rapidity with which an economy adjusts to remove it.

As the readings in Part Three make clear, empirical analyses of rural employment have been preoccupied with aspects only cursorily treated, if at all, in the theoretical literature. The theoretical literature has largely concentrated on the extent to which labour could be withdrawn from the rural areas without output falling. Empirical studies of rural employment have stressed the crucial importance of seasonal fluctuations in the demand for labour, in turn closely related to weather, crop patterns, mechanization, the type of seed, and in part the institutional structure of landholding. Far from finding evidence of general labour surplus, most empirical research has tended to emphasize a period of labour scarcity at peak seasons of planting and harvesting. This would suggest that changes in land ownership, crop patterns and mechanization are important for changing the pattern of labour demand throughout the year and are the precondition for permanently withdrawing labour without a reduction in output.

In any case, the real problem is to increase agricultural output and employment, rather than withdraw labour and merely maintain output. The pattern of landholding is of crucial importance for these reasons. In part, it determines what crops can and will be grown. Secondly, it determines how the product is distributed, with effects both on incentives for production and on the extent and the place to which the surplus is re-invested. Third, the pattern of land tenure is important because of its links with the pattern of work-sharing, within the family, the large estate, the commune or the cooperative.

Perhaps the three most emphasized causes of unemployment in the rural sector are the system of land tenure, the invasion of inappropriate technology, and physical deficiencies in the supply of human resources. Quite apart from the inequities in the existing structure of land holding in many countries, particularly in Latin America and Asia, the *rigidity* of land tenure has limited adjustments to the rapid growth of population, often leaving the poorest sections of the population to eke out an income on ever-declining plots of land.

Technology in the rural areas has proved a two-edged sword. The new seeds, new crops and certain types of mechanization (or mechanization at certain seasons) have undoubtedly helped to even out the fluctuations of labour demand over the agricultural year, thereby *increasing* demand in the slack seasons and partially at least helping to eliminate some underemployment. But other parts of mechanization and technology have been labour-saving, *removing* some of the demand for labour by replacing it with tractors, weedicides and other labour-saving methods, often subsidized. Perhaps most important of all have been the effects of technological advance in the rich countries, replacing primary products with synthetics, thereby cutting demand for the basic exports from developing countries and lowering the returns to agriculture in terms of foreign exchange.

In the urban setting technology has played a similar role, particularly in contributing to the slow growth of industrial employment even when manufacturing output has been moving rapidly ahead. (See the Readings in Parts Six and Seven.) But again, the influence of technology goes far beyond its simple effects on production possibilities. The dominance of technology has provided the power for international corporations to establish other forms of dominance, in bargaining over prices, export supplies, the share of profits and the payment of royalties. The superiority of advanced technology has wiped out producers of more traditional products even when competition has been fair, but often in addition the products of the new technologies have been pushed by various forms of advertising, special fiscal concessions and other forms of market intervention usually operated in a way which discriminates against the traditional producer.[4]

Related to these changes in the structure of production have been parallel changes in the structure of consumer demand, reflecting the pattern of income distribution (see Readings in Part Three). Extreme inequalities of income distribution have tended to raise the level of demand for luxury goods, usually the demand for imports and sometimes also the demand for capital-intensive goods domestically produced.

Finally, distortions in factor prices over a wide field have contributed to underutilization of labour and excessive demand for capital and imports. Here empirical work is more closely aligned with the theoretical models. Subsidies to capital, upward pressures on wage rates, downward pressures on agricultural prices, inappropriate exchange rates have all distorted key prices from those required for an efficient use of the available resources.

Common to the analysis of many of the above factors is a strong emphasis in empirical studies on the wide-ranging importance of international influences (see Reading 32 in Part Eight). In some cases, international influence is the direct result of the vast disparities in income and economic power between the rich and poor countries of the world – as for example in the technological power possessed by the industrialized countries, in part the result of the fact that 98 per cent of expenditure on technological research and development in the world takes place outside the Third World. Other analysts however see this form of international influence as simply one part of a much wider structure of dependence. From this viewpoint most countries of the Third World are caught in a complex web of economic, social and political dependence, operating through a wide range of inter-relationships between power groups in the rich countries and key interest groups in the poorer countries, but all combining to produce structures of underdevelopment. The increasing power of the international corporation is an important theme in this analysis. Dependence between the centre and the periphery internationally is under this analysis carried forward into dependence between the centre and the periphery within the developing countries themselves. Many specific aspects of dependence could be analysed – in relation to trade, private overseas investment and aid, many of which seem to operate with a bias against employment generation in developing countries.

The emphasis on interest groups in the international setting is simply one area of such relationships given by general inequalities in power and wealth. A general weakness of many of the empirical analyses, even when they are not bound to a particular economic model, is that they have too often been

4. Moreover both international and internal terms of trade effects operate in ways which suggest that not only may income distribution be worsened but even the level of total national product may be affected.

conducted within a limited framework of economic analysis rather than of political economy. It is true that a few of the Readings give explicit attention to the underlying economic and political interest groups and to their roles in supporting the existing situation or inhibiting the changes necessary to remove rural and urban unemployment. But such analysis in employment studies are, so far at least, the exception rather than the rule and ideally the inclusion of political and social factors should be part and parcel of the analyses of all the factors treated in other Readings. But this is a deficiency which can only be solved by improving the standards of social sciences not simply by more careful selection from existing work.

Poverty, income distribution and the process of adjustment

Apart from identifying crucial elements in the expansion of unemployment, there is a need to analyse the process of adjustment to deal with it. How adequate are the mechanisms of adjustment in the theoretical models when judged by the analysis of the empirical literature?

The theoretical models emphasize two main processes of adjustment: first, capital accumulation and growth of demand in the modern sector, leading to absorption of the supply of labour; second, adjustments in wages (and other factor prices), leading to the use of relatively more labour in relation to other factors of production.

The empirical literature suggests that changes in other factors are of equal if not greater importance. Analysis of a specific case almost always enlarges the range of factors with which policy must be concerned. Empirical work also suggests that changes in the two main factors of the theoretical literature – simple increases in capital accumulation or adjustment in factor prices – will not necessarily lead towards full employment rather than away from it since technology is largely given by the requirements of the rich countries, not by domestic conditions in the poor. Interest groups may defend their present advantages even in situations where the welfare of the majority is diminished; although group attitudes may often adjust to realities, in some circumstances they can be dysfunctional and only make the situation worse. In all these respects, the operation of these variables can take one further from a situation of equilibrium in the labour market.

Even if this were not true, concern with poverty and income distribution raises the possibility that some types of adjustment in the labour market to achieve full employment may not be satisfactory. There is some evidence for example that higher rates of open unemployment lead to lower rates of participation in the labour force or to greater amounts of disguised unemployment (Urrutia, 1968). To the extent that lower participation leads to an inadequate level of income in the families concerned, the market adjustment is not acceptable when judged against social objectives. Similarly, the achievement of an increase in employment by lowering the minimum wage may well not lead to a satisfactory state of income distribution. Since it is often not possible in a less developed country to achieve a subsequent redistribution of income through tax, subsidy, social services or price policy, the achievement of full employment by such labour market adjustments may not be desirable.

Conclusions

It may be worth pausing at this point to see where this introductory discussion has led. In moving from the current economic models to empirical analyses the approach to the employment problem has been broadened in a number of respects. Conceptually 'the employment problem', has been greatly expanded, to become as much a problem of income distribution and poverty as of shortage of work and underutilization of labour. The employment problem has also been disaggregated into its constituent parts, e.g. identifying different types of underutilized labour and different attitudes to work, especially between the educated and the less educated. The closed system of the economic models of unemployment has been opened, to set the analysis more realistically within a highly unequal world economy in which the developing countries are largely at the mercy of rich country power, technology and economic influence. The economist's preoccupation with politically and socially disembodied economic variables has given way to broader analyses taking account of the viewpoints of other disciplines.

It is only too obvious that the simple elegance and coherence of the original models has been lost in this process of widening the frame of analysis. To some extent this is inevitable, if one is to draw upon analyses of unemployment in fundamentally different situations. This could be remedied by recognizing that one seeks not one model but a tool kit of models, each relevant to a particular aspect of the employment problem as it emerges in a particular context. Can such models be created? Hopefully, yes, though there is still a long way to go. But as Lloyd Reynolds concluded:

Before investing much effort in further model-building . . . intensive empirical work . . . is the most urgent task in the state of economic development. Without this, useful analytical models cannot be formulated or tested (1969).

This is the task ahead, as relevant for future theorists as for practitioners striving to grapple with one of the most important development problems of the 1970s. The welfare of perhaps one third of mankind could be affected by how seriously social scientists respond to this challenge and on how willing and able the industrialized countries are to permit a change in the balance of world power and income.

In putting together this collection of readings we have had in mind two types of reader: practitioners of development in both developing and developed countries; and students of development, some of whom will be among the practitioners of the future.

Many of the items chosen have been used in our teaching of study seminars and graduate courses at the Institute of Development Studies and in the University of Sussex. Although we have begun by selecting *economic* readings, it seems obvious to us that the issues involved in unemployment in the Third World go far beyond the confines of economic analysis as traditionally pursued. We have therefore included a number of sociological or political items – and some with no particular disciplinary focus – to help show the wider issues involved.

We owe thanks to a number of people – first to the authors of items included in this volume, for their permission to include them. But we thank also the authors of many other pieces which we have not been able to include but which have stimulated our ideas and influenced our thinking about the subject.

Making the selections has been a joint enterprise amongst the four of us, an important point since we wished to take account of different disciplinary viewpoints. At the final stage of selection and editing, we were greatly helped by Gordon MacKerron. Most of the joint work was done during a week together at Plaw Hatch Hall, a trade union country club and conference centre in Sussex. We are grateful to the staff of Plaw Hatch Hall for what they did to make our time there an enjoyable blend of work and leisure – a good example of the long-run objective for work in all parts of the world. Finally, we would like to thank those who helped with the production of the book, particularly Sue Evans, Caroline Jardine and Molly Beirne of the IDS staff.

References

BLAUG, M., LAYARD, P. R. G., and WOODHALL, M. (1969), *The Causes of Graduate Unemployment in India*, Allen Lane.

ECKAUS, R. S. (1955), 'The factor proportion problem in underdeveloped areas', *Amer. econ. Rev.*, vol. 45 pp. 539–65.

FEI, J. H. C., and RANIS, G. (1964), *Development of the Labor Surplus Economy: Theory and Policy*, Irwin.

LEWIS, W. A. (1954), 'Economic development with unlimited supplies of labour', *Manchester School*, vol. 22, pp. 139–91.

LEWIS, W. A. (1958), 'Unlimited labour: further notes', *Manchester School*, vol. 26, pp. 1–32.

REYNOLDS, L. G. (1969), 'Economic development with surplus labour: some complications', *Oxford econ. Paps*, vol. 21, no. 1.

SEN, A. K. (ed.) (1970), *Growth economics*, Penguin.

TURNHAM, D., and JAEGER, I. (1971), *The Employment Problem in Less Developed Countries*, OECD.

URRUTIA, M. (1968), 'El desempleo disfrazado en Bogota', in *Empleo y Desempleo en Colombia*, CEDE.

Part One
Concepts and Dimensions of the Employment Problem

As the Introduction to this volume makes clear, the employment problem in less developed countries covers much more than the existence of open unemployment, large and growing as this often is. The employment problem is also a matter of insufficiency of work opportunities of particular sorts – especially well paid, secure white-collar jobs and reasonably secure opportunities for self-employment; of underutilized or inefficiently utilized labour resources; and of aspirations for work, particularly among the young and educated, which are often sharply at variance with the type of work available.

Closely related to unemployment is the whole question of income distribution, particularly the levels of income of the poorest sections of the population. The provision of jobs for the unemployed is a necessary but by no means sufficient condition for achieving a more satisfactory distribution of income in a country.

One cannot however simply accept the pattern of work opportunities thrown up by the labour market as it currently operates in many developing countries. Major changes in development strategy will often be required if future growth, particularly in the rural areas, is to improve the living standards of the mass of the population in a rapid and balanced fashion. If these changes in strategy take place, they will alter both the pattern of labour demand and of labour supply.

Reading 1 – from the ILO Mission Report *Towards Full Employment* – illustrates the different dimensions of the employment problem as they appeared in Colombia in 1970, the beginning of the United Nations Second Development decade. Although the selection refers to one country, the approach is more general and the data probably typical of the situation in a number of developing countries. Particularly significant is the estimate that in Colombia open unemployment, the more readily measurable part of the wider employment problem, formed at most about half of the estimated size of the whole employment problem from whatever viewpoint it was approached. But note also the tenuous basis of the statistical estimates of the magnitude of the other parts of the employment problem.

Reading 2 – from an exhaustive review of recent evidence on unemployment by Turnham – gives data on the extent of open unemployment in more than twenty developing countries. These show that in much of the Third World, urban unemployment now approaches levels comparable to those of the worst periods of unemployment in the industrialized countries in the 1930s. Moreover, unemployment in developing countries today occurs at a time of rapid growth in world trade and comparative prosperity in the industrialized countries. One cannot therefore look simply to an expansion in the industrialized economies to cure Third World unemployment.

A major theme in the economic literature on unemployment in developing countries has been concerned with the existence of 'disguised unemployment'. The conceptual and theoretical difficulties of this literature have been increased by differences and confusions in the terminology used by different authors.[1]

Myrdal's classic, *Asian Drama*, includes what is perhaps the most thorough critique of the applicability of Western concepts of employment and unemployment in the context of many developing countries. Part Five and Appendix 6 of his monumental study are essential reading for anyone working in this field, though unfortunately too lengthy to be included in the present selection. Instead, we have included two short pieces, the first by Professor Streeten (Reading 3), one of Myrdal's collaborators on *Asian Drama*, in which he briefly summarizes the arguments against a simple transfer of Western concepts of unemployment to less-developed countries. The main thrust of this piece is a succinct exposition of an alternative approach based on the disaggregation of total employment into key components which are conceptually important and empirically measurable.

Reading 4 by Weeks is a lively attack on the use of conventional concepts of unemployment within the African context. The *general* problem he argues is not unemployment but poverty, not involuntary idleness but marginal income – in part because the vast majority of urban dwellers, though working long hours in a debilitating climate, are burdened by energy-draining diseases and parasites.

It may seem odd that the four readings primarily concentrate on unemployment and underemployment, with no reading on overall employment structure. This is because the main purpose of the Readings in

1. A brief but useful discussion of various concepts of disguised unemployment – and results of attempts to measure it – is Kao, Anschel and Eicher (1964). The International Labour Office published in 1966 a report: *The Measurement of Underemployment: Concept and Methods*, suggesting standard terminology and definitions.

this volume is to direct attention to the shortfalls in employment creation and what can be done about them. But, of course, the issues involved in defining and measuring unemployment are very close to those which arise in defining and measuring the labour force or employment considered separately.

One major practical problem of measuring employment is that an important section of the employed labour force is unenumerated. This is generally true of employment in the 'informal sector' – the mass of small-scale, labour intensive, often one or two person operations in, for instance, tailoring, shoe repair, house building, beer brewing, food preparation and trade. This wide range of activities includes the so-called 'underemployed' street hawkers and shoe-shine boys and is therefore often considered unproductive – though many in fact are very productive and economically highly efficient, in the sense of being well adapted to the local economic environment. Hart (Reading 5) provides a well documented analysis of informal sector employment in Accra which makes clear the danger of examining employment issues without reference to this important and often dynamic sector.

Certain other readings in this volume expand further on concepts and measurement of different parts of the employment problem identified in this section – most notably the readings on population and the labour force, agricultural employment, educated unemployment and unemployment and poverty. The latter is of particular importance because in the last resort, the social urgency of dealing with the problem of employment is so closely related to the objective of abolishing poverty and of improving income distribution.

Reference

KAO, C. H. C., ANSCHEL, K. R., and EICHER, C. K. (1964), 'Disguised unemployment in agriculture: a survey', in C. K. Eicher and L. Witt (eds.), *Agriculture in Economic Development*, McGraw-Hill.

1 International Labour Office

The Nature and Extent of the Employment Problem

From International Labour Office, *Towards Full Employment. A Programme for Colombia*, prepared by an inter-agency team, I L O Geneva, 1970, pp. 15–28, 13–14.

There are three distinct but related dimensions to the employment problem:

1. Many people are frustrated by lack of employment opportunities; they include both those without work and those who have jobs but want to work longer hours or more intensively.

2. A large fraction of the labour force, both urban and rural, lack a source of income both reliable and adequate for the basic needs of themselves and their dependants.

3. A considerable volume of unutilized or underutilized labour forms a potential productive resource, which ought to be brought into use.

Although the term 'unemployment' is most commonly applied to the first of these categories, we cannot ignore the second way in which the employment provided by the economy is inadequate. For in the last resort, the real tragedy of those without jobs is the poverty into which they slip, and which they share with all those with very low incomes. After all, the ultimate object of policy is not just to provide more jobs, but to provide work which is socially productive *and yields enough income for a reasonable standard of living*.

Access to reasonable levels of income has received emphasis as part of the employment problem in recent years, particularly in studies of Latin America and other developing areas,[1] but the justification for this approach should perhaps be spelled out. Raising the incomes of the poor involves many of the same issues as providing work opportunities, when they are regarded as objectives of policy, and to some extent to achieve one is to

1. A recent study by the Organization for Economic Cooperation and Development on employment treated 'the ability to earn an adequate living as the crucial feature of the employment problem, rather than unemployment or underemployment as such' (Turnham, 1970, p. 7). A similar approach to the measurement of underemployment was formally recommended by the Ninth International Conference of Labour Statisticians meeting at the ILO in Geneva in 1964. Their report, containing specific recommendations on appropriate methods for collecting data on underemployment, is an important reference (ILO, 1966).

achieve the other. So it is reasonable to treat them together. But they may also be incompatible at times: for example, the higher wages are, the more difficult it may be to increase the number of jobs. To emphasize the two dimensions of the employment problem does not tell one how to handle such dilemmas, but it does help to prevent a misleading preoccupation with just one facet of it.

The third dimension is also important, but from a different viewpoint. Removal of this sort of wastage is not an objective of policy *per se*, but should rather be considered a means of raising output and thus providing the resources for eliminating poverty.

The extent of the employment problem must therefore be judged by all these three yardsticks, not just by one alone. As far as possible, moreover, each needs to be applied separately in urban and rural contexts, because it has both different causes and different effects in the two cases. Actually, we were able, because of shortage of data, to analyse only the three aspects of the employment problem for urban areas, though we have added a short section on the same aspects of the problem as they appear in rural areas.

Urban employment in Colombia
The shortage of urban work opportunities

Two groups of people suffer from shortage of work opportunities: those without work and those in work but working short hours. In both cases, the numbers involved are almost certainly a good deal larger than the observed numbers actively seeking work or longer hours, because of the 'disguised element' – the unemployed (or underemployed) who are not openly seeking work (or more work) but would do so if open unemployment were to decrease. Table 1 gives estimates of the order of magnitude of both open and disguised rates in urban areas for persons lacking work opportunities in Colombia in 1967. (The year 1967 was one of rather low economic activity, but the general scale of the problem is too big for the figures to be greatly affected by year-to-year economic fluctuations.)

While the table suggests that open unemployment of the total labour force is probably the largest element, it accounts – at least among men – for less than half the total lack of work opportunities. (Among women, the rate of open unemployment in 1967 was extremely high, having apparently increased sharply over the previous three years.)

By its very nature, disguised unemployment is, of course, difficult to quantify. To make estimates which are at all adequate one needs detailed sample surveys covering work motivation and intentions. In the absence of these, rather sweeping assumptions have to be made. However, the rates of labour participation in Colombia – i.e. the proportion of the population of working age which is in the labour force – provide a clue to its extent

Table 1 The extent of urban work opportunities, 1967
(percentage of active urban labour force)

	Total	Males	Females
1. *Open unemployment* (persons without work and seeking it)	14	12	19
2. *Disguised unemployment* (persons without work and who would probably seek it if unemployment were much lower)	(7)*	10	—†
3. *Open underemployment*‡ (persons working less than thirty-two hours per week and seeking to work longer)	2	2	1
4. *Disguised underemployment*‡ (persons working less than thirty-two hours per week, who would probably seek longer hours if the opportunity were available)	3	2	4
Total**	(25)*	25	(25)*

* Incomplete total (see note †).

† No estimate possible but probably substantial.

‡ The proportion of the labour force working less than thirty-two hours a week is larger than this figure which is obtained by expressing the number of hours of underemployment in units of forty-eight hours (i.e. in its full-time equivalent) before the percentage is worked out.

** Totals may differ from the sums of items because of rounding.

Source: surveys of eight of the largest cities.

These are low in comparison with many other Latin American countries[2] (let alone with countries enjoying higher income levels) or even compared with what they used to be in Colombia, and the declines in these rates since 1951 strongly suggest that disguised unemployment has grown in recent years.[3]

These suspicions are strengthened by more careful studies showing that the higher the level of unemployment the lower the tendency for people to seek work.[4] The estimates in Table 1 therefore, though inevitably very rough,

2. See Centro Latinoamericano de Demografía (CELADE) (1968). Comparing recent censuses, rates in Colombia were lower than those of Peru or Venezuela for almost all age groups, male or female.

3. An exception here was that participation rates apparently rose for women between 1964 and 1967, seemingly because disguised unemployment came out into the open (which helps to explain the sharp increase in female unemployment rates in the same period). The data come from different sources, however, and are not entirely comparable.

4. Regressions of changes over time in age-specific participation rates against rates of open unemployment show negative correlation. The same relation can also be observed between cities.

derived from changes in labour participation rates, give perhaps a reasonable order of magnitude.

On underemployment, data can be found in the periodic sample surveys carried out by a number of universities. This is not as large as one might expect; the full-time equivalent of short hours is in total only about 5 per cent of total employment, as items 3 and 4 in Table 1 indicate. Fewer than half of those working short hours are openly seeking more work, though no doubt more would do so if they had any prospects of finding it, i.e. there must be some further (disguised) underemployment among those working part time.[5]

In any case the figures are misleadingly low. Part of the explanation for the small extent of underemployment shown reflects the definition used – the data are of hours worked per week, and not the time usefully employed in earning money. If statistics based on the latter approach were available, we would undoubtedly find larger numbers for this item, since in many occupations (e.g. shining shoes) people have to wait long intervals between opportunities of earning incomes.

However, there are reasons to believe that the working of 'short time' in most jobs is rather limited. Employers are encouraged by labour legislation (often with the support of their employees and the unions) to employ their existing labour force for longer hours rather than to take on more people. It is also no doubt true that many of those who are self-employed (such as shopkeepers) work very long hours to obtain an income at all adequate. The result is not only that underemployment is small, but also that this very situation makes unemployment somewhat larger.

The total effect of all four elements of work shortage is considerable – a lack of opportunities equivalent to some 25 per cent of the urban labour force in 1967, even on the incomplete figures available.

Unemployment is subject to cyclical fluctuations and, at least so far as open unemployment in Bogotá was concerned, 1967 was a particularly bad year. But for reasons given later in the report, there is no doubt that the long-run trend in unemployment is upward. This is confirmed by data for Bogotá (the only city for which there is a regular series), though these probably have a downward bias.[6] They show open unemployment at 7 per cent of the labour force for 1964 and 10 per cent for 1969, despite relatively prosperous conditions in the latter year. But figures for other cities at various dates also suggest a rising trend.

5. For the purposes of the table it is assumed that all those working part time would work full time if the opportunity for doing so presented itself.

6. They are derived from the sample surveys of the Research Centre for Economic Development of the University of the Andes (CEDE). People in the poorest areas, who have the heaviest unemployment and are probably growing as a proportion of the total population, are very incompletely covered.

Inadequate urban incomes

The second approach to the problem of employment is to measure the active labour force with very low incomes. This aspect of the problem is of particular importance in a country where the majority of families in the urban areas have no other source of income than what they can earn. The Government has but a limited capacity to redistribute income by direct transfer payments and the provision of free or subsidized services – and this would be true even if taxation were increased as we suggest later. So relieving the poverty of the poorest sections of the population – which is acute – depends heavily on the provision of jobs, with reasonable wages.

Purely in order to indicate the magnitude of urban poverty in Colombia, we show in Table 2 estimates for 1967 of the proportion of the labour force with incomes of less than 200 pesos monthly, a daily equivalent of less than 8 pesos (or about 50 US cents), assuming employment of twenty-six days a month. (Taking this particular level does not by any means imply that 200 pesos is considered to have been, even in 1967, an adequate income for a single person, let alone for a family – data in the source are tabulated by 100-peso intervals and 200 happens to be the highest figure shown below the lowest minimum wage.)

The figures show that a third of the urban labour force received less than 200 pesos a month (indeed more than half received less than 400 pesos). The 'hard core' was the open unemployed, with no earnings at all.

Ideally, one would like to relate figures on income distribution to data on size of family and to some measure of family needs for basic expenditure

Table 2 **The extent of extreme urban poverty, 1967**
(percentage of the active labour force)

	Total	Males	Females
Unemployed – open	14	12	19
– disguised	(7)*	10	—†
Occupied but with incomes below 200 pesos monthly‡	12	6	24
Total – all with incomes below 200 pesos monthly	(33)*	28	(44)*

* Incomplete total (see note †).

† No estimate possible but probably substantial.

‡ Including those under fifteen years of age. These account, however, for only about 2 per cent of the total urban labour force; to exclude them from the data on earnings would thus make very little difference to the overall picture.

Source: Numbers unemployed: see Table 1. Those with low incomes: see CEDE: *Encuestas urbanas de empleo y desempleo*, 1969 (averages for eight cities).

on food, clothing and shelter. Unfortunately, no such statistics exist at present, although there is evidence that the diet of a big fraction of the urban population is inadequate (in terms of basic nutritional needs) and their housing well below minimum standards of public health.

One can, however, relate the levels of earnings to minimum wages. In 1967 the lowest levels of non-agricultural minimum wages were 9·80 pesos daily in the 'low cost' areas and 11·20 pesos in the 'high cost' cities, such as Bogotá or Medellín. (The highest levels of minimum wages applied to the larger manufacturing firms were 11·20 pesos in the 'low cost' areas and 14 pesos in the 'high'.) Thus, in 1967, a third of the urban labour force received at the very most about three quarters of the lowest of the minimum wage rates.

A major conclusion can therefore be deduced, in spite of the margins of uncertainty in the figures. A very large proportion of the active labour force has an inadequate income, by any standards, and this proportion is considerably more than that of the unemployed or underemployed. Poverty therefore emerges as the most compelling aspect of the whole employment problem in Colombia.

Unutilized or underutilized reserves of urban labour

This is the third dimension of the employment problem. Here, the point of concern is not with the human consequences of lack of work or low income but with the economic potential of labour not used to the full. From this point of view, unemployment need not necessarily be considered a burden for policy makers. It can be looked on as a potential asset. To treat it as a liability is one indication of how one's values become distorted during a period of large-scale unemployment. There is this reserve of human resources available, if only the will and the way could be found to mobilize them for national development; certainly the long-term outlook for reaching high living standards would be in some ways more bleak if there were neither spare labour nor spare land to be brought into production. (Still, it is also understandable that in present circumstances large-scale unemployment should be considered a problem rather than an opportunity.)

Table 1 has already indicated part of Colombia's surplus labour reserves in 1967. This showed the proportions lacking the opportunities to work as much as they were willing and able to do. Taking all groups together, the total proportion in 1967 was the full-time equivalent of a quarter of the active labour force. The other component consists in another form of disguised underemployment, namely persons employed full time but in work where their contribution to output is low or even zero, even though they statistically appear as occupied in the sector. Where there is chronic unemployment, some workers, usually in family businesses, substitute their own production for part of someone else's. This is particularly common in the service sector, but it can be found in other sectors, too.

By its very nature, it is almost impossible to obtain adequate evidence on this phenomenon. There is first the difficulty of distinguishing low productivity due to this cause from low productivity due to shortage of complementary capital or land or to lack of motivation or to ill health. Even if one can make this distinction, a measure of the *extent* of this form of disguised underemployment would require making an estimate of the amount by which labour productivity could be raised *before* it reached a ceiling set by the supply of the other factors of production.[7] The whole question raises a series of difficult conceptual and empirical issues, which could be quantified only if we had data from inquiries in depth.

But the difficulties of measurement should not lead one to ignore the problem, particularly as various clues suggest it is both large and of growing importance. It has been estimated that in 1964 the equivalent of 13·5 per cent of the non-agricultural labour force was underemployed in this sense (Zschock, 1967) and the percentage could well be larger in other countries.[8] One should admit, however, that almost any figure is possible, depending on the breadth of one's definition and the boldness of one's guesswork. To the extent that one can rely on the national income data for commerce and finance, productivity in these sectors fell by 8 per cent from 1951 to 1964 and by a further 4 per cent in the whole service sector over the following three years. This alone would suggest considerable and growing surpluses of labour in the service sector, quite apart from underutilized labour elsewhere.

Thus, the third approach to the problem of employment suggests that in 1967 there was a pool of unemployed, underemployed or unproductively employed labour, equivalent to at least a third of the whole urban labour force. This total pool of surplus labour has tended to grow over the years; it is clear that the part we can measure (very roughly), open unemployment, has risen since 1964, and it seems very likely that the remainder has too.

Rural employment in Colombia

Even fewer and weaker statistics are available on the employment problem in the rural areas than for the towns. This is a serious hindrance to policy making; special surveys and the regular collection of basic data should be instituted as a matter of urgency.

7. More strictly, before the marginal productivity of labour in all sectors became the same.

8. Studies in Chile and Peru, for instance, have suggested that in those countries almost 30 per cent of the nonagricultural labour force was underemployed. See Lederman (1969, p. 13).

In the absence of hard statistics, one can only surmise on the facts. But one can begin with three broad generalizations. The first is that the rural situation varies sharply from area to area. Differences in rates of unemployment between towns have already been noted: patterns of land ownership, crops, marketing and communications are so dissimilar between different parts of the country that it is absurd to talk of the rural situation as if it were everywhere the same.

The second point is that rural employment varies considerably over the year. While agriculture's natural cycle from planting to harvesting creates peaks of labour demand, at which periods almost any additional labour (longer hours or more people) can add to the yield, much less labour is needed during the slack seasons. To some extent, the peaks and troughs occur at different times for different crops, so the total demand for agricultural labour shows less seasonal variation. But this is truer for the country as a whole than for separate regions. There is a marked pattern of local specialization, leading to temporary migration from one area to another which mitigates the extremes of imbalance between the supply and demand for rural labour over the year. Small-scale handicrafts and local industry also provide work for some people during the slack periods in agriculture, particularly in the rural areas and in the small towns, although such possibilities are insufficient to remove seasonal fluctuations in the rural employment pattern. Thirdly, the nature of rural life often makes nonsense of over-precise urban concepts like 'active labour force' or even 'unemployment'. Using our three approaches to the employment problem avoids some of the worst confusions, but great difficulties of definition still remain.

The shortage of work opportunities

Census results tell us nothing, really, about how much surplus labour there is in rural areas, because of the great difficulty of interpreting them.[9] At any one date, the surplus will differ from one district to another, anyway, according to local crop patterns and the movement of migrant labour. It is likely, however, that in most areas there are some periods in the year, at least, when labour is scarce; investigations in other countries have shown that this is normally the case.

Thus the real problem of shortage of work opportunities occurs during seasonally slack periods – though we do not know how long they last or how severe they are. It then often takes the form of part-time work, especially on the family farm, rather than unemployment in the sense of seeking work. (In many rural areas, there would really be no point in 'seeking

9. The 1964 census shows open unemployment in agriculture as 2·9 per cent, with underemployment at 17 per cent.

work' – everyone will know whether or not the local large-scale farmers are offering jobs.)[10]

Inadequate incomes

Migration, whether temporary or permanent, is also evidence of the low income of many of those living in the country areas.[11] Here we do have some rough data – in Table 3 (though for *agricultural* rather than *rural* incomes). It shows that many people have a very low income indeed, even in relation to the minimum wage in rural areas, which amounted to about 1100 pesos in 1960, in annual terms. Perhaps one in six of the agriculturally occupied (wage earners plus self-employed) received less than this, which was equivalent to less than US$200.

A major reason for these low incomes is that 40 per cent of families are estimated to have less than two hectares each, and 6 per cent to have none at all. Although many of them work part of the year as labourers on other people's farms, this still does not provide an adequate income.

What makes this poverty much more serious is the limited availability in the rural areas of any of the basic government services. In terms of health, education, basic sanitation or clean water, many of these rural communities have only the barest minimum, if that.

Table 3 **Income distribution of the occupied labour force in agriculture, 1960** (percentages)

Annual income* (Thousand pesos)	Percentage of those occupied in agriculture	Cumulative percentage of those occupied in agriculture	Cumulative percentage of incomes
0 – 1	9	9	2
1 – 1·5	33	42	13
1·5 – 2	22	64	23
2 – 3	12	76	30
3 – 5	10	86	41
5 – 10	9	95	57
Over 10	5	100	100

* 'Income' refers only to incomes from agriculture (though subsequent research shows that it makes little difference when other rural incomes are covered). Income in kind is included.
Source: unpublished estimates.

10. It may well be the case that, precisely because there is unemployment, people stay on smallholdings which they work intensively, for long hours. This underlines the importance of the income approach.

11. A study in the Río Suárez Valley shows the pressures on persons with very low agricultural incomes to supplement their incomes from other sources. See Reyes *et alia* (1965).

We just do not know how this situation has changed over the last decade, important though it would be to have such information, but there are reasons for suspecting that at any rate it has not improved much. Government measures to provide additional land and aid to production have benefited only a small proportion of poor farmers. Moreover, though physical output (excluding coffee) has risen by nearly 3·5 per cent per year between 1960 and 1967, much of the increase seems to have come from the large producers.[12] It has been estimated that real wages in the countryside have changed little since 1935 – a fall in the following fifteen to twenty years being made up by a rise which, however, apparently ended in 1963. It is worth noting that rapid migration to the towns has continued in spite of growing urban unemployment.

Unutilized or underutilized labour

We start here, as for urban labour, with the volume of open unemployment and underemployment – though we have no data for these categories. Because of the fluctuation in activity, there is a labour reserve at certain times of the year which could be temporarily employed. Some labour indeed is, through migration, working on nearby farms or taking jobs in other industries, but the unused capacity is still considerable – because of the facts that peak demands on various farms in areas specializing in coffee or other crops coincide, that rural industry scarcely exists, and that rural public works are not on a large scale.

In addition, there is 'disguised' underemployment, even harder to define, let alone measure, in the rural context. In principle there are certainly people, very large numbers in fact, who are working with low productivity because family holdings are too small, or the land is too poor. In some areas, at least, they could be moved to adjacent land which is being underused and could be cultivated without big needs of capital; where this could be done without causing crops in the neighbourhood, which they would otherwise have picked, to go to waste (which raises the problem of the seasonal peak again), we could call this another facet of disguised unemployment. One would imagine that the small proprietor would often be able both to produce more, if he had the land, and yet also at certain times of the year help with the harvest of others. The relatively very low yields per man currently obtained on minifundia are a clue that the net effect could be a rise in output.

12. Moreover, although prices of agricultural products have risen somewhat faster than those of manufactures, the variation between different products is considerable. It is precisely those products in which output rises fastest which are most likely to suffer price declines. If the big producers are raising their output rapidly the effect may well be that while their income rises, that of the small producer declines.

There clearly is therefore a labour reserve in agriculture bigger than just the open unemployment, though its dimensions are unknown. Judging from the slow rise of productivity in agriculture (about 2 per cent a year), disguised unemployment, at least, is almost certainly growing – indeed one could expect little else since there are greater and greater numbers of people per hectare on the smallholdings as the population rises. Because of its seasonality and other special characteristics of the rural sector, there are particular problems about mobilizing the labour surplus at all fully. They almost all involve serious issues of institutional change.

Who are the unemployed?

We need to know something about the composition of the unemployed – their age, education levels, family status, whether they are migrants from the countryside, their occupation, period unemployed, reasons for leaving previous jobs, etc. Such characteristics provide essential information about the nature of the problem: who are the people primarily affected and why it has arisen. Both questions must be answered if sensible policies are to be framed.

In fact the *main* reason that chronic unemployment exists in Colombia is widespread imbalance throughout the economy, which only in minor respects can be attributed to the individual characteristics of the unemployed themselves. Such characteristics are important, but as determinants of *who* are unemployed, not of *why* unemployment exists.

As regards the composition of the rural unemployed, we again know virtually nothing. Our only information is about the migrants to the towns, who tend to be younger and slightly more educated than those who stay behind, and who are pulled by hopes of higher incomes in the towns and pushed by lack of economic opportunities in the countryside, particularly lack of sufficient land. In the towns, they seem to have both higher rates of participation and lower rates of unemployment than urban-born persons – interesting and important points, which raise a number of further questions on which research could usefully be focused.

Some information about the urban unemployed is available from sample survey data. Mostly the urban unemployed are young: about two-fifths under twenty-five and a further fifth under thirty-five. A high proportion are new entrants to the labour force. Indeed, looking at the same figures from another point of view, more than one in four young people (aged from fifteen to twenty-four) are openly unemployed; this is true of both males and females.[13]

On average, unemployed who have just entered the labour force are

13. This proportion does not include other types of unemployment discussed above; however, these may be less severe among younger people than among those who are older.

significantly better educated than the other unemployed and indeed than those who have jobs. This does not mean that education is a handicap. On the contrary, we can surmise from the census that more educated persons have lower – but by no means negligible – rates of open unemployment and underemployment than less educated persons. It is primarily a reflection of the larger number of educated persons coming on the market in recent years.

Unemployment rates seem fairly evenly spread over sectors, apart from construction, where (in 1967 anyway) it was especially high. In terms of occupations sought, unemployment is especially heavy among those seeking work as clerical workers – though many of these will in fact lack the necessary qualifications. One significant feature is the downgrading in job ambitions which seems to occur once a person loses a job; many of the former employed are trying for jobs in occupations of lower status and pay (e.g. domestic service) than the ones they previously held.

From the point of view of social policy, those unemployed for long periods and the older persons with dependants are particularly important. In most cities, a quarter of the unemployed have been without work for at least a year, one half for more than three months. Unskilled workers have to wait a particularly long time to get jobs.

It is not clear what proportion of the unemployed are heads of families, although we know that about two-fifths of all previously employed males have families. Unemployment must present very severe hardships to these men (and unemployed women in the same position) and their dependants.

Nevertheless, unemployment in Colombia may as yet be less serious for the individual, in two respects, than it ever is in more industrial societies. Since families are still large, many of the unemployed can survive by living off their relatives and so avoid the worst extremes of poverty. This is probably true of most of the younger unemployed, who are numerous, but it can also apply to a good part of the older as well, a whole family often feeding on the earnings of the one or two children lucky enough to have a job. Secondly, those who have only recently migrated to a town can return to their family if their situation becomes desperate.

The extent to which the bite of unemployment is eased in these ways is conjectural, and in any case less reliance can be placed on these safety mechanisms for the future, since traditional forms of family solidarity are no doubt weakening as the urban population becomes more settled. Moreover, much of the rural population has little food to spare, now that land holdings have been subdivided into such small plots.

We must never forget, when we are dealing with statistics in hundreds of thousands, that each person who is unemployed is a tragic individual case, the cause of poverty for himself (or herself) and the family. There is no escape from the psychological damage of unemployment – the demoralizing daily round looking for work, and the even more demoralizing series of refusals, increasing a man's disillusionment with himself and with society as the months tick by, and undermining his family's respect for him as an individual. Thousands of women and young girls are compelled to prostitute their bodies to support themselves and their dependants.

Even those with jobs are affected by unemployment when it is on the scale that can be found in Colombia – apart altogether from the need to maintain unemployed members of their families (and at times the families of neighbours). They are insecure, dependent on the goodwill of foremen and managers and on the defensive against those who might take their posts away from them; their bargaining strength is sapped by the existence of so many willing to take work at almost any wages.

Measured open unemployment is only the most noticeable symptom of a much bigger problem, that a large section of the population is struggling to survive on incomes which are well below what is necessary for reasonable health and nutrition, let alone comfortable living.

The whole analysis of these problems of unemployment leads one to conclude that they are part and parcel of certain broad tendencies in the process of growth in the Colombian economy over recent decades. The plain truth is that the poorest sections of the population have gained little, if anything, from the growth of some 5 per cent per year (in real terms) of the economy since the mid-1950s; the bottom third of the rural population may well be no better off than in the 1930s.

This is the outcome of a complex of political, social and economic forces, which are at work not only within Colombia but also in the outside world. The fact that unemployment is a major and growing problem in the majority of developing countries suggests that some of its causes are common – and that we must look for them not only inside each country (though certainly we should look there first) but also in the relations between developing countries and those more highly developed.

References

CENTRO LATINOAMERICANO DE DEMOGRAFIA (CELADE) (1968), *Boletin Demográfico*, Year 2, vol. 3.

ILO (1966), *Measurement of Underemployment: Concepts and Methods*, Report 4, Eleventh International Conference of Labour Statisticians, Geneva.

LEDERMAN, E. (1969), *Los recursos humanos en el desarollo de América latina*, Cuadernos del Instituto Latinoamericano de Planificación Económica y Social, no. 9, Santiago de Chile.

TURNHAM, D. (1970), *The Employment Problem in Less Developed Countries: A Review*, OECD, Paris.

REYES, M., PRIETO, R., and HANNESON, B. (1965), *Estudio agroeconómica de la Hóya del Rio Suárez*, CEDE.

ZSCHÖCK, D. K. (1967), *Manpower Perspective of Colombia*, Princeton University.

2 D. Turnham

Empirical Evidence of Open Unemployment in Developing Countries

From D. Turnham, *The Employment Problem in Less Developed Countries*, OECD, Paris, 1970.

Data relating to the full-time unemployed for less developed countries which keep or have kept a regular survey are shown in Table 1. It is to be emphasized that in regard to the trend in unemployment in less developed countries, this table includes very nearly all the information we have, and even here changes in sample design and date of inquiry affect the results. Nevertheless, if we compare these rates with those available for developed countries over a similar period, only Canada and Ireland have experienced, for any length of time, rates like those for Chile, Korea or the Philippines; and Puerto Rico or Bogotá are entirely outside the range.[1]

It is worth emphasizing that these rates are high *despite* problems of measurement and that with labour force growing at 2 or 3 per cent, even a constant percentage rate of unemployment implies considerable growth in the number of unemployed.

Much more information is available on a cross-section basis, as many countries have undertaken one or more special surveys, especially in urban areas. Some information is available from population census statistics as well, especially in the post 1960 period when more questions about unemployment were introduced. However, in many of the surveys rather special definitions of employment and unemployment are used and the differences in unemployment rates probably owe a good deal to these factors as well as to differences in the underlying reality.

In particular, considerable differences are frequently observed between rates of unemployment derived from Census and Survey data. Because of these difficulties, it is probably a waste of time to analyse in detail differences in levels of unemployment between countries and most of our attention is directed to an examination of the structural characteristics of unemployment.

There seems little doubt that surveys directed to conditions in urban

1. 1958, the last depression year, produced the highest rates of unemployment in developed countries; 9·6 per cent in Denmark, 6·6 per cent in Italy and 6·8 per cent in the United States for example; in the same years the rate in Puerto Rico was 13·9 per cent and in Chile (Gran Santiago) 9·5 per cent.

Table 1 Unemployment as a percentage of the labour force: sample survey statistics

	1957	1958	1959	1960	1961	1962	1963	1964	1965	1966	1967	1968
Africa												
UAR	5·1	3·4	4·9	4·8	3·2	1·8	—	<u>1·5</u>	—	—	—	3·2
Asia												
Korea*	7·9		3·8	4·8	2·3	8·4	8·1	7·7	7·4	7·1	6·2	5·1
Philippines		8·2	6·8	6·3	7·5	8·0	6·3	6·4	7·1	7·1	8·0	7·8
Taiwan							<u>5·3</u>	<u>4·4</u>	3·4	3·1	2·3	<u>1·7</u>
America												
Argentine (Gran Buenos Aires)	6·4	9·5	7·4	<u>7·4</u>	6·7	5·3	5·1	5·3	5·3	5·6	6·4	5·0
Chile (Gran Santiago)									5·4	5·4	6·1	6·0
Colombia (Bogotá)†							8·7	7·2	8·8	11·5	12·7	11·6
Panama							5·8	<u>7·4</u>	7·6	5·1	6·2	9·1
Puerto Rico‡	13·0	13·9	13·8	12·1	12·6	12·6	11·8	<u>11·1</u>	12·0	12·3	12·2	11·6
Trinidad and Tobago									14·0	14·0	15·0	14·0

Note: underlined figures are at monthly dates different from those used elsewhere in the series.
 * New series from 1962.
 † 14 plus until 1965, thereafter 10 plus.
 ‡ Revised series after 1960.
Source: International Yearbook of Labour Statistics, 1968, 1969, except Bogotá from the CEDE Surveys.

areas have most chance of providing useful information and the discussion which follows is based on results from about twenty such inquiries. From them a surprising similarity in the characteristics of the unemployed group seems to emerge.[2]

Table 2 indicates perhaps the major common feature which is the preponderance of young workers in the unemployed group.

In most cases the rate of unemployment among young workers is double or more than double that applying to the labour force as a whole. It is worth pointing out that the difference between rates found for the 15–24 groups and groups over 24 is a good deal bigger than this. In Malayan towns for example, the overall rate of 9·8 per cent is made up from rates of 21·0 per cent for 15–24 age group and only 4·6 per cent for workers over 24, so that the rate for the former group is four and a half times greater than the rate for the latter group. Our cut off point – age 15 – admittedly arbitrary, is intended to remove the effect of the inclusion of very young workers who are often anyway excluded by definition and which in some inquiries only seem to get included if they are employed. In some countries, however, unemployment rates (whether meaningful or not) are extremely heavy among this group – in Taiwan, for example, the unemployment rate for 12 to 14 year olds can be calculated as 16 per cent.

A number of other striking characteristics of the unemployed group of workers tend to follow directly from the relative young average age of the group.

The proportion of 'inexperienced' workers tends to be considerable. Lack of experience is variously defined from e.g. having never worked before, to having never held a particular job more than two or three weeks. Depending partly on definition, the proportion of inexperienced unemployed to total unemployed seems to vary from about 20 per cent to over 60 per cent.[3] Inexperienced workers are very heavily concentrated at the young end of the age distribution (though slightly more so for men than for women).

Relative to the whole working population, the unemployed as a group tend to be better educated, especially where young and inexperienced unemployed are numerous. Thus, there are often considerable differences in rates of unemployment among labour force groups of different educational level, with particularly low rates among the illiterate urban population – often only 1 per cent or 2 per cent in Asia (Ceylon, Thailand, India and Taiwan for example) and nowhere more than 4 per cent or 5 per cent,

2. The surveys do not, however, include big countries like Mexico, Brazil, Pakistan and Indonesia, or most of Africa.

3. Of surveys in some twenty countries, we found seven cases with between 20 per cent and 30 per cent inexperienced unemployed, three between 30 per cent and 50 per cent and ten over 50 per cent. The larger percentages tended to occur in Asia.

Table 2 Rates of urban unemployment* by sex and age

	15–24	15 and over total	Notes
	(a)	(b)	

Africa
Ghana, 1960 Large towns

	15–24	15 and over total	Notes
Total	21·9	11·6	Census tabulation
Males	22·1	11·5	
Females	21·5	11·8	

America
Bogotá, Colombia, 1968

	15–24	15 and over total	Notes
Total	23·1	13·6	March 1968 survey
Males	21·8	10·3	
Females	24·3	18·5	

Buenos Aires, Argentina, 1965

	15–24	15 and over total	Notes
Total	6·3	4·2	(a) 14–29 age group
Males	4·3	2·9	(b) 14 plus
Females	9·0	7·0	1965 survey

Chile, 1968 (urban areas)

	15–24	15 and over total	Notes
Total	12	6	(b) 12 plus age group Survey December 1968

Caracas, 1966

	15–24	15 and over total	Notes
Total	37·7	18·8	Survey data

Guyana, 1965 (mainly urban areas)

	15–24	15 and over total	Notes
Total	40·4	21·0	(b) Over 14 age group
Males	36·5	18·4	Survey data, 1965
Females	49·0	27·7	

Panama, 1963–4 (urban areas)

	15–24	15 and over total	Notes
Total	17·9	10·4	(a) 15–29 age group
Males	17·5	8·9	Survey data, 1963–4
Females	18·5	13·3	

Puerto Rico, 1969 (all areas)

	15–24	15 and over total	Notes
Total	15·3	10·2	(a) 14–24 age group
Males	16·1	11·2	(b) 14 plus age group
Females	13·4	7·8	Survey July, 1969

* Some well conducted survey estimates which do not distinguish rural and urban areas are included.

Table 2 – *continued*

		15–24	15 and over total	Notes
		(a)	(b)	
Trinidad and Tobago, 1968 (all areas)				
	Total	26	14	Survey data,
	Males	26	14	January–June 1968
	Females	26	16	
Uruguay, 1963 (mainly urban)				
	Total	18·5	11·8	Census tabulation
Venezuela, 1969 (urban areas)				
	Total	14·8	7·9	Survey data March 1969

Asia

Bangkok, Thailand, 1966				
	Total	7·7	3·4	Survey data,
	Males	8·0	3·2	August–November 1966.
	Females	7·3	3·4	Bangkok–Thonburi municipal areas
Ceylon, 1968 (urban areas)				
	Total	39·0	15·0	Survey data,
	Males	36·1	12·9	January 1968
	Females	48·4	25·9	
China (Taiwan), 1966 (whole island)				
	Total	6·9	2·6	Survey data, 1966
	Males	5·8	2·1	
	Females	8·1	6·8	
India, 1961–2 (urban areas)				
	Total	8·0	3·2	(b) 15–60 age group
	Males	8·1	3·4	Survey data, 17th
	Females	7·7	3·2	round, 1961–2
Korea, 1966 (non-farm households)				
	Total	23·6	12·6	Survey data,
	Males	25·6	13·2	average of four
	Females	21·5	11·3	quarters, 1966
Malaya, 1965 (urban areas)				
	Total	21·0	9·8	Survey data,
	Males	17·7	7·4	metropolitan
	Females	26·8	16·7	towns, 1965

	15–24	15 and over total	Notes
	(a)	(b)	

Philippines, 1965 (urban areas)

		(a)	(b)	Notes
	Total	20·6	11·6	(a) 10–24 age group
	Males	23·8	10·8	(b) 10 plus
	Females	16·9	12·9	Survey data, May 1965

Singapore, 1966

| | Total | 15·7 | 9·2 | (a) 15–29 age group |
| | | | | Survey data |

Syria, 1967 (whole area)

	Total	8·6	6·0	Survey data,
	Males	10·9	6·2	November 1967
	Females	3·7	5·2	

Tehran City, Iran, 1966

	Total	9·4	4·6	Census tabulation
	Males	9·3	4·6	
	Females	10·3	4·0	

Note: where possible, the labour force under 15 has been excluded.

except in Puerto Rico. These results could of course reflect a measurement problem in dealing with illiterate populations, but the finding seems fairly general.

Puerto Rico (whole country) is also the only example we have found where rates of unemployment are higher among illiterate groups than others. Differences are smaller when urban and rural areas are taken together.

It is clearly impossible to provide more than illustrative comparisons of the pattern of unemployment by education partly because educational systems vary so widely and partly also because few surveys provide the detail required. Some findings for a number of countries are shown in Table 3.

One other generalization suggested by these illustrations (and we have not seen this contradicted by other evidence) is that rates of unemployment are relatively low among highly educated people.[4] It seems that it is among the middle group – primary and secondary school leavers – where unemployment rates are highest. In the case of Malaya, where age group specific rates of unemployment are presented, one is struck by the extraordinary

4. It is not always possible to distinguish between those who graduate or otherwise successfully complete a course of higher education and those who do not, but data in a few cases suggest that rates of unemployment are typically much higher among high level 'drop-outs'.

Table 3 Education and unemployment, selected countries

	Rates of unemployment			
	Illiterate	1 to 5 years education	6 to 11 years education	12 or more years education
Bogotá, Colombia, April 1967				
Total labour force				
Males	11·5	15·3	14·9	13·2
Females	4·1	22·0	16·3	11·3

	Illiterate	Primary	Secondary	Post Secondary
Buenos Aires, Argentina, 1965				
Total labour force	3·8	4·3	5·7	3·3
Venezuela, 1969 (urban areas)				
Total labour force	4·3*	7·0	10·2	2·3

	Illiterate	Below matriculation	Matriculation	Graduates
India, 1960–61 (urban areas)				
Total labour force	1·2	2·7	7·0	2·8

	Illiterate and primary grades 1 to 4	Secondary grades 5 to 8	Ordinary certificate	Higher certificate and above
Ceylon, 1963 (urban areas)				
Total labour force	7·1	7·3	11·8	2·3

	Illiterate	Primary	Secondary grades 1 to 4	Higher certificate and above
Malaya, 1965 (urban areas)				
Total labour force 15–24:				
Male	10·4	19·5	30·9	15·5
Female	17·2	32·4	69·7	27·5

	Illiterate	Literate	Elementary to secondary	Graduate
Syria, 1967 (all areas)				
Total labour force	4·3	5·2	11·7	4·4

* Includes others not classified.

high rates among some of the groups distinguished; note also that illiterates are still, on the age specific basis, less likely to be unemployed than others.

Finally, an interesting (but seemingly almost unique) tabulation in the Indian Sample Surveys indicates a very sharp difference in the *duration* of unemployment by educational groupings of unemployment. Other surveys also indicate that the average duration of unemployment can be extraordinarily long,[5] though the phenomenon is less striking in Latin America than in Asia.

Table 4 **Education and duration of unemployment: urban India 1961–2**

	Duration of unemployment		
Educational group	Less than one month	1 to 9 months	More than 9 months
Secondary	9	39	52
Literate, below secondary	15	37	48
Illiterate	47	34	19
Overall average*	21	38	41

* Includes groups other than those shown.
Source: National Sample Survey No. 127, 17th Round, September 1961–July 1962.

Persons of dependent status or not heads of households tend to be relatively heavily represented among the urban unemployed. Again, the statement can only be supported by fragmentary evidence, but is not contradicted by any evidence that we know about.

Interpretations of the evidence about open (urban) unemployment

How do we interpret these findings and what is their significance in relation to the general employment problem? Why is open unemployment so concentrated in these particular socioeconomic groupings? These are not questions to which much attention seems to have been given either at theoretical or empirical level although different explanations yield rather different implications for an assessment of the 'size' of the unemployment problem and the remedial policies needed. Two interpretations seem possible. One could simply argue that 15 per cent open unemployment does indicate the magnitude of the overall gap between supply and demand for labour and that young and inexperienced people are particularly affected

5. In Singapore, Oshima's data indicate that almost two-thirds of first time job seekers were unemployed longer than a year. See Oshima (1967).

because these are the most vulnerable groups in the labour surplus economy; older people cling to their jobs and previous work experience commands a premium which in a more balanced market would be translated into a wage differential, but in the surplus economy enables jobs to be got and

Table 5 Unemployment by status

	Heads of household		Dependants	
	---	---	---	---
	Married	Not married	Married	Not married
Rates of unemployment				
Philippines, 1965, urban areas				
Males	3·7	7·4	9·4	22·9
Females	11·7	2·9	10·3	15·3

		Married		Not married	
	---	---	---	---	---
	Total	Had job	Never had job	Had job	Never had job
Percentages of unemployed persons					
Malaya, 1965, urban areas					
Males	100	22	1	24	53
Females	100	10	11	15	64

	Rates of unemployment
Puerto Rico, 1969 (whole area)	
Heads of household	7·5
Wives of household heads	3·3
Married (not separated)	6·7
Single	18·0
Children of household heads	18·4
Other dependants	20·8

held. Standard explanations for high unemployment then follow, e.g. that rates of increase in the demand for labour are insufficient in relation to increases in the supply because capital accumulation does not proceed fast enough. Capital requirements per unit of output are inelastic because of technical rigidities and/or rigidities in respect of complementary human capital in the form of management expertise or other skills acquired by work training and experience.

A different interpretation of the unemployment problem begins from the proposition or assumption that some work is always available in the traditional sector and that additional numbers can be accommodated there partly through work sharing and partly through accepting lower income for a given effort. The question to focus on therefore, according to this argument, is the reason why some groups prefer open unemployment to disguised unemployment or low productivity working. A number of possible answers suggest themselves.

Having regard either to past trends in wage increases in 'modern' sector employments or to current wage differentials between these employments and those available in the traditional sector, the decision of a school leaver to spend time looking or waiting for the 'right' job is in many countries a perfectly sensible one. It may, similarly, be perfectly rational for parents or others to maintain the school leaver during the process in the hope of later 'pay-off'. As family responsibilities grow or when family support is no longer forthcoming, the unsuccessful job hunter is absorbed into the traditional sector where some income generating occupation can be got, albeit less satisfying and less financially rewarding.

This argument is more closely related to the special characteristics of the structure of open unemployment – the importance of young and relatively well educated people, and of persons of dependent status. It also receives some support from the findings of a few surveys which have directly investigated job aspirations. These tend to show a marked preference among school leavers for non-manual work which is considerably at variance with the existing structure of occupations. For example, in Bogotá in 1966, over 60 per cent of first time job seekers were looking for 'white collar' work and rather less than 20 per cent for industrial 'blue collar' occupations. 'White collar' male workers, however, accounted for only about 40 per cent of the total employed labour force – less than 'blue collar' workers at about 45 per cent.[6] A similar, if not more extreme, situation is suggested by the Indian sample survey inquiries,[7] where out of the total of first time job seekers over 60 per cent sought 'white collar' work and less than 30 per cent industrial work, while less than 20 per cent of the employed population actually had 'white collar' jobs. It may be objected that these questionnaires throw little light on what work would in fact be accepted if it were offered and may reflect no more than an expression

6. See C E D E (1969), Section 4, Table 16 and Appendix Table 7. Data relate to March 1966. Regarding new entrants, a further 20 per cent sought jobs in 'services', the army, the police force etc, compared with about 15 per cent employed in these categories among men and over 50 per cent among women.

7. Data quoted are derived from the 17th round – urban labour force, September 1961–July 1962.

of wishful thinking of little relevance to economic behaviour; nevertheless, the findings, while scattered, are fairly generally observed.

There is, no doubt, a massive gap between the aspirations of increasingly modern-minded young job seekers and the opportunities which can be provided.

Finally, this explanation for open unemployment enables us to interpret the otherwise puzzling finding of a few surveys showing rates of unemployment separately for natives and migrants into urban areas. These surveys tend to show *lower* rates of unemployment especially at young age groups, for migrants than for native born workers. Statistics quoted by Herrick (1965) for Chile and by CEDE (1969) for Bogotá provide an illustration.[8]

Table 6 Rates of unemployment among natives and migrants, Greater Santiago, 1963 and Bogotá, 1967

	Natives		Migrants		
	Chile	Bogotá	Chile	Bogotá (*)	(†)
15–19	14·0		8·8		
20–29	6·4		4·8		
Total	6·4	22·5	4·0	11·6	14·9
Total men	7·2	20·5	4·6	11·0	14·1
Total women	4·9	26·5	3·1	12·5	16·3

* Migrants from the same department.
† Migrants from other departments.

A conclusion to this line of argument, pushed sufficiently strongly, would be that the existence of a high wage, high status, modern sector in the towns together with a level of family income high enough to support the young adult job seeker are sufficient to explain why urban unemployment is so high. It would follow from this argument that a tendency for urban unemployment to grow would be closely linked, on the one hand, to educational developments and, on the other, to the existence of relatively high wages in favoured job categories and growing real income among urban family groups.[9]

8. Other detailed surveys reporting similar results include the Indian Sample Survey for Urban Areas no. 53.
9. The existence of a high wage sector besides encouraging unemployment by creating excess demand for the favoured job categories may also directly provide a support

Again, the qualification in respect of generality is important; the tendency is for the distributions of unemployment with respect to the characteristics examined to be more striking or extreme in the poorer countries than in cities like Buenos Aires which are more like those of developed countries.

It is perhaps clear on the basis of existing empirical knowledge that no very firm conclusion can be justified. In particular, studies which relate unemployment among young persons to family income and social level are one obvious gap in current knowledge.[10] Furthermore, one might question whether the traditional sector is open to all new entrants to the labour force; in getting jobs, at any level, in less developed countries much depends on the infrastructure of personal and family connections. Thus, if those from families whose connections are with the organized or modern sector of the labour market cannot find jobs in this sector, perhaps it is impossible for them to get jobs elsewhere. Lastly, even if, having regard to the special structure of the urban unemployed,[11] urban rates of 10 per cent or 15 per cent unemployed do not represent the major crisis which they would in developed countries nevertheless the corresponding rates of 20 per cent or 30 per cent among young people constitute a very serious waste of potential resources and an invitation to violence and political unrest.

---

base for the unemployed. This point is perhaps particularly important in Sub-Saharan Africa and is strikingly illustrated by Pfefferman (1968) in the case of Senegal: his sample of 188 industrial wage workers were maintaining 'at least 1614 persons, excluding themselves, permanently at their homes: the average size of the extended family is ... 9·63 persons (including the wage earners themselves)'. Figures do not include temporary guests. Pfefferman's data also indicate that the size of the group supported is related to the level of individual wage earnings; in Berg's phrase – 'increments of income are followed by increments of kinsmen to share it' (Berg, 1966).

10. One study for Puerto Rico in 1959 did however show that family income tended to be higher than average for the families to which unemployed workers belonged and that such families, on average, included more working members (Elizaga, 1967).

11. This point should not be overemphasized: in the United States, for example, unemployment is also relatively heavy among young age groups and a significant fraction of the total is accounted for by first time job seekers. However, one would hardly expect the United States to furnish an unemployment structure typical of a labour surplus economy.

References

BERG, E. J. (1966), 'Major issues of wage policy in Africa', in A. M. Ross (ed.) *Industrial Relations and Economic Development*, Macmillan.

CEDE (1969), *Encuestas urbanas de empleo y desempleo, analysis y resultados*, Centro de Estudios sobre Desarrollo Economico, Universidad de los Andes, Facultad de Economica.

ELIZAGA, J. C. (1967), 'The demographic aspects of unemployment and underemployment in Latin America', World Population Conference 1965, vol. 4, *Migration, Urbanization, Economic Development*, UN Dept. of Economic and Social Affairs.

HERRICK, B. (1965), *Urban Migration and Economic Development in Chile*, MIT.

OSHIMA, T. (1967), 'Growth and unemployment in Singapore', *Malayan econ. Rev.*, vol. 12, no. 2, October.

PFEFFERMAN, G. (1968), *Industrial Labour in the Republic of Senegal*, Praeger.

3 P. P. Streeten

A Critique of Concepts of Employment and Unemployment

Extract from 'A critique of development concepts', *European Journal of Sociology*, vol. 11, no. 1, 1970.

[. . .] Most less developed countries have what is commonly described as a serious and growing problem of surplus labour, unemployment, disguised unemployment and underemployment. Whatever the precise interpretation of these somewhat vague and ill-defined terms, there can be no doubt that development policies must give a high priority to a fuller mobilization and utilization of what is sometimes thought to be their most abundant factor of production – unskilled labour. It is worth considering briefly the notions of unemployment, disguised unemployment and underemployment.

Unemployment, underemployment and disguised unemployment are often considered both a cause of poverty and a potential source of development. Approaches in terms of 'employment', 'unemployment' and 'underemployment' are misleading because they suggest that an increase in effective demand and the provision of equipment are all that is needed to absorb labour and raise production, while all other conditions are adapted or easily and quickly adaptable to full labour utilization. In fact, a number of other measures are necessary for a full mobilization and utilization of manpower: better feeding, improvements in health, training and education, transport and housing, and fundamental attacks on prevailing attitudes to life and work (e.g. women's participation, a contempt for certain kinds of work, the desire to minimize work, lack of discipline) and on institutions (introduction of standard working week and working day, creation of labour market, provision of information, readiness to move from one place to another or to change one's occupation, etc.).

As a first step, it is helpful to break down the multiplicity of dimensions of Income (or Product) per Head of the Population into four categories. These should aid the collection of data, the organization of thought, and the formulation of policies.[1]

1. A similar identity was first used by Michael Lipton in a working paper for Myrdal's *Asian Drama* in April 1961. See also Barber (1966).

$$\frac{\text{Income}}{\text{Population}} = \frac{\text{Production}}{\text{Hours worked}} \cdot \frac{\text{Hours worked}}{\text{Labour force}} \cdot$$

$$\frac{\text{Labour force}}{\text{People of working age}} \cdot \frac{\text{People of working age}}{\text{Population}} \cdot$$

The identity brings out four distinct aspects of the Level of Living (= Income per head) on which more information would be useful for framing policies for the multidimensional aspects of labour utilization. It is important to note that the ratios are not independent of one another.

$\dfrac{\text{Production}}{\text{Hours worked}}$ *or hourly productivity* **1**

depends, in any given activity in any given sector, on a large number of factors, including other terms in the identity, such as: hours worked and participation rate (see below **2** and **3**); also on equipment, fuel, raw materials and other complementary productive factors; education and training; health affecting work such as intestinal parasites, amoebas, onchocerciasis or schistosomiasis; intensity of application, itself a function of morale; industrial relations; motivation; incentives, etc.; organization of work, management, etc.

This category covers numerous aspects, some of the most important of which are difficult to measure. It should be analysed in greater detail. For the country as a whole, it is an average of all sectors, each weighted by its share in the total number of hours worked. If we denote the sectors as 1, 2, 3, etc., and their shares in total working hours as h_1, h_2, etc.,

$$\frac{\text{Output}}{\text{Hours}} = h_1 \frac{Y_1}{H_1} + h_2 \frac{Y_2}{H_2} + \ldots$$

Hourly productivity can be raised if all other things remain constant, either by transferring workers from low-productivity to high-productivity sectors, or by raising productivity within sectors.

$\dfrac{\text{Hours}}{\text{Labour force}}$ *or working time rate* **2**

depends on organizational and institutional factors; whether there is a standard working day and working week; whether overtime is worked; whether multiple shifts exist; whether time is wasted in idleness, waiting for materials and components, or spent on holidays, weddings, funerals and at feasts. It also depends on natural factors such as the weather and the require- ments of harvest seasons. The ratio will depend both upon the level of demand and on the availability of essential supplies. A shift of rural labour to urban industry raises output not only by changing the weights attached to low- and high-productivity sectors, but also by raising hours per labour force. Unemployment of people both willing and able to work will show up as low hours/labour force. But the distinction between ability to work and willingness to work in any occupation outside the home may not always be easy to draw or even logically legitimate (e.g. Moslem women). Much time is spent in an underdeveloped country moving from one place to another: peasants walk from one piece of their land to another; women walk back and forth to draw water; migrant workers walk from one region to another to collect the harvest, etc. In so far as these movements are necessary to carry out specific tasks, given the prevailing institutions, transport facilities and cooperating factors, it is a factor accounting for low hourly productivity. But if the movements are in search of work, they come under low working time.

$$\frac{\text{Labour force}}{\text{People of working age}} \quad \textit{or participation rate} \qquad 3$$

depends on attitudes to work and to gainful activities (their dignity or ignominy), housing and transport facilities, legislation about minimum working age, compulsory full-time education, etc. Removal of the objections to certain kinds of work, increased incentives to earn money, emancipation of women, improved mobility, etc. will raise participation rates.

Education is by no means necessarily an investment with positive returns. It can result in reduced labour force participation. The educated unemployed, a widespread phenomenon in South Asia, figure prominently in unemployment statistics. While their geographical mobility between urban areas is high, their occupational mobility is small. They are not prepared to accept manual work. From a sample survey of unemployment in Calcutta in 1953 it appears that only 10 per cent of the unemployed were illiterate and 27 per cent had enjoyed higher education. Only 43 per cent of the total sample were seeking work involving manual labour.

The attitude to work appropriate for one who has enjoyed education is rooted in traditional attitudes and reinforced by the colonial heritage and possibly even by technical assistance. It is by no means just a matter of the wrong curriculum, for there is large and growing unemployment of engineers in India. It is estimated that there are now about 50,000 fully qualified engineers unemployed in 1970. The shortage exists in the same occupation for less qualified people, e.g. for semi-skilled technicians.

Both in Asia and in Africa, education reflects and instills an anti-rural bias; indeed the pressures for education arise from a desire on the part of parents to free their children from the miseries and hardships of rural life. Attitudes towards work among the educated – often ill-educated – are deeply rooted in the social structure and cannot easily be eliminated by restoring 'equilibrium' between supply and demand, by changing curricula or by exhortation.

There are parallels between the participation rate of the unemployed and the participation rate of women. Non-participation of women is linked with status and prestige, particularly in the higher strata of society.

$$\frac{\text{People of working age}}{\text{Population}} \quad is\ a \text{ demographic ratio} \qquad\qquad 4$$

and will depend on the age structure of the population, which can be predicted with a fair degree of accuracy. All those of working age in fourteen years' time are already alive and only mortality and migration rates have to be allowed for.

Since each of our four categories, viz. **1** hourly productivity, **2** working time rate, **3** participation rate and **4** demographic ratio, is an average of sectoral ratios, each sector appropriately weighted, the identity can be rewritten as:

$$\frac{Y}{P} = \left[h_1 \frac{Y_1}{H_1} + h_2 \frac{Y_2}{H_2} + \dots \right]. \quad \left[l_1 \frac{H_1}{L_1} + l_2 \frac{H_2}{L_2} + \dots \right].$$
$$\left[p_1 \frac{L_1}{W_1} + p_2 \frac{L_2}{W_2} + \dots \right]. \quad \left[s_1 \frac{W_1}{P_1} + s_2 \frac{W_2}{P_2} + \dots \right].$$

where Y is total income (output)
H is total hours worked
L is labour force
W is working age group
P is population
h is share in total hours worked
l is share in labour force
p is share in age group
s is share in population

and the suffixes indicate the different sectors.

The conventional presentation suffers from the fact that intensity of work, skill, organization, education, health, labour markets, transport, information, etc. are assumed given. Thus the only variables are demand and equipment. Furthermore, the assumption is usually made that unemployment and underemployment are 'involuntary'[2] This implies that

2. Currie (1966, p. 168): '[. . .] there is a great deal of idleness, voluntary, and involuntary' [in Colombia]. In the Ivory Coast, the essence of the primitive methods of producing coffee is described by Professor Barna as minimizing the amount of work necessary for obtaining a coffee crop of any sort.

willingness and ability to work are present. It also presupposes Labour Exchanges or some other objective test of voluntariness. Without such a test, it is impossible to tell. Some men work with dysentery, others don't. Some may not seek work because they know or believe that none is available. In the absence of an organized market for labour, the distinction between voluntary and involuntary unemployment breaks down. Unemployment and underemployment must also be defined with reference to some standard of working hours per day and working days per week. But such standards do not exist in large parts of traditional societies and are therefore introduced, usually implicitly, from outside. The whole set of questions relating to participation and organized work is thereby begged and a number of important relationships are concealed.

Once the relevant distinctions are drawn, policies can then be classified according to whether they use compulsive, permissive, or persuasive measures.[3] Table 1 provides illustrations.

Table 1

	Compulsive measures	Permissive measures	Persuasive measures (incentives)
Output/hour	Make pay depend on minimum output	Forbid trade union restrictions	Piece rates
Hours/lab. force	Fix eight-hour day	Improve diet	Overtime rates
Lab. force/ people of working age	Lock up workless, conscript, poll tax	Raise demand, provide equipment	Raise wages, supply incentive goods
People of working age/ population	Draconian measures against large families, forced late marriage	Birth control advice and contraceptives supplied	Birth control campaigns, a transistor for a vasectomy, child tax

The main lesson of this brief discussion is that the utilization of labour in developing countries has many dimensions and it is not warranted to assume that attitudes, aptitudes and institutions are adapted to full labour utilization or that consumption at low levels of living has no effect on productivity. Measures which raise labour productivity may reduce hours

3. The distinction is due to P. Sargant Florence (1953). The application to the theory of controls was suggested by Michael Lipton to Gunnar Myrdal. Further subdivisions are possible by combining the general-specific and positive-negative distinctions with those in in the table.

worked or participation rates[4] and measures which raise participation rates may lead to work-spreading and less intensive or to otherwise less productive work. Only a simultaneous attack on several of the relevant variables can bring about fuller utilization of labour.

The analysis also bears on the argument that there is a surplus of unskilled labour to draw on for any alternative activities and that labour opportunity costs are therefore low or zero. If these alternatives require attitudes, motivations, responses, work habits or institutions different from those to be found in, say, coffee growing, the fact that coffee growers dispose over spare time is irrelevant to the availability of labour supply for these alternatives. It would be dangerous to argue from the premise that coffee growing does not take up all the potential working hours of the farmers to the conclusion that alternative work opportunities, either elsewhere or in the place of residence, would automatically be taken up and result in larger production. Proposals for alternatives must be accompanied by detailed specification as to what measures of reform with respect of human attitudes to work and life and to social and commercial institutions, such as land reform, or reform of the civil service, or the creation of a labour market, or of credit channels, or of marketing outlets, have to accompany this shift in resources.

The main causes of the gross underutilization of labour are to be found in rural underemployment, combined with an industrial sector which, though often growing very rapidly in terms of production, is too small and often uses techniques inappropriate to absorb even a fraction of the rapidly growing potential labour force. Underutilization reflects the attitudes and institutions of a backward society and can therefore not be treated as a source for its transformation.

4. Currie (1966, p. 156): '[. . .] The relative high productivity of the machine, and the use of better techniques in commercial farming lower the return the colonial-type farmer can gain and make it even less practical for him to do all the costly things that would increase his productivity'.

References

BARBER, W. J. (1966), 'Some questions about labour force analysis in agrarian economies', *East African econ. Rev.*, vol. 2, new series, no. 1, pp. 23–37.
CURRIE, L. (1966), *Accelerating Development*, McGraw-Hill.
SARGANT FLORENCE, P. (1953), *The Logic of British and American Industry*, Routledge & Kegan Paul.

4. J. Weeks

Does Employment Matter?

From *Manpower and Unemployment Research in Africa*, Centre for Developing Area Studies, Montreal, 1971, vol. 4, no. 1.

The view that 'unemployment' is the central problem in less developed countries has swept aside all objections in its path. This is despite the absence of empirical data (Turnham and Jaeger, 1969) and despite the overwhelming theoretical and practical objections to the use of the term in the third world context[1] (Myrdal, 1968). At this stage, the literature on 'unemployment' in less developed countries is too extensive and the investment by international organizations in the implied analysis too great to hope for a reversal of the tidal wave. Therefore, this paper can hope to do little more than register a protest. My argument shall be: (a) it has not been established that 'unemployment' is in fact a general problem in less developed countries, (b) while there is a serious international crisis resulting from the relative impoverishment of the third world, it is misleading and of negative instrumental value to define this crisis as one of 'growing unemployment', and (c) defining the problem in this way implies a solution which will increase the dependence of the third world on the industrial countries. Finally, since it is this very dependence which has fostered the growing relative impoverishment, defining the crisis as one of unemployment precludes any solution.

Unemployment in the statistical sense refers to a situation in which a person has no substantial source of earned income, is looking actively for work, will accept a job at the going wage, and has been unable to find work. In the context of a developed country, this means quite simply, that a person has lost his job and is looking for another job. The condition is largely cyclical in nature – 'aggregate demand unemployment' – and for all practical purposes limited to the wage employed. This concept has little applicability outside the context of an economy wherein the vast majority of the population is obliged to sell its labor to others on a regular basis. In Africa south of the Sahara the entire rural labor force, and the vast majority of the urban labor force, does not sell its labor to others on a regular basis.

1. In constructing a case for the unemployment problem, the authors demonstrate how little data there actually are.

Further, the majority of urban Africans alive today will go their entire lives without a wage job of significant duration.

This is not to say that unemployment does not exist in some third world countries – it does, but in particular circumstances. It exists as a widespread phenomenon only in those countries with serious land shortage, either due to population pressure or to the proletarianization of the rural population as a consequence of plantation agriculture – Mauritius is the classic example of the former, and the West Indies of the latter, while Ceylon is a case where both elements play an important part. In other countries, it is a particularized phenomenon restricted (as far as we know) to certain social and occupational groups. In this case, we have no idea of the extent of the phenomenon, even among so-called 'school-leavers' – though ignorance has not prevented amazing generalizations.

The mistake by economists and other social scientists has been to conclude that because an individual in an urban area of a developing country is seeking a wage job but unable to find it, he is unemployed. In an industrial country, this is valid for the reason that casual wage employment and self-employment opportunities are severely limited, and those that exist would provide an income far less than that of the vast majority of the working population.[2] This is not true in developing countries. In most, the possibilities for casual and self-employment are extensive (indeed, such employment is the basis of the economy), and while the income derived from these pursuits in many cases is less than that for wage jobs, it approximates to that earned by peasants on the land, where most of the population is. If all those without wage jobs in African towns are to be considered unemployed, then we are not talking about rates of 20–25 per cent (Green 1969) but of 70–90 per cent. But, of course, it is absurd to define the employment norm in terms of the conditions enjoyed by a tiny majority of the labor force – this has not, however, deterred social scientists from doing so (Todaro, 1969) – better the irrelevant concept one can fit easily into *a priori* models than the relevant one that is not subject to partial differentiation.

The relevant concept in developing countries is poverty. The problem is not that manpower is being wasted because of involuntary idleness, but that the vast majority of urban dwellers are working long hours in a debilitating climate while burdened by energy-draining diseases and parasites to earn a marginal income. To say 'unemployment' is a major problem in urban Africa is not only incorrect, it is insulting to most of the labor force. Further, until sound studies are forthcoming on hours of work in urban self-employ-

2. The best example of this is the casual employment or part-time employment most married women are forced to accept. It is interesting that this is rarely considered to be 'unemployment'.

ment, it is mere speculation that 'underemployment' is prevalent in the sense of part-time involuntary idleness.[3]

Some have sought to get around the sticky problem of defining 'idleness' (ILO, 1970, p. 15) by suggesting that 'unemployment' be defined in terms of income. This cuts to the heart of the matter, and in doing so, renders 'unemployment' analytically redundant. For once it is conceded that the problem is income, or the inadequacy of income, we have granted that we are dealing with what has been called in the United States the 'working poor'. Of what use is it to call those who toil (for inadequate incomes) 'unemployed'? I suggest that the reason for this is political. Most of those who take this approach are well intentioned, but as is so often the case with well-intentioned fabrications, the broader consequences are disastrous, for developing countries in this case.

The use of the 'unemployment crisis' comes in large part from an attempt to stir the conscience of the wealthy countries at a time when political support for foreign aid (particularly in the US and the UK) is on the wane.[4] There is little hope these days of pricking any eleemosynary instincts by invoking images of poverty-stricken masses, so it is hoped that an image of endless queues at factory gates will have a greater impact (particularly if an implied threat is included that the 'unemployed' are a source of 'political instability')[5]

Unfortunately, if the hoped-for aid is forthcoming from the wealthy countries, by virtue of defining the problem in terms of 'unemployment' instead of poverty, it is unlikely that the aid can solve it.

If the problem is one of 'unemployment' then the solution is 'employment'. And if by employment, we mean 'wage employment', then the solution is clear – faster growth of the foreign-owned 'modern' (i.e. imported from the West) sector. This is not a solution; it is the problem itself. The logical consequence of the 'unemployment' crisis is that less-developed countries shall have to remake their economies in our (Western) image – the best sales pitch for the Western capital goods industries imaginable.[6]

The 'unemployment' problem is the consequence of the existence within third world economies of industry able to pay wages far in excess of the

3. It is open to question whether underemployment is a useful concept by any definition. Weeks (1971).

4. For a feeble attempt to invoke the same sentiments with the spectre of third world famine, see Dumont and Rosier (1969).

5. Space does not permit me to pursue the central role of 'political unrest' as the trump card of the 'unemployment crisis-makers', other than to note its obvious relevance to cold warriors. It seems largely to be a non-issue. See Nelson (1969).

6. For a much more coherent version of this argument, applied to the relationship between developed and underdeveloped countries in general, see the numerous articles by Ivan Illich in the *New York Review of Books* over the last two years.

income of the population as a whole, and able to pay these wages by virtue of competitive advantages denied indigenous small-scale enterprise – tax 'holidays', import tax rebates, tariff protection, accelerated depreciation concessions, and many others. The presence of these enterprises is no accident – in many cases, they cater to the consumption demands of a Western-educated elite.[7] This wage sector is an 'attractive nuisance', in that it provides a level of income for a tiny portion of the population which is extravagantly beyond the capacity of the economy to provide for the rest of the work force.

Explicitly or implicitly, this is the sector that most 'unemployment crisis' analysts would expand to provide employment for the 'unemployed' which must mean the entire population earning less than the 'alien' sector wage.[8] Yet it is inconceivable that under present conditions this sector could grow at a rate which would do much more than maintain its share of the urban employment market – indeed, doing this would be an improvement on past African experience (Weeks 1971). This is not because this sector's output is not growing – it is (given the extensive government concessions, any other result would be remarkable), but incremental output-employment ratios are remarkably high. This dilemma is generally recognized and attributed to the following causes: (a) foreign aid policies of industrial countries which frequently restrict use of aid to the capital (i.e. imported) component of projects, which, of course, encourages the maximization of this component; (b) artificially low interest rates and overvalued exchange rates which cheapen capital and encourage use of labor-saving technology; (c) tax concessions on investment expenditure which encourage excessive capital intensity; (d) shortage of supervisory labor complementary with unskilled and semi-skilled labor; (e) the industrial country monopoly on the supply of capital goods, which results in a growing labor-saving bias to industrial techniques; (f) a distribution of income in less developed countries which biases the structure of demand toward capital and skill intensive elite-goods.

The diagnosis has been turned on its head, however. These are not causes at all – they are symptoms, symptoms of a development strategy which seeks to reproduce a Western consumer goods economy in Africa. Such a strategy will only be fostered by a Western-oriented elite with a bias in its own consumption toward capital-intensive goods (see (f) above).

7. To take an extreme example, the Nigerian 1970–74 development plan calls for a privately owned '*passenger* vehicle assembly plant'. It is not referring to buses.

8. The expanding sector would not have to absorb the entire self-employed sector, for presumably as the 'modern' sector expanded, incomes would at some point begin so rise in the other sector due to shortage of labor. This theoretical point is irrelevant, tince the 'modern' sector is unlikely to expand fast enough to absorb large amounts of labor in any case. See below.

These goods must be produced with Western technology which is capital- and skill-intensive (d) and (e), and this foreign capital will only be attracted if the enterprises are made profitable through extensive government concessions (e), and the resulting importation of capital equipment and intermediate goods will perpetuate a balance of payments crisis, leading to continually overvalued exchange rates (b), and the reliance on capital biased foreign aid (a).

The solution clearly is not a piecemeal attack on these problems, which are inherent in the developing strategy, and in many cases beyond the control of the developing country, but to reject the strategy itself.[9] Once the strategy is rejected, 'unemployment', which was the result of the presence of the alien sector, is gone, and poverty remains.

The crisis of the relative impoverishment of the third world is essentially a political crisis – given the present distribution of income and political power. The elites are incapable of generating a development strategy which is appropriate to the resource endowments of the economies in question. In the process of solving this problem, employment does not matter.

9. To its great credit, the Colombia Report recognizes this, and eloquently argues that the 'employment' problem in Colombia cannot be solved without a redistribution of income and wealth in order to change the structure of consumer demand, so that it is consistent with the resource endowment of Colombia, rather than with that of the United States and other industrial countries. This is another way of saying a new development strategy is called for. I would take issue only with the use of 'unemployment' and 'employment' as the key analytical variables. This emphasis, I believe, seriously dilutes the strength of an otherwise path-breaking document.

References

DUMONT, R., and ROSIER, B. (1969), *The Hungry Future*, Deutsch.
GREEN, R. H. (1969), 'Wage levels, employment, productivity and consumption', in J. R. Sheffield, *Education, Employment and Rural Development*, East African Publishing House.
ILO (1970), *Towards Full Employment: A Programme for Colombia, Prepared by an Inter-Agency Team Organized by the International Labor Office*, Geneva, ILO.
MYRDAL, G. (1968), *Asian Drama*, © Twentieth Century Fund, Penguin 1968.
NELSON, J. M. (1969), 'Migrants, urban poverty and instability in developing nations', *Harvard University Occasional Papers in International Affairs*, no. 22, September.
TODARO, M. (1969), 'A model of labor migration and urban unemployment in less developed countries', *Amer. econ. Rev.*, vol. 59, no. 1.
TURNHAM, D., and JAEGER, I. (1971), *The Employment Problem in Less Developed Countries: A Review*, ch. 3, OECD.
WEEKS, J. F. (1971), 'Wage policy and the colonial legacy – a comparative study', *J. Mod. African Studies*, vol. 9, no. 3, pp. 361–387.

5 K. Hart

Informal Income Opportunities and Urban Employment in Ghana[1]

Extract from K. Hart 'Informal income opportunities and urban employment in
Ghana', paper delivered to Conference on Urban unemployment in Africa, Institute
of Development Studies, University of Sussex, 12–16 September 1971.

The informal opportunity structure

The definitional distinction being drawn here is between activities classified
as formal, i.e. wage-earning employment, and informal, i.e. self-employment. This parallels that drawn between the organized and unorganized
sections of the urban labour force, common synonyms for the latter being
'the reserve army of underemployed and unemployed', 'those who are self-
employed in small enterprises', etc. Often one is talking of those workers
who are enumerated by surveys of establishments and the remainder who are
not. It is sometimes estimated for African cities that the latter group is at
least as large as the first. There is wider variance, however, in estimations
of the significance of these informal activities; the semi-automatic classification of unorganized workers as 'underemployed', 'shoeshine boys,
sellers of matches etc.' contrasts with the view which stresses the important
part played by these workers in providing many of the essential services on
which life in the city is dependent. Clearly, therefore, when we address
ourselves to this aspect of urban economic life, we must be careful to
encompass a wide-ranging scale, from the marginal activities of the 'unemployed', housewives and other part-time workers to more substantial
enterprises.

Moreover, if we are to consider income opportunities outside formal
employment, we must include certain kinds of crime. The incidence of

1. This case-study arose from anthropological fieldwork towards a University of
Cambridge PhD in 1965–8. The ethnographic present, whenever used, refers to this
period. I am much indebted to John Bryden of the University of East Anglia, Norwich,
for many insights into the relevance of these findings for modern economic approaches
to unemployment in developing countries.
The paper describes the economic activities of the low-income section of the urban
labour force in Accra, the urban proletariat into which the unskilled and illiterate
majority of Frafra migrants are drawn. Many of these mobile workers are housed in
the slum area on the city's northern outskirts, of which the centre is Nima. In the late
1960s over a third of the Accra labour force lived in areas like Nima (such as New
Town, Sabon Zongo, etc.), but the Nima district alone in 1960 constituted some 8 per
cent of the city's population.

illegitimate activity in Nima was all-pervasive. It was difficult indeed to find anyone who had not at some time transgressed the law, usually with some profitable result if undetected. In classifying the opportunity structure for members of the urban proletariat, a distinction is made in the informal sector between legitimate and illegitimate activities. The following constitutes an attempted typology:

1. Formal income opportunities
(a) public sector wages
(b) private sector wages
(c) transfer payments – pensions, unemployment benefits (if any) etc.

2. Informal income opportunities (Legitimate)
(a) primary and secondary activities – farming, market-gardening, building contractors and associated activities, self-employed artisans, shoe-makers, tailors, etc., manufacturers of beers and spirits.
(b) tertiary enterprises with relatively large capital inputs – housing, transport, utilities, commodity speculation, rentier activities, etc.
(c) small-scale distribution – market operatives, petty trade, streethawkers, caterers in food and drink, bars, carriers (*kayakaya*), commission agents and dealers.
(d) other services – musicians, launderers, shoeshiners, barbers, night soil removers, photographers, etc.; brokerage and middlemanship (the *maigida* system in markets, law courts etc.[2]); ritual services, magic and medicine.
(e) private transfer payments – gifts and similar flows of money and goods between persons; borrowing, begging.

3. Informal income opportunities (Illegitimate)
(a) services – 'spivvery' in general; receiving stolen goods, usury and pawn-broking (at illegal interest rates), drug-pushing, prostitution, poncing ('pilot boy'), smuggling, bribery, political corruption Tammany Hall-style, protection rackets.
(b) transfers – petty theft (pickpockets, etc.), larceny (burglary and armed robbery), peculation and embezzlement, confidence tricksters (money doubling, etc.), gambling.

This list is by no means exhaustive, but serves to illustrate the range of income opportunities widely available to the urban proletariat living in areas such as Nima. The exception is political corruption and racketeering, which were included for reasons of completeness and comparison with similar areas where crime is organized at a higher level than in Ghana.

2. *Maigida* (Hausa = houseowner) is not only a high status category in Ghana, but also a remunerative profession in certain trading and legal networks where the ownership of a house is a part-qualification for brokerage activities. See e.g. Hill (1966).

[. . .] We are in a position now to make some general points. The first relates to variations in the availability of both formal and informal opportunities between different tribes, socioeconomic classes and other social groupings (such as the educated and the illiterate). Economic opportunities are distributed extremely unevenly over the regions and ethnic groups of Ghana. Thus, while 21 per cent of Gas (the dominant tribe of Accra) had a white-collar job in 1960, only 1 per cent of the northern Mole–Dagbani group of tribes fell into this category. The extremes are well illustrated by comparing the 200 Frafra white-collar workers with the 5000 from the smaller Akwapim group in Southern Ghana; the latter rate is seventy-five times the former. These differences, which add an explosive regional/tribal element to Ghana's emergent class structure, are largely attributable to differing lengths of exposure to colonial rule and the spread of Western education.

Frafras and other groups like them when seeking employment in the South, are very conservative – few will apply for a job where they have no particularistic relationship, such as a previously employed kinsman; and perhaps their view of the recruitment process is justified. Information about vacancies tends to travel along informal social networks rather than through employment exchanges and nepotism is not unknown in Ghana. The result is that migrants from one village or area tend to be clustered occupationally – twenty cooks out of twenty-two Accra residents from one section, half of another section employed as construction workers and so on. This is perhaps why virtually no Frafras throughout Accra–Tema (and there were about 10,000 of them) were employed in factories during the mid-1960s. We have already seen the same phenomenon in specialized commodity trading. Thus, a significant constraint limiting access to urban employment of all kinds is the actor's perception of the competitive advantage or disadvantage to himself of ethnic- or kin-group membership.

All types of work in the city are, therefore, viewed differently according to the social position of the job-seeker. The status-ranking of occupations varies between social groups and, while some (such as the Islamic community) may accord high prestige to commercial success, others may look down on all informal occupations. An independent variable in this is undoubtedly the degree of exposure to western-style education, the means by which we may say that many younger Ghanaians are socialized into rejecting opportunities outside the conventional framework of a bureaucratic career. If, to the illiterate Frafra migrant, informal opportunities offer a ladder out of poverty, to the educated youth with his eyes on conventional advancement, such employment may be both socially inferior and undesirable. An interesting corollary to this analysis is the observation that, as an increasing proportion of middle-school leavers find their qualifications inadequate for scarce white-collar jobs and therefore must compete with illiterates for manual work, their reluctance to envisage informal occupational roles as desirable is diminished.

A further group of general remarks relates to the combination of a number of income sources by individuals. If job duplication in the formal sector is common, multiple informal employment both with and without simultaneous wage employment is almost universal in the economic behaviour of Accra's proletariat. Only rarely is one individual or family dependent on one source of income. This preference for diversity of income streams has its roots in the traditional risk aversion of peasants under conditions of extreme uncertainty and is justified by the insecurity of urban workers today.[3] The most salient characteristic of wage employment in the eyes of the urban proletariat is not the absolute amount of income receipts but its reliability. For informal employment, even of the legitimate variety, is risky and expected rewards highly variable. Thus, for subsistence purposes alone, regular wage employment, however badly paid, has some solid advantages; and hence men who derive substantial incomes from informal activities may still retain or desire formal employment. In all the previous discussion of informal occupations, perhaps the paramount issue has been, 'How easy is it for someone who lacks alternative means of supporting himself to find work of this kind?' The answer is, of course, dependent on the type of work. But [. . .] the range of opportunities available outside the organized labour market is so wide that no one need be totally without income of some kind, however irregular.

Aggregate perspectives

The activities described so far are widely acknowledged as typical of economic life in the city slums of developing and developed countries. But they are usually perceived as being of little consequence except to the individuals forced to live in this way. [. . .] Can we say, from an aggregate rather than individual perspective, that there is more to the 'informal economy' of the slum than this?

[. . .] We must confront the question, 'Is the informal economy homogeneous in its relationship with movements in formal labour demand, as measured by total wage expenditure?' If it is, and the relationship is a direct one, then urban income opportunities may be summarized by an indicator composed of the volume of urban jobs and current wage levels in the organized labour market. But, if the relationship is complex and all informal sectors are *not* alike in their response to variations in employment levels, such an indicator alone would be inadequate.

We may begin by hypothesizing that numbers engaged (or man/hours)

3. See Hart (1970).

in all informal activities would rise if pressure on the number of wage jobs (let us say, 'unemployment') rose. But an increase in labour supply is likely only to reduce returns to individuals rather than raise aggregate production of informal goods and services. [. . .] But if unemployment rose because of increases in the supply of unskilled labour to the urban market, no relaxation in demand (for informal goods and services) need be anticipated. This argument holds with force for income gained through the redistribution of wealth via illegitimate transfers (e.g. burglary in the suburbs), which is independent of demand factors and which, by virtue of resultant expenditure within the informal economy, has important spread effects throughout the urban proletariat.

It is, therefore, far from obvious that fluctuations in the demand for and supply of informal goods and services within the urban proletariat are a function of variations in formal employment levels. Whereas the supply of labour to the informal economy is likely to vary inversely with the level of employment, in some sectors this may lead to a simultaneous rise in the aggregate production of informal goods and services or in the volume of transfers, thus counteracting the income effects of increasing residual underemployment and unemployment among proletarians. In other words, having observed how informal activities may act as a buffer against unemployment from the individual's point of view, we may proceed to argue that the informal economy in aggregate possibly acts to countervail the full effects of increasing urban unemployment. Indeed, the informal economy, with its emphasis on tertiary activities may be developing at a rate faster than other sectors of the economy and thus taking up some of the slack created by inadequate rates of growth in the well-documented modern sector.

[. . .] The main point is that this whole area of analysis has been neglected because of the elusive nature of the subject matter. When half of the urban labour force falls outside the organized labour market it cannot be disputed that serious investigation of their economic behaviour is long overdue.

References

HART, K. (1970), 'Small-scale entrepreneurs in Ghana and development planning', *J. Devel. Stud.*, vol. 6, no. 4, pp. 104–20.

HILL, P. (1966), 'Landlords and brokers', *Markets and Marketing in Africa*, published by the Centre for African Studies, Edinburgh, pp. 1–14.

Part Two
Population: Growth, and Migration

The rapid growth in population in most developing countries over the
last few decades has increased the labour force – i.e. the number of
people for whom remunerated work has to be found – by unprecedented
proportions. No discussion of development problems is conceivable
without reference to the consequences of the population explosion. In
this section readings are included which discuss first of all the
dimensions of total population growth and the arguments for a
population policy; and secondly the changes in the distribution of
population which are taking place through migration.

This section opens with a summary statement prepared by the ILO
of the world labour force situation at the beginning of the 1970s
(Reading 6). One important aspect of labour supply mentioned but not
explored in this reading is the participation rate. It is evident that
participation rates do not remain constant over time. In the first reading
of this volume – on the unemployment situation in Colombia – it was
pointed out that participation rates fall as unemployment rises:
overall more people are discouraged from trying to find work. But such
aggregate figures often conceal more subtle changes within sub-groups.
Urrutia (1968), in fact, found in his meticulous analysis of figures for
Bogotá that some categories – in his case younger unmarried women
and women over forty-five years of age – who usually do *not* participate
in the labour force, will enter the labour market in search of work
when unemployment is high, in order to make up for the lost earnings
of the family's usual breadwinners. This is an important finding, not to
be lost sight of.

We then turn more specifically to the consequences of the population
explosion for people's chances of employment, income and a decent
standard of living. The extract from Myrdal's balanced discussion of
population trends in Asia (Reading 7) should dispel any doubts about
their economic effects. It is true that changes in the rate of population
increase do not have an impact on the labour force for many years: at
any point in time those who will be part of the working population fifteen

years hence have already been born. But this lag does not make the problem any less urgent. As Myrdal points out, the long run cumulative effects of continued high population increase are nothing short of disastrous, especially with regard to employment.

On the other hand, some less cautious commentators, forgetful of all other problems, would have one believe that no more is needed for the poor countries to become rich than a massive distribution of pills and condoms. In reaction, some circles in the developing world have come to see the efforts to spread family planning in their countries as no more than a wicked imperialist plot.

Myrdal tries to disentangle the effects on family planning practices of economic development on the one hand, and of government policies and public ideologies on the other. The relevant experience of now industrialized countries demonstrates that spontaneous family planning seems to be more a by-product of the former. It is true that ethos as well as ignorance and lack of access – not to speak of enforced legal impediments to birth control – can make a substantial difference, but socio-economic and associated educational factors are at least equally important. Widespread poverty and unemployment are not conditions in which the spontaneous adoption of family planning practices is likely; an active population policy is, in this context, all the more urgent.

Turning to the way in which the distribution of population within the country is changing: the United Nations estimated that between 1920 and 1960 the world's urban population (living in centres of 20,000 inhabitants or more) increased from sixty-eight million to 320 million, and the population living in large cities (that is, in centres of over 500,000 inhabitants) increased from fifteen million to 139 million.[1] The growth of towns in Africa between the early 1950s and the 1960s is illustrated by Table 1 of Frank (Reading 24). The data is extremely uncertain but the annual average rate of growth of the urban centres shown is about 7 per cent though with the growth rates of individual cities apparently ranging from barely 2 per cent to about 15 per cent. This high rate of urban growth characteristic of most Third World countries reflects the importance of the migration movement and what is more, it usually demonstrates that migration streams focus predominantly on only one or at most a few towns within each country.

Migration patterns in the present day are complex, with the predominant pattern being rural to urban migration. The migrant may stay for a relatively brief spell in the city, he may stay until retirement before returning home, or the move may be permanent. In Reading 9

1. Figures from United Nations (1968).

Elkan discusses such temporary stays in towns in his analysis of
'circular' migration in Africa. Substantial migration flows may
develop between rural areas: people being attracted to areas where
there are agricultural schemes which provide more jobs. Empirical
evidence shows that return migration is much more significant in many
countries than was previously imagined. As Caldwell (1969) found in
his detailed survey of migration in Ghana, many of the young people
will go between rural home and the towns several times.

Central to an understanding of the decision to migrate is the role of
information. The rate of migration depends on the potential migrant's
perception of his own environment and how he sees it in relation to
that in other parts of the country. Differences in income, jobs and
opportunities not only must exist, but they must be seen to exist, before
migration will take place on a large scale. Hutton (1970) has argued
that it is this felt cash need and level of aspiration which will account
for migration. The spread of education over a country has played an
important part in diffusing general information of the urban way of
life, but propensity to migrate will also be related to the degree of
contact a particular community has with the town. The greater the
number of people who have gone to look for work, education, or
opportunities, in a town, the more likely it is that friends and relatives will
follow. Such personal information flows will determine when a migrant
will move and where he will move to. The different degree of accessibility
and contact that exists between places can help account for the seemingly
paradoxical situation mentioned by Hutton: the richer rural community
where cash crop production is relatively profitable may supply a greater
number of migrants than a rural area where incomes and opportunities
are much lower but which is more remote from the flows of information
concerning the other parts of the country.

Turning to the demand for labour, employment in the high
productivity jobs in the 'modern' or 'formal' sector has not expanded
at the same rate as output – employment needs may even decline in
certain sectors – and yet migration persists. As Todaro (Reading 8)
argues, there is now a substantial disparity in the wage level between
the jobs in the 'modern' sector and jobs in the other sectors. Also
important is the fact that wage employment is often a more reliable
source of income than either agriculture or the 'informal' or
unenumerated sector. It is rational for the migrant to go to the urban
centre and risk a period of unemployment or underemployment in the
'informal' sector in the hopes of getting a regular well-paid job. In
Todaro's thesis the migration decision rests on the probability of
employment in the formal sector: thus if new employment opportunities

are created in the city, the effect might well be to increase the numbers who are unemployed or underemployed there – because the new opportunities will attract many more migrants who judge the new situation to be more favourable.

References

CALDWELL, J. C. (1969), *African rural-urban migration: the movement to Ghana's towns*, Australian National University Press.

HUTTON, C. (1970), 'Rates of labour migration', in J. Gugler (ed.), *Urban Growth in Sub-saharan Africa*, Makerere Institute of Social Research.

UNITED NATIONS (1968), 'Urbanization: development policies and planning', *Int. Social Devel. Rev.*, no. 1.

URRUTIA, M. (1968), 'El desempleo disfrazado en Bogotá' in *Empleo y Desempleo en Colombia*, CEDE.

6 International Labour Office

The Employment Prospect for the 1970s[1]

From *The World Employment Programme*, International Labour Conference,
Fifty-sixth Session, Report 4, ILO, 1971.

The rapid population growth which the world has been experiencing for the past quarter century has two main effects on the employment situation. First, it is causing an almost explosive growth of population of working age and since it appears more and more clearly that economic development will not of itself necessarily bring about a sufficient increase in employment, it is resulting in a widening gap between the supply of and the demand for labour. Second, an increasing scarcity of land in relation to population tends – other things being equal – to accentuate rural–urban migration, thus intensifying the problem of urban unemployment. The Report on the World Employment Programme submitted to the 53rd Session of the Conference in 1969 already showed the magnitude of the problem facing the world and in particular the developing countries. Since then, further studies and projects have only confirmed the seriousness of the situation. These make it possible to up-date the information presented in 1969 on the expected growth of the world population and labour force, and to compare these figures with expectations concerning the growth of employment.

Total population

The United Nations produced in 1970 new projections of total population by country, by sex and by age group as assessed in 1968 (earlier United Nations projections, produced in 1966, corresponded to the situation as assessed in 1963).

As Table 1 indicates, the world's population, excluding the People's Republic of China, which numbered almost 2350 million persons in 1960, was estimated at close to 2900 million in 1970 and is expected to reach almost 3600 million by 1980. In the more developed regions of the world the observed growth of almost 12 million persons a year is expected to continue at much the same pace during the coming decade. In the less developed regions, however, where the population had been growing at about 42 million persons a year during the past decade, it is now expected

1. New data, made available by the Employment Planning and Promotion Department of the ILO, have been incorporated in this reading.

Table 1 **Total population in the more developed and less developed regions of the world 1960–80**

	Population (*millions*)			Annual growth rates	
	1960	*1970*	*1980*	*1960–70*	*1970–80*
More developed regions*	964·6	1078·0	1198·1	1·1	1·1
Less developed regions	1381·1	1797·6	2375·3	2·7	2·8
Asia†	916·2	1192·7	1570·8	2·7	2·8
Africa	251·4	321·7	427·3	2·5	2·9
Latin America	213·4	283·3	377·2	2·9	2·9
Total†	2345·7	2875·6	3573·4	2·1	2·2

* Europe, North America, USSR, Oceania, Southern Africa, Japan.
† Excluding the People's Republic of China.

Source: UN Population Division and ILO Statistical Branch.

to grow by almost 58 million persons a year during the decade 1970–80. As a result, the population in the less developed regions of the world in 1980 will number close to 2400 million persons, more than the population of the entire world in 1960, (in both cases again excluding the People's Republic of China).

The world labour force

[. . .] New data on the world labour force have been prepared by the ILO on the basis of the new United Nations population projections and ILO estimates and projections of labour force activity rates by country, by sex and by age-group as assessed in 1970.[2]

The labour force of the world, excluding the People's Republic of China, in 1970 is now estimated at about 1150 million persons (see Table 2), of whom over 650 million are in the less developed regions of the world.

[. . .] Table 2 shows also that the rate of growth of the labour force in the less developed regions during the past decade was almost twice that experienced in the more developed regions. During the present decade the rate of growth in the former regions is expected to increase from its present level of 2·1 per cent a year to 2·3 per cent, while in the more developed regions it will remain at a level of about 1·1 per cent a year.

2. The earlier ILO estimates and projections of labour force were based on earlier United Nations population data and on ILO labour force activity rates as assessed in 1965. The new regional data on the labour force have been derived by aggregating the estimates and projections obtained independently for each of the countries within a given region. In addition, the ILO methodology for projecting activity rates has undergone considerable revision and refinement. These new estimates and projections also take into account more recent data and more detailed information.

Table 2 Labour force in the more developed and less developed regions of the world, 1960–80

	Active population (millions)			Annual growth rates	
	1960	1970	1980	1960–70	1970–80
More developed regions*	435·7	484·0	538·5	1·1	1·1
Less developed regions	542·3	665·0	838·0	2·1	2·3
Asia†	370·2	452·5	569·1	2·0	2·3
Africa	102·0	124·3	155·4	2·0	2·3
Latin America	70·1	88·2	113·6	2·3	2·6
Total†	978·0	1149·0	1376·5	1·6	1·8
	Participation rates (percentages)				
More developed regions*	45·2	44·9	44·9		
Less developed regions	39·3	37·0	35·3		
Asia†	40·4	37·9	36·2		
Africa	40·6	38·6	36·4		
Latin America	32·8	31·1	30·1		
Total†	41·7	40·0	38·5		

* Europe, USSR, Japan, North America, Southern Africa, Oceania.
† Excluding the People's Republic of China.
Source: ILO Statistical Branch.

During the past decade the world's labour force, still excluding the People's Republic of China, grew by approximately 17 million workers a year, that is 5 million in the more developed regions and 12 million in the less developed regions. During the present decade it is expected to rise by some 23 million workers a year, including 5·5 million in the more developed regions and 17·3 million in the less developed regions. Thus, more people will be added to the labour force of the less developed regions during the period 1970–80 than were added to the entire labour force of the world (without China) between 1960 and 1970, while by 1980 the labour force of the less developed regions of the world will equal in size that of the entire world (without China) in 1960.

The employment outlook

In the light of the impressive increase in the labour force in the developing countries to be anticipated for the present decade, what is the outlook for the development of employment?

The concepts employed are so ambiguous and the available statistics so scanty[3] that any answer to this question must be in very general terms, but it is important to attempt to give some figures in connection with the probable trends. It is essential to have some idea of the extent of the employment problem in order to determine the effort to be undertaken, and to judge whether the situation is getting better or worse and how it is affected by various forms of action.

One of the methods that can be used for this purpose – even if, for reasons explained below, it is far from perfect – consists of attempting to establish employment growth projections and to compare the resulting figures with the forecasts for labour force trends.

The manpower projections given above are based on relatively reliable estimates of the total population but they remain subject to uncertainty in regard to the evolution of activity rates and the ambiguity surrounding the whole concept in the developing countries. Nevertheless, since the persons who will be of working age between 1970 and 1980 have already been born, these projections are free from other elements of uncertainty such as might result from substantial variation in fertility rates.

On the other hand, any employment projection, even in the relatively short term (for example up to 1980), is much more open to question. It is nevertheless worthwhile attempting to outline the major trends in employment for the decade 1970–80. The estimates given below are the result of summary projections based on international comparison and convey no more than a rough idea of the magnitude of the various factors.[4] They correspond, by and large, to an extrapolation of tendencies observed during the preceding decade, assuming the absence of any policy directed towards systematic expansion of employment. These projections (covering thirteen sub-regions and seven major economic sectors) will be presented for the three major developing regions: Asia (excluding the People's Republic of China), Africa (excluding Southern Africa) and Latin America, and according to the three major traditional economic sectors, namely agriculture (including agriculture, forestry and fishing), industry and construction (including mining and quarrying, energy and construction) and services (including commerce, transport and communications and miscellaneous services).

Table 3 shows in respect of the three major regions the estimated employment figures for 1960 and 1970 (since many developing countries have no

3. For detailed indications regarding the method followed, see Sabolo (1969) and ILO (1969).
4. The projections for the labour force and for employment, though covering the same geographical regions, should *not* be used to arrive at unemployment figures by simple subtraction.

Table 3 **Estimated employment in 1960 and 1970** (in millions)

| | Employment | | Increase |
	1960	1970	
Asia*	343	420	77
Africa†	95	115	20
Latin America	67	87	20
Total	505	622	117

* Excluding the People's Republic of China.
† Excluding Southern Africa.

employment statistics the figure can only be estimated by using various factors).

Thus total employment in these regions probably increased between 1960 and 1970 by slightly less than 120 million, the annual growth rate being about 2 per cent. This compares with an increase in the labour force of the same countries amounting to a total of 127 million.

The same estimates suggest that in 1970 the percentage distribution of employment by principal sectors was roughly as follows:

Table 4 **Estimated distribution of employment by sector, 1970**

	Agriculture		Industry and construction		Services		Total	
	%	millions	%	millions	%	millions	%	millions
Asia*	66	277	12	50	22	93	100	420
Africa†	67	77	12	14	21	24	100	115
Latin America	34	30	27	23	39	34	100	87
Total	61	384	14	87	25	151	100	622

* Excluding the People's Republic of China.
† Excluding Southern Africa.

The projections for 1980 show a probable increase of about 180 million in the number of jobs, bringing the total up to some 800 million, distributed as follows:

Table 5 **Estimated employment in 1980** (in millions)

	Employment in 1980	Increase from 1970 to 1980
Asia*	535	115
Africa†	149	34
Latin America	115	28
Total	799	177

* Excluding the People's Republic of China.
† Excluding Southern Africa.

For all the countries covered by these projections of employment in 1980, the total labour force will probably amount to about 856 million.

The distribution of employment by major economic sector in 1980 would not appear likely to differ essentially from the situation in 1970, to judge from the estimates in Table 6:

Table 6 **Estimated distribution of employment by sector, 1980**

	Agriculture		Industry and construction		Services		Total	
	%	millions	%	millions	%	millions	%	millions
Asia*	59	316	15	80	26	139	100	535
Africa†	57	85	16	24	27	40	100	149
Latin America	26	30	30	34	44	51	100	115
Total	54	431	17	138	29	230	100	799

* Excluding the People's Republic of China.
† Excluding Southern Africa.

Certain conclusions can be drawn from these figures provided it is borne in mind that they are estimates based on the projection of past tendencies.

In Asia the proportion of agricultural employment, although declining, will probably still continue to account for about 60 per cent of total employment. The breakdown of overall employment growth in Asia should be as follows: 30 per cent in agriculture, 30 per cent in industry and construction, and 40 per cent in services.

In Africa agricultural employment may be expected to follow the same lines as in Asia; agriculture will provide some 35 per cent of the new jobs, industry and construction barely more than 25 per cent and services around 40 per cent.

In Latin America the share of agricultural employment will probably decline until it represents only slightly more than one quarter of the total employed population, while the number of jobs in agriculture will most likely remain stable from 1970 to 1980, continuing the trend that began during the past decade. Thus the jobs created between 1970 and 1980 will be distributed between industry and construction on the one hand (about 40 per cent) and services on the other (about 60 per cent), which will bring up service employment to nearly 45 per cent of total employment.

These rough estimates point to certain major trends. Except in Latin America, agriculture will probably continue to use a large proportion of the total employed, absorbing about one third of the new jobs created during the decade 1970–80.

Employment in industry and construction will rise fairly rapidly, and faster than employment in services. Nevertheless, in view of the meagre proportion it represents in 1970 (about 15 per cent) it can make only a very slight contribution to the absorption of manpower. If it is found necessary to use labour-intensive or progressive technologies it might be wisest not to expect very spectacular results, at least during the forthcoming decade, seeing how small a proportion of total employment this sector represents. (See Marsden, Reading 25.)

Employment in services will certainly not increase at an annual rate amounting to as much as 4 per cent, and will therefore fall short of the equivalent figure in industry and construction, but the proportion of the total number of jobs created will be greater.

These projections suggest strongly that employment is likely to grow less rapidly than the labour force during the 1970s. But from the procedural viewpoint a comparison between labour force (or labour supply) projections and employment (or labour demand) projections is an unsatisfactory way of attempting to measure the magnitude of the employment problem. There will not simply be a certain increase in the labour force, a certain (smaller) increase in the number of jobs and a certain number of additional people left jobless or unemployed. There may, indeed, be a substantial increase in overt unemployment, but this is likely to be overshadowed in importance by increases in underemployment. Thus, employment increases such as those expected in the services sector in Latin America seem very likely to exceed the actual needs of that sector, and therefore to result in additional underemployment.

It is well known that underemployment is already widespread throughout the developing world. This situation was reviewed in detail in the Report on the World Employment Programme submitted to the 53rd (1969) Session of the Conference. Attempts to quantify underemployment and to describe its characteristics in numerical terms have not, however, met with great success in the past: the very nature of underemployment – and, in fact, of unemployment – in developing countries is such that the concepts derived in developed countries and hitherto also employed in analysing employment in them are rarely adapted to the entirely different situation prevailing in the developing countries.

For instance, the distinction between members of the labour force and dependants is not clear in most parts of most developing countries. This is particularly true in many rural areas where men and women, and children above a fairly young age, all devote a part of their time to productive activities. Even in urban areas there are large numbers of people who carry on certain kinds of work sporadically, but who are also at least partly dependent on others. [. . .]

References

Sabolo, Y. (1969), 'Sectoral employment growth: the outlook for 1980', *Int. Labour Rev.*, vol. 100, no. 5.

ILO (1969), *Sectoral Growth of Employment*, mimeo. document D.5, ILO

7 Gunnar Myrdal

Population Trends and Population Policies

Extract from G. Myrdal, *Asian Drama*, vol. 2, ch. 28, © 1968 by the Twentieth Century Fund, Penguin, 1968.

Two types of effects

Basic to our analysis of the economic consequences of population trends is the fact, demonstrated by Coale and Hoover (1958, p. 232), that a decline in fertility rates would have no substantial influence on the size of the labour force in underdeveloped countries, for as long as twenty or even thirty years. For fifteen years ahead this is self-evident; but even for some fifteen years beyond that, Coale and Hoover's calculations indicate the effect to be gradual and slow.[1] Thus the impact of a decline in fertility on the number of producers is delayed for almost a generation. Its impact on the number of consumers, however, is immediate: the relative number *outside* the labour force begins to fall as soon as the fertility rate declines.

An analysis of the influence of population trends on economic development must therefore distinguish between two types of effects, one arising from *changes in the size of the labour force* and the other from *changes in the age distribution* [. . .].

Change in the age structure

As a result of the very high fertility rates experienced in the relevant past period, the age distribution of the populations of the South Asian countries is skewed in the direction of a high dependency burden. The proportion of children in these populations is large. Reduction of fertility rates would have the direct effect of decreasing the dependency burden. There would

1. Coale and Hoover estimated in this study that a decline of 50 per cent in fertility in India between 1956 and 1986 would reduce the number in the 15–64 age group at the end of the period by only about 8 per cent below what it would be under conditions of constant fertility throughout the thirty years.

Age limits for the labour force cannot be rigidly demarcated. The custom of defining the range as 15 to 60 or 65 years is not altogether realistic. In the Western countries more and more young people attend school beyond 15 years of age, thus remaining outside the labour force, and many people over 60 or 65 are productively employed. In South Asia as well the limits are, for different reasons, far from clear-cut. As we have observed elsewhere (appendix 16 and chapters 22 and 23), many of the very young and very old work, particularly in agriculture, at least during certain periods of the year, while many in the normal working ages are idle or work very little.

immediately be fewer children to support, and if the lower fertility were maintained, this decrease in the dependency burden would continue until the children began to reach working age. The decrease in the proportion of children would be progressive if the decline in fertility rates were gradually intensified. A couple of decades hence, when the depleted age cohorts entered the reproductive period, there would also be a decline in the relative number of people in the reproductive ages. Still further ahead, if fertility should be stabilized, at a lower level than now, the age distribution would tend to become 'normal', it would not return to the present high dependency ratio.

With a lower dependency burden, income per head, however we calculate it, would rise. If all of the rise in average income were devoted to increased consumption, if the average child and adult maintained the same relative shares of consumption, and if public expenditure for consumption purposes were kept at a constant figure, there would be a general rise in levels of living corresponding to the increase in income per head. Everyone would eat better and be better housed; all would have a larger share in the educational and health facilities and other benefits provided for in the public budget.[2]

The static assumptions made above are, of course, not realistic because of the cumulative effects of circular causation. Thus a secondary effect of the higher consumption levels would be to raise productivity by increasing both labour input and labour efficiency. This effect would be most pronounced in the poorest countries, where particularly low levels of nutrition, health, and education depress the duration and efficiency of work, and participation in work, even more than elsewhere. Moreover, at progressively higher levels of income per head, more could be saved or devoted to direct investment, and the government could squeeze out more in 'forced savings' through taxation or other means. Both forms of saving would, after some delay, tend to increase income per head still further, with cumulative effects similar to those of the initial rise in income per head due to lower fertility. With lower fertility rates, costs and interruptions of work incidental to births would also decrease. We have, in addition, to reckon with other, more

2. As children require food, clothing, and services but are assumed not to produce anything, every prevented birth would imply a yearly 'saving' of expenditure, until the new generation entered the labour force. Taking into account that children consume less than adults in rough proportion to their age group, and discounting future 'saved' consumption by a rate of interest of 10 per cent, Enke (1960, 1966) calculates the value of 'saved' consumption per birth for twenty years ahead in India at 537·6 rupees ($113) and for fifteen years at 442·3 rupees ($93). In those South Asian countries with higher average incomes and levels of living the figures would be correspondingly higher. Enke's figures are minimum figures since his calculation does not allow for the cumulative effects of circular causation, discussed below.

subtle effects of rising levels of living. The great poverty in India and Pakistan and in large sections of the population in the other South Asian countries must account, at least in part, for the apathy of the masses and their unresponsiveness to efforts to change attitudes and institutions, spread modern technology, improve hygiene, and so on.

Also, relatively more of total national income could then be devoted to raising the living levels of children, with especially beneficial effects on productivity in the long run. Thus public expenditures for educational and training facilities could be increased. Larger efforts could also be devoted to improving health facilities. Better health standards for adults as well as children would result, and still further improvements of labour input and efficiency would be possible. Finally, we must note that nearly all these direct and indirect effects of a decline in fertility would facilitate the productive integration of the expanding labour force into the economy.

We have so far disregarded the effects that a decline in fertility rates would have on mortality rates. Lower fertility rates could be expected to speed up the decline in the mortality rate for several reasons: fewer maternal and infant deaths, higher levels of living, and with progressively higher income levels, a broadened financial base for public health work. Declining mortality rates, in turn, tend to raise economic levels because of the decrease in illness associated therewith. And not to be entirely overlooked are the economic inconveniences and the costs following upon every death, among them funeral costs – which, as in all poor countries, are inordinately high in South Asia.

It seems apparent, then, that *the effects of a decline in fertility would be favourable in both economic and more broadly human terms and that these effects are very considerable and cumulative, gaining momentum over the years*. They would also be *independent of the man/land ratio*: the same causal mechanism must operate in sparsely as in densely populated countries.

Increase in the labour force

In all South Asian countries the labour force is now increasing much more rapidly than it ever did previously in these countries, and two or three times as fast as it did in Western Europe before the effects of birth control made their influence felt; and the increase will accelerate. Coale and Hoover's estimates for India, published in 1958, indicated an increase in the labour force over three decades, beginning in 1956, of 87 per cent (Coale and Hoover, 1958, p. 232). This projection was based on the highest fertility rate Coale and Hoover used, but today it is a conservative projection since mortality has declined faster than they assumed while fertility has not fallen. For Pakistan they projected an increase of the same order. For Burma and Indonesia the projected increase was even greater. In the other Southeast

Asian countries and Ceylon the growth in the labour force by 1986 would be still higher.

When we inquire into the significance of these projections for the economies of the South Asian countries, one brute fact already alluded to must be remembered: whether our vantage point is 1956 or 1966, most of those who will be of working age fifteen or twenty years hence are already born. For a generation ahead, indeed, the size of the labour force will not be very greatly changed by any reduction in fertility rates that might occur. The labour force in the South Asian countries is certain to increase rapidly during the next few decades because of the high birth rates in the recent past, and its increase will be magnified by the continuing decline in mortality. It is possible, therefore, to isolate the problem of the growth in the labour force from the question of a possible decrease in fertility.

[. . .] Typically in South Asia today, the labour force is greatly under-utilized. Efforts to raise labour input and efficiency, and thereby the productivity of the labour force, meet with extreme difficulties, political, institutional and attitudinal. A rapid increase in the labour force must aggravate these difficulties of planning for development, particularly as, by itself, this increase tends to make the social and economic structure more inegalitarian and rigid. [. . .]

Combining the two types of effects

We must now combine the conclusions we have reached in the two last sections. In Section 2 we found that a decline in fertility would raise average incomes and levels of living; it would also help in many ways to raise labour utilization and productivity. It would thus help to counteract – and in some countries perhaps more than counteract – the adverse effects on labour utilization and productivity, and thereby on income, exerted by the growth in the labour force due to high fertility in earlier years and declining mortality rates as discussed in Section 3. We know that the favourable effects of a lower fertility rate along the first-mentioned line of causation are very substantial and cumulative. They would mount for at least fifteen years if the lower rate were kept low; if birth control were gradually intensified, the gains would become progressively bigger and continue longer.

[. . .] In the longer time perspective, a decline in fertility would be even more advantageous. This is true, first of all, because some of its effects are cumulative: circular causation does not occur instantaneously; it takes time to gather momentum. Secondly, as the smaller cohorts of children reached working age, a brake would begin to be put on the growth in the labour force. Thirdly, growth in the size of the procreative age group would also begin to be slowed down – and more rapidly, since a woman's child bearing period is over earlier than the normal working life – with the result that fewer children would be born even at a given age-specific fertility rate.

Population policy by its very nature needs to be viewed in the very long time perspective, and the need is the greater in South Asia because of the youthfulness of the population. As some 40 per cent of the population in South Asia is below fifteen years of age, contrasted with 20–25 per cent in Western countries, and as the age distribution even in the procreative age group is correspondingly skewed, the braking distance is extremely long before population growth and, especially, labour force growth can be significantly slowed down. Even if for one or another of the South Asian countries, the prospective growth in the labour force would not seem likely to cause great difficulties for some period ahead, this could not be an argument for postponing efforts to reduce the birth rate. And it must not be forgotten that a period of mass education will be needed before a policy of spreading birth control can have significant effects on fertility rates.

The danger is that the long 'running-in' period of any policy to induce a decline in fertility will be underestimated. If a major and successful effort in population policy, corresponding to Coale and Hoover's most optimistic assumption in regard to fertility, were begun in India in fifteen years, reckoned from 1956, as opposed to five, there would be a difference of about 7 per cent in the size of the total population after thirty years. This difference may appear trivial, particularly as the labour force thirty years hence would be almost the same in both cases. But the population increase thereafter would be significantly slowed down ten years earlier, and what is certainly not trivial is the considerable savings on the maintenance burden in the average family that would immediately follow a decline in fertility and the cumulative effects of this change that would follow. The sooner fertility is reduced, the sooner will the cumulative effects of the decrease in the dependency burden be felt. Moreover, each postponement of effective birth control measures increases the potential growth rates in later years because, as the larger cohorts of children grow up, it allows the continued rapid increase in the procreative age group – which is, after all, the basic determinant of the future size of population. The longer time perspective – far on the other side of any perspective planning actually attempted in any South Asian country – is the only realistic one.

Although our treatment of the problem has been in general terms, and although we have consistently avoided making it more specific than our knowledge of the facts and the relationships between the facts permits, we believe we can conclude that *a consideration of the economic effects of population trends should give the governments of the South Asian countries strong reasons for instituting as soon and as vigorously as possible policy measures to get birth control practised among the masses of the people.*

The world setting of the emergent population policy in South Asia

[. . .] *The deliberate choice of a restrictive population policy based on contraception was unique in modern world history.* Japan is the only country outside South Asia that has made such a choice, but it did so after India and in the beginning not as explicitly. The dramatic decline in fertility in the Western countries since the last quarter of the nineteenth century, and the earlier manifestations of this trend in France and elsewhere, were not the result of a restrictive population policy. On the contrary, all the forces of organized society – the law, officialdom, the clergy, educators, the press, the medical profession – were mobilized to prevent birth control from spreading.

For a rather long time, obstruction was firmer in Protestant than in Catholic countries, mainly because the former were more demanding of conformism, in public if not in private behaviour, and better organized to enforce it.[3] In consequence, both public policy and public opinion diverged sharply from private morality.[4] In Sweden, for example, a statute counteracting the sale of contraceptives remained on the books until the latter part of the 1930s, although the birth rate, reflecting private attitudes and behaviour, had by then reached a low point that did not even guarantee replacement of the population. The law was finally repealed after the blatant contradiction between public and private morals was exposed in a lively debate on family questions. Now that Protestant clergymen no longer formally oppose birth control, Catholic action groups have sought to carry on the fight in the predominantly Protestant countries (Fagley, 1960).

[. . .] Yet one may safely predict that official Catholic ideology will not succeed in blocking the spread of birth control practices any more than Puritan doctrine did. The somewhat higher fertility rates in Catholic countries and among Catholics in Protestant countries are probably due only to a time lag, in part the consequence of poverty and ignorance. This is borne out by statistics on fertility in Italy. Italy's crude birth rate was 36 per thousand in 1890 and above 30 per thousand in the early 1920s. Thereafter, despite the Catholic Church's strong disapproval of birth control and despite Mussolini's pro-natalist policies, the birth rate began to decline. By 1940 it was 24 per thousand. Fertility actually fell more rapidly in Italy in the inter-war period than it did in Sweden at a corresponding stage (approximately 1875–1910). Even after the Second World War the decline

3. In England, John Stuart Mill found it inadvisable to advocate birth control after a dismaying experience in his youth. See Himes (1929, pp. 457–84 and 1963, pp. 301; 310).

4. About the distinction between public and private opinions, see Myrdal (1944, pp. 1139 ff).

continued, uninterrupted by the 'baby boom' that took place in other countries. Since 1951 the birth rate has been fairly stable at around 18 per thousand, about the same as in France. In Spain, where the influence of the Church is probably even stronger and the people poorer, the trend has been essentially similar despite irregularities during and after the Civil War. The birth rate in Spain has been stabilized in recent years at around 21 per thousand (Population Reference Bureau, 1962, pp. 25, 32, 33). Among the underdeveloped countries, Catholic Puerto Rico is one of the few in which birth control has spread rapidly, largely by means of female sterilization. As one writer has pointed out in reference to the government-sponsored family planning service, 'It is now quite evident that in this matter the Roman Catholic laity will not be guided by the priests' (Cadbury, 1962).

[. . .] In the Communist world the history of population policy and development has not been altogether dissimilar. Their ideological heritage has, for the most part, prevented the governments in the Soviet orbit from committing themselves to birth control policies. Long before Marx, the main strand of socialist thinking ascribed 'overpopulation' to the defects, social and economic, of the non-socialist society. Marx merely reinforced this doctrine and brought it into his system of 'scientific socialism'. A contemporary adaptation of this theory is the statement of a prominent member of the USSR Academy of Sciences, Vasily Nemchinov:

Food shortages in many countries spring from defects in their social and economic systems. If the survivals of semi-feudal relationships in agriculture are eliminated, and if agriculture is freed from the insupportable burden of land rent, the situation will change . . . Soviet people believe that, given a rational social system, the achievements of modern science and technology should make it possible to attain a genuine abundance of food in each country and throughout the world . . . The solution of the world's food problem lies not in reducing the growth of the population, but in the radical re-organization of the economic and technical aspects of agricultural production (PEP, 1955).

In this sense, economic policy can undoubtedly be at least a temporary substitute for a population policy, when the conditions for development are favourable. Since Communist governments are prepared to apply more radical policy measures, and are confident they can raise labour productivity substantially, they need naturally be less concerned about population growth than non-Communist governments, under comparable conditions.

However, another strand of socialist thinking, which also antedated Marx, considers voluntary parenthood an ideal fully realizable only in the 'realm of freedom' in a socialist society. Often this other view includes the tenet that under socialism even fertility would be brought under rational control. As on many other points, Engels was somewhat less restrained than Marx in predicting what would happen after the revolution:

There is, of course, the abstract possibility that the number of people will become so great that limits will have to be set to their increase. But if at some stage communist society finds itself obliged to regulate the production of human beings, just as it has already come to regulate the production of things, it will be precisely this society, and this society alone, which can carry this out without difficulty. It does not seem to me that it would be at all difficult in such a society to achieve by planning a result which has already been produced spontaneously, without planning, in France and Lower Austria. At any rate, it is for the people in the communist society themselves to decide whether, when, and how this is to be done, and what means they wish to employ for the purpose. I do not feel called upon to make proposals or give them advice about it. These people, in any case, will surely not be any less intelligent than we are.[5]

There is no reason to believe that Marx would have taken exception to this statement. As Engels went on to say, the problem had little immediacy in view of the rapidly increasing production in the Western countries on which his and Marx's analysis was premised.

Immediately after the revolution in Russia there was much shifting between these two ideological positions, but for the first fifteen years Soviet policy rather reflected the second one. That the ideal of voluntary parenthood held sway for so long – well after the short spurt of radicalism in general family matters had died down – may perhaps be attributed in part to the severe economic difficulties the country was enduring. By the middle of the 1930s, as a result of legalized abortion, promotion of contraception, and ease of divorce, the birth rate in the Soviet Union had fallen by about a third (Lorimer, 1947, pp. 126, 134). To the by then monolithic Soviet government, bent on rapid economic development as formulated in the five-year plans, so low a rate did not seem desirable. There followed an abrupt change in policy, encompassing measures both to hamper the spread of birth control, particularly abortion, and to encourage families to have many children. This new policy quickly raised the birth rate to almost its previous level (Lorimer, 1947, pp. 128–30, 134).

The official Communist policy line was thereafter uncompromisingly linked to the dominant 'Marxist' position that a socialist state has no need for birth control. At the 1954 World Population Conference in Rome, delegates from the Soviet bloc and Catholic scholars engaged in a curious competition, each group vying with the other in arguing that there was no real population problem anywhere in the world but only a need for huge social and economic reform (United Nations, 1954, pp. 131, 139). This official doctrine did not, however, prevent a decline in birth rates. As against 38·3 per thousand in 1938, the reported crude birth rate in the Soviet Union varied in the 1950s between 26·7 (in 1950) and 25·0 (in 1959). It dropped also

5. From Engels' letter to Kautsky of 1 February 1881, in Meek (ed.) (1953, p. 109).

in the other European Communist countries, with the exception of Albania, and in several was not markedly different from rates prevailing in the United Kingdom, France, Belgium and Denmark in the 1950s (United Nations, 1962, p. 6; Lorimer, 1947, p. 134). The decline in fertility, as in the Western countries, has been entirely due to private initiative, running counter to public policy, which has remained pro-natalist.[6] The fact that women in Eastern Europe constitute so large and effective a part of the labour force and that their earnings are so important to the family budget has probably speeded the downturn.

Probably as an incidental effect of de-Stalinization, but more fundamentally as a reflection of a felt need to bring public policy into closer conformity with private morals (an issue that is bound to come to the fore in any country), we are now witnessing a softening of the 'Marxist' doctrine on the population issue in the Soviet Union and the other European Communist states; what is important, the trend is particularly visible in regard to policy in the underdeveloped countries.[7] When countries that are obedient to the Catholic Church – and that have associated themselves with the position taken by the European Communist countries on the population issue in inter-governmental organizations – are beginning to feel they can modify their position in regard to birth control, it does not seem likely that the European Communist countries will stand firm in their old doctrinal position.

[. . .] Disregarding China, where the policy line seems as yet undecided, the spread of birth control was not a response to public policy either in the Western Protestant or Catholic countries or in the Communist countries except for a short interlude in Russia immediately after the revolution. On the contrary, public policy strove to inhibit its practice.[8] Particularly because

6. A few years ago the Soviet Union – followed by the other countries in the Soviet orbit, except for Albania and East Germany – again legalized abortion because illicit operations were becoming so prevalent as to constitute a serious public health danger and legalization was the only means of insuring proper medical control. In this instance, the development of private morals forced a change in public policy.

7. 'A population policy is . . . becoming an increasingly notable feature in the social life of the young national states. In principle this testifies to a more mature approach to problems of economic development. The overwhelming majority of newly liberated states are planning their economic development, but this cannot be achieved unless population factors are taken into account and efforts are made to influence them so as to ensure a better combination of population growth and economic progress'. (Guzevaty, 1966, p. 58). See also 'Population Growth – Two Conflicting Points of View' (those of Academician Stanislav Strumilin and Candidate of Philosophy E. Arab-Ogly), *Soviet News*, no. 5307, 18 August 1966, p. 78; Ogly supports his stand by reference to Engels' views and what we called the second strand of Socialist thinking.

8. To Western criticism of India's dilatory population policy, Jawaharlal Nehru occasionally replied that he knew of no government anywhere that had done more.

of its possible relevance for South Asian countries, the exceptional case of Japan should be noted. In the imperialist era, Japanese policy was strongly pro-natalist. But after the Second World War, with the return of some five million nationals from Japan's former colonial empire and a baby boom, there was a sudden change in public policy, supported, after some hesitancy, by American occupation officials. As a result, the birth rate dropped from 34·3 per thousand in 1947 to 17·2 in 1957 (United Nations, 1955, 1960). The decisive factor in this 50 per cent drop in ten years was not prevention of births through contraception but the practice of abortion, which is estimated to have been responsible for about 70 per cent of the reduction in the fertility rate in the mid-1950s.[9] The policy measure that made this possible was the government's decision to permit legal abortion without restriction. The government, while remaining permissive towards abortion, has actively promoted contraception as a more humane and less wasteful means of birth control. With this new emphasis, Japan shifted to the population policy initiated by India.

9. In 1954 the proportion of reported abortions to live births was 64 per cent for all women, and very much higher in the age groups over 35. According to the official estimate, 35·4 per cent of all conceptions ended in abortion; but the real percentage was probably considerably higher. See Taeuber (1958, pp. 276, 277).

References

CADBURY, G. W. (1962), 'Outlook for government action in family planning in the West Indies', in C. V. Kiser (ed.), *Research in Family Planning*, Princeton University Press.

COALE, A. J., and HOOVER, E. M. (1958), *Population Growth and Economic Development in Low-Income Countries*, Princeton University Press.

ENKE, S. (1960), 'The gains to India from population control: some money measures and incentive schemes', *Rev. Econ. Stats.*, vol. 42, pp. 117 ff.

ENKE, S. (1966), 'The economic aspects of slowing population growth', *Econ. J.*, vol. 76, pp. 44 ff.

FAGLEY, R. M. (1960), 'A Protestant view of population control', *Law and Contemp. Probs.*, vol. 25, no. 3, pp. 470 ff.

GUZEVATY, Y. (1966), 'Population problems in developing countries', *International Affairs*, no. 9.

HIMES, N. E. (1929), 'John Stuart Mill's attitude toward neo-malthusianism', *Econ. J.*, Economic History Series, no. 4, pp. 457–84.

HIMES, N. E. (1963), *Medical History of Contraception*, Gamut Press.

LORIMER, F. (1947), *The Population of the Soviet Union*, League of Nations.

MEEK, R. L. (ed.) (1953), *Marx and Engels on Malthus*, Lawrence & Wishart.

MYRDAL, G. (1944), *An American Dilemma*, Harper & Row.

PEP (1955), 'Food and population', in *World Population and Resources*, Allen & Unwin.

POPULATION REFERENCE BUREAU (1962), 'Low birth rates of European Catholic countries', *Pop. Bull.*, vol. 18, no. 2, Washington.

TAEUBER, I. B. (1958), *The Population of Japan*, Princeton University Press.

UNITED NATIONS (1955), *Proceedings of the World Population Conference* 1954, summary report, United Nations.
UNITED NATIONS (1955), *Demographic Yearbook*, p. 615, United Nations.
UNITED NATIONS (1962), *Monthly Bulletin of Statistics*, vol. 16, no. 12, Table 2.

8 Michael P. Todaro

Income Expectations, Rural–Urban Migration and Employment in Africa

Extract from M. P. Todaro 'Income expectations, rural-urban migration and employment in Africa', *International Labour Review*, vol. 104, 1971, pp. 387–413.

In the few short years since independence, the nations of tropical Africa have experienced an unprecedented increase in the size of their urban populations. From Abidjan to Brazzaville to Nairobi, recorded urban population growth rates of 7 to 10 per cent per annum are a common phenomenon (see Table 1 Reading 24). Part of this growth is due to the rather rapid rates of overall population increase in Africa, rates typically around 3 per cent per annum.[1] However, by far the most important contributing factor has been the massive increase in the number of migrants arriving from surrounding rural areas. Numerous factors, both economic and non-economic, underlie the decision of peasant farmers and educated youths to seek the 'better life' in the rapidly growing urban centres. [. . .]

Urban unemployment: a major dilemma

Before turning to a theoretical examination of the economics of rural–urban migration, it should be pointed out that rural-urban migration is by no means an undesirable phenomenon. In fact most of the theories of economic development, which are based largely on the historical experience of Western industrialized nations, emphasize the transformation of an economy from a rural agrarian base to one with an industrial, urban-oriented focus. This process is made possible by the gradual but continuous absorption of 'redundant' or 'surplus' rural labourers into the growing industrial economy. Under ideal circumstances, the rate of growth of modern sector industries then provides a sufficient number of newly created employment opportunities to bring about a more productive and efficient allocation of human resources in the economy as a whole. Unfortunately, real work conditions do not always conform to the hypothetical framework of the economist's development scenario.

In tropical Africa the magnitude of rural-urban migration has greatly exceeded the capacity of the modern industrial sector to absorb the persons concerned, so that it can only employ productively a small proportion of them. Part of the problem relates to the nature of the African industrializa-

1. For a useful review of African demographic data, see Som (1968, pp. 187–9).

tion process itself, a process which has typically failed to produce a growth of job opportunities at anything near the rate of output growth. If one uses the standard criterion of output growth as the measuring rod for the success of the industrial development effort, many African economies with output growth rates of 5 to 8 per cent per annum have not done that poorly under the circumstances. However, as Table 2 Reading 24 reveals, the growth rate of non-agricultural employment has typically been negligible and, in many cases, negative.

It is in this context of slowly growing urban employment opportunities accompanied by a disproportionately high rate of rural-urban migration that the chronic urban unemployment and underemployment problem has emerged in tropical Africa. Although there are few hard data on the magnitude of African urban unemployment, owing both to conceptual difficulties in defining unemployment and, more importantly, to the fact that very few studies have been directed to the problem, the limited evidence available provides ample empirical confirmation of what any informed observer already knows – namely that urban unemployment is an extremely serious problem (see Table 1 for a summary of available data on urban unemployment rates in African cities). However, in spite of these rising levels of overt unemployment and even higher levels of underemployment, the rate of rural–urban migration shows no sign of deceleration. To the extent that many newly arrived migrants are likely to join the growing pools of unemployed and highly underemployed workers, and to the extent that

Table 1 **Urban unemployment rates in Africa** (%)

Country (*urban centres*)	Unemployment rate	Country (*urban centres*)	Unemployment rate
Algeria (1966)	26·6	Kenya (1969)	
		Eight urban areas	17·4
Cameroon (1966)			
Douala	13·0	Morocco (1960)	20·5
Yaoundé	17·0		
		Nigeria (1963)	
Congo (1958)		Lagos	15·5
Léopoldville (Kinshasa)	15·0	Ife	19·7
Ghana (1960)		Onitsha	26·3
Large towns	11·6	Kaduna	30·8
Ivory Coast (1963)		Abeokuta	34·6
Abidjan	20·0	Tanzania (1965)	12·6

Sources: Algeria, Ghana, Morocco and Tanzania – Turnham (Reading 2). Cameroon and Ivory Coast – Clignet (1969). Nigeria – Gutkind (1967). Congo – Raymachers (1958). Kenya – Rempel and Todaro (1972).

an increasingly large proportion of these migrants represent the more educated segments of society whose productive potential is largely being dissipated, the process of continued rural-urban migration at present levels can no longer be said to represent a desirable economic phenomenon. Until something positive is done to relieve this problem, the African development effort will be only partially successful.

A theoretical framework for analysing the economics of rural-urban migration in Africa

In this section I would like to set forth briefly a theoretical framework which yields some important insights into the causes and mechanisms of rural-urban migration in tropical Africa. No attempt will be made to describe this model in any great detail since that has been done elsewhere (Todaro, 1968, 1969; Harris and Todaro, 1970). I believe that the model can usefully serve two purposes: first, to demonstrate why the continued existence of rural-urban migration in the face of rising levels of urban unemployment often represents a rational economic decision from the point of view of the private individual; and second, to demonstrate how such a theoretical framework can be used in an analysis and evaluation of alternative public policies to alleviate the growing urban unemployment problem.

The individual decision to migrate: some behavioural assumptions

The basic behavioural assumption of the model is that each potential migrant decides whether or not to move to the city on the basis of an implicit, 'expected' income maximization objective. There are two principal economic factors involved in this decision to migrate. The first relates to the existing urban-rural real wage differential that prevails for different skill and educational categories of workers. The existence of large disparities between wages paid to urban workers and those paid to comparably skilled rural labourers has long been recognized as a crucial factor in the decision to migrate.[2] The increasing divergence between urban and rural incomes has arisen both as a result of the relative stagnation of agricultural earnings (partly as a direct outgrowth of post-war bias towards industrialization at the expense of agricultural expansion) and the concomitant phenomenon of rapidly rising urban wage rates for unskilled workers. For example, in Nigeria Arthur Lewis noted that 'urban wages' are typically at levels twice as high as average farm incomes. Between 1950 and 1963

2. Some of the more recent studies identifying economic forces as principal factors affecting the decision to migrate include Beals, Levy and Moses (1967); Caldwell (1969); Gallaway (1967); Gugler (1969); Harris and Todaro (1968); and Rempel (1970). See also Frank, Jr (Reading 24), for a useful review of the literature on urban unemployment in Africa.

prices received by farmers through marketing boards in southern Nigeria fell by 25 per cent while at the same time the minimum wage scales of the Federal Government increased by 200 per cent (Lewis, 1967, p. 42).

In Kenya average earnings of African employees in the non-agricultural sector rose from £97 in 1960 to £180 in 1966, a growth rate of nearly 11 per cent per annum. During the same period the small farm sector of Kenya experienced a growth of estimated family income of only 5 per cent per annum, rising from £57 in 1960 to £77 in 1966. Consequently, urban wages rose more than twice as fast as agricultural incomes in Kenya so that in 1966 average wages in the urban sector were approximately two-and-a-half times as high as average farm family incomes (Ghai, Reading 14). Moreover, the urban-rural income differential in Kenya in 1968 varied considerably by level of educational attainment. For example, whereas farm income was approximately £85 in 1968, individuals with zero to four years of primary education in urban areas earned on the average £102, those with five to eight years of primary education earned £156, while migrants who had completed from one to six years of secondary education earned on the average £290 per annum in 1968.[3]

A final example of the growing disparity between urban and rural incomes can be gleaned from Uganda data. During the period 1954–1964 agricultural incomes remained essentially unchanged while minimum wages in government employment in Kampala rose by almost 200 per cent from £31 to £90 per annum (Knight, 1967). It should be noted that in Uganda as in most other African nations the minimum wage often acts as the effective rate which determines the level at which more than 50 per cent of urban unskilled workers are paid. It is also the key weight in the overall wage structure since when the minimum wage changes, the entire wage structure tends to move with it (Berg, 1970).

The second crucial element, which for the most part has not been formally included in other models of rural–urban migration, relates to the degree of probability that a migrant will be successful in securing an urban job. Without introducing the probability variable it would be extremely difficult to explain the continued and often accelerated rate of migration in the face of sizeable and growing pools of urban unemployed. Arguments about the irrationality of rural peasants who unwittingly migrate to urban areas permeated by widespread unemployment are as ill-conceived and culture-bound as earlier assertions that peasant subsistence farmers were unresponsive to price incentives. The key, in my opinion, to an understanding of the seemingly paradoxical phenomenon of continued migration to centres of high unemployment lies in viewing the migration process from an

3. For an analysis of the relationship between education and migration in Africa, see Todaro (1971, pp. 16–30).

'expected' or permanent income approach where expected income relates not only to the actual wage paid to an urban worker, but also to the probability that he will be successful in securing wage employment in any given period of time. It is the combination and interaction of these two variables – the urban-rural real income differential and the probability of securing an urban job – which I believe determine the rate and magnitude of rural-urban migration in tropical Africa.

Consider the following illustration. Suppose the average unskilled or semi-skilled rural worker has a choice between being a farm labourer (or working his own land) for an annual average real income of, say, 50 units, or migrating to the city where a worker with his skill or educational background can obtain wage employment yielding an annual real income of 100 units. The more commonly used economic models of migration, which place exclusive emphasis on the income differential factor as the determinant of the decision to migrate, would indicate a clear choice in this situation. The worker should seek the higher-paying urban job. It is important to recognize, however, that these migration models were developed largely in the context of advanced industrial economies and, as such, implicitly assume the existence of full employment or near-full employment. In a full employment environment the decision to migrate can in fact be predicated solely on securing the highest-paying job wherever it becomes available. Simple economic theory would then indicate that such migration should lead to a reduction in wage differentials through the interaction of the forces of supply and demand, both in areas of out-migration and in points of in-migration.

Unfortunately, such an analysis is not very realistic in the context of the institutional and economic framework of most of the nations of tropical Africa. First of all, these countries are beset by a chronic and serious unemployment problem with the result that a typical migrant cannot expect to secure a high-paying urban job immediately. In fact, it is much more likely that upon entering the urban labour market the migrant will either become totally unemployed or will seek casual and part-time employment in the urban traditional sector. Consequently, in his decision to migrate the individual in effect must balance the probabilities and risks of being unemployed or underemployed for a considerable period of time against the positive urban-rural real income differential. The fact that a typical migrant can expect to earn twice the annual real income in an urban area than he can in a rural environment may be of little consequence if his actual probability of securing the higher-paying job within, say, a one-year period is one chance in five. In such a situation we could say that his actual probability of being successful in securing the higher-paying urban job is 20 per cent, so that his 'expected' urban income for the one-year period is in fact

20 units and not the 100 units that the fully employed urban worker receives. Thus, with a one-period time horizon and a probability of success of 20 per cent it would be irrational for this migrant to seek an urban job even though the differential between urban and rural earnings capacity is 100 per cent. On the other hand, if the probability of success were, say, 60 per cent, so that the expected urban income is 60 units, then it would be entirely rational for our migrant with his one-period time horizon to try his luck in the urban area even though urban unemployment may be extremely high.

If we now approach the situation more realistically by assuming a considerably longer time horizon, especially in view of the fact that the vast majority of migrants are between the ages of fifteen and twenty-three years, then the decision to migrate should be represented on the basis of a longer-term, more permanent income calculation. If the migrant anticipates a relatively low probability of finding regular wage employment in the initial period but expects this probability to increase over time as he is able to broaden his urban contacts, then it would still be rational for him to migrate even though expected urban income during the initial period or periods might be lower than expected rural income. As long as the present value of the net stream of expected urban income over the migrant's planning horizon exceeds that of the expected rural income, the decision to migrate is justified.

The mathematical details of our model of rural–urban migration are set forth in the Appendix to this article. For our present purposes, suffice it to say that the model attempts to demonstrate the conditions under which the urban–rural 'expected' income differential can act to exacerbate the urban *unemployment* situation even though urban *employment* might expand as a direct result of government policy. It all depends on the relationship between migration flows and the expected income differential as expressed in an 'elasticity of migration response' term developed in the Appendix.

Since the elasticity of response will itself be directly related to the probability of finding a job and the size of the urban-rural real income differential, the model illustrates the paradox of a completely urban solution to the urban unemployment problem. Policies which operate solely on urban labour demand are not likely to be of much assistance in reducing urban unemployment since, in accordance with our expected income hypothesis, the growth of urban employment *ceteris paribus* also increases the rate of rural–urban migration. If the increase in the growth of the urban labour force caused by migration exceeds the increase in the growth of employment, the level of unemployment in absolute numbers will increase and the unemployment rate itself might also increase. This result will be accentuated if, for any increase in job creation, the urban real wage is permitted to expand at a greater rate than rural real income. A reduction or at least a slow growth in urban wages, therefore, has a dual beneficial effect in that it tends to reduce the rate of rural–urban migration and increase the demand for labour.

A second implication of the above model is that traditional methods of estimating the 'shadow' price of rural labour to the urban sector will tend to have a downward bias if the migration response parameter is not taken into account. Typically, this shadow price has been expressed in terms of the marginal product of the rural worker who migrates to the city to secure the additional urban job. However, if for every additional urban job that is created more than one rural worker is induced to migrate, then the opportunity cost will reflect the combined loss of agricultural production of all those induced to migrate, not just the one who is fortunate enough to secure the urban position. It also follows that whenever there are sizeable pools of urban unemployed, traditional estimates of the shadow price of urban labour will reflect an upward bias.

Appendix

A mathematical model of rural–urban migration

Consider the following formulation of the theory of rural–urban migration used in this article. I begin by assuming that individuals base their decision to migrate on considerations of income maximization and that their calculations are founded on what they perceive to be their expected income streams in urban and rural areas. It is further assumed that the individual who chooses to migrate is attempting to achieve the prevailing average income for his level of education or skill attainment in the urban centre of his choice. Nevertheless, he is assumed to be aware of his limited chances of immediately securing wage employment and the likelihood that he will be unemployed or underemployed for a certain period of time. It follows that the migrant's expected income stream is determined both by the prevailing income in the modern sector and the probability of being employed there, rather than being underemployed in the traditional sector or totally unemployed.

If we let $V(0)$ be the discounted present value of the expected 'net' urban-rural income stream over the migrant's time horizon; $Yu(t)$, $Yr(t)$ the average real incomes of individuals employed in the urban and the rural economy; n the number of time periods in the migrant's planning horizon; and r the discount rate reflecting the migrant's degree of time preference, then the decision to migrate or not will depend on whether

$$V(0) = \int_{t=0}^{n} [p(t)\,Y_u(t) - Y_r(t)]e^{-rt}\,dt - C(0)$$

is positive or negative, where
$C(0)$ represents the cost of migration, and
$p(t)$ is the probability that a migrant will have secured an urban job at the average income level in period t.

In any one time period, the probability of being employed in the modern sector, $p(t)$, will be directly related to the probability π of having been selected in that or any previous period from a given stock of unemployed or underemployed job seekers. If we assume that for most migrants the selection procedure is random, then the probability of having a job in the modern sector within x periods after migration, $p(x)$, is:

$$p(1) = \pi(1)$$

and

$$p(2) = \pi(1) + [1 - \pi(1)]\pi(2)$$

so that

$$p(x) = \pi(x-1) + [1 - \pi(x-1)]\pi(x)$$

or

$$p(x) = \pi(1) + \sum_{t=2}^{x} \pi(t) \prod_{s=1}^{t-1} \left[1 - \pi(s) \right]$$

where $\pi(t)$ equals the ratio of new job openings relative to the number of accumulated job aspirants in period t.
It follows from this probability formulation that for any given level of $Y_u(t)$ and $Y_r(t)$, the longer the migrant has been in the city the higher his probability p of having a job and the higher, therefore, is his expected income in that period.

Formulating the probability variable in this way has two advantages:
1. It avoids the 'all or nothing' problem of having to assume that the migrant either earns the average income or earns nothing in the periods immediately following migration: consequently, it reflects the fact that many

underemployed migrants will be able to generate some income in the urban traditional sector while searching for a regular job; and

2. it modifies somewhat the assumption of random selection since the probability of a migrant having been selected varies directly with the time he has been in the city. This permits adjustments for the fact that longer-term migrants usually have more contacts and better information systems so that their expected incomes should be higher than those of newly arrived migrants with similar skills.

Suppose we now incorporate this behaviouristic theory of migration into a simple aggregate dynamic equilibrium model of urban labour demand and supply in the following manner. We once again define the probability π of obtaining a job in the urban sector in any one time period as being directly related to the rate of new employment creation and inversely related to the ratio of unemployed job seekers to the number of existing job opportunities, that is

$$\pi = \frac{yN}{S-N} \qquad\qquad 1$$

where y is the net rate of urban new job creation, N is the level of urban employment, and S is the total urban labour force.

If w is the urban real wage rate and r represents average rural real income, then the 'expected' urban-rural real income differential d is

$$d = w \,.\, \pi - r \qquad\qquad 2$$

or, substituting 1 into 2

$$d = w \,.\, \frac{yN}{S-N} - r \qquad\qquad 3$$

The basic assumption of our model once again is that the supply of labour to the urban sector is a function of the urban-rural *expected* real income differential, i.e.

$$S = f_s(d) \qquad\qquad 4$$

If the rate of urban job creation is a function of the urban wage w and a policy parameter a, e.g. a concentrated governmental effort to increase employment through a comprehensive programme of industrial import substitution or, as in the case of Kenya, the 1964 and 1970 Tripartite Agreements to raise employment levels, both of which operate on labour demand, we have

$$\gamma = f_d\,(w;\,a) \qquad\qquad 5$$

where it is assumed that $\partial y / \partial a > 0$. If the growth in the urban labour demand is increased as a result of the governmental policy shift, the increase in the urban labour supply is

$$\frac{\partial S}{\partial a} = \frac{\partial S}{\partial d}\frac{\partial d}{\partial \gamma}\frac{\partial \gamma}{\partial a} \qquad\qquad 6$$

Differentiating 3 and substituting into 6, we obtain

$$\frac{\partial S}{\partial a} = \frac{\partial S}{\delta d}\, w\, \frac{N}{S-N} \cdot \frac{\partial \gamma}{\partial a} \qquad\qquad 7$$

The absolute number of urban unemployed will increase if the increase in labour supply exceeds the increase in the number of new jobs created, i.e. if

$$\frac{\partial S}{\partial a} > \frac{\partial(\gamma N)}{\partial a} = \frac{N\partial \gamma}{\partial a} \qquad\qquad 8$$

Combining 7 and 8, we get

$$\frac{\partial S}{\partial d}\, w\, \frac{N}{S-N} \cdot \frac{\partial \gamma}{\partial a} > \frac{N\partial \gamma}{\partial a} \qquad\qquad 9$$

or

$$\frac{\partial S/S}{\partial d/d} > \frac{d}{w} \cdot \frac{(S-N)}{S} \qquad\qquad 10$$

or, finally, substituting for d

$$\frac{\partial S/S}{\partial d/d} > \frac{w \cdot \pi - r}{w} \cdot \frac{(S-N)}{S} \qquad\qquad 11$$

Expression 11 reveals that the absolute level of unemployment will rise if the elasticity of urban labour supply with respect to the expected urban-rural income differential,

$$\frac{\partial S/S}{\partial d/d}\ ,$$

(what I have called elsewhere the 'migration response function') exceeds the urban-rural differential as a proportion of the urban wage times the unemployment rate,

$$\frac{S-N}{S}\ .$$

Alternatively, equation 11 shows that the higher the unemployment rate, the higher must be the elasticity to increase the level of unemployment for any expected real income differential. But note that in most developing nations the inequality 11 will be satisfied by a very low elasticity of supply when realistic figures are used. For example, if the urban real wage is 60, average rural real income is 20, the probability of getting a job is 0·50 and the unemployment rate is 20 per cent, then the level of unemployment will increase if the elasticity of urban labour supply is greater than 0·033, i.e. substituting into 11 we get

$$\frac{\partial S/S}{\partial d/d} = \frac{0·50 \times 60 - 20}{60} \times 0·20 = 0·033$$

Clearly, much more needs to be known about the empirical value of this elasticity coefficient in different African nations before one can realistically predict what the impact of a policy to generate more urban *employment* will be on the overall level of urban *unemployment*.

References

BEALS, R. E., LEVY, M. B., and MOSES, L. N. (1967), 'Rationality and migration in Ghana', in *Rev. econ. Stat.*, vol. 49, pp. 480–86.

BERG, E. J. (1970), 'Wage policy and employment in less developed countries', paper prepared for the Overseas Study Committee Conference; *Prospects for Employment Opportunities in the Nineteen-seventies*, University of Cambridge.

CALDWELL, J. C. (1969), *African Rural–Urban Migration. The Movement to Ghana's Towns*, Columbia University Press.

CLIGNET, R. (1969), 'Preliminary notes of a study of unemployment in modern African urban centres', in *Manpower and Unemployment Research in Africa*, vol. 2, April.

GALLAWAY, L. E. (1967), 'Industry variations in geographic labor mobility patterns', *J. Hum. Res.*, vol. 2, pp. 461–74.

GUGLER, J. (1969), 'On the theory of rural–urban migration: the case of sub-Saharan Africa', in J. A. Jackson (ed.), *Sociological Studies Two: Migration*, Cambridge University Press, pp. 134–55.

GUTKIND, P. C. W. (1967), 'The energy of despair: social organization of the unemployed in two African cities: Lagos and Nairobi', in *Civilizations*, vol. 17, pp. 186–211.

HARRIS, J. R., and TODARO, M. P. (1968), 'Urban unemployment in East Africa: an economic analysis of policy alternatives', *East African econ. Rev.*, vol. 4, pp. 17–36.

HARRIS J. R., and TODARO, M. P. (1970), 'Migration, unemployment and development: a two-sector analysis', *Amer. econ. Rev.*, vol. 60, pp. 126–42.

KNIGHT, J. B. (1967), 'The determination of wages and salaries in Uganda', *Bull. Oxford Univ. Inst. econ. Stat.*, vol. 29, pp. 233–64.

LEWIS, W. A. (1967), *Reflections on Nigeria's Economic Growth*, OECD.

RAYMACHERS, P. (1958), *Étude par sondage de la main d'oeuvre à Léopoldville*, Ministère du Plan et de la coopération économique.

REMPEL, H. (1970), 'Labor migration into urban centers and urban unemployment in Kenya', unpublished Ph.D dissertation, University of Wisconsin.

REMPEL, H., and TODARO, M. P. (1972), 'Rural–urban labour migration in Kenya: some preliminary findings of a large-scale survey', in S. Ominde and C. N. Ejiogu (eds.), *Population Growth and Economic Development in Africa*, Heinemann.

SOM, R. K. (1968), 'Some demographic indicators for Africa', in J. C. Caldwell and C. Okoanjo (eds.), *The Population of Tropical Africa*, Longman.

TODARO, M. P. (1968), 'The urban employment problem in less developed countries: an analysis of demand and supply', in *Yale Economic Essays*, vol. 8, pp. 331–402.

TODARO, M. P. (1969), 'A model of labor migration and urban unemployment in less developed countries', *Amer. econ. Rev.*, vol. 59, pp. 138–48.

TODARO, M. P. (1971), *Education and rural–urban migration: theoretical constructs and empirical evidence from Kenya*, paper prepared for the Conference on Urban Unemployment in Africa, Institute of Development Studies, University of Sussex.

9 Walter Elkan

Circular Migration and the Growth of Towns in East Africa

W. Elkan 'Circular migration and the growth of towns in East Africa',
International Labour Review, vol. 96, 1967, pp. 581–9.

For many people the process of economic development conjures up a picture of peasant families – once prosperous – leaving their villages in stark poverty to stream into the towns, there to man new industries and so become transformed into a new urban working class. This is what is often said to have happened in England and elsewhere in Europe in the eighteenth and nineteenth centuries, and it is tacitly assumed that in Africa history must repeat itself. But in East Africa the evidence points to a more complicated process. Not only has a great deal of economic development already been accomplished by an expansion of agriculture, often by adding new cash crops to the subsistence crops grown on small 'peasant' farms, but the growth of towns itself has been different in character. Part of the urban populations in East Africa and elsewhere in the continent consists of people who continue to have closer connections with their villages of origin, to which they may ultimately return. Compared with the familiar pattern of migration, all in one direction, there is another and important movement back to the countryside. Despite growing numbers who regard the town as their permanent home a significant part of the population continues to be born and buried in the villages. These people go to the towns to earn a living, but only a few remain town-dwellers all their lives. This fact has important policy implications for all those concerned with social security and urban growth in Africa.

What follows should be regarded as an 'essay' – and it is no more than that – on just one facet of the movement into the towns of East Africa, drawing particularly on the author's own earlier work in Uganda. He makes no attempt to describe or quantify labour migration as a whole. He is more concerned to suggest ways of looking at the process of urban growth than to document the process in detail. Although the discussion is primarily concerned with East Africa reference will be made to studies elsewhere. The process of what will be called *circular migration* has been observed in Central Africa, and recent work by Elliot Berg in West Africa shows that the basic forces there may also be very similar (Berg, 1965a).

The growth of towns

It is sometimes assumed to be almost part of the order of nature that economic development must be associated with the growth of an impoverished urban working class. If, as in East Africa, the great majority of town-dwellers are manifestly *not* permanent inhabitants, cut off from the country, this is said to be a purely temporary phenomenon to be explained either by an excessive attachment to a tribal countryside, which is bound sooner or later to break down, or to the unpleasantness of towns which looked attractive only from a distance. Everyone has noticed the drift into the towns; the subsequent return to the countryside has received less attention because it does not pose parallel social or economic problems. The growth of towns in East Africa is treated as though it were exactly like the growth of towns in Europe, and especially in Great Britain a century or more ago.

But even for Great Britain this model of a simple transfer of rural populations into the newly developing towns is something of a myth. In the early nineteenth century it was really only the Irish who moved directly from their country dwellings to the new industrial towns along the western seaboard of England and Scotland, whilst Englishmen tended to move much less directly. The English movement is best described as leapfrogging, in which people in the south left agriculture to work in nearby towns whilst others already there moved to larger towns farther north and so on until eventually those who went to live in the newly developing industrial towns of northern England were often people with long experience of town life as such (Ashton, 1948, p. 123). But at any rate it is perfectly true that all these population movements were in one direction, whereas it is essential to notice from the outset that this has not been the case in East Africa, where a circular movement has accompanied the growth of towns. In other words, the distinguishing feature of migration in East Africa as elsewhere in Africa is that, in contrast with England in the early nineteenth century, it has not always involved a permanent withdrawal from the countryside.

This is sometimes obscured by the growth of towns. It is obvious to all that towns in Africa have grown very greatly, especially in the past twenty years (United Nations, 1957, p. 145; Hance, 1964, p. 54), and it has therefore often been taken for granted that this growth has been brought about almost entirely by an increase in permanent town-dwellers. But the growth of towns can take place in many ways: an increase in the number of permanent inhabitants, growing numbers of temporary migrants, or longer stays by migrants. In East Africa the growing number of migrants was probably the main cause of the growth of towns until the late 1950s; but since then the two other causes appear to have predominated. Recent investigations suggest that the period spent in town has been getting longer (United Nations, 1963, and Ministry of Economic Affairs and Development Planning, 1966), but there is nothing to indicate that there has been any basic change in the pattern of circular migration. The permanent inhabitants are characteristically of two types: those in the coastal towns such as Mombasa or Dar es Salaam, which have long had a nucleus of settled town-dwellers – Arab, Swahili or Zaramu – and, second, the established workers whose landholdings are within easy reach of town. In Kampala and Jinja my earlier study revealed that those who remained much longer in employment tended to be Buganda or Basoga who had smallholdings within cycling distance of the towns (now of course the distance is extended, since many have scooters or other motorized transport) and were thus able to combine some farming with wage employment without migrating from home (Elkan, 1960). The proportion of settled urban immigrants who have severed ties with the country – 'committed town-dwellers' – is difficult to determine. Clearly a town that has had less than thirty years of rapid growth will be inhabited predominantly by first-generation immigrants and it is easy to infer from this that as time passes the proportion of second- and third-generation inhabitants will increase dramatically. As a corollary, circular movement is seen as a feature of transition, which will quickly disappear. However, the rapid growth of towns, such as has occurred in East and Central Africa, is also compatible with continued circular migration, and the possibility of its persistence should be taken into account in planning the urban development.

To sum up, then, the typical pattern of migration in East Africa includes a circular movement. A significant proportion of workers do not move permanently but only for a time, so that the very word 'worker' may be misleading since many of those who work for wages do so only for a limited part of their lives and continue to have homes in the countryside even during the period when they are urban wage earners. It may therefore also be misleading to think of urban wage earners as constituting a 'working class'.

Explanations of circular migration

Over the years a number of explanations of circular migration have been put forward. Each may have been true in relation to a given time or place but none is wholly satisfactory today. Some of the more widespread are considered in the following paragraphs.

First, it has sometimes been said that the reason why men come to the towns is that a spell of work away from home has become a kind of initiation rite. The supporters of the argument assumed that Africans had a preference for rural life, which was imagined to be a life of indolence interrupted only by the need for initiation. In the past, it was said, young men proved their strength in battle to show that they were fit to marry; now that inter-tribal wars were no longer, they spent a period at work away from home to prove their manhood (Schapera, 1947, pp. 116–17). Professor Clyde Mitchell has also suggested that 'in many tribes a trip to the towns has become a recognized symbol of boys becoming men' (Mitchell, 1961, p. 234). If 'initiation' is the object of migration in search of work, one would not expect the movement to be anything other than circular. Initiation could hardly, however, account for more than a very small part of the movement today.

Another type of explanation focuses attention on the occasional need to save, and the difficulty of doing so at home because of the demands made on people by their extended families. It is said that the only way to keep the money they earn for themselves without being obliged to share it with their relations is to leave home until they have saved the appropriate sum. No doubt there have been, and are, instances where employment at a distance is preferred to work nearer home for that very reason. Most African societies are built around extended rather than nuclear families and this places on Africans both the advantages and obligations of an extended network of kinship relations. The difference between African and western societies in this respect has probably been exaggerated, and recent sociological studies in England show that there too, for many working people, kinship obligations stretch well beyond the nuclear family (Young and Willmott, 1959). But in any case, important as the desire to escape kinship obligations may be as a possible motive for seeking work away from home it is unlikely to be the sole explanation for circular migration.

These explanations, couched in terms of initiation rites and the peculiarities of extended family systems, emphasize non-economic factors. Most recent studies of labour migration have, however, laid stress on straightforward economical factors of one kind or another; but even so the explanations differ greatly from one another. For one thing, over time, much has changed. Thus there is no reason to doubt that in the early part of this century one major reason why Africans went to seek wage employment was that this was the only way in which they could earn the hut or poll taxes imposed on them by governments. Indeed these very taxes were sometimes imposed in order to encourage people to enter paid employment (Powesland, 1957; Berg, 1965b, pp. 403–5). Where this was the motive for seeking a job, the explanation of why people did not move permanently is only too obvious. As soon as enough had been earned to pay the tax they went back home. Later other motives for seeking employment were added to this basic one. People wanted to buy clothes and other consumer goods and in order to do so they were often obliged to find a job because this was the only, or at any rate the most advantageous, way for them to earn the necessary money. Where the objectives of employment were so clearly defined, people were often spoken of as 'target workers', and again the explanation why they were target workers or why migration to work was only temporary was part of the very reason for this type of movement. It was said that Africans had only limited wants; once satisfied, there was no longer any reason for continuing in employment, so they returned home. The targets gradually became bigger and more diverse. To clothes were added sewing machines and later bicycles. Today wants are no longer limited in this way, but there is one modern version of the target worker. This is the young man who works to save enough capital to set up as a farmer sooner than he could by waiting for the normal processes of inheritance.[1] This was tremendously important in the 1950s, when the income to be earned from growing cash crops, especially in Uganda, was much greater than that to be derived from unskilled or semi-skilled work in towns, but since then a rapid rise in urban wages and a simultaneous decline in the prices of the primary products grown by small cultivators has turned the tables, and consequently this reason for moving to and from the towns is no longer so important.

The conditions of employment

The explanations for circular migration that have been considered so far have been couched in terms of the motives that impel people to seek employment. Perhaps the most widespread explanation and the one for which most evidence has been assembled looks rather at the conditions of employment. Defined in the widest sense, these include wages, housing, and provision against ill-health, unemployment and old age; and conditions in this sense are said to make it impossible for most Africans to contemplate a permanent shift from village to wage employment in mine, plantation, or town. In the Republic of South Africa it is, of course, deliberate policy to prevent Africans from settling in the towns. But in East Africa this has not been the case for many years and any impediments to permanent settlement are certainly not the result of deliberate government action.

It is, however, frequently said that the reason why few people settled permanently in towns is a result of policy in another sense: governments have been blamed for not making the necessary provisions to enable people to become permanent wage earners (ILO, 1958, p. 152; Van Velsen, 1961).

It is averred that the conditions of work are geared to the needs of young bachelors. Wages are said to be barely sufficient to support a single man,

1. See Richards (ed.) (1954, p. 213), for evidence that 'in peasant economies a man requires the greatest capital outlay in youth'.

let alone a family. Workers are not insured against unemployment, sickness or even accident and, although some employers have a provident fund, the proceeds from it, even after a lifetime of service, would not be sufficient, by themselves, to support a man and his wife in old age. In contrast the rural areas still provide a measure of social security, both by the widespread distribution of land and by the network of social relations, which places an obligation on those whose age and health permit, to maintain those who are less lucky. However, even in 1955 the East African Royal Commission pointed out that the security provided by tribal areas was becoming steadily less. This is true both in absolute terms, as population pressure on the land that provides the security increases, and relatively, in the sense that as urban standards of living rise so the 'security' of the villages appears progressively less adequate. Nevertheless, for the moment the rural areas in most parts of Africa still provide a kind of cushion which has hardly begun to exist in the towns, and severe shortage of land is fortunately rare.

While it is true that employment conditions in the towns are far from attractive, excessive emphasis on this aspect is liable to obscure the important fact that for many workers their wage is only part of the total family income. The latter must include, besides the wage, any income that accrues in the countryside, for example the subsistence and perhaps even cash income from farming. E. H. Winter found that amongst the Bwamba of Western Uganda families maximized their incomes when the head of the household was away working for wages and wives and relatives continued farming (Winter, 1955). Under these conditions, however highly paid a man may be in employment, there is no obvious advantage in giving up the other part of his income, provided by his farm. If this is the case, then clearly the size of the wage plus fringe benefits may be largely irrelevant to a worker's decision ultimately to return home. There must, of course, come a point when a man's rural income is so small a proportion of his total income that he is prepared to sacrifice it without compensation for the sake of having his family in town with him. At what point this is likely to happen no one can at present say because no data on the rural income of urban employees exist, but it will clearly vary according to the agricultural potential of the worker's home area.

Two types of explanation of why people do not remain permanently in employment have been considered. The first, the idea that Africans have only limited wants, may indeed have been true at one time but finds virtually no support in contemporary evidence. Most of this evidence points to a normal supply curve of effort. Thus farmers have responded positively to increased opportunities to earn incomes from farming, and where the supply curve of labour to industry has been carefully investigated the evidence has suggested a normal, positive relationship. The notion of the quickly backward-bending supply curve of effort has been largely discredited in the writings of those who have given time to careful study (Berg, 1961, pp. 468–92; Neumark, 1958, pp. 55–63).

At the same time there is a growing support for the argument that inadequate wages and unsatisfactory conditions of employment are the true explanations of the failure to settle in towns. There is evidence that as these conditions improve larger numbers are in fact leaving their villages for good. Wages have increased very considerably, especially for unskilled work, in most parts of East and Central Africa during the past decade, but it is easier to quote figures of the increase than to construct a satisfactory index of the degree of permanence in employment (Elkan, 1960, p. 4). In Kampala the latest annual inquiry into the patterns of income and expenditure of unskilled workers shows that the proportion of unskilled wage earners who have dependent wives and children living with them has risen from 27 per cent in 1957 to 43 per cent in 1964, which may be taken as an indication of greater stability (Uganda Protectorate, 1957, p. 4). There also appears to have been a decline in labour turnover in secondary industries in some towns, but the evidence for urban employment as a whole either does not exist or is ambiguous (Commission for Technical Cooperation in Africa South of the Sahara, 1962). In one case the increase in the average length of service resulting from a decline in labour turnover was accompanied by a substantial increase in the proportion of workers from areas nearby. This is significant because even ten years ago workers from areas nearby had shown a marked propensity to remain longer in employment than migrants from a distance.[2] It is of course possible to argue that these workers are semi-rural rather than truly urban, and in any case it is unwise to generalize from the experience of one firm.

It is important to realize that neither the increase in the number of dependants nor the decline in labour turnover is unequivocal evidence in favour of the growth of the permanent urban population. With the increase in wages more workers can now afford to maintain a wife in town as well as one on their rural farms and they may still return to the country in the end. A more important point is that a reduction in labour turnover can well be caused by greater competition for jobs, and recent trends in employment figures suggest that this is at least part of the explanation. Total employment appears to have reached a plateau and in some instances has actually declined. In all three countries of East Africa total employment was higher

2. Private communication from Dr Roger Scott concerning employment in the Jute factory of the East African Tobacco Company, which had been investigated ten years previously and reported upon in Elkan (1955).

in 1960 than in the most recent year for which statistics are available (ILO, 1966).

At the same time, there is no doubt that higher urban wages combined with the fall in many cash crop prices have tipped the balance in favour of urban life for increasing numbers. For example, in her study of men seeking jobs in Kampala and Jinja, Caroline Hutton found little evidence of the prejudice against farming which is often said to be characteristic of school leavers. What she was told, time and again, is that the attraction of urban employment was not only the much higher income than was to be obtained in agriculture, but also the fact that it was paid regularly each month in contrast with agriculture, where it comes seasonally and is in any case unpredictable owing to the vagaries of weather and world market prices (Hutton, 1966, pp. 5–7).

Conclusion

In contrast with the migrants of nineteenth-century England those who move to the growing towns of East Africa are not landless poor. Many continue to enjoy the security of a land holding and the addition to their income that it brings. All the same it is clear that, as conditions in the towns improve, more and more people will feel able to abandon their rural ties. The question is, how far and how fast can such a process go without doing more harm than good to countries like those of East Africa? Resources are scarce and if governments choose to ignore the fact that they have an indigenous social security system, and attempt to provide full-scale services in towns, there is no doubt that increasing numbers will want to settle permanently in the towns. The cost will, however, be great. If the number of jobs does not grow as fast as the number wanting to settle in the towns, urban unemployment will grow. Improving urban conditions does not create additional employment, but if it is financed from funds that might have been used to improve the profitability of agriculture it will merely serve to tilt the balance of advantages still more in favour of working in town as opposed to remaining in agriculture. If instead these funds were used to make agriculture pay more, this would lead to a better balance between new jobs in towns and the demand for them. Meanwhile circular migration, while it lasts, should be seen not as an evil or a concomitant of backwardness but as a process that lowers the cost of development.

References

ASHTON, T. S. (1948), *The Industrial Revolution*, Hutchinson.
BERG, E. J. (1965a), 'The economics of the migrant labour system', in H. Kuper (ed.), *Urbanization and Migration in West Africa*, University of California Press.

BERG, E. J. (1965b), 'The development of a labour force in sub-Saharan Africa', *econ. Devel. Cult. Change*, vol. 13, pp. 403–5.

BERG, E. J. (1961), 'Backward-sloping labour supply functions in dual economies – the Africa case', in *Q.J. Econ.*, vol. 75, pp. 468–92.

COMMISSION for TECHNICAL COOPERATION in AFRICA SOUTH of the SAHARA (1962), *Absenteeism and Labour Turnover*, Joint Project no. 7, from Proceedings of the Sixth Inter-African Labour Conference, Abidjan.

ELKAN, W. (1955), *An African Labour Force*, East African Studies no. 7, Kampala.

ELKAN, W. (1960), *Migrants and Proletarians: Urban Labour in the Economic Development of Uganda*, OUP.

HANCE, W. A. (1964), *Geography of Modern Africa*, Columbia University Press.

HUTTON, C. (1966), 'Aspects of urban unemployment in Uganda', in *East African Institute of Social Research Conference Papers*, January 1966, Kampala.

ILO (1958), *African Labour Survey*, Studies and Reports, no. 48.

ILO (1966), *Yearbook of Labour Statistics*, Geneva.

MINISTRY OF ECONOMIC AFFAIRS AND DEVELOPMENT PLANNING, TANZANIA (1966): Labour force survey, mimeo, p. 108.

MITCHELL, J. C. (1961), 'Labour and population movements in Central Africa', in K. N. Barbour and R. M. Prother (eds.), *Essays on African Population*, Routledge and Kegan Paul.

NEUMARK, S. D. (1958), 'Economic development and economic incentives', *South African J. Econ.*, vol. 26, pp. 55–63.

POWESLAND, P. (1957), *Economic Policy and Labour*, East African Studies, no. 10, Kampala.

RICHARDS, A. I. (ed.) (1954), *Economic Development and Tribal Change*, Cambridge University Press.

SCHAPERA, I. (1947), *Migrant Labour and Tribal Life: a Study of Conditions in the Bechuanaland Protectorate*, OUP.

UGANDA PROTECTORATE (1957), *The Patterns of Income, Expenditure and Consumption of African Unskilled Workers in Kampala, February, 1957*, East African Statistical Department.

UNITED NATIONS (1957), *Report on the World Social Situation*, New York.

ECONOMIC COMMISSION FOR AFRICA (1963), *Social Factors Affecting Labour Stability in Uganda*, United Nations.

VAN VELSEN, J. (1961), 'Labour migration as a positive factor in the continuity of Tonga tribal society', in A. Southal (ed.), *Social Change in Modern Africa*, Manchester University Press.

WINTER, E. H. (1955), *Bwamba Economy*, East African Studies no. 5, Kampala.

YOUNG, M., and WILLMOT, P. (1959), *Family and Kinship in East London*, Penguin.

Part Three
Poverty, Income Distribution and Factor Prices

The unemployed in developing countries are also the poor: they are, in a sense, primarily the poor. The short excerpt – unduly short, perhaps – from the careful study of Dandekar and Rath (Reading 10) provides a first approach to the nature and magnitude of the problem. In rural areas the absence of opportunities for productive work during much of the year is often experienced as part of an immutable order of things, and the social institutions of peasant life – for example, the family, kinship and *compadrazgo*, patron–dependent ties – are supposed and expected to alleviate the most extreme consequences of poverty. In fact, almost everywhere in the developing world rural poverty is greater than urban poverty. But it is the latter that is more visible to policy-makers and researchers alike, in part because it is *experienced* as a greater problem, also by the poor themselves. When rural migrants move to the towns they drop some of the attitudes and behaviour patterns that were 'typical' of their rural milieu, and which in fact helped them apparently to cope with poverty. But the structure of economic opportunities they encounter in the towns is usually very unfavourable, and the resulting set of adaptations highly ambivalent. Dandekar's deduction that the measure of improvement which Indian rural–urban migrants can expect has drastically declined over the last decade is very disturbing. This *could* mean corroboration, in Indian circumstances, of Todaro's model, reproduced in Part Two, with its suggestion that more urban employment only leads to more urban poverty.

The extracts that follow from Gutkind (Reading 11) on the unemployed in urban Africa show an aspect of such a process of adaptation: the breakdown of traditional mutual aid based on kinship obligations, in the face of the increasing demands made upon those with jobs by recently arrived relatives from the countryside who are unable to find work.[1] Gutkind documents the emergence of new types of

1. It is very worthwhile to consult the original articles, which contain a wealth of material from field reports. For lack of space this has had to be largely omitted.

class-based associations, and his work points clearly to the usefulness of regarding those who are unable to find anything but occasional short-term employment as a group with highly distinctive class interests. But it is also obvious from this extract that great difficulties stand in the way of concerted action by the jobless to promote their interests as a class. In virtually all developing countries there is a growing number of persons (and certainly a growing proportion of the labour force) for whom work, and income, is rapidly becoming a mirage. But equally large numbers experience some measure of improvement in living conditions, at times more apparent than real, but in any case enough to keep the hope alive that poverty or joblessness will not be a permanent condition, certainly not for their children.

After these readings on the poorest and most vulnerable groups, wider issues of income distribution are examined. To move towards a more satisfactory distribution of income is an obvious objective of economic policy, particularly in countries where a sizeable fraction of the population is living on the margins of poverty. But apart from being an end in itself, it is increasingly being realized that changes in income distribution are themselves a *means* of achieving other objectives, particularly the objective of expanding employment.

Reading 12 from the ILO mission to Colombia explores the connections between income distribution and employment. In the past, development literature has tended to concentrate on the links between income distribution and the propensity to save and the level of investment. This reading is noteworthy because of the much broader perspective with which it approaches the relationships involved, emphasizing particularly the connection between income distribution and the whole structure of consumption demand – on *what* is produced as well as *how*. The direction and extent of these effects is an important area for empirical research – there are only a few examples of such research, often reaching different conclusions in different countries. But to the extent that consumption patterns differ between different income groups, a change in income distribution will change the overall structure of demand, both for goods and the labour to produce them.

Issues on the supply side have been more commonly considered in the past, primarily in terms of the links between wage levels and incentives for employers to adopt capital-intensive techniques. In Reading 13, Ranis takes a broad view of the influence of factor prices, considering not only the price of labour but also the price of capital goods, foreign exchange and urban goods in terms of rural – as judged respectively by interest rates, foreign exchange and the rural-urban terms of trade. There is strong evidence in Asia as in many other parts of the Third World that these three price levels often diverge significantly from equilibrium. Ranis goes beyond an analysis of the damaging effects on employment of factor price distortions. His article is also a succinct example of the case for dealing with distortions not by controls but by allowing market prices to reflect factor endowments as closely as possible.

Wages and salaries, both money and real have risen rapidly in many less-developed countries over the last decade, even in the presence of substantial open unemployment.[2] Ghai (Reading 14), focuses on facts such as this in terms of their implications for incomes policy. Although written in terms of Kenya, Ghai's approach is essentially analytical and identifies the general elements for an incomes and wages policy directed towards the objectives of employment creation and improving income distribution. In spite of the disappointing experience in many countries with previous (though often partial) attempts at such policies, the growing realization of the need for action in this area – and the inadequacies of alternative policy instruments – makes this an important field for future analysis.

2. Of course there are exceptions – but interesting evidence on the general proposition is provided in Turner and Jackson (1970).

Reference

TURNER, H. A., and JACKSON, D. A. S. (1970), 'On the determination of the general wage level – a world analysis', *Econ. J.*, vol. 80, pp.827–49.

10 V. M. Dandekar and N. Rath

Poverty in India

Extract from V. M. Dandekar and N. Rath 'Poverty in India: I – dimensions and trends', *Economic and Political Weekly*, vol. 6, 1971, pp. 32–3, 39–40.

An inquiry of the National Sample Survey of India in 1960–61 provided extensive data on private consumer expenditure. Both in urban and rural areas households living only a little below the national average spent between 70 per cent and 75 per cent of their total expenditure on food. Their diets were far from adequate. It was estimated that in 1960–61 42 million urban people, which is about 54 per cent of the total urban population, lived on diets inadequate even in respect of calories. Adding this number to the estimate of rural population living on inadequate diets, namely 135 million, it seems that in 1960–61, between 175 million to 180 million people in the country lived on diets inadequate even in respect of calories. This briefly is the measure of the extent of poverty prevailing in the country at the beginning of the last decade.

Not enough is known about these people who were so poor as not to be able to afford a diet adequate even in terms of calories. In the following, we shall present what little fragmentary data are available regarding the characteristics of the poor which may also indicate the causes underlying their poverty.

Size of the households

One of the reasons of poverty is the unduly large number of dependants to be supported per earner in a household. There are no direct data available to support this proposition. But it may be indirectly inferred by examining the size of households (number of persons per household) in different sections of the population.

The average size of household in the poorest 10 per cent of the rural population is 5·87. As we move through the successive ten per cent sections of the population with increasing *per capita* consumer expenditure, the average size of the household steadily declines until for the richest 5 per cent of the population, it is as low as 3·78. The phenomenon is even more marked in the urban area. Here, in the poorest 10 per cent of the population, the size of the household is as large as 6·09. It declines steadily and rapidly as we move to the better sections until for the richest 5 per cent of the population, the size of household is as small as 2·25. There is therefore little doubt that the size of a household is an important factor pushing it down the ladder.

It should be noted that a larger household does not necessarily mean a larger number of dependants per earner. A larger household may also have more earners as in a joint family; but in that case, it would also have a larger income and the fact of a mere large size would not reduce its *per capita* consumption. When a large household has low *per capita* consumption, it is evident that it has more dependants per earner. This would be particularly true of rural households. These households may not necessarily be marked by destitution, disability or old age. They may be perfectly normal households, with normal earners but burdened with too large a number of dependants. Nonetheless, for that reason, they will need to be given special assistance in one form or another.

The urban situation is likely to be somewhat different. Here a large household may have more than one earner in the formal sense of the term. However, they earn little. These are cases of the rural poor who have drifted into the cities in search of a living but have not yet been able to secure an adequate one. The mere fact of poverty may bring them together and for want of adequate living room, they may huddle together to constitute a 'household' for the purpose of the census or the National Sample Survey. Their problem is one of employment opportunity for their working members and not so much of special assistance.

The rural poor

Little more information is available on the rural poor. In rural areas, an important cause of poverty is lack of land resources. A number of rural households have no land at all. They live entirely by the personal labour of their members. They constitute some of the poorest sections of rural population. It will be useful to examine what proportion of rural poverty is accounted for by the landless.

The relevant data are available from the Eighteenth Round of the National Sample Survey which refers to the period from February 1963 to January 1964. However, only a few summary tabulations of data from this round are presently available in published form. Therefore we shall supplement these data with the more detailed data earlier collected and published in the Eleventh and Twelfth Rounds of the National Sample Survey which covered the period from August 1956 to August 1957.

In the Eleventh and Twelfth rounds covering 1956–7, besides the general inquiry into the consumer expenditure of a sample of all rural households, a special inquiry was conducted into the employment, earnings and consumer expenditure of a sample of agricultural labour households. For this purpose, an agricultural labour household was defined as one for which agricultural wage employment constituted the major source of income. In the Eighteenth Round covering 1963–4, the special inquiry was extended to cover all rural labour households and a distinction was made between agricultural labour households and non-agricultural labour households depending upon the major source of their wage income. It seems that in 1956–7, about 25 per cent of the rural households were agricultural labour households. In 1963–4, only about 20 per cent of the rural households were agricultural labour households but, in addition, about 5 per cent of the rural households were classified as non-agricultural labour households. It is possible therefore that there was a decline in the proportion of agricultural labour households. However, it seems more likely that, though the inquiry in 1956–7 was confined to agricultural labour households, it in fact covered all rural labour households as was explicitly done in the inquiry during 1963–4. In that case, the proportion of labour households seems to have remained more or less constant over the seven years from 1956–7 to 1963–4. In both the periods, about 60 per cent of the labour households had no land and hence they depended almost entirely on the personal labour of their members. They had no other means of livelihood. The remaining 40 per cent cultivated small pieces of land; nevertheless their main dependence was on wage employment in agriculture or outside agriculture. Nearly three fourths of the labour households worked as casual labourers, that is, they worked if and when work was available. Otherwise they were unemployed. The remaining one fourth were attached labourers, that is, they worked for a single employer under some kind of a contract extending to at least a period of one year. The nature of this contract would vary from a proper agreement of an annual farm servant to the feudal tie of a bonded labourer. But all of them had some kind of regular employment. In a sense, they were never unemployed during the year. [. . .]

The incidence of rural labour is very high in the South, namely in Kerala, Tamil Nadu and Andhra Pradesh where more than one third of all rural households are labour households. The incidence is also high in West Bengal, Bihar and Orissa where nearly one third of all rural households are labour households. In Maharashtra, about 30 per cent of all rural households are labour households. In the remaining States, the incidence of rural labour is much lower. The States with high incidence of rural labour are also generally the States with large proportions of the rural population living below the minimum. [. . .]

In spite of these rather old and fragmentary data, it is clear that the rural poor consist predominantly of agricultural labour households and small landholders with cultivated holdings of less than 5·0 acres and particularly less than 2·5 acres. The two groups would also include village artisans progressively thrown out of their traditional employment. The urban poor are only an overflow of the rural poor into the urban area. Fundamentally, they belong to the same class as the rural poor. However, as they live long enough in urban poverty, they acquire characteristics of their own. Little is known of their life and labour in the growing cities. [. . .]

Deepening of urban poverty

During the period from 1960–61 to 1967–8, the rural-urban disparity has narrowed down a little. Thus, while in 1960–61 the *per capita* urban consumer expenditure was 37·7 per cent higher than the *per capita* rural consumer expenditure, in 1967–8 the urban *per capita* expenditure was only 35·9 per cent higher than the rural *per capita* expenditure. We shall now examine how this slight reduction in the rural-urban differential came about. In particular, we shall ask whether the reduction in the rural-urban differential has come about because of a reduction in the differential between the rural-urban rich or the rural-urban poor. [. . .]

Even in 1960–61, the rural-urban differential was much greater between the rural-urban rich than between the rural-urban poor. For instance, the *per capita* consumer expenditure of the 30 per cent urban poor was then about 27 per cent higher than the *per capita* consumer expenditure of their rural counterparts. [. . .]

What has happened (by 1967–8) to the 10 per cent poorest in rural and urban areas is the most striking. The 10 per cent rural poor have stayed practically where they were at the beginning of the decade. On the other hand, the 10 per cent urban poor have definitely suffered. As a result, they have moved close to the rural poor. In 1960–61, the consumption of the urban 5 per cent poorest was 27·2 per cent higher than the consumption of their rural counterparts, in 1967–8, it was only 4·5 per cent higher. The same is true of the 5 per cent poor next above them. In 1960–61, their consumption was 29·2 per cent higher than their counterparts in the rural areas; in 1967–8, it was only 10·2 per cent higher. These small margins are certainly not adequate to compensate for the higher cost of urban living at this level. It means that in 1967–8 the living standard of the 10 per cent urban poor was worse than that of their rural counterparts.

It is necessary to understand the meaning of this deterioration in the living standards of the urban poor. It does not necessarily mean that the same people were worse off in 1967–8 in comparison with their condition in 1960–61. This is not impossible. But more generally it means that new migrants have moved from the rural area into the growing urban centres and have been compelled to accept life at a level much below what used to be the case a decade ago and hardly distinguishable from the life they left behind and to escape which they moved into the cities. It is thus that the rural-urban disparities have somewhat narrowed down.

Conclusion

We should conclude. During the past decade, the *per capita* private consumer expenditure increased by less than half a per cent per annum. Moreover, the small gains have not been equitably distributed among all sections of the population. The condition of the bottom 20 per cent rural poor has remained more or less stagnant. The condition of the bottom 20 per cent urban poor has definitely deteriorated; and for another 20 per cent of the urban population, it has remained more or less stagnant. Thus, while the character of rural poverty has remained the same as before, the character of urban poverty has deepened further. This is the consequence of the continuous migration of the rural poor into the urban areas in search of a livelihood, their failure to find adequate means to support themselves there and the resulting growth of roadside and slum life in the cities. All the latent dissatisfaction about the slow progress of the economy and the silent frustration about its failure to give the poor a fair deal, let alone special attention, appear to be gathering in this form. Its shape today is probably no more than hideous; allowed to grow unheeded and unrelieved, it will inevitably turn ugly.

11 P. C. W. Gutkind

The Unemployed and Poor in Urban Africa

Extract from P. C. W. Gutkind, 'The energy of despair: social organization of the
unemployed in two African cities: Lagos and Nairobi; preliminary account',
Civilizations, vol. 17, 1967, pp. 380–405, and 'The poor in urban Africa: a prologue
to modernization, conflict and the unfinished revolution', in *Power, Poverty and
Urban Policy*, vol. 2, Urban Affairs, Sage Publications, Inc., 1968, pp. 370–92.

Introduction

[. . .] In this article my main interest is in the social organization of the
urban-resident unemployed in Lagos and Nairobi.[1] To begin with, we make
certain assumptions about the nature of African social organization, and
the operation of kinship and reciprocity which leads us to question whether
unemployment in Africa is not a fiction rather than a fact. Even those who
recognize that unemployment in Africa is a fact, and that it is a condition
increasing in intensity, will almost invariably suggest that Africans are
rooted to the land, i.e. an African can always return to the land and farm,
and, further, African family life and the rules of kinship and reciprocity are
such that, while many Africans may be out of work, they are protected
against total dependency by being part of a complex network of mutual
aid and support. But this argument, too, attributes to African societies in
transition certain immutable features alleged to be universal and characteristic of traditional African social organization – an organization somehow highly flexible in its adaptive potential to meet the pressures and
demands of modernization. In part this is true and, indeed, African leaders
are fully aware that certain characteristics of African social organization
provide an important safety valve at this critical moment in change and
modernization. But, as we shall see below, these are arguments and attitudes
based on the perception of an idealized system rather than on the way people
actually perceive their family obligations. While ties of blood and marriage
are still significant, not in general terms but under specifically defined and
structured situations, the desire to individualize achievements and to be
more selective in one's aid to others injects a highly competitive and
entrepreneurial element. 'The more the opportunities become individual
and competitive,' Marris (1966) writes 'the less appropriate are family
claims that would frustrate individual achievement . . .' In African urban
society in particular, Marris observes, there are not 'likely to be any very

1. Although I recognize that the problems faced by unemployed women are also of
considerable importance, particularly in West Africa, my observations and interviews
were predominantly with young men in the age group 16–45.

telling communal sanctions that might force the prosperous to give to their poor relations. The successful man is free to decide for himself the nature of his obligations.' In this respect 'the advantages of family solidarity are no longer reciprocal'. A telling point made by Marris, writing about Lagos and Nairobi, and one frequently ignored, is while it might still be correct to observe that an African, particularly if he is well off, 'has a duty to provide the opportunity to as many members of his family as he can afford . . . he is not required to protect them from the failure to make use of that opportunity. If they cannot compete successfully, they must find their own level.' Clearly this formulation is a product of changing conceptions regarding family responsibilities and, possibly, the basis of incipient class formation.

The implications of this, as we shall see, for the economic and social life of the unemployed is far reaching as compatibility of education, type of work, earnings and residence have become the basis of new personal and group networks which are 'association' rather than 'kin-based' (Gutkind, 1965; 1966).[2] The unemployed are progressively forced into associational networks and institutional structures which exist as enclaves within Africa's urban areas.

[. . .] The unemployed as a collective category exist at the margins of African urban society. Their hope of effective participation in this society is rapidly declining. While their political power has considerable potential, econ-omically they are weak due to the fact that most unemployed men are unskilled and thus not readily placed in employment. The prospects of absorbing the totally unskilled in a gradually increasing labour market are slim indeed. If this observation is correct, African urban society will before long show clear signs of stratification (Wilson and Mafeje, 1963; Pauw, 1963; Mitchell and Epstein, 1959). On the one hand, there will be those with the required skills, resources and opportunities, and, on the other, those to whom mobility is denied. For some time to come, this group will have to depend on aid from family and friends and, progressively, on their own ingenuity. Mutual aid and reciprocity is a two way process. The more advantaged see their help as of only limited reciprocal value to themselves – as those whom they support can offer little in return – other than turn some of their dependents into servants. The probable consequences will likely be that the unemployed, the unskilled, the illiterate and the primary and lower secondary school-leavers, will devote their energy – the energy of despair – to draw inward for their own salvation and as means of protecting their self-respect. [. . .]

Whether or not migrants are 'pushed' out of the rural areas for environ-mental, economic, or social and personal reasons, or whether they are

2. See particularly footnote 2, p. 51 of Gutkind, (1966).

'pulled' into the towns for similar reasons, they all come with the expectation of finding employment. Those able to write often take the trouble to give advance notice of their pending arrival by writing to a relative or friend asking him to secure work in advance. The following letter was received by a junior civil servant from his brother, a Luo from Western Kenya, who had been resident in Nairobi for just over two years. The writer had just finished primary school and had taken a three month typing course at a secretarial college in Kisumu (a town of some 24,000 in 1962).

June 1966.

Dear Ezikiel,

I hope that you are well. I hope that your health is good and that you are eating well. We have had much rain recently. My work is now completed and I am ready to job [sic]. I have done my work of learning to type and have reached a speed of 97 words per minute. I think that I can do better. My shorthand is not so very fine because the teacher was not good and I did not learn so good [sic]. I must now earn my own money but I have not been lucky to find job in Kisumu. I have used all the money I had to put [sic] on bus tickets and now I have no more to buy new clothes. I would like you to sent [sic] some money to me so that I can buy my ticket to come to Nairobi. Please find work for me in your office. I want to come on saturday or monday and will come to your home. Samuel has told me that he will give me some food to bring to you. Please sent [sic] me money because I have no more shillings left in my pocket.
Charles.[3]

[. . .] In the course of interviewing some 120 unemployed men in Nairobi, and an equal number in Lagos, only 27 in the former and 13 in the latter had given written warning to relatives or friends that they were about to arrive and needed shelter and work. All others simply arrived unexpectedly. This is a source of very considerable annoyance to the hosts, a number of whom respond to this imposition with considerable hostility. Although the majority will allow such unexpected visitors to stay with them, a good many unemployed men, particularly in Lagos and among the Yoruba, complained that they were treated with considerable rudeness (particularly by the wife of the host if the latter was away and if the visitor was not related to the wife) and either sent on their way or told that they could sleep on a verandah or in the yard.

[. . .] The housing and family circumstances of the host often place enormous strain on both the host and the job seeker. Many hosts complain bitterly that they must cut back on their own standard of living, and that of their own family, to meet the expenses of their guest. While some of the latter are sensitive to the additional burden they impose on their hosts, quite a few feel that their relatives and friends owe them a living. Such an attitude readily breeds frequent quarrels and their cumulative effect is that

3. Field data notes, Nairobi, August–Sept. 1966.

the guest moves on to the next person willing to look after him. [. . .] In this way many of the unemployed circulate from one relative to another. During this time such persons use the network of family and kin to the fullest possible extent. Many of them seek out lines of consanguinity and affinal kin, although more of the former than the latter, which are then activated only to be broken again a few weeks or months later. While the job seeker moves in this network he continues to be, to a certain extent, under the watchful eye of members of the kin group. While this is so his contacts are more restricted and he feels highly dependent on them for help. Particularly older members of his kin group generally demand that he submit to their advice and wishes. Failure to do so may result in being reprimanded or expelled from the home of the host. Many young job seekers resent that the greater authority of their host, and the often condescending attitude they display, results in their being exploited in the home.

Association-based networks

When a man has exploited every possible aid that he could obtain from his relatives, over a period of months or several years, while he tried to find employment but failed, he then starts to cultivate friends and progressively turns his back on his kin. What contacts he continues to maintain with the latter in the urban area are generally restricted to occasional visits and to more formal occasions, such as births, marriages and deaths when his absence would have been noted.

Once an unemployed person has decided to turn to his friends, rather than return to his village, he has made an important decision. He can now no longer expect or demand help but must adjust to a highly flexible structure. He is now incorporated into an association of persons most of whom care little for him. But at the same time he is free to go his own way. While he cannot make demands, his friends cannot order him about. Goodwill and a sympathetic attitude allows him to stay in the home of his host. Generally, friends accept fewer responsibilities for their guest. He can come and go as he pleases. Most often a friend will offer no more than a bed space, although some generous friends will also offer food and money. This rather depends on the previous duration and the quality of the friendship. [. . .] The bond of reciprocity has been replaced by a greater emphasis on individual initiative and enterprise. What contacts a man makes are judged by him to promote his own interest and to give him an advantage in his efforts to obtain work. Thus he might join an ethnic or recreation association, a church, or a political party. This further broadens his contacts which he uses as a means to find work. Unlike the contacts he had within the limits of the kin-based network, his new associations constantly proliferate. His working host introduces him to his friends, and these in turn introduce him to their friends. The conscientious job seeker usually follows each of the leads suggested. Thus new contacts are made, new avenues explored and old contacts lapse. The search for work involves the job seeker in a network of contacts which vary in strength and durability. Yet these networks have continuity and the kind of flexibility which make them particularly suitable under urban conditions. [. . .]

When an unemployed man has exhausted his contacts among those of his friends who have work, and hence can look after him, his situation becomes precarious. Not only does he become discouraged but his friends find him a burden and no longer offer him hospitality. At that point an unemployed person has to make yet another important decision. The choice is between returning to his village community or staying on in the town in a desperate last bid to find work. What determines a man's decision at this point might be crucial for his future. It is difficult to know why some men give up, for the time being, and return to the land and others refuse to do so. Up to a point this appears to be determined by length of urban residence and degree of involvement in urban life. Returning to the village might be understood as a sign of defeat and failure. [. . .]

Men who have looked for work for more than a year have often given up hope that they will ever find employment. Their friends, and even their kin, who are fortunate to have jobs, gradually drift away from them and restrict their contacts. Class attitudes then begin to manifest themselves. This was clearly expressed by a Benin man, a highly placed civil servant in Lagos, who talked about his younger brother (who had not succeeded in finding employment for over a year) in the following terms:

I have done what I could to help Isole. He lived in my home for almost ten months and I gave him letters to my friends who were willing to help him. But he complained all the time that he wanted a better job than people were willing to offer him. When he lived with me in my home my friends asked me about Isole and wondered why I had not been able to find work for him. He was even begging money from my friends. He has now become lazy and there is nothing more that I can do to help him. I think that he must join his own friends.[4]

The unemployed person is not insensitive to such sentiments and, as the prospect of his upward mobility appears to diminish, he more readily interprets his predicament in class terms.

[. . .] Unemployed men who have been out of work for long, particularly those whose education and skills are very limited, can hope for little more than irregular and casual work. Time has given them the stigma of being unemployable. Year by year they are pushed further to the fringes of urban life, they are the disaffiliated – the outsiders – unable to participate in economic change. [. . .] Industrial development can make little use of this

4. Field data notes, Nairobi, August–Sept. 1966.

vast pool of readily available manpower – and an increasing number of unemployed recognize this predicament.

[. . .] When a job seeker has thus reached the stage when employers treat him as unemployable, and his relatives and friends no longer offer him dependable aid, he is relegated to a new social milieu. The network of his contacts and associations, his friends and the social groups he selects, now comprise predominantly other unemployed men. While he will continue to visit his working friends and relatives, the greater part of his time is spent on activities no longer designed to help him find employment. Thus many job seekers have given up calling regularly at the Employment Exchanges or visiting factories, offices or ministries. Some might take to individual entrepreneurship such as petty street trading but the rewards are so small that many give up in frustration. Few can raise the capital to secure and expand their efforts. Those who peddle goods for others also gain little reward quite apart from needing some cash as a deposit with the owner of the merchandise. Some adjust their lives to the very irregular employment available and others lower their expectations, although for the Primary School Leaver this is somewhat unusual. Junior Secondary Leavers tend to spend their time scanning the newspapers for advertisements and writing applications (one such young person, an Ibo, had filed copies of some 131 applications written over a period of 14 months).

Associations of unemployed

To promote their interests the urban unemployed in Africa have at times attempted – mostly unsuccessfully thus far – to organize. The various associations which they have formed have as yet been able to do little to advance the interest of their membership. Most of them have lacked skilled and powerful leadership and have been torn by internal dissensions. Because of this inability to organize themselves and develop a sense of corporateness, many unemployed have participated in the pre- and post-independence political movements, serving the leaders of these movements whenever called upon for mass rallies and demonstrations. [. . .]

Many of the younger unemployed men formed the core of the various 'youth wings' of the parties which rallied them in very large numbers. These age-homogeneous movements produced their own 'band' leaders and acted as political socialization structures for the membership. In the absence of alternative channels for the expression of economic, social, and political grievances, they attracted a good deal of support from many unschooled and schooled unemployed. However, a sense of disillusionment over lack of achievement by mere membership also set in very quickly, particularly as political instability increased and political parties were restricted in their activities.

Although the unemployed have formed a distinct stratum in the economic structure, they have yet to become a major political force in Africa. It is perhaps remarkable that no political leader in the post-independence era has as yet attempted to organize them into a vocal political pressure group. The few leaders who have tried to do this have risen from among the unemployed. Generally, the response by government to this leadership has been to treat it as potentially subversive, or to 'offer' employment to those attempting to organize the unemployed. [. . .]

Faced with such a situation, the unemployed are forced to deal with their economic and personal predicaments in their own terms. It is at this point of breakdown of traditional mutual aid that the unemployed, both individually and collectively, redefine their place in the social order in more political terms. Indeed, it appears that only when they are conscious of their exposed social and economic position do they become aware of the existence of large numbers of other men whose situation does not differ greatly from their own. Although in the early weeks or months of their job hunting they tend very much to keep to themselves and not reveal to others the opportunities they hear about, after months of looking for work they will register at the Employment Exchange (not having done so initially since they had heard that few people obtain work by referral from the Exchange, an agency which the majority of private employers refuse to use in any case). Here they come into contact with a large number of other men and here their political socialization takes place as they sit outside the offices of the Exchange passing the time in conversation. It is therefore not surprising that associations of unemployed have come into being as a result of acquaintances first made at the Lagos and Nairobi Exchanges. [. . .]

But few, if any, of the numerous attempts to form associations of unemployed men have had any staying power. The reasons for this are complicated since they are rooted in the very complexity of the yet imperfectly understood change and modernization processes. However, there are several possible explanations. First, to be effective such associations must cut across ethnic lines in order to avoid extensive fragmentation of the political effort and for the sake of concerted action. Instead, the unemployed use their ethnicity, as members of tribal associations, as an instrument of competition for employment. Secondly, no association can operate effectively without an established organizational structure which has continuity over time and whose officers are wholly committed to the activities and objectives of the group. Such a body requires financial support from the membership and skilled, i.e. educated and trained, organizers. Neither of these conditions have been met in the various associations. [. . .]

More fundamentally, however, associations of unemployed will only become self-sustaining when they develop into protest movements with objectives closely related to the establishment of a more equitable economic and political order. At present many unemployed men believe that jobs will eventually become available and their individual efforts rewarded. Many believe these opportunities will arise at the moment political leaders representing their ethnic groups come to power, or at such a time when they have established a personal contact with a political leader or a civil servant. Few unemployed men understand that the barriers to their sought-after opportunities spring from economic and technological characteristics of modernization rather than from their inability to cultivate political relations with members of the elite.

The unemployed and the trade unions

[. . .] Faced with mounting unemployment, the trade union movement has been placed in a difficult position. Many unemployed men feel that its leaders have erected political and economic barriers designed to protect the interests of the few, of those who have work, while using the unemployed when it suits them. Thus, in the widespread strike in Nigeria in June 1964, it was said that the unemployed were in the vanguard of the rioters at Port Harcourt and that the trade union leaders were prepared to let the blame fall on them for the damage done and the tensions which were generated. Likewise, in the Congo (Brazzaville), Ivory Coast, Dahomey, Tanganyika, and the Central African Republic, the trade unions have been identified with attempts to overthrow African governments, often using as their spearhead the urban-resident unemployed.

However, more fundamentally, the trade unions view the large pool of unemployed as a constant threat to their bargaining position. Small-scale employers in the construction industry, for example, are ever ready to hire the unemployed at wages well below the statutory minimum. Sometimes when unemployed men assemble outside factory gates or building sites, employers will ask them whether they are or ever were members of a union. On two occasions, in Lagos in July, 1966, fights broke out at a building site and outside a factory between those willing to work for lower pay and those who insisted on the minimum wage. [. . .]

Diversity and convergence of interests among the unemployed

Although the unemployed lack much needed political leadership, they are the first significant manifestation in contemporary African society of incipient economic, social and political stratification along class lines. They highlight the enormous differences between the elite and the poor and exhibit a real difference of life style from the rest of the society, a difference which is particularly obvious in the urban areas. For many their style of life is dominated not merely by severe poverty but also by a total lack of

upward mobility and the real fear that they are forever 'fixed' in the incipient class system. Although they actively compete for work, they lack
the education and skills which could give them the initial anchorage and
'push' they desire. Particularly in West Africa, personal and social aspirations are high, fanned by a large degree of political involvement and an
extensive and articulate group of politicians able to exploit grievances. Yet
the life style of the unemployed has progressively removed them from the
bulk of the population about whose predicaments and aspirations they
know little. As such, all the manifestations of class conflict exist. Exclusive
recruitment from the elite categories diminishes economic opportunities
for all, while at the same time educational opportunities and standards
are on the increase. [. . .]

The emergence of political groupings designed to express popular discontent is, of course, restricted in the context of current African political
structures. In the one-party African state, it is assumed that all categories
of the population will bend their energies and support towards the party
of 'national integration'. The activities by any group of men that impedes
this objective are viewed with suspicion and hostility. It would not be
surprising, therefore, that those who demand work are likely to look to more
revolutionary ideologies and, initially, to express their demands in un-
coordinated attacks against the government and the politicians. The cynical
attitude expressed by many unemployed men is channelled into an increasing political awareness that the present course of national development has
brought major benefits to the few at the expense of the majority.

But the poor lack the instrumental channels to express their grievances.
What channels they have, such as ethnic and voluntary associations, do not
provide the ideological and political framework required to press the
urgency of their case. Instead, these groups concentrate their political
efforts along traditional and ethnic lines. Lloyd summarizes the argument
as follows:

    . . . the institutionalized channels for the expression of . . . grievances are
    becoming less effective, so that protests are not directed against the structure of
    society by organized political movements. Instead individual frustrations are
    expressed through charges of tribalism and corruption, of witchcraft and sorcery.
    Action lies in developing one's own relationships with influential patrons and in
    seeking from supernatural agencies protection against evil forces and support
    in one's aspirations. Outbreaks of aggressive behaviour tend to lack coherent
    leadership or organization, to be without any class ideology or goal – save a
    general attitude of destruction directed against those with wealth, power or
    property (Lloyd, 1967, p. 317).

Furthermore, so long as the unemployed are dependent on their close
and far kin and friends, and as long as they can, if they wish, return to the

rural areas to (try to) obtain a living from the land, they remain immune to the intensive social and economic pressures which might make them a more active political community. Thus, political parties and politicians, such as the Eastern Nigerian-based Socialist Workers and Farmers Party, have not yet been able to develop a strong sense of class consciousness among the disadvantaged urbanites and to place class loyalty above tribalism or regionalism. [. . .]

Africa's unemployed, and those who are today underemployed but tomorrow join the pool of the work seekers, are part of the debris of modernization and exploitation. More significantly, they stand as a monument to the unfinished revolution which a few short years ago swept the continent into the rough waters of a dubious sovereignty.

As Stanley Diamond writes:

Millions of Africans, radically disengaged from their own traditions, are being rapidly proletarianized in both rural and urban areas, and are being forced to substitute a mere strategy of poverty and survival for authentic cultural expression. Put another way, they are being rapidly converted into marginal producers and marginal consumers on the remotest fringes of contemporary industrial society (Diamond, 1963, p. 178).

References

DIAMOND, S. (1963), 'Modern Africa: the pains of birth', *Dissent*, vol. 10, p. 178.
GUTKIND, P. C. W. (1965), 'Network analysis and urbanism in Africa: the use of micro and macro analysis', *Canad. Rev. Sociol. Anthrop.*, vol. 2, pp. 123–31.
GUTKIND, P. C. W. (1966), 'African urban family life and the urban system', *J. Asian African Stud.*, vol. 1, pp. 35–42.
LLOYD, P. C. (1967), *Africa in Social Change: Changing Traditional Societies in the Modern World*, Penguin.
MARRIS, P. (1966), *Individual Achievement and Family Ties, Some International Comparisons*, mimeographed paper.
MITCHELL, J. C., and EPSTEIN, A. L. (1959), 'Occupational prestige and social status among urban Africans in Northern Rhodesia', *Africa*, vol. 29, pp. 22–40.
PAUW, B. A. (1963), *The Second Generation, A Study of the Family among Urbanized Bantu in East London*, OUP.
WILSON, M., and MAFEJE, A. (1963), *Langa, A Study of Social Groups in an African Township*, OUP.

12 International Labour Office

Income Distribution and Employment

From International Labour Office, *Towards Full Employment; A Programme for Colombia*, prepared by an inter-agency team, ILO Geneva, 1970, pp. 139–51.

There are many links between levels of employment and the distribution of income. In economies where the rates of unemployment and under-employment of the labour force are high and rising – as in Colombia – to achieve a higher level of employment is to redistribute income; it is in fact almost the only way of providing the poorest groups of the population with the opportunity to obtain a larger share of the total. A policy of full employment is the first and most effective component of a programme to eliminate extreme poverty.

Nevertheless, what is important for our present task is the effect of the distribution. This can be approached in many ways. One can examine it from the viewpoint of justice – is it a fair distribution? Or again from the point of view of incentives – will it encourage hard and careful work, in the right place and the right job, with adequate rewards for those who study and in other ways increase their capacity to contribute to development? [. . .]

Our concern here is, however, the relation between distribution and employment. This raises, of course, the need for savings and incentives, but, as we shall see, some other aspects of the Colombian income structure turn out to be more important, especially its effect on the pattern of consumption.

The distribution of income

The first point to establish is: what is the shape of the income distribution? Little reliable statistical information exists about the patterns and trends of income distribution in most developing countries. Thus, to mention just one obvious example, those estimating the distribution of personal income face considerable difficulties in countries where the legal obligation to pay income taxes affects only a small fraction of the population or where evasion of tax laws is easy and widespread. To some degree, however, statistical weaknesses reflect lack of political interest. Much more could be discovered about income distribution, despite the restricted coverage of the tax system, if there were the will to do so.

Until last year the data in Colombia were poor, worse even than for most other countries in Latin America. [. . .]

In 1969, however, two carefully designed and executed studies were written, one on the distribution of income in agriculture and the other on distribution in urban centres (see Table 1). Of course this does not mean that the data they provide are sufficient either in quantity or in quality. In particular, it is not possible to add together the data of the two studies: the studies refer to different years and they overlap.[1] Moreover, there is a limit to what can be done with the poor basic statistics on income.

Nevertheless, and in spite of these and other qualifications about the data, one fundamental conclusion clearly emerges from all the information available, namely that income in Colombia is heavily concentrated in a very few hands. It also appears from other sources (but less definitely) that, on the whole, this concentration of income has not lessened during the last fifteen years: it might even have increased.[2]

Whichever estimate is taken, the poorest 50 per cent obtain only about one sixth of all income, while according to the most recent estimates, the people included in the 5 per cent of the population with the largest incomes receive between one third and somewhat more than two fifths of total income.

Table 1 **Estimates of the distribution of personal income in agriculture (1960) and in urban centres (1964)**
(cumulative percentages from the bottom)

People	Incomes	
	Berry (Agriculture) 1960	Urrutia-Villalba (Urban centres) 1964
50	14	12
60	21	17
70	26	26
80	34	37
90	46	53
95	57	67
100	100	100

Sources: Berry (1969, Tables 1 and 2); Urrutia and Villalba (1969).

1. For example, incomes which originate in agriculture (and are therefore included in the Berry estimates) but are also received by residents of the cities (and are consequently included in the Urrutia-Villalba study).

2. See, for instance, Urrutia and Villalba (1969, pp. 1277–9), and especially Slighton (1968). Slighton thinks that 'within the non-agricultural sector, at least the degree of inequality in income distribution has been widening over the past fifteen years' (p. 5).

Looking at Table 1, the concentration of income among the very rich seems to be much greater in agricultural than in the urban centres. In the former, the 5 per cent of the population with the largest incomes receives over 40 per cent of total farm income, and has an average income which is twenty times as high as the median income of the agricultural population – a truly exceptional ratio. The corresponding figures for the cities, although high, are much more moderate: one third and nine.

Table 2 **Percentage of total income received by poorest and richest income groups in various countries**

	5 per cent with highest incomes	50 per cent with lowest incomes
Latin American Countries		
Brazil	40	15
Costa Rica	35	18
Panama	34	21
El Salvador	33	16
Argentina	31	21
Mexico	29	15
Venezuela	26	14
Industrialized countries		
Netherlands	24	21
United States	20	23
United Kingdom	20	23
Norway	15	25

Source: E C L A (1969).

Table 2 shows roughly comparable data for other Latin American countries for which information is available. It depends which Colombian distribution one takes, but probably the concentration in the hands of the rich in Colombia is comparable with that in Brazil and El Salvador which have a somewhat similar level of income, rather than with that in Argentina, Mexico or Venezuela, which have all reached levels of income per head considerably higher than in Colombia.[3]

The degree of inequality that characterizes the distribution of income in Colombia is apparently not much modified by the tax system. The combined effects of the different taxes made the tax system nearly 'neutral' in 1966, so far as its effects were concerned – i.e. the distributions of income

3. The 'Gini coefficient' also suggests a greater degree of inequality in Colombia than in Argentina or Mexico. The difference is sufficiently striking to be of interest, despite the weakness of the basic statistics. Compare Jaffe (1969) with estimates by Berry (1969) and Urrutia-Villalba (1969), for Colombia.

before and after taxes were practically the same, the 'progressive' nature of direct taxes being more or less balanced by the 'regressive' incidence of indirect taxes. Despite the arbitrary nature of the assumptions on which the table is based, the conclusions are probably broadly valid.

It is not possible to discuss here at length all the factors which generate the very uneven distribution of income which prevails in Colombia. Nevertheless, employment policy cannot be properly discussed unless we mention some of the most important and obvious causes. The first is the extremely unequal distribution of property. Although marked enough in all sectors of the economy, it is specially so in the case of agriculture. This is clearly brought out by the data of Table 3 in which we can see the enormous spread

Table 3 Average income of producers by farm size, 1960

Farm size (hectares)*	Average income (thousand pesos)	Number of producers (thousands)
1–2	1·2	191
2–3	1·8	117
3–4	2·3	92
4–5	2·7	58
5–10	3·7	169
10–20	5·9	114
20–30	7·1	44
30–40	8·8	27
40–50	10·8	16
50–100	13·5	40
100–200	24·8	22
200–500	42·5	14
500–1 000	106·0	4
1 000–2 000	193·0	2
2 000 and more	553·0	1

* Farms of less than one hectare are excluded since most of the 300,000 people with such plots earn the majority of their income working for someone else.
Source: Berry (1969).

of the incomes of farmers and the close relation between income and farm size. The highly skewed distribution of agricultural income must derive essentially from the heavy concentration of land holding. The distribution of company shares is also heavily concentrated: a mere 0·2 per cent of shareholders (themselves a very small group) own 61 per cent of all shares.[4]

4. ILO PREALC (1969, vol. 4). The figures cover two thirds of all the corporations registered at the Superintendencia de Sociedades Anónimas.

Other factors strongly influencing the distribution of income in the direction of inequality are highly uneven access to the higher levels of education and to employment in the modern sector. Both of these elements are crucial in determining the distribution of labour income (understood in a wide sense that includes any return on human capital). In developing countries, where the general level of education is low and where there is a dual economy, with modern and traditional sectors, the distribution of income from work is also very uneven. Relatively very high incomes (sometimes high also in absolute terms) are received by professional and technical personnel, by highly skilled workers, and by the small fraction of unskilled labourers who work in the modern sector. Of course, this fact need not in itself make the overall distribution of income more uneven.

But in Colombia, as in other developing economies, the probability of a person reaching the highest levels of education or even of entering the modern sector is strongly correlated with his family's income. In other words, those with high incomes from property are also more likely to obtain higher incomes from work, thus reinforcing the inequality of the overall distribution of income which arises from the skewness of the distribution of property.

Income distribution, the structure of consumption and the level of employment

The main way in which income distribution affects the level of employment in Colombia is through its effect on the pattern of consumption. This works in two ways: the first is through the different import content of the expenditures of the rich and the poor; the second is through the different direct labour content of those expenditures.

The relation between the first element and the level of employment can be explained as follows. If we assume that the tendency to consume imported products is higher among the rich than among the poor[5] then the greater the degree of inequality in income distribution, the higher the demand for foreign goods and less foreign exchange is left for the capital goods and intermediate products needed to expand employment.

Because of shortages of both time and data, it was not possible for us to determine even approximately the relation between these tendencies and income levels. At first sight they do not differ very greatly between rich and poor. After all, imports of consumer goods are extremely low in Colombia; in fact, during the period 1964–8 they accounted for only about 1 per cent of total consumption. Under these circumstances, a change in the distribution of income could have only marginal effects on imports.

There are, however, three reasons for doubting this conclusion. The first

5. Strictly we are talking about the *marginal* propensity to consume imported goods.

is the amount of contraband imports; the second, the volume of tourist expenditure; and finally the import content of different domestically produced consumer goods.

The low level of imports of consumer goods is due to import controls rather than to a lack of demand for them. The demand is there, but it is suppressed – and is continually bedevilling the administration of import policy. One symptom of this is the apparent impossibility of staunching the flow of foreign exchange for contraband goods. Official estimates of this form of illegal trade, suggest that during the period 1962–8 the value of contraband imports hovered around 40 million dollars, a sum one third higher than the value of imported consumer goods in the same period. And, as the National Planning Department has stated, it is safe to assume that 'import contraband is formed in its immense majority by consumer goods' (1969, pp. 1–15). It is reasonable to assume that a high proportion of these goods are bought by people with high incomes.

Expenditure on foreign travel surpassed by about 60 per cent the total of imports of consumer goods during the period 1964–7. In fact, it is rather remarkable that over those years, when the Colombian economy faced severe balance-of-payments problems, expenditure on tourism took on the average slightly over one tenth of the foreign exchange accruing from exports. Of course, not all this expenditure can be regarded as a form of luxury consumption by the rich, but clearly a good deal is.[6]

The link between economic equality and the demand for imported commodities is more indirect in the case of the last factor mentioned above. The available information only allows one to make rough estimates of the 'import content' of the different consumer goods produced in Colombia. Nevertheless, differences in the amount of imported inputs required per unit of output seem to be sufficiently large for different products to permit making some broad generalizations. Thus the import content is extremely low (less than 5 per cent) in the production of basic industrial consumer goods like clothing, footwear, beverages, furniture, etc., but much higher (about 30 per cent) for electrical consumer durables which are bought very largely by the rich (given the level of average incomes in Colombia).

In addition, it must be noted that the method we have used to estimate the import content of output understates the proportion of their value which in the end flows abroad. This is so partly because the domestic inputs themselves have an import content, but also because many of these goods are produced in Colombia – as in other Latin American countries – by foreign firms or require the use of foreign industrial licences. So part of the value added in their production is transferred abroad in the form of profit remittances, interest payments, royalties, etc. These are no doubt more

6. Tourism is also one of the chief sources of contraband.

important in the case of sophisticated luxuries than of consumer goods for the public as a whole.

For all the reasons previously mentioned, one of the direct consequences of a more equal distribution of income would be the reduction of the pressure on the supply of foreign exchange now being used to finance contraband, tourism and foreign inputs for the domestic production of non-essential consumer goods. As we show later, the scarcity of foreign exchange has been in the past and is likely to be in the future a major constraint on the process of capital accumulation and hence on the rates of growth of both output and employment in the long run. So all measures which, like the redistribution of income, increase the amount of foreign exchange available for the purchase of imported investment goods permit an acceleration in growth of capital accumulation[7] and therefore also in the rate at which jobs can be created in the longer run.

But this is only one of the links between equality and employment. A more direct influence is that the basic goods which are widely purchased by those on low incomes – essentially food and rather simple manufactures like clothing and footwear – are precisely the goods which are (or can be) produced with techniques considerably more labour intensive than those used in the production of the goods demanded by the rich. To produce the latter usually requires high capital intensity. A given amount of income will thus generate more employment when spent in the purchase of wage goods than in the acquisition of consumer durables. Since, broadly speaking, these goods for mass consumption can be produced with simple techniques, the greater the increase in their sales the greater the demand for unskilled labour which is in particularly ample supply.

There is a further link. Since the poorer classes spend a high proportion of their income on food, the bigger their share of total income, the greater the demand for agricultural goods, and the greater the check on the pace of urbanization – a check which we believe would help a full employment strategy. (Agriculture also has rather low capital needs.)

Income distribution and savings

There are many ways, therefore, in which the pattern of consumer demand that would prevail if income were less unequally distributed would contribute to generating a higher level of employment. It can be argued, however, that although a highly unequal income distribution may harm employment in the short run, it may help in the long run, by providing the savings which are needed to buy the capital equipment that makes higher employment possible.

7. Of course, for this to happen, it would also be necessary that the rate of saving (private plus public) should rise.

This hypothesis – of old, indeed classical, origin – is in principle persuasive. In Colombia, as elsewhere, the higher the income levels the higher the proportion saved. There are, however, a number of reasons for thinking that this argument does not carry a great deal of weight in Colombia.

In the first place, notwithstanding the extreme degree of economic inequality that has prevailed in Colombia, total personal savings appear to be quite low. Data on savings are notoriously unreliable, but for what they are worth, they show savings averaging 2 per cent in the period 1961–7.[8] Thus, a high price has been paid, in terms of welfare and equity, for a fairly disappointing result in terms of savings. The owners of *latifundia* in particular appear to be keener on maintaining high standards of consumption than on accumulating funds to develop their properties.[9]

Secondly, it must be noted that even if a highly uneven distribution of income did induce a higher rate of personal saving, it would not be obvious that Colombia would benefit. To a considerable, but unknown, extent savings flow abroad. Indeed, if the distribution of income became still more unequal, this would almost inevitably be accompanied by greater unrest, which would stimulate the outflow of capital. (There is also a question whether such savings as do remain in Colombia are used in the most productive way.)

One can finally speculate about the consequences for the growth of employment of a regressive redistribution of income that *did* lead to higher levels of *both* savings and domestic investment. In principle, this should have a positive effect on the creation of new work opportunities. Nevertheless, if one keeps in mind the previous discussion, showing the pattern of demand that would emerge in such a case, it is not evident that employment would rise. The rich will at best save only part of any increases in their income. So a still higher concentration of income in their hands would tend to raise the demand for sophisticated consumer durables and for foreign travel.

For the reasons mentioned earlier, this shift in the structure of private consumption would, on the one hand, increase the import content per unit of expenditure and, on the other hand, raise the capital requirements of employment. With both these changes acting as limitations on the expansion of employment opportunities, the benefit from a higher rate of capital formation would be partly, or wholly, or more than wholly lost.

8. *Cuentas nacionales, 1960–67.*
9. This argument frequently found in economic writings (since Ricardo!) needs much empirical research in Colombia, especially because of the recent growth in large-scale commercial agriculture. Berry (1969, p. 2) states that 'the evidence that small farms produce more per hectare [than large ones] also works against the "necessary inequality" argument'.

On balance, then, it does not seem that the consideration of the hypothetically favourable effect on savings of greater economic inequality changes our earlier conclusion. The best way to raise the level of investment, as will certainly be necessary to accelerate the growth of various sectors of the economy, is through taxation, and it would appear that this would have the least damping impact on the current demand for labour if taxes were raised on the upper rather than the lower income groups.

Income distribution and incentives

Finally, there is also the incentive argument. Some mechanisms are certainly needed in any society to ensure that people making different contributions to the production of goods and services also obtain different rewards. But we question whether the high degree of economic inequality that actually exists in Colombia is needed to induce adequate responses from the population in effort or self-improvement, any more than in saving.

Changing the distribution of income

Because of the gravity of the unemployment problem, and the need for much higher levels of public investment, fiscal and other policies need to be followed which will in their total effect not merely contain, but in many cases reduce, the consumption of the rich. Of course, it would be less hurtful and therefore politically easier to pursue a set of policies that merely let the incomes of the poor grow at a faster rate than those of the rich – broadly speaking, what has been the historical process in Western Europe. An additional argument in favour of this process is that a sudden change would require economic readjustments which impose their own social costs, at least in the short run – for example, the closing of some establishments catering primarily for the rich. On the other hand, a shift towards more equality would not merely bring economic benefits mitigating in fact the poverty which is an integral part of the employment problem; it would also produce a much more favourable political climate for obtaining the cooperation of wage earners in some aspects of an employment policy, which would involve from them patience, perhaps for some even sacrifice.

We know that there are limits in practical politics to the shift in income distribution that can be achieved by government action. Nevertheless it is hard for us to envisage much fall in the proportion of the population which is unemployed or a real reduction in poverty, without policies being adopted which shift the income distribution, both soon and decisively, towards those who would spend it on the goods which can be produced in Colombia.

We can classify these policies into three groups, namely (a) those which alter the pre-tax distribution of income, (b) those which influence the distribution of disposable income, and (c) those which affect the real income of different groups by changes in the relative prices of goods and services.

References

BERRY, A. (1969), *The Distribution of Agriculturally Based Income in Colombia, 1960,* mimeograph.

ECLA (1969), *La distribución del ingreso en América Latina,* mimeograph.

ILO PREALC (1969), *Antecedentes para políticas de empleo en Colombia,* vol. 4, mimeograph.

JAFFE, A. J. (1969), *Notes on Family Income Distribution in Developing Countries in Relation to Population and Economic Changes,* paper read at the meeting of the International Association for Research in Income and Wealth, unpublished.

NATIONAL PLANNING DEPARTMENT (Colombia) (1969), *Planes y programas de desarollo, 1969–72.*

SLIGHTON, R. L. (1968), *Relative Wages, Skill Shortages and Changes in Income Distribution in Colombia,* Rand.

URRUTIA, M., and VILLALBA, C. E. (1969), 'La distribución del ingreso urbano para Colombia en 1964', in *Revista del Banco de la República.*

13 Gustav Ranis

Unemployment and Factor Price Distortions

From Gustav Ranis, 'Output and employment in the seventies: conflict or complements', in R. G. Ridker and H. Lubell, *Employment and Unemployment Problems of the Near East and South Asia*, vol. 1, Vikas, 1971.

In looking at the evidence of the 50s and 60s and in trying to learn what is transferable from the experience of the success cases, the inevitable question remains 'how'. The short answer is the adoption of policies which permit the changing factor endowment of society to be 'heard' over time. A successfully growing developing economy can be said to be moving from a land intensive to a labor and ultimately a skill and capital intensive phase of development. But the growth path within these various regimes and, more importantly, the transition from one to the other, are much facilitated if, in fact, the signals reflecting changes in factor endowment over time are permitted to be transmitted to the decision-making units in society. Letting the changing endowment speak, in other words, means permitting a closer relationship between the market prices of the factors of production and their equilibrium levels.

Viewed from an historical perspective, it should be clear that most of the developing countries initially adopted a policy of import substitution, including typically a combination of overvalued exchange rates, low interest rates, favourable internal terms of trade for industry, all intended to provide protection to the new domestic industrial sector and the emerging industrial entrepreneurs. There are some persuasive reasons why such an import substitution phase may be a historical necessity in countries just emerging from colonialism. The difficulty, however, resides both in the type of import substitution package adopted and, second, in the method of dismantling these protective devices once the minimum necessary entrepreneurial capacity in the true infant industries has been created. Inevitably, strong vested interests, in the form of inefficient firms and civil servants who hate to give up the power bestowed through the control system, make it very difficult to dismantle the very controls which were initially established with a supposedly temporary purpose. As a consequence, it usually becomes increasingly difficult to differentiate between *bona fide* and non *bona fide* residents in the infant industry compound. The distortion of the three sets of relative prices, the interest rate, the exchange rate, and the internal terms of trade, artificially induce capital and import intensity. For example, interest rates which should reflect the universally scarce availability of capital are normally kept at artificially low levels. Consequently, capital is artificially undervalued, credit is rationed rather than allocated by price, and the factor endowment is not permitted to 'come through' when decisions are made on either technology or output choice. An additional very serious consequence of artificially low interest rates, i.e. in addition to allocative inefficiency, is the fact that private savings are discouraged.

The normally overvalued exchange rate artificially encourages both capital and imports by undervaluing the price of imported capital goods and acts as a deterrent to the use of domestic inputs, especially of the labor intensive variety. Exports are discouraged, imports encouraged, and once again an artificial wall is erected between the factor endowment and factor utilization.

With respect to the domestic terms of trade, agricultural production incentives are sacrificed at the altar of speeding industrial development by keeping food artificially cheap. The whole package bestows larger and larger windfall profits on the industrial 'in' group and those civil servants which benefit from the direct rationing system which has long replaced any price determined allocation. Increasingly, especially as inflation pressures assert themselves with continuing government deficits, these disparities between the market prices and equilibrium prices become more and more pronounced, and more and more serious in terms of exacerbating the employment/output conflict.

We have been silent so far on the subject of wages – another distorted price – and this is because it is a horse of a somewhat different color. For one thing, no one in his right mind would recommend a reduction of the real wages of unskilled workers that brings them anywhere close to their equilibrium levels. But what might be strongly suggested is that any continuing increase in real wages as a consequence of union and/or government pressure via minimum wage legislation is bound to be highly unfavourable to the maximum utilization of the relatively abundant unskilled labor supply along the economy's production functions. We all know that governments often take the lead in granting wage increases to their own civil servants and that such increases are then copied by the private sector and supported by union pressure. As economists and policy makers all we can do is tell the politician what the costs of such policies are. If wages are rising in spite of a substantial overhang of unskilled labor, and if there is fear of more such rises in the future, we can only expect entrepreneurs and/or public officials to continue to react more and more in a labor-saving direction. The course of real wages is a very sensitive issue in most countries, and politicians have to make the choices themselves once the costs of various policies are made clear to them. But it should be remembered once again that while no union leader will go to his constituents to advise them on wage restraint, it is someone's responsibility, presumably the government's, to worry about the disenfranchised people who are unemployed and unemployed outside of union membership.

No one, in other words, would argue for reducing real wages to anything close to the equilibrium price for labor: but no one should be concerned with wage restraint in the sense of avoiding increases in real wages for unskilled workers, as long as there exists a tremendous overhang of unemployed and underemployed workers in the labor market, and substantial potential future inflows into that market from prospective population growth can be anticipated.

It is, moreover, abundantly clear that the gap in real wages as between the agricultural and industrial sectors, which seems to be growing in many parts of the region, has led to an increase in the so-called rate of urban drift ahead of urban job opportunities which is extremely costly, not only in terms of the extra economic costs of displacing disguised rural unemployment with open urban unemployment – due to the higher cost of urbanization, etc. – but also politically and socially. While there are inevitable wage and amenity differentials between agricultural and urban workers, any widening in that gap exacerbates an already serious problem of wage distortion.

To let the endowment speak under these circumstances clearly requires a turning down of the temperatures in the aforementioned industrial hothouse. Substantial adjustments of the interest rate, the exchange rate and the terms of trade may be required. It should be clear, however, that a simple elimination, or at least diminution, of the distortions in these various relative prices may not be sufficient. A devaluation, for example, to bring the exchange rate into line with the real cost of foreign exchange, may have to be accompanied by a change in the rationing system, in this case the import control regime, if, in fact, a more price determined allocation is to become possible. Even a re-examination of the tariff structure underneath the quantitative restrictions, often quite haphazard in character, may be necessary. Similarly, a high interest rate often needs to be accompanied by the greater willingness of banks to take risks even when the borrower does not have a prime signature. Thus, liberalization in a number of markets may be needed, i.e. both an adjustment of the signals and a willingness to permit greater play for the market and a lesser role for discretionary action by officials.

It should be emphasized in passing that the attempt to improve any of these signals in the attempt to let the endowment speak for itself is not to be interpreted as a call for free enterprise, capitalism or any other particular social system. As is well known, socialist countries are themselves increasingly coming to rely on the market mechanism as a tool for improving their own allocation and thus furthering their own development. What we are concerned with here is a better set of signals as propelling or inducing and coordinating devices to get the proper economic response, rather than the support of any particular social system. Such advice is equally valid when a society has determined, in its own wisdom, to follow either a socialist, a capitalist or a mixed economy path. What we are saying is that as long as certain groups, public or private, enjoy windfall profits bestowed upon them through a direct allocation process which is unable to clear the markets, the choice of technologies and output mixes is likely to be inefficient, not only because the signals are wrong, but also because there is no need to be efficient when the very possession of an import license or a line of credit provides ample profits without requiring any entrepreneurial energy or productive ingenuity.

I am also not suggesting that the government should take its hands off and go back to a textbook *laissez faire* nineteenth century stance. Markets themselves are admittedly imperfect; private returns do not equal social returns. The time horizon of private entrepreneurs may be too short. The question rather is, what role the government should play in lessening the impact of these imperfections without returning the society to colonialism or a rampant market mechanism. In my view, that role is one of trying to bridge the gap between social and private returns and of trying to perfect the markets just a little, by indirect rather than direct means. In other words, once it has decided, for one reason or another, what activities should be in the public sector, in affecting what goes on in the rest of the economy it should attempt to work through taxes, tariffs, and subsidies, and as even handedly as possible, e.g. uniform tariffs, rather than through the low interest rate, over-valued exchange cum licensing packages which are bound to be inefficient and whimsical.

Just because it is the conventional wisdom there is no need to abandon our view that government must also provide the overheads, must see to it that markets operate better, must provide information to ensure that weaker elements in the market are not disadvantaged by monopoly or oligopoly power. It must provide information on new technologies, including intermediate technology; it should be in a position to provide technical assistance when entrepreneurs have little at their disposal but the blueprints of the advanced countries and those made available by avid salesmen from abroad. Government cannot simply step aside and let the signals speak for themselves. It has a tremendous responsibility to direct the development effort. It is merely a question of what tools are more effective for that purpose.

It should be made emphatically clear that the failure to move quickly enough to permit the factor endowment to make itself felt cannot be laid entirely at the doorstep of the developing countries. The blame, if that is a proper term, must clearly be shared with the advanced countries who, through the proclivities of private investors as well as the official policies with respect to foreign aid, often encourage the adoption of capital and import intensive technology in the recipient countries. Both recipient and donor country engineers are all too ready to accept the blueprints they are most familiar with, i.e. those of the advanced donor country, especially when there is a belief, without much investigation, that the latest technology usually dominates in every respect. Multi-national corporations, for example, are typically unlikely to spend much time in investigating technologies alternative to those used in the mother plants. On the aid side, the practice of tying to the donor country typically prevents developing countries from obtaining their capital goods in the cheapest market. But with respect to both the private and public flow of capital, perhaps the most important problem emanates from the normal project orientation which induces developing countries to maximize the import and thus the capital content of projects proposed for foreign financing.

It should, moreover, be readily admitted that both the recipient and the donor are customarily subject to the prestige appeal of large shiny modern factories and of other latter-day monuments, which provide a much better press both to the visiting donor congressman and to the recipient governing élite.

In some quarters, sometimes quite respectable, all this talk about letting the factor endowment influence the choice of technology is considered rather irrelevant. This is due to the fact that the choices actually available are viewed as few or non-existent. In other words, if there exist objectively very few possibilities for substituting labor for capital, then all this talk about factor-price distortions and their impact on output and employment generation is misplaced – so the argument goes.

This argument can be met on two levels. First, even if we conceded that there are absolutely no technological choices, i.e. there is only one way of producing a particular commodity, there is still the question of changes in output mix which should make it possible to adjust one's productive structure in line with one's changing factor endowment. We seriously underestimate, I think, the ability to increase trade between the developing and the developed world, in spite of the ample evidence that developed countries have not done enough in terms of opening up their own markets to the labor intensive products of the developing countries. Even more importantly, trade among the developing countries is still absolutely at a very low level and could expand very rapidly, given substantial growth in the less developed world as a whole – with or without special regional trade arrangements.

But let me get to the heart of the matter, i.e. the uneasiness concerning the range of technological choice within given industries. What is this new intermediate technology people are talking about, one is frequently asked? Are you trying to foist obsolete machinery on the developing countries? Or, alternatively, the only machinery that can be procured is the very latest; there is only one kind of machinery which dominates and the amount of labor and other complementary domestic resources that can be combined with it is fairly well spelled out. Those are the arguments. If one thinks about them for a moment from the logical standpoint, they state, in their extreme form, that since developing countries normally draw their technology from the advanced world, the only choice is the very latest and from the most advanced of the rich countries. You cannot, as a minimal choice, import either last year's technology from the United States or this year's from Japan or Germany as an alternative. Thus, in the extreme, the argument is patently absurd. We know that in the advanced countries themselves we see a substantial variety of technological choices in the same industry in different parts of the country, utilizing capital stock of different vintages.

That aside, one must be willing to acknowledge that there may be only one best way to build a bridge, that there may be a rather restrictive set of technological choices in such continuous process industries as petrochemicals. But this is not true for most of the industrial sector and certainly not true in agriculture which still constitutes the preponderant sector in most developing countries.

What I think is important to remember is that intermediate technology does not mean the use of second hand, outmoded or obsolete machinery. It means innovative, modern, labor-intensive technology, i.e. using one's ingenuity to accommodate one's factor endowment each step of the way. These are not just words, for such technological flexibility has been demonstrated to be feasible both in historical Japan and in such contemporary contexts as Korea, Taiwan and West Pakistan. Take Japan, for example. In the nineteenth century Japanese spinning industry the number of workers per identical spindle was seven times that used in the US. The Japanese increased the speed of their machines, used cheaper raw materials, i.e. a lower staple cotton, and compensated by putting more workers to the task of repair and maintenance. Not only on the machine proper, but also in such machine-peripheral activities as inspection, handling between machines and transportation between plant sites, a tremendous amount of substitution between labor and capital can be accomplished. In construction, for example, this is evident to the naked eye. One thing that the tourist is often impressed by in the Indian sub-continent is the evidence of machine-paced labor intensity, as cement is passed from the mixer from hand to hand along a human conveyor belt until it is poured into concrete just before it hardens. Such flexibility in substituting unskilled labor for capital has been demonstrated even in metal working, for example in the Soviet Union.

Another important type of capital-saving or labor-using innovation is the use of the putting-out or cottage system, a plant-saving innovation taking advantage of economies of scale at certain stages of processing and permitting much of the production to be done, as appropriate, in homes, adjoining sheds and small workshops. This requires relatively little capital for plant and thus permits radically different capital intensities and different vintages of capital to be used at different stages of processing. Such contracting was used extensively, in the case of historical Japan, in silk production, in cotton weaving, and later, in bicycle, rubber and electrical goods production. Its importance may be demonstrated by the twin facts that more than 60 per cent of Japanese industrial output at the turn of the century was in medium and small-scale industries involved in a form of putting-out as described; and that plant rather than equipment typically makes up more than 50 per cent of total capital formation in developing countries.

The historical examples above can be duplicated in the contemporary developing world. The Koreans and the Taiwanese, for example, are showing a wide range of technological choice in textiles, in electronics and in plywood industries, during the last decade. What the Japanese were doing relative to British and American machinery in the nineteenth century, the Koreans and Taiwanese are now doing relative to the Japanese as well as the American technology. They are producing the same quality textile or plywood or transistors with three to four times as much labor input per unit of capital. The sub-contracting which can be so important a feature of labor-using technological change is being used increasingly at an international level as exemplified by the export-bonded processing schemes in both Korea and Taiwan. While the United States, five or ten years ago, used to send raw materials to Japan to be worked up, with cheap labor added, and then re-exported to the United States, the Koreans are now handling such materials for Japan. In fact, there are some situations which find the United States sending raw materials to Japan, where some processing takes place as skilled labor is added; then the semi-finished materials are re-exported to Korea where unskilled labor is added before the final product is re-exported to the United States. All these are examples of substantial technological adaptation in response to international differences in factor endowment, when these differences in factor endowment are permitted to be reflected in the relative price signals which entrepreneurs face. In West Pakistan the medium and small scale engineering industries which grew up in the Punjab in the wake of the Green Revolution, have shown remarkable adaptations in a labor and domestic material using direction. There are clearly substitution possibilities, not only in Korea, but in Japan and Taiwan, which some people may call special cases but which exist in other parts of the developing world as well. It is this evidence and this evidence only which gives one comfort that the crisis of the 70s and 80s can be met.

The overall contours of that Japanese success story are well-known and need not be repeated here. What is less well-known is that the Japanese started with a relatively short period of import substitution for very much the same reason contemporary developing countries do, i.e. in order to build sufficient industrial infrastructure and provide for a training period for its entrepreneurs. But, unlike in contemporary developing countries, the import substitution package never took on an extreme form and didn't last very long. Tariffs were instituted but remained very low, partly because Japan was 'lucky' enough to be deprived of fully independent tariff policies by extra-territoriality arrangements. The government was heavily involved in many of the early infant industries, either by direct participation or through the establishment of pilot plants and experimental structures, but Japan also managed to dismantle the hothouse and move toward a greater reliance on the market by 1890 when most government enterprises were sold off to the private sector, reforms took place on the monetary side and the participation of medium and small scale industrial entrepreneurs as well as agriculturalists was considerably enhanced.

Perhaps even more to the point are the contemporary success stories. In Korea, for example, the first effort to shift from import substitution to a market and export oriented pattern of growth took place in the early 60s. In May 1964, Korea substantially devalued her currency and simultaneously unified a complicated multiple exchange system. Moreover, imports were liberalized, i.e. the licensing system broadened through the widening of import quotas, the introduction of export retention schemes and, later, a quasi-automatic licensing system to cover an expanding volume of imports. The effects of a change in the signals via a change in this crucial relative price have been startling. Exports, which had grown at annual rates of less than 15 per cent during the 1958–62 period, have been growing at 30–40 per cent annual rates since 1964. Moreover, this export boom has been especially pronounced in the area of light industry where value added in the form of pure unskilled labor could play an increasingly important role. In 1962, 75 per cent of Korea's exports were land-based raw materials and primary goods; by 1968 77 per cent of her exports were industrial labor-based products. Especially noteworthy is that the participation of the small-scale industrial sector (less than 10 workers), which is most labor-intensive, rose from 19 per cent to 32 per cent of the total during that same period.

In 1965, relative prices in the sector complementary to the foreign trade sector, i.e. the credit sector, were changed dramatically. Interest rates, which had been kept at artificially low levels, were drastically raised in 1965, and the huge gap between the low official rates, actually available only to established prime borrowers, and the astronomically high rates facing ordinary people on the curb market was substantially narrowed. Interest rates on saving deposits doubled and deposits responded by rising by more than 200 per cent between 1964 and the end of 1965, and by more than 700 per cent by September 1968. To indicate that this was not just a shift from one form of saving to another, we should note that the overall saving rate which had been negative in the 1958–62 period and had stood at only 5·8 per cent as late as 1962–4, reached 13·6 per cent in 1968 and is currently in the 15 per cent range.

It can be said that the changes in these two relative prices, the exchange rate and the interest rate, more than anything else, have led to the spectacular turn-around in the performance of the Korean economy summarized above. As a direct consequence, Korea was placed in a position to put her abundant human resources to use in an export-led rather than import substitution dominated industrialization effort. Increasingly also, with time, her domestic skill and innovative ingenuity could be incorporated with unskilled domestic labor, as medium and small-scale entrepreneurs had an opportunity really, for the first time, to gain access to resources and participate broadly in the development process.

14 Dharam P. Ghai

Incomes Policy in Kenya: Need, Criteria and Machinery

D. P. Ghai 'Incomes policy in Kenya: need, criteria and machinery', paper presented at the University of East Africa Social Science Conference, University College, Dar es Salaam, January 1968.

Need for an incomes policy

The current interest in incomes policy in East Africa has been stimulated by concern over the failure of employment to expand over the last decade and the widening of rural/urban differentials. It is felt that a continuation of the above trends would jeopardize the achievement of national economic and social goals such as a high rate of growth of the economy, rapid expansion of employment opportunities and equitable distribution of incomes. Incomes policy is, therefore, being advocated to achieve the following objectives:

1. Promotion of a more equitable income distribution.
2. Rapid expansion of employment opportunities.
3. Prevention of inflation and balance of payments difficulties.

We shall consider each of these objectives in the context of the Kenya economy.

1 Income distribution

Gross inequalities of income distribution are a relatively well known and reasonably well documented feature of the East African economies (Ghai, 1964; Salaries Review Commission, 1967; Green, 1967).

From the point of view of incomes policy, two aspects of this question are of particular interest: income differentials between unskilled urban workers and peasant farmers, and the differentials between skilled persons (salariat) and capitalists on the one hand, and wage earners and peasant farmers on the other.[1] The nature of the problem may be vividly illustrated with a few key statistics.

1. In the terminology used here, skilled persons (salariat) are defined to include professional, managerial, administrative and technical personnel; while wage earners comprise the rest of the employees including not only the unskilled workers but also what is often called the middle-level manpower such as clerks, salesmen, primary school teachers, artisans, minor technicians etc.; where the argument relates to unskilled workers among wage earners, they are so distinguished in the paper.

Peasant-unskilled worker income differentials. The income differentials between peasants and urban unskilled workers are considerable and have been increasing in recent years. The average earnings of African employees in Kenya rose from £68 in 1960 to £135 per annum in 1966.[2] This represents a cumulative increase of about 12 per cent per annum. If we exclude agricultural employees, average urban African earnings rose from £97 in 1960 to £180 in 1966 – a compound increase of nearly 11 per cent per annum. These figures cannot be taken as a measure of the increase in average wages of unskilled African employees. They have been affected, on the one hand, by the additional coverage of 1964, which had the effect of lowering average earnings by 2·7 per cent.[3] On the other hand, the upgrading of African employees during this period, the most obvious and most important example of which is Africanization of better paid jobs, had the effect of raising average African earnings. Unfortunately, since no data are available on the distribution of African earnings since 1960, it is difficult to separate out the effect of the latter movement on average earnings. It appears reasonable to assume that wages for unskilled urban workers have probably increased at a rate of about 10 per cent per annum since 1960.[4] Since the Nairobi cost of living index for wage earners has risen merely by 14 per cent between 1960 and 1966, most of the increase being concentrated in 1965–6, it is clear that the real income of unskilled urban workers has risen by about 8 per cent per annum over this period.

In contrast to this, the gross domestic product (GDP) measured at current prices rose by 41 per cent or at an annual rate of 6·0 per cent over the same period, while monetary GDP increased at a slightly lower rate of 5·7 per cent per annum.[5] Thus wages for unskilled urban workers have increased by slightly less than double the rate of GDP growth since 1960.[6] It is notoriously difficult to make similar calculations for the small farm sector.

2. All these figures unless otherwise stated are obtained from Economic Survey, Kenya, various years.

3. In 1964, the average earnings of the additional coverage of 39,300 African employees was £56 compared with £70 for other employees. Since the additional coverage represented an increase of 13·5 per cent in the enumeration of African employees, it pulled the average earnings down by 2·7 per cent.

4. Analysis of the Industrial Court wage awards since its establishment in 1964, and of four important firms since 1960 shows that wages of unskilled employees have increased by about 10 per cent per annum.

5. This apparently surprising result is due to the fact that whereas subsistence output was depressed in 1960, it was at a record level in 1966. All these figures are based on the old GDP estimates.

6. The same sort of picture emerges both in Uganda and Tanzania. In Tanzania the average yearly increase in cash wages has been 17 per cent between 1960 and 1966, while GDP at current prices has risen annually by 6·7 per cent; ILO (1967, p. 4); Background to the Budget, 1967–8 (Government Printer, Dar es Salaam).

Nevertheless, some rough estimates must be presented for illustrative purposes. In 1960, the subsistence output was estimated at £50·2m, while the cash income of the small farm sector amounted to about £9·5m.[7] On the assumption that in 1960 a total of 1·04 million adult males derived their livelihood from cash or subsistence agriculture, the per family income comes to £57, the cash component of which amounts to £9·1.[8] The corresponding 1966 figures for subsistence and cash income are £75·3m and £19·7m. Assuming an adult male population of 1·24 millions, this gives us per household income of £77·4, the cash component of which amounts to £15·9. Thus average peasant household income went up by nearly 36 per cent between 1960 and 1966, while the cash income increased by about 75 per cent; the annual growth rates, therefore, amount to about 5 and 10 per cent respectively. It will, therefore, be seen that while their cash incomes have grown at roughly the same rate, average total income of farmers has risen at about half the rate of unskilled urban workers. In absolute terms, the average wage of the urban unskilled worker would appear to be twice that of the average peasant household.[9] The above estimates are subject to a considerable margin of error.[10] Nevertheless, the overall picture they reveal of wide and increasing differentials between peasant farmers and unskilled urban workers is almost certainly true.[11]

Salariat and Capitalists. The second aspect of inequalities in income distribution relates to income differentials between skilled persons and capitalists, on the one hand, and unskilled workers and peasants on the other. Following Green's definition of salaries as employee incomes above £50 per month, then the 41,000 salariat, comprising about 7 per cent of recorded employment of 589,000, received nearly 44 per cent of total employment income in Kenya in 1964 (Green, 1967, Tables 1 and 2). Another measure

7. For a variety of reasons such as the failure to estimate rental income and the inadequate coverage of cash sales, this is almost certainly an underestimate of the real income of peasant farmers.

8. Calculated from the Revised Development Plan, Kenya, p. 102.

9. It must also be remembered that whereas average wage represents the earnings of a single person, the average peasant income is a return to the labour (and land) of the entire household. Thus the differences in the average income of the unskilled urban worker and the peasant are substantially greater than suggested by the above figures.

10. Apart from statistical weaknesses, there are many other factors which make a simple comparison between incomes of peasant and urban workers hazardous; see Salaries Review Commission (1967, pp. 20–21).

11. Similar trends are observable in Uganda and Tanzania: see Knight (1967, pp. 233–64), and ILO (1967, p. 5): 'There seems no doubt that there is a very large discrepancy between the living standards of the average wage earner and the average smallholder, and that this discrepancy has substantially increased in recent years.' According to the Report whereas wage earners in 1966 were over twice as well off in terms of real income as in 1960, 'it does not appear that the smallholder's average real income for 1966 is likely to be more than 5 per cent above 1960–62 figure'.

of the tremendous differentials between the earnings of skilled and unskilled employees, is given by the fact that whereas in the public sector the current wage for subordinate staff in large urban areas is £120 per annum, the starting salary for graduates is about £804, or about seven times as much. The fringe benefits, particularly pension schemes and housing subsidy, further reinforce the differential between salary and wage earners. In addition, while virtually all the salary earners are on incremental salary scales, wage earners in the lowest income brackets do not receive any automatic annual increases. In the private sector, annual increments in general are not automatic for salary earners, but the end result is not much different from that in the public sector.

We have unfortunately much less information on the distribution of income among unincorporated businesses (including professionals) and owners of corporate enterprises. The only readily available source of data are the income tax statistics. These show that the average income of unincorporated businesses in 1964 was £1783, while that of 'controlled companies' was £4297. Assuming an average of three persons per controlled company, average income per person in 'controlled companies' comes to £1432.[12] These figures illustrate the enormous gap between the incomes of capitalists and of skilled persons, on the one hand, and of unskilled workers and peasant farmers on the other.[13]

An important objective of public economic policy is to move towards a more equal income distribution.[14] It can be argued that fiscal rather than incomes policy is the appropriate means to achieve a desired pattern of income distribution. Indeed fiscal policy is inherently a more effective instrument of income redistribution since it takes into account individual ability to pay whereas incomes policy works largely by affecting group or factor incomes; and there may be considerable inequalities of income distribution within a group, such as peasants or capitalists, which cannot be reduced directly by incomes policy. However, in actual practice because of the political and administrative difficulties encountered in devising an appropriately progressive tax structure, fiscal policy cannot serve as a complete substitute for incomes policy in reducing relative income differentials; this is particularly true of the gap between the incomes of wage

12. A company is controlled unless there is a public holding of more than 25 per cent of the voting power and of equity; public for this purpose excludes relations and nominees of other persons. This distinction between controlled and non-controlled companies has now been abolished.

13. The figure on average capitalist income must be treated with caution. Income tax statistics exclude very small enterprises and thus exaggerate the average income of unincorporated enterprises. On the other hand, they almost certainly understate the true income of both unincorporated enterprises and controlled companies.

14. This is defined as bending inwards of the Lorenz Curve of income distribution.

earners and farmers. Moreover, even if there were no case in equity for initiating an incomes policy, the need for securing a rapid growth in employment would necessitate some sort of incomes policy. We now turn to this aspect of the argument.

2 Employment and incomes policy

Expansion of employment opportunities, along with economic growth, is an important social and economic objective of the East African countries. Yet experience in this respect has been disappointing: recorded employment in Kenya in 1965 was 10 per cent lower than in 1960, in Uganda it had marginally declined between 1960 and 1965, and in Tanzania it fell by 14 per cent over the same period. This despite the near boom conditions throughout East Africa since 1963. The phenomenon of stagnation in employment in the face of substantial increases in production has excited much academic speculation but so far little hard empirical research. However, there appears to be widespread agreement that the rapid increase in wages of unskilled workers in recent years has contributed in an important way to stagnation in recorded employment.[15]

More specifically, it has been argued that the rapid increase in wage rates has forced employers generally to economize on labour by using it more efficiently, has stimulated the adoption of more capital intensive techniques of production, and has probably resulted in the relative shrinkage of the labour intensive product and services sectors.

It would appear that a continuation of the past trend in wage rate increases would make it virtually impossible to achieve the target rate of increase in employment laid down in Kenya's Development Plan. In an open, predominantly agricultural economy such as that of Kenya, wage rate increases in excess of productivity increases may be expected to have an adverse effect on employment. Let us classify employees into three sectors: export sector, public sector and the rest of the economy. Employment in the export sector, and more particularly in the agricultural export sector, is likely to be very sensitive to changes in wage rates. Given constant or in some cases falling prices, excessive wage rate increases will lead to a fall in employment, caused partly by a fall in production and partly by substitution of capital for labour. In the public sector, employment in local

15. See, for instance, *Economic Survey*, 1967, Kenya, pp. 85–6; *Work for Progress*, Uganda's second Five-Year Plan, p. 146; ILO (1967, pp. 8–9), where it is stated that econometric analysis shows that at current levels of labour efficiency in Tanzania, and, at the recent rates of improvement in labour efficiency, if average wages and salaries etc. rise by 15 per cent per annum, employment will fall by 5 per cent per annum; if the former rise by 10 per cent per annum, the latter will fall by 2½ per cent per annum, and if they rise by 5 per cent per annum, employment will rise by 5 per cent per annum, Baryaruha (1967, p. 80).

government will also be adversely affected by a substantial rise in wage rates, as local authorities typically have highly inelastic tax systems. These two sources provide a very substantial proportion of the total recorded employment in Kenya. Employment in the other sectors of the economy may not be so sensitive to excessive wage rate increases, as it is possible to pass on the increased labour costs in the form of higher prices for goods and services. But even here, the combination of the depressive effect of fall in export earnings and competition from foreign imports, may limit price rise and hence lead to a fall in employment. It will, therefore, be seen that excessive wage rate increases will lead to a fall in employment in the short-run, and in the longer run will lower the rate of expansion of employment.

3 Inflation and balance of payments

Owing to lack of data, it is not possible to assess the effect on the prices of domestically produced goods and services of wage rate increases of recent years. Even if in the past, rapid wage rate increases have been absorbed through advances in productivity, the scope for similar striking improvements in productivity in the future will be less. It is, therefore, quite likely that wage rate increases of a magnitude experienced in the last six years could generate wage inflation.[16]

The likely implications for balance of payments follow directly from our discussion of the employment effects of excessive wage rate increases. The main adverse effects are likely to flow from a fall in agricultural exports and a loss in the competitive position of domestic manufactures *vis-à-vis* foreign imports in the East African market. There might also be a reduction in capital inflows owing to lower profitability of investment in new projects.[17] However, to the extent that foreign prices rise at the same rate as domestic prices, the effect of rapid wage increases will be felt largely through decline in agricultural export earnings. Although balance of payments is not a current constraint on the growth of the economy, it is likely to become one in the not too distant future.[18] This, therefore, is an additional reason for initiating a policy of restraint in wage and salary increases.

The arguments presented in the preceding sections have attempted to show that it would be desirable to initiate an incomes policy in Kenya in order to promote a more equitable distribution of incomes, to secure rapid expansion

16. It appears that this may already have started in Tanzania: see ILO (1967, p. 11).
17. The force of all these arguments is increased by the recent devaluation of sterling and the non-devaluation of East African currencies.
18. According to the projections made in the Development Plan, the 1964 surplus on current account of £10·6m. is expected to be converted into a deficit of £26·5m. by 1970.

in employment opportunities, and finally to prevent inflation and balance of payments difficulties. The following sections are devoted to a discussion of the criteria and machinery needed to implement an incomes policy designed to achieve the above objectives. We start with wages, and then proceed to a consideration of salaries, profits and prices.

National wages policy

The main characteristics of the market for unskilled labour in Kenya may be restated and summarized as follows:

1. The existence of excess supply at the existing wage rate, i.e. unemployment of unskilled persons;

2. Considerable divergence in wage rates as between different industries and different firms within an industry;

3. A substantial rate of increase in wage rates in recent years despite the existence of unemployment;

4. Stagnation in the volume of recorded employment.

The phenomenon of increasing wages in the face of considerable and growing volume of unemployment is to be explained by the passage of successive minimum wage laws and more recently by the power of trade unions to wrest wage increases from the employers.[19]

All three objectives of incomes policy listed earlier would be furthered by a moderation of wage rate increases for unskilled persons. Can we say anything about the appropriate size of increase in wage rates? The Paretian criteria for optimum resource allocation would imply a fall in the price of labour. This is clearly unrealistic. In the predominantly private sector economy of the Kenya type, the most that can realistically be achieved is a substantial lowering of the rate of wage increases experienced in recent years. The two obvious methods of determining the advance of the incomes of unskilled workers are increases in productivity and the growth of peasant incomes. The rationale behind the productivity criterion presumably is that its application will ensure price stability. This makes sense in fully employed, developed economies where the main problem is external equilibrium; hence it is vital to secure price stability. In economies with considerable unemployment, the productivity criterion does not make much theoretical sense, especially if productivity increases are brought about largely by substitution of capital for labour. In addition, there are also practical difficulties in the application of this criterion. Statistical data on

19. I have discussed this phenomenon in some detail in my paper (Ghai, 1967, pp. 7–10). For a similar explanation of rising wages in conditions of excess supply of unskilled labour in Uganda, see Knight (1967). He attributes the rise to government policy, trade union pressures and employers' enlightenment.

productivity are scanty and for some important sectors non-existent. While, therefore, it may be difficult to base wage rate increases on productivity increases at a macro level, the productivity criterion, as will be shown below, has a role to play in providing continuing incentives for increasing labour efficiency and flexibility in wage structure at the micro level.

Since one of the objectives of an incomes policy is to reduce differentials between the incomes of smallholders and unskilled urban employees, and since the supply of labour in the employment sector is affected most fundamentally by peasant incomes, it is natural to relate wage rate increases to growth in peasant incomes. According to the Kenya Development Plan, peasant cash crop production, livestock and subsistence output are projected to increase at 1964 prices, at an annual rate of 17·8 per cent, 10·3 per cent and 3·2 per cent respectively. This works out to an annual growth in peasant incomes of about 6 per cent.[20] Allowing for a 3 per cent annual increase in the peasant population, average peasant (household) income has been projected to rise by 3 per cent per annum. This figure does not make any allowance for the decline in prices of agricultural products. In actual practice, peasant incomes have increased by about 7·4 per cent per annum since 1964 at current prices, and possibly more at 1964 prices.[21] It may, therefore, be more realistic to assume an increase in average peasant income of 4–5 per cent per annum. If we are able to prevent a widening of the relative gap in rural/urban incomes, and hopefully to narrow it in the future, the overall increase in the wage rate of unskilled employees must be limited to 4 per cent per annum. The essence of the proposal made here is to base wage rate increases on a moving average of increase in average peasant income over the last three to four years. This will have the advantage of tying wage rate increases to increases in peasant incomes, while at the same time eliminating difficulties arising from frequent fluctuations of farm incomes.[22] Moreover, the permitted increase in wage rates can be determined fairly easily from the regularly published statistics.

20.		1964: £m	1970: £m
Subsistence output		68·5	82·4
Cash crop production		10·5	28·1
Livestock		3·4	6·1
Total		82·4	116·6

21. Based on old calculations of GDP.

22. The ILO Report recommends that *minimum* wages should be fixed in relation to smallholder's income. But it proposes a different system – the proficiency wage – for determining wages above the minimum. The overall ceiling of 5 per cent annual increase presumably reflects the maximum increase in wages and salaries bill consistent with projected increases in employment.

Three obvious objections against the above proposal are that (a) it will have an adverse effect on the supply of labour to the employment sector, (b) it will impair incentives to raise productivity, and (c) it will introduce undesirable rigidity into the wage structure. Under the present conditions of excess supply of unskilled labour and overwhelming attraction of urban jobs, the first objection is largely academic. Should there be a scarcity of unskilled labour in the future, the problem could be met easily by permitting wages to rise faster. The other two objections are more serious and a way must be found of incorporating incentives and flexibility in the operation of the wages policy. One way of doing this would be to have a system under which wage rate increases up to a certain figure, say 3 per cent, would continue to be subject to negotiations between employers and unions as at present; but any demands for wage increases above 3 per cent would be submitted to a government appointed board. The board would have a discretion to award wage increases in excess of 3 per cent and up to a maximum of 6 per cent. In deciding on wage awards, it should be guided by the following principles:

1. If productivity increases are in excess of the permitted increases in wage rates, and if these increases could be attributed directly to increased efficiency or effort of workers, then higher increases in wage rates could be justified. This would have the important effect of providing continuing incentives for productivity increases on the part of workers.[23] Although it is difficult to state in general terms the operational rules for attributing productivity increases to different factors of production, the detailed study of individual cases should reveal the main agents of improvements in productivity.

2. If there is a scarcity of certain types of labour, extra wage rate increases could be awarded to induce workers to take up these jobs. This would make for a more efficient working of the labour market.

3. Higher increases might be awarded to workers at the lowest rung of the wage scale for unskilled workers, in order to reduce income differentials amongst workers themselves.

Two further points should be made: the overall annual increase in wage rates should not exceed 4 per cent, and wages should be defined as including

23. Productivity may increase for several reasons: additional effort or efficiency of workers, more and better equipment per worker, and improved management. There is no reason why workers should get extra benefits for productivity increases brought about solely by more capital and better management. It is one of the weaknesses of the I L O Report that in arguing for a closer relation between wage and productivity increases, it does not distinguish among different causes of increases in productivity.

all fringe benefits such as holiday, working time, social security contributions etc.

Apart from the advantages of incentives and flexibility, the scheme outlined here has the virtue of involving minimal departure from the established system of wage negotiations. For its successful working, it will be necessary to provide deterrents to ensure that all wage claims are not automatically taken to the board for settlement. These could take the form of a fee, or an obligation to meet expenses, etc. in the event of no award decision by the board.

Machinery for wages policy

It is proposed that a National Incomes Board be established to implement the government's incomes policy. As far as wages are concerned, the board will be charged with the responsibility of considering wage demands in excess of the permitted increment. In addition, it will be required to formulate minimum wages and orders relating to wages and conditions of service in particular industries. The board will thus take over the functions of the Wages Council and of the Ministry of Labour in determining certain wages and conditions of service. The board should consist of three independent members of high competence and standing appointed by the government. Because of the technical nature of its functions, it will be necessary to provide it with a small professional staff with expertise in statistics, accountancy and economics. The board will keep under review trends in such significant variables as national income, peasant incomes, employment, wages, productivity, profits and prices. It will be required to issue six-monthly reports, reviewing the progress of its work.

It is an open question whether the existing Industrial Court could be transformed into the National Incomes Board. The Court was established in 1964 to arbitrate on the disputes between unions and employers. However, as currently constituted, it suffers from the fact that it operates without the benefit of centrally issued criteria on wages policy. Thus inevitably the Court's decisions are influenced by a desire to resolve conflicts in terms which would be acceptable to both parties. In the first two years of its operation, the wage rate increases granted often amounted to 10 per cent or more. It has thus added to the upward bias in wage settlement already inherent in the existing machinery of wage determination. It has also suffered from the fact that it has lacked access to expert advice. If the court is to serve as an instrument of national incomes policy, it will be necessary to effect drastic changes in its present functions, staff and membership.[24]

24. For a detailed analysis of the working of the Industrial Court, see Ghai and Hollen (forthcoming).

Salaries policy

Most of the discussions on incomes policy have tended to concentrate on wages to the exclusion of salaries and other types of income. This is unfortunate not only because of the great disparities in incomes between capitalists and salariat on the one hand, and peasants and unskilled workers on the other, but also because neglect of other incomes will seriously jeopardize the acceptance of a national wages policy on the lines indicated earlier. Before discussing the policy alternatives for salaries, it may be useful to summarize the main characteristics of the market for skilled labour in Kenya.[25]

In contrast to unskilled workers, the market for skilled labour is characterized by excessive demand. The total stock of skilled labour force may be divided into three categories: local persons, expatriates provided to the public sector by foreign governments and international organizations at prices considerably below their true supply price, and expatriates recruited in the world market. Expatriates constitute a significant proportion of the total stock of skilled manpower. The public sector is by far the most important employer of skilled labour and as such effectively determines the salary and terms of service for skilled persons. Whereas the wages of unskilled workers are determined in the domestic economy, the salaries for skilled labour reflect the market conditions in Europe. The expatriate salaries are in general substantially higher than those of their local counterparts. Finally, although there continues to be a tightness in the skilled labour market, the supply position is changing rapidly with an increasing flow of local skilled persons coming on the market. Most of the following discussion about salaries is concerned with local skilled persons.

Because of the large differentials in the remuneration of skilled and unskilled employees, there is a strong equity case for reducing these differentials either by a freeze on salaries, or more effectively by an actual reduction in salary scales. However, in view of the continuing shortage of skilled manpower, we must weigh the equity requirements against the economic costs, if any, of such a policy. These may conveniently be considered under two heads: effect on the demand and the supply of skilled labour. On theoretical grounds, one would expect an increase in quantity demanded of skilled labour both because of substitution of skilled for unskilled labour and because the demand for products where skilled labour is an important input will increase relative to the demand for other products. The ability of the public sector to employ more skilled persons will also be enhanced. It is clearly not possible to estimate the magnitude of this effect. Provided the barriers to inflow of foreign skilled manpower are eased,

25. These are described in detail in my paper (Ghai, n.d.).

there need be no intensification of the excess demand for labour. The economic costs of reducing the salaries of local skilled persons are, therefore, confined to the inefficient use of skilled labour, i.e. the substitution of skilled for unskilled persons. It is a matter of judgement as to how strong this effect might be. Considering the large differentials in the remuneration of skilled and other employees, it can be argued that the substitution effect may be quantitatively insignificant.

Another argument against lowering the relative price of skilled labour that is often put forward relates to the adverse effect this will have on its supply. There are two aspects of this question: effect on the existing stock and on the future flow of unskilled labour. It is not possible to say *a priori* how sensitive is the international mobility of local skilled labour to changes in salaries. Because of the close links among the three East African countries, one would expect a certain amount of mobility within East Africa. But Tanzanian salaries for local skilled persons are already considerably below their counterparts in Kenya and Uganda. It is, therefore, doubtful whether there would be much outflow of skilled persons from Kenya to other parts of East Africa. Similarly, unless there is a drastic reduction of salaries, say by 50 per cent, it would appear that the outflow of local skilled persons in the foreseeable future to countries outside East Africa need not present much of a problem.[26] Should there, however, be a serious drain of local skilled manpower, it is open to the government to raise the price of emigration by say, the imposition of an emigration tax.[27]

The adverse effect of a reduction in salaries on the future supply of skilled labour is likely to be negligible. Not only are the returns to skills so relatively high that only a drastic reduction of salaries will significantly affect the attractiveness of acquiring skills, but under the present system in Kenya most of the costs of higher training and education are borne by the state. The main constraint on the supply of skilled labour is provided by the capacity of the training institutions and not by lack of demand for such facilities. It seems unlikely, therefore, that say a 10 to 15 per cent reduction in the salaries will have much of an impact on the flow of skilled manpower.

26. It would be interesting to see the extent of outflow of skilled manpower in Tanzania following the recent reduction in salaries of senior Civil Servants. My own impression is that it has been negligible. It is doubtful whether there has even been a net flow from the public to the private sector where salaries have been maintained at their old level.

27. Several developing countries, such as UAR and India, which have suffered considerably from 'brain drain', do already operate some controls on the flow of skilled labour. If developed countries do not permit the inflow of unskilled labour in the 'interests' of their economy, is it that outrageous to suggest that developing countries might impose controls on the outflow of skilled labour to safeguard their economies?

It does not, therefore, seem to me that the economic costs of a reduction in salaries will be significant. To the extent that there are marginal adverse effects, they are likely to be outweighed by the gains resulting from this policy. These gains are: (a) a more equal distribution of income; (b) greater acceptance of controls on wages; (c) enhancement of the ability of the public sector to expand its social and economic services and undertake development projects; (d) favourable impact on imports of consumer goods.

As far as the existing stock of local skilled labour is concerned, any proposal for reduction in salaries will naturally generate fierce opposition. Moreover, the salariat are strongly entrenched in positions of power and policy-making; in the absence of a powerful political leadership, dedicated to egalitarian principles, it may prove virtually impossible to enforce a reduction in the earnings of the salaried group.[28] The second best alternative of a freeze in salary scales may prove more acceptable. But under the present system, this automatically ensures to most salary earners, at any rate in the public sector, an annual increment of 2 to 5 per cent.[29] Thus if incomes policy is to be effective in reducing differentials between skilled and unskilled persons, it is essential to reform the salary structure either by abolishing the principle of automatic increments and equating increments up the scale to promotion, or by granting increments every three years or so, thus effectively reducing the annual increment.

The prospects of enforcing a reduction in the salaries of new entrants to the labour force appear more favourable. This may be achieved effectively by any of the following three methods: (a) lowering of the current salary scales, either by having lower salary or higher qualifications for the same job; (b) financing of higher education by loans, which would be repayable over a specified period and carry a rate of interest;[30] (c) a compulsory national service for a specified period, at a salary below the current rates.[31]

28. This is no doubt the reason why, barring a few exceptions, most African countries have failed in their attempts to reform their salary structures inherited from the colonial era.

29. The annual increments built into various salary scales appear to be quite haphazard; they bear no relation to considerations of equity or economic efficiency.

30. For a detailed discussion, in the Kenya context, of the financing of higher education through loans, see Rogers (1968).

31. Tanzania has utilized both lower salary scales and national service to reduce the earnings of skilled workers. In October, 1966 the Tanzanian government announced salary reductions ranging from 20 per cent in the case of ministers and top civil servants down to 3 per cent in the case of civil servants earning from £660 to £900 a year. At the same time, national service was introduced; college and university leavers were required to serve for two years at 60 per cent of their normal salary. The first proposal applies to both the existing stock of local skilled force as well as to new entrants; while the second proposal applies only to the latter.

If the objective is to reduce the present value of the stream of earnings of skilled labour by a certain figure, this could be achieved theoretically by all three methods.[32] However, there are some important differences among them with respect to incidence, equity and administrative and economic efficiency.

The first alternative of a straight salary cut will presumably apply in the first instance to new employees in the public sector; it may prove difficult to enforce the cut on the private sector directly. On the other hand, since it is the public sector which effectively determines the salaries for skilled employees, the salaries in the private sector may be adjusted downwards in line with those in the public sector. From an administrative point of view, this alternative is superior to loans and national service. Likewise, it would appear to involve smaller 'psychological costs' for those affected by it than the other alternatives. National service could be so devised as to be applicable to all new entrants to the skilled labour force. While it has this advantage over other alternatives, it is likely to raise considerable administrative problems, and if experience in other countries is any guide it may also be wasteful in the use of the skills made available. Furthermore, it will probably

---

32. Let the stream of earnings under the present salary scale be represented by $X_1, X_2, \ldots X_n$

The present value (PV) of earnings $= \dfrac{X_1}{(1+r)} + \dfrac{X_2}{(1+Y)^2} + \cdots \dfrac{X_n}{(1+r)_n} = X.$

Let us assume that it is proposed to reduce the PV of this stream of earnings by Y. This can be done either by a straight salary cut, by loan financing of education, or by national service.

Alternative 1: salary reduction. Let us assume a proportionate salary reduction of m per cent.

Therefore, PV of salary reduction $= \dfrac{mX_1}{(1+r)} + \dfrac{mX_2}{(1+r)^2} + \cdots \dfrac{mXn}{(1+r)^n} = Y.$

The value of m can be determined from the above equation.

Alternative 2: loan scheme. Let i be equal annual instalments for h years towards loan repayment.

Therefore, PV of loan instalments $= \dfrac{i}{(1+r)} + \dfrac{i}{(1+r)^2} + \cdots \dfrac{i}{(1+r)^h} = Y.$

The value of i can be determined from the above equation.

Alternative 3: national service. Let national service rate represent p per cent reduction in salary over f years.

Therefore, PV of reduction in salaries $= \dfrac{pX_1}{(1+r)} + \dfrac{pX_2}{(1+r)^2} + \cdots \dfrac{pXf}{(1+r)^f} = Y.$

The value of p can be determined from the above equation. The maximum reduction in salaries cannot exceed the amount of the loan granted. In the above analysis, we have abstracted from the complications introduced by taxes.

be less acceptable to those affected by it than the other schemes in so far as the latter interfere less with the individual choice of occupation.

The loan scheme can only apply to those whose higher education has been financed by the state. Thus a considerable number of those taking up salaried jobs will, therefore, be outside its scope.[33] This in itself might generate considerable resentment and hostility to the scheme. It is also likely that a loan scheme might involve greater psychological costs and thus have a more adverse effect on the supply of skilled manpower than the other methods of reducing the earnings of skilled labour. Finally, there is a lag of several years before a loan scheme can become effective in reducing salaries.

The weight of the arguments presented above is in favour of relying on direct salary cuts as a means of reducing the income of new entrants to the skilled labour force in preference to national service or loan financing of education. A reasonable figure for salary reduction might be 10 to 20 per cent, the rates increasing progressively for higher salaries. Most of the entrants to the skilled labour force would in fact fall in the lower brackets of the salary structure in the early years. The initiative for salary revision would clearly have to come from the Government and would in the first instance apply to the public sector. The National Board would be charged with the function of reviewing matters relating to salaries, and one of its first tasks in this connection would be to devise techniques and procedures for extending the revised salary scales to new skilled employees in the private sector.

Profits and prices policy

It is more difficult and less desirable to have the same sort of controls on profits as have been proposed for wages and salaries. For one thing, profits fluctuate a good deal from year to year, rising sharply in boom years and falling in recession. Secondly, the rate of profit on the capital employed varies enormously from firm to firm, and from industry to industry, reflecting differences in risk, managerial efficiency and sheer luck. Thirdly, since profits are the main source of investment funds in the private sector, any kind of direct control over them could have serious adverse effects on private investment. It would, therefore, be preferable to adopt indirect measures to achieve the main objectives of incomes policy with respect to profits.

If the proposed policies on wages and salaries are accepted and implemented, it is possible that there may be a rise in the share of profits in

33. Strictly speaking, this will be true only if training and educational institutions charge true economic costs to the students. Under the present system, even those who are supposed to be paying their own way, do in fact enjoy considerable hidden subsidy from the state.

national income. This would probably be acceptable in a largely socialist economy. But in a predominantly private enterprise economy such as that of Kenya, a rise in the share of profits, while desirable from the growth point of view, will worsen income distribution and jeopardize wages policy. In order to deal with this situation, it will be necessary to rely on fiscal and prices policy. The corporate tax is already quite high in East Africa, amounting to 40 per cent of net profits. Taking into account the surtax on distributed dividends, the effective rate of taxation of business profits probably amounts to more than 50 per cent. Thus the government will be one of the principal beneficiaries of a rise in the share of profits. It is doubtful whether corporate tax can be raised much further without affecting foreign private investment in the country. On the other hand, there is considerable scope for further reform of the business tax system. The most urgent need in this area is the improvement of procedures for the assessment of income of private companies and unincorporated enterprises, in order to reduce tax evasion through underdeclaration of incomes.

The role of the price policy is to ensure stability in the worker's cost of living index, which is essential for the success of the wages policy, and to prevent the earnings of excess profits by firms enjoying monopolistic powers. The government is already responsible for the fixing of prices of a wide range of goods, which figure heavily in the budgets of low income groups. Supplemented by selective subsidies of a temporary nature, this should enable the government to achieve reasonable stability in the low income cost of living index.

It is more difficult to devise means to control the pricing policies of monopolistic firms. A substantial proportion of the manufacturing and services sector is dominated by monopolistic and oligopolistic structures. Unlike many industrial countries, East African countries do not have any public bodies whose function is to keep a check on the activities of monopolistic firms. This role could be performed by the proposed National Incomes Board. The main objectives here are to ensure that the market power is not used to raise prices when there is no adequate justification for it, and more positively to induce firms to reduce prices when productivity increases are in excess of wage rate increases and other costs have not risen. The implementation of these policies, however, is likely to prove extremely difficult. It is easier to prevent unjustified price increases than to secure price reductions.[34] If the board is to discharge its functions adequately in this respect, it would need to have access to detailed data on the cost and price structure of a wide range of industries. Planned variations in import duties and direct pressure on firms would be the main means of influencing

34. This certainly appears to have been the experience of the National Board for Prices and Incomes in UK; See National Board for Prices and Incomes (1965–6).

the price policy of firms. In addition the government could use its immense powers as a purchaser of these goods and services to encourage price reductions.

Conclusion

It has been argued above that in the interests of equity and a rapid expansion of employment, it is desirable to introduce controls to slow down the increase in wage rates to 4 per cent per annum. A proposal designed to achieve this objective involving minimum interference with the existing machinery of wage negotiation was put forward. With respect to salaries, the best practicable alternative would appear to be to freeze the salary scale at its existing level for the present holders of salaried jobs, and to lower the salaries for future entrants to the skilled labour force. Profits should be regulated through a combination of fiscal and price policies.

References

BARYARUHA, A. (1967), *Factors Affecting Industrial Employment. A Study of Ugandan Experience 1954–64*, Nairobi, OUP.

GHAI, D. P. (1964), *Some Aspects of Income Distribution in East Africa*, paper 52, East African Institute of Social Research.

GHAI, D. P. (1967), *Analytical aspects of an incomes policy for Kenya*, discussion paper no. 50 (mimeo.), Institute for Development Studies, University College, Nairobi, Kenya.

GHAI, D. P. (n.d.), *Some notes on labour markets in East Africa*, Staff Paper, Institute for Development Studies, University College, Nairobi, Kenya.

GHAI, D. P., and HOLLEN, C. (forthcoming), *Kenya's Industrial Court – an economic analysis*, discussion paper, Institute for Development Studies, University College, Nairobi, Kenya.

GREEN, R. H, (1967), 'Wage levels, employment, productivity and consumption', in J. R. Sheffield (ed.), *Education, Employment and Rural Development*, East African Publishing House.

ILO (1967), *Report to the Government of the United Republic of Tanzania on Wages, Incomes and Prices Policy*, Government Printer.

KNIGHT, J. B., (n.d.), 'The determination of wages and salaries in Uganda', *Bull. Oxford Univ. Inst. econ. Stat.*, vol. 29, pp. 233–64.

NATIONAL BOARD for PRICES and INCOMES (1965–6), *General Report*, pp. 18–21, cmnd. 3087, HMSO.

ROGERS, D. C. (1968), *The returns to investment in higher levels of education in Kenya*, discussion paper no. 59 (mimeo), Institute for Development Studies, University College, Nairobi, Kenya.

SALARIES REVIEW COMMISSION (1967), *Report of the Salaries Review Commission*, Kenya Government, Government Printer.

Part Four
Education and Employment

The unemployment of the educated is a much emphasized and
particularly important part of the wider problem of general
unemployment. Exactly who is included within this specific group
varies but there is hardly a less developed country which is not
experiencing difficulty, and often considerable alarm, in finding enough
jobs for all its school leavers – or at least, enough jobs of the sort which
education has led them to aspire to and expect. In Asia, the problem
groups are usually university and secondary school graduates; in
Africa, mainly primary and secondary school leavers. But in almost all
countries, the unemployed educated form a large and growing section
of the total unemployed, amounting to a third or more of the urban
unemployed. Their importance often springs less from their numerical
size than from their position as an articulate and politically-conscious
group, with the ability to mobilize public opinion and government
opposition.

At first sight one may wonder whether any special explanation of
unemployment of the educated is required. Since unemployment is
widespread it is hardly surprising that the unemployed include some
educated persons along with the uneducated. But this approach is too
simple since it fails to explain why rates of unemployment usually differ
among groups with different levels of education. There is thus a need
for separate or at least additional analysis to account for the existence
of unemployment among the educated in general.

Reading 15 is an analysis of unemployment among the educated in
Ceylon. This brings out with startling clarity the differences which can
exist in the rates of unemployment among persons with differing levels
of education. The cause of these differences is structural as distinct from
the overall imbalance between the total supply and demand for labour.
In this situation, the types of work which people are willing and able to
undertake, do not match the job opportunities available. In Ceylon,
these structural problems have become increasingly pronounced over
time, as a greater proportion of the population has been exposed to

education, which has had the effect of implanting certain aspirations and felt needs. The substantial majority of the new entrants aspire to white collar jobs. This is not simply for reasons of status but largely it is in response to a wage and income structure which still seems to bear the imprint of a colonial ancestry by favouring administrative and clerical jobs as opposed to professions such as architects, engineers and health officers.

In Reading 16 Coombs emphasizes a basic factor in the explanation of structural imbalance – the extremely rapid rates at which education at all levels in most developing countries has expanded in the last decade, rates far in excess of the growth of wage employment or other job opportunities. Coombs elaborates on the urgency of the problem of unemployment among the educated and draws some of the implications for educational policy.

After this, we present two readings concerned with unemployment among the educated in India each stressing a further aspect of structural imbalance in explanation of the way education can lead to unemployment. Myrdal (Reading 17), in a wide-ranging discussion of political and social traditions in Asia, emphasizes the cultural factors which discourage educated persons from taking manual and other jobs which they believe to be beneath their dignity. This is perhaps the clearest statement of the viewpoint which places most emphasis on white collar attitudes.[1]

In contrast, Blaug (Reading 18) stresses economic rationality in job seeking as the main explanation of unemployment among the educated. This is less the result of a gap between total labour demand and supply than the result of an adjustment lag in the period before the unemployed educated take jobs. The pool of unemployed educated is thus a revolving queue in which an individual may be unemployed for two or three years while searching for the best available job opportunity. Blaug's explanation emphasizes a reduction in the real wage of this group as the main factor tending to bring the total demand and supply for educated labour into balance – though equilibrium may never in fact be reached because both demand and supply are continually expanding.

Other analysts, among them many manpower planners, have put primary emphasis neither on attitudes nor wage adjustments, but on disparities in the growth of demand and supply in recent years. For

1. An opposite view is taken by Foster (1966). In a study based on job aspirations and expectations of secondary students in Ghana, Foster strongly disagrees with 'the white collar myth', arguing that a preference for white collar jobs reflects a realistic appreciation of actual prospects in the job market, not prejudice.

example, in India the supply of engineers increased four fold in the 1960s, rapidly transforming a position of shortage to a position of surplus. According to the analysis, a main part of the cure for educated unemployment is to bring relative growth rates into balance. That this is a relevant approach for many developing countries is indicated by the data in Coombs's article showing high rates of educational expansion in all parts of the Third World.

Each of these authors reveals a certain tendency to emphasize his own part of the explanation to the exclusion of the others. In fact a full explanation in most countries of the phenomenon of unemployment among the educated seems to require something of each of the three elements identified; disparities in the rates at which the supply and demand for educated manpower are growing; lags in the speed at which wages and salaries of educated persons adjust to clear the market; prejudices in the attitudes of the educated against taking certain types of jobs. Moreover, in varying degrees, each of these elements is also part of the explanation of the general problem of unemployment and of other particular elements within it: unemployment among youth, among migrants, among minority ethnic groups, to name just three groups of obvious interest. (On this, see also the readings in Part Two).

To what extent do the educated get jobs at the expense of the uneducated? To what extent are the educated the privileged of society, even in countries where unemployment among the educated is heavy? These are important questions which as yet have been too little explored. Blaug's data clearly show that the private financial returns to education are considerable, even after allowing for the effects of a period of unemployment. It may be that the priority given to measures which reduce educated unemployment has in fact increased inequality within these countries. In this respect, the emphasis on finding jobs for the educated unemployed may have been at the expense of improving the living standards of those in greater poverty. Far from improving income distribution, higher education and policies to provide jobs for the educated unemployed may well have worsened it. Although not explored further here, some of the readings in Part Three on Income Distribution and Wages and Incomes carry these issues somewhat further.

Reference

FOSTER, P. J. (1966), 'The vocational school fallacy in development planning', reprinted in M. Blaug (ed.), *Economics of Education*, vol. 1, 1970, Penguin.

15 International Labour Office

Unemployment of the Educated in Ceylon

Extract from International Labour Office, 'Unemployment of the educated in Ceylon', from *Matching Employment Opportunities and Expectations. A Programme of Action for Ceylon*, ILO Geneva, vol. 1 (1971) pp.20–33 and 117–120.

Two types of imbalance

It may help if we begin with a rather formal and oversimplified statement of the causes of the problem. Basically the different parts of Ceylon's employment problem encompass two types of imbalance:

1. An *overall* difference between the total supply and demand for labour (measurable, for instance, in man-hours);

2. A *structural* imbalance, in which the types of work which people are willing and able to do do not match the pattern of opportunities available. This arises because the opportunities for additional work occur at the wrong season or in the wrong place, require special skills, compared with what the various types of labour can offer, or carry lower income or status than people will accept.

We emphasize the structural problems, because they are so severe in Ceylon, and because they seem to have been rather underemphasized in developing countries. But we must not forget that even if the attitudes and skills of the Ceylonese labour force could be magically changed overnight, so as to fit the pattern of demand for labour, there would still be an overall imbalance, due to the shortage of foreign exchange and capital – ultimately to the composition of production and the distribution of income.[1]

The process of adjustment

[. . .] Let us consider the processes by which structural imbalances grow and become chronic.

In no country are employment opportunities easily matched with job-seekers. But in time, changes occur on both sides of the labour market which help to eliminate the unemployment due to structural mis-matching. Square pegs have their sharp edges knocked off and the round holes are adapted to a better fit. Not always happily and not very efficiently, human aspirations and job requirements begin to mesh with one another. A process of structural

1. So, in a sense, our approach to the overall imbalance is 'structuralist' too.

adjustment takes place. The important questions concern the *incentives* which encourage this adjustment and the *time* it takes.

Adjustments in job openings and work opportunities are not rapid. They depend on the level and structure of the economy and on techniques of production, which change only slowly. Individuals adjust themselves more quickly, provided incentives exist. Although attitudes and preferences may appear to be strongly held, evidence from other countries suggests that these reflect objective circumstances more than irrational prejudices.

It is not unreasonable to prefer a secure job with a reasonable income. Educated Ceylonese have in the past had a high chance of obtaining this type of job and find it still pays to wait for it. The free rice ration and other social benefits all give some chance to do this, including many whose families are barely able to support them. Besides, young people can more easily afford to wait because most of them have no family responsibilities. Moreover, those who take at an early date one of the jobs available find that they then lose their chance of what they really want – they become typed as manual workers, and in any case cease to have the time to search for better jobs. But in time most of those who wait also accept what they realize to be inevitable.

Of course the labour market also gradually changes. The gap between salaries and wages narrows, and a whole array of other institutional changes take place – in the hiring practices of employers and in labour legislation, for example – some changes speeding the process of adjustment, others slowing it down or obstructing it completely.

[. . .] Table 1 shows the breakdown of the labour force by level of education. About a fifth of the urban population and just over an eighth of the rural had passed GCE 'O' level examinations.[2]

For the purpose of understanding the origins of Ceylon's unemployment, rising educational levels are of fundamental significance. The rapid increase in the numbers leaving school has already been mentioned. As can be calculated from the data given in Table 2, the increase in the numbers of educated people in the younger age groups of the non-estate labour force has

2. This category was defined fairly precisely in the Survey to include those who had obtained five passes in the GCE 'O' level examination, taken at the end of grade 10. In principle this would be after ten years of schooling but because of repetition, it is usually more. Those with 'A' levels or above include persons who have passed the 'A' level examination taken at the end of grade 12 normally two years later, but again because of repetition often more. This category also includes persons with higher degrees, together with those whose university education is incomplete. Of course, some respondents may be claiming more education than they actually received. For the sake of brevity, tables showing distribution by level of education refer to the highest level attained – thus 'passed "O" level' excludes those who have passed 'A' or higher levels of examination.

Table 1 Educational structure of active labour force by sector, 1969–70
(percentages of sector totals)

	Urban	Rural	Estate	Total
No schooling	7	10	43	16
Primary, grades 1–5	30	39	48	39
Middle, grades 6–10	40	37	8	32
Passed 'O' level	19	13	1	12
Passed 'A' level or above	3	1	—	1
Total*	100	100	100	100

* May not equal the sum of items, because of rounding.
Source: *Socio-Economic Survey, 1969–70*, First Round.

Table 2 Non-estate labour force by education and age, 1969–70
(thousands)

Age groups	15–24	25–34	35–44	45–54	55–59
No schooling	51	43	106	77	29
Primary, grades 1–5	316	232	289	239	73
Middle, grades 6–10	460	286	228	163	43
Passed 'O' level	167	140	78	47	10
Passed 'A' level or above	15	23	7	3	1
Total	1009	724	708	529	156

Source: *Socio-Economic Survey, 1969–70*, First Round.

been dramatic, e.g. the fraction with 'O' levels rising from under 10 per cent of the 45 to 54 year age-group to over 19 per cent of the 25 to 34.[3]

In brief, this is due to three causes:

1. The growth of the school population over the last decade;

2. The increasing proportion of school children going on to higher levels of education;

3. The higher rates of participation in the labour force among educated people, particularly women.

Nevertheless the net rise in the educational levels of the labour force appears most clearly not in relation to the general average within the population but in relation to the educational levels of the older age groups who are retiring. A comparison between the first and last columns of Table 2 gives a

3. Indeed, the full effect of these factors is understated in Table 2, because many in the lowest age group who will shortly qualify for 'O' level (or 'A' level) certificates are still at school.

rough indication of the margin by which the educational levels of the new entrants to the labour force exceed the levels of those who are retiring. This sharp contrast is a prime source of imbalance in the labour market, requiring, as it does, a reduction in the wage differentials enjoyed by the more educated groups faster and more far-reaching than the flexibility of the system – and the interests it benefits – will permit.

Table 3 Those seeking work by age, sex and sector, with and without GCE 'O' level qualifications,* 1969–70
(percentage of the active labour force)

	Urban		Rural		Estate†		Total	
Both sexes	−O	O+	−O	O+	−O		−O	O+
15–19	48	87	37	93	32		38	92
20–24	34	43	28	71	11		25	64
25–34	16	17	6	18	1		6	17
35–44	4	4	1	7	1		1	6
45–54	2	0	1	0	0		1	0
55–59	1	(0)	2	(0)	0		1	0
Total	19	20	12	39	7		12	32
Males								
15–19	49	(86)	35	(80)	44		39	81
20–24	26	39	23	60	16		23	54
25–34	13	11	5	7	1		5	8
35–44	4	5	0	6	2		1	5
45–54	2	0	1	0	0		1	0
55–59	0	(0)	0	(0)	0		0	0
Total	16	15	10	24	10		11	21
Females								
15–19	47	(88)	41	(100)	19		34	98
20–24	67	50	44	81	5		32	76
25–34	38	38	16	38	1		10	38
35–44	4	0	6	10	0		4	8
45–54	2	(0)	3	(0)	0		2	0
55–59	10	(−)	10	(−)	0		8	(−)
Total		32	36	21	57	4	16	53

* O+ refers to those recorded as having passed five subjects for the 'O' level examination (normally taken after at least ten years of schooling) or some higher qualification. −O refers to all others.

† Very few on the estates have passed 'O' level.

Brackets round an entry indicate that it is based on a sample of less than 10 observations. (−) indicates no observations of either employment *or* unemployment.
Source: *Socio-Economic Survey, 1969–70*, First Round.

[. . .] Table 3 brings out the high rates of unemployment among the young and the more educated (those having passed at least five subjects in the 'O' level examination). As pointed out above, there may be some overstatement of educational qualifications; even for the younger age groups the figures are deceptively large because of the delay before new recruits to the labour force find their first job.[4] But whatever allowance one makes for these

Table 4 **Those seeking work by education, age, sex and sector,* 1969–70** (percentage of the active labour force)

	Aged 15–19				Aged 20–24			
	U	R	E	T	U	R	E	T
Both sexes								
No schooling	13	(11)	31	23	29	8	5	8
Primary	44	34	27	34	16	17	12	15
Middle	57	41	71	46	44	38	25	39
Passed 'O' level	87	93	(—)	92	45	69	(—)	63
Passed 'A' level†	(—)	(—)	(—)	(—)	(22)	(83)	(—)	69
Total	51	41	32	41	37	39	11	34
Males								
No schooling	(14)	(11)	46	26	(17)	(0)	18	11
Primary	48	39	35	40	11	13	12	12
Middle	52	36	79	41	34	33	39	33
Passed 'O' level	(86)	(80)	(—)	81	41	61	(33)	55
Passed 'A' level†	(—)	(—)	(—)	(—)	(20)	(50)	(—)	(40)
Total	50	37	44	40	29	30	17	28
Females								
No schooling	(11)	(—)	22	20	(38)	(14)	0	6
Primary	28	19	16	19	(56)	(36)	12	24
Middle	73	54	(33)	56	77	54	(0)	55
Passed 'O' level	(88)	(100)	(—)	98	54	78	(—)	74
Passed 'A' level†	(—)	(—)	(—)	(—)	(25)	(100)	(—)	(88)
Total	52	51	19	42	61	59	5	44

* U = Urban, R = Rural, E = Estate, T = Total for the three sectors.
† Or a higher qualification.
Brackets round an entry indicate that it is based on a sample of less than 10 observations. (—) indicates no observation of either employment *or* unemployment.
Source: *Socio-Economic Survey, 1969–70*, First Round, special tabulation.

4. Because those with 'O' levels enter the labour force at a later age, they show higher rates of unemployment.

points the proportions unemployed of those with 'O' levels aged 15 to 19, especially women, are indeed staggering – even in the age group 20 to 24, the figures were still over 50 per cent for men and over 75 per cent for women.

Table 4 gives a more detailed breakdown for the vulnerable age groups 15 to 19 and 20 to 24. What stands out here is that, generally speaking, the more a young person has been educated, the greater the likelihood that he or she will be unemployed, up to 'A' level – where the rates drop, except for young women in rural areas. Figure 1 brings out clearly the association between education and unemployment.

There is not much difference between urban and rural areas in the shape of this relation, but there is between the sexes. Figure 2 brings out one of

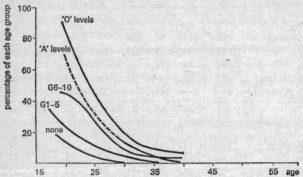

Figure 1 Unemployment by education and age (percentage of active labour force openly employed)

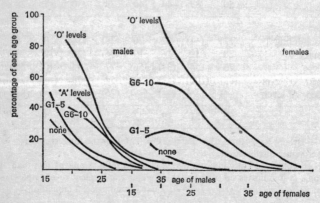

Figure 2 Unemployment by age, sex and education
Source: *Socio-Economic Survey, 1969–70*, First Round

the conclusions to be drawn from Table 4, namely that unemployment is higher among women at all educational levels, especially the highest, and that this difference persists into older age groups.

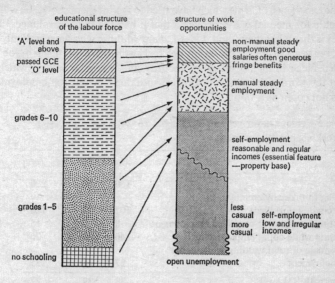

Figure 3 The imbalance in aspirations and opportunities, 1968
Key: arrows – focus of aspirations for jobs
Source: educational structure of the labour force – *Socio-Economic Survey, 1969-70.* Structure of work opportunities – approximate calculations based on 1968 Labour Force Survey data

[. . .] The dramatic rise in educational levels in recent years has brought a rapid change in the prospects facing educated school-leavers and the need for rapid and continuing change in their evaluation of their employment prospects. This is not to suggest that the *basic* aspirations of young persons with different levels of education differ fundamentally. Although we have no general data on the point, it is reasonable to suppose that people in Ceylon, just as anywhere else, would like work offering at least three things: a reasonable income, reasonable security, and reasonable conditions on the job, including status amongst their fellows.

These aims are not absolute, but relative to what people think they have a fair chance of achieving, which in turn depends largely on their educational level. Among new entrants to the labour force aged 15 to 24 in 1968, three quarters of those who had passed 'O' levels aspired to white-collar jobs. Table 5 provides more detailed figures.

It is a mistake to interpret these figures as a snobbish preference for white-collar status. White-collar jobs also pay more, and they are more secure, both in terms of regularity of income and in terms of having lower risks of being out of work. Many of those who have 'O' level passes would, as the experience of firms which have tried to recruit them shows, be willing to settle for manual work, provided that it had the same advantages. The point is that what they – and, indeed, many of those who have had only six or seven years of education – want and feel justified in expecting is a 'job': a settled niche in an organization, security and a regular salary (which is what the word 'job' means in English-speaking Ceylon: self-employment does not count as a 'job').

Table 5 **Persons never yet employed aged 15–24, by sex and type of work sought** (thousands)

	Males	Females	Total
Total	150	70	220
Willing to take any employment (including unskilled)	102	27	124
Wanting semi-skilled or skilled employment	8	7	15
Wanting white-collar employment*	40	36	76
Percentage of total wanting white-collar employment	27	51	35
Those with 'O' level	38	39	77
Willing to take any employment (including unskilled)	8	6	14
Wanting semi-skilled or skilled employment*	1	3	4
Wanting white-collar employment[1]	29	30	59
Percentage of total wanting white-collar employment	76	77	76

* Covers clerical, teaching, technical training and professional occupations.
Source: calculated from data given in *1968 Labour Force Survey*.

And 'jobs' are clearly scarce. Of the total labour force outside the estates today, about one third, say 1 million, have jobs in this sense (not all of them by any means, very secure or well paid). Allowing, generously, for a 2 per cent retirement in the labour force and a 5 per cent growth rate, there are 70,000 new jobs each year, to be shared among some 220,000 school-leavers newly entering the labour force outside of the estates.

Perhaps some 30,000 to 40,000 of that 220,000, certainly not more than 50,000, are able to settle down, at home, fairly happily, into fairly secure, what we might call 'property-based' self-employment backed by sufficient land or capital, or the goodwill of an established clientele, to provide a reliable source of income at a reasonable level – in agriculture, for instance, wet zone rice farms larger than about 3 or 4 acres. That still leaves 100,000, some of whom will easily reconcile themselves to more meagre opportunities for self-employment or for casual wage employment, but the majority of whom now have sufficient education to feel themselves qualified for a 'job'. Figure 3 brings out the extreme imbalance between the structures of opportunities and of aspirations.

Reforming the wage and salary structure

[. . .] The starting point for reform is to change the whole structure of incentives influencing the relative desirability of different types of work. These incentives are in part a matter of income differentials – the difference in average earnings and fringe benefits which a person can reasonably expect to receive from one type of work compared with those from another. But, as shown above, the relative attractiveness of different types of work is only partly a matter of earnings. The security of a job, the regularity of employment, the pleasantness of the work and the social status it brings are all attractions additional to income. Particularly important are differences in the security of employment and the relative difficulty of finding another job if unemployed. Indeed, it is in part the prevalence of unemployment which induces people to put such a premium on secure jobs – particularly those in government or large enterprises, from which dismissal is rare, or in certain forms of property-based self-employment, where income compares well with alternatives and is fairly regular.

The present pattern of wages and salaries in Ceylon sustains a structure of incentives which in these terms is often perverse – perverse in the sense of over-encouraging the search (or waiting) for certain types of work, so that the numbers are well beyond those the occupation concerned can absorb. Even more perverse are differentials encouraging types of education and training which are of low priority for future development.

This has often been pointed out in Ceylon. But in spite of many recommendations and some – rather piecemeal – action,[5] the existing structure of wages and salaries still reveals remnants of its colonial ancestry. Government scales embody considerable differentials in favour of administrative and clerical occupations and against those which are professional and

5. This point is well revealed in the work of the committee recently charged with drafting regulations on wages and salaries in the state corporations. Apparently very few of the memoranda submitted to the committee dealt adequately with wages in relation to the general structure of incentives in the country. Although proposals were submitted to make clerical and skilled manual scales comparable, no consideration seems to have been given yet to revising educational differentials (e.g. extra salaries for degrees), even though this is probably the most serious anomaly in the whole incentive structure.

technical – such as engineers, health officers and architects. It is true that since 1948 the gaps have been narrowed – but often to a small extent in relation to those which remain. Moreover, the wide variety of fringe benefits, not shown in the table, make the pattern even more extreme.

Between government, public corporations and the private sector, other anomalies persist. Sometimes the private sector pays more, sometimes less, than government, but with little obvious rationale. The public corporations have set wages and salaries by a variety of conflicting criteria, usually following government in the level of clerical pay (and the practice of paying annual increments on a scale) but taking labourers' scales from collective agreements between workers' organizations and the Employers' Federation. Variations in fringe benefits are wide and haphazard: sometimes these benefits are very large, especially those which are free of tax, such as season-ticket concessions or free housing.

More serious, however, are differences between the level and regularity of the earnings of those with and those without steady jobs: on the one hand, broadly most employees; on the other, those in casual and agricultural employment, and also the bulk of those in self-employment.[6] It is true, as mentioned earlier, that small-scale craftsmen with reasonable capital or agriculturalists with a reasonable acreage of land – the property-based producers – can look forward to a reasonable and steady income. But they are a minority and from the viewpoint of incentives their success is often not such as to encourage emulation. Indeed those without access to capital are more likely to think that the best way to successful self-employment is to accumulate it while in a regular wage earning job. Thus the differentials in favour of wage earning, and often white-collar, employment dominate the scene.

This is even truer of incentives for seeking further education as a step towards a steady, paying job. Substantial differentials exist in favour of formal qualifications. Again they have narrowed slowly over time but far too slowly in relation to the flood of educated unemployed joining the labour market and the numbers seeking to go on to higher education. Table 6 shows the differentials in 1969–70 and how they have changed since 1953.

Such differentials evidently far exceed what would be necessary to attract sufficient qualified applicants for further study – particularly since education is largely free. Even after allowing for the risks of unemployment,

6. On the other hand, rural–urban differentials between comparable occupations or activities are less of a *general* problem in Ceylon than in many developing countries, in part because of the cheap transport and short distances between towns. Important differences in basic wages sometimes arise, however, in different parts of the country at particular seasons – though these are usually indicative of a genuine labour shortage.

education in Ceylon is still richly rewarding for those who reach the higher levels. These excessive differentials must bear a large part of the blame for the continuing pressures for secondary and higher education, even after educated unemployment has become so severe.

Table 6 **Differentials in earnings by level of education, 1953, 1963 and 1969–70** (earnings as a multiple of those received by workers with no schooling)

Level of education	1953	1963	1969–70 Age groups			
			15–59	15–19	20–24	25–29
Primary 1–5	1·6	1·5	1·6	1·0	1·4	1·3
Primary 6 or above but below 'O' level	3·6	2·4	2·4	1·2	2·0	1·9
'O' level	5·0	3·9	4·2	2·2	3·0	2·3
'A' level and above	8·6	6·8	6·8	3·9	3·7	4·2*

* 6·7 for degree holders in this age group.
Sources: Bank of Ceylon (1963), and *1969–70 Socio-Economic Survey*, First Round (special tabulations).

As in so many other areas, the policies needed to narrow (and in some cases reverse) these differentials have been documented in detail within Ceylon in the various reports produced over the years. The essential recommendations in reports have largely gone unimplemented – even though most of the reports we studied had in our view already leaned over too far in compromising with the existing wage structures and the interest groups behind them, instead of recommending more fundamental changes.

But if employment strategy is to be taken seriously – and educational reform – fundamental changes cannot be avoided. Some instruments for implementing policy are already available – notably the Government's control over its own pay scales and its influence on those in public corporations. Moreover, if a strong line were taken in the public sector, private employers would follow, particularly since many of the most urgent changes correspond to what market forces would tend to produce anyway.

Reference
BANK of CEYLON (1963), *Survey of Ceylon's Commerce Finances*, Sri Lanka.

16 P. H. Coombs

The World Educational Crisis: A Systems Analysis

Extract from P. H. Coombs, *The World Educational Crisis: A Systems Analysis*, OUP, 1968.

[. . .] There are three main reasons why the social demand for education has been rising rapidly since the end of the Second World War. The first is the mounting educational aspirations of parents and their children. The second is the new stress of public policy almost everywhere on educational development as a precondition for overall national development, and the parallel stress on the democratic imperative of increased 'educational participation rates' – which means sending a higher proportion of each age group to school, and for more years. The third reason is the population explosion, which has acted as a quantitative multiplier of the social demand.

The interaction among these forces since 1950 accounts for the phenomenon that is depicted in Figure 1. World-wide primary school enrolments have increased by more than 50 per cent, and secondary and higher education enrolments by more than 100 per cent. Since the developing countries started from a smaller base, their *percentage* increase, especially at the primary level, has been much greater than is the case in the developed countries. In absolute numbers, however, the developed countries have had a much greater increase in secondary and higher education.

The whole of these enrolment figures, showing that compared with a generation ago, twice the proportion and number of the world's children are today being exposed to formal schooling, forms the bright side of the case. The figures, however, are silent about the dark side. They do not reveal the vast social waste and the human tragedy in the high rate of dropouts and failures. They hide the large number of costly 'repeaters'. And, most important, they say nothing about the nature, quality and usefulness of the education received.

More will be said later about all these matters. What must be noted here is a dual aspect of the increased demand for education. The rising enrolment curves reflect the compounded effect of an overall expansion in the *absolute size* of each age group, and a rise in the *percentage* of each age group participating at each educational level.

[. . .] Our main concern thus far has been with the question: 'Can edu-

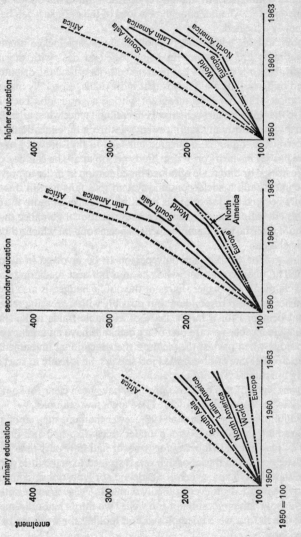

Figure 1 Sharp rises in enrolments, particularly in developing regions

cation – in respect of its output – overcome or avert specific human resource shortages that hamper national development?' We turn now to what is fast emerging as a more serious manpower question, quite the opposite of the foregoing one. It is whether enough new jobs of the right sort can be found for the newly educated.

The point at issue has a potential political hurricane locked up inside it, and economists are not alone in being asked to deal with the matter. Education is also a party to the matter, with its attendant disputes over plans and budgets. The plain fact is that individuals, especially males, look on education primarily as a means of getting a good job. They are interested in the 'investment' benefits of education. Hence when an individual after hard work and many sacrifices emerges from an educational system with a certificate, diploma, or degree but fails to find the kind of job on which he has set his heart or, worse, finds no job at all, he can be expected to feel frustrated or bitter. He obtained his education in order to prevent his unemployment, and a socioeconomic system that fails him in this regard may easily become the target of his hostility. This is even more the case if, during his education, he received no sound vocational guidance that gave him a more realistic set of employment expectations on which to base his academic choices.

But this graduate is not the only person to be involved in a counter-reaction. The finance minister, who sits in a hot seat mediating amongst the rival claimants for bigger shares of the public budget, is also involved. The minister has been responding, but possibly with increasing reluctance, to annual demands for a larger share of available funds to be spent on education. He has been aware that other demands have an urgency of their own. So now, when part of the yield on the educational investment turns out to be a picket line of disgruntled job-seekers, he is likely to start asking searching questions.

The overt signs of this ominous problem have been clear for some time, especially in the developing nations. Here are a few examples.

In the Philippines, as far back as 1961, fewer than one quarter of all high school graduates in the age group under thirty-five had full-time jobs; another 44 per cent were looking for work or had only part-time jobs; the rest had stepped out of the labor market. It seemed to make little difference whether they had taken general, academic, or vocational courses; the unemployment rate dealt evenhandedly with all. *University graduates* were doing relatively better, yet still not too well. Two thirds had full-time jobs – but over one in four were unemployed and looking for work, or had only part-time jobs.

In the United Arab Republic, a research study reports that, as of the mid-sixties.

about 70 per cent of the university enrolment is in the Faculties of Arts, Law and Commerce, and for the vast majority of these there is no demand . . . [such] graduates . . . constitute a large and rapidly growing group whose skills are largely substandard and unwanted (Kerr, 1965, p. 187).

In India, between 1956 and 1962, the number of job-seeking 'matriculates' and 'intermediates' on the live registers of employment exchanges (which tend to understate the real case) rose from about 217,000 to over 644,000. In the same seven years, university graduates on these registers rose from under 27,000 to over 63,000. The Indian Education Commission (1966) recently estimated that the total of educated unemployed in all categories was one million in round figures. From this pool of one million, of course, some were constantly being drained off to employment. But they were just as constantly being replaced by the next crop from the schools and universities. It is especially noteworthy in India's case that there is now significant, and rising, unemployment in such a specialized 'shortage' category as engineering.

In Burma, according to Hunter,

there was in 1962 and 1963 a 'surplus' of university graduates – that is to say, considerable numbers (up to 40 per cent in some mechanical and electrical branches of engineering) of newly-graduated students were unable to find employment in the type of work for which they felt themselves qualified. Similarly, there was a 'surplus' of graduates from the technical institutes, of about 20 per cent, and even unemployment from the trade schools (Hunter, 1967).

In most of Latin America there has been heavy unemployment and underemployment for some years among secondary and university graduates. Africa has seen a heavy accumulation of unemployed among those who have left primary school (this group used to get clerical jobs fairly readily in the 'old days'). Nigerian authorities, troubled by this problem for some years, have now started worrying over the prospect of an imminent 'surplus' of university graduates. Production of graduates is sharply up, but the seemingly unquenchable demand for them of only a few years ago has eased off, especially with the filling up of government posts.

[. . .] What causes the paradox of developing nations who clearly need more educated manpower but who are unable to use it when they get it? Is education somehow at fault? Has it expanded *too* rapidly? Has it produced the wrong kinds of manpower? Or does the fault lie elsewhere – perhaps in the economy, or in economic development policies and plans? Where are the solutions to be found? Indeed, is there any solution?

The earlier history of today's industrialized nations sheds light on certain of the problems and prospects of today's developing countries. This does not mean, of course, that the latter countries should follow precisely the same path, or take as long to travel it. But there are certain inescapable stages and processes that must be gone through, whatever a particular country's philosophy or form, as it moves from a relatively low state of economic development to a more balanced industrial economy.

One of these processes is a gradual change in the composition of its labor force. Starting with a large component of unskilled, common labor and a very small component of skilled and high-level manpower, the profile of the labor force progressively alters as it comes to consist less and less of unskilled workers and more and more of skilled and high-level manpower. To put the same thing differently, a modernizing economy gradually moves from being a low-wage, low-productivity, labor-intensive economy, toward being a higher productivity, higher wage, capital-intensive, labor-saving economy with a better qualified manpower. It is at best a long transition process.

Education and training play a major role in the progression by developing an educated labor force that has a higher productivity than uneducated labor. And as the process continues, education moves from being a 'scarce' commodity to being an 'abundant' one, from being a relative luxury, available to only the few, to being a basic need for everyone who wants to escape the shrinking unskilled sector of the labor force.

In the early stages – roughly where western Europe and North America were one hundred years ago – the national structure of incomes has a very large spread between the bottom and top, reflecting among other things the high scarcity value of education. But with time and the expansion of both the economy and education, the bottom incomes move upwards faster than the top incomes (which may even move down as a result of very high inheritance and progressive income taxes).

Today, for example, the income spread in Africa between what a common laborer receives and the salary of a top civil servant or businessman may be in the ratio of 1 to 100 or higher. The income spread in the United States has never been as large as it is in Africa, but the distance between the take-home pay of an average factory worker and that of a fairly high-level business executive has now narrowed to a ratio of something like 1 to 5. The western European income spread is moving toward a similarly narrow band.

The relevance of all this to our discussion of employment and unemployment is that as more and more people become educated, the supply of new *top* jobs becomes scarcer relative to the number of educated people seeking them. These educated people then adapt to the situation (though not always gracefully) by stepping down on their 'job preference scale' until they find a job they can actually get, something less than their first choice. If the preferred civil service posts are filled, for example, they may turn to teaching, and education starts getting a better quality manpower. Eventually, as happened in Japan, for example, high school graduates overcome what reluctance they may have had for manual labor and take factory jobs. *But they become more productive factory workers* because of their education. They produce more, and eventually get paid more, and the bottom of the income pyramid moves upward.

The key to this adjustment process is that the jobs become upgraded. They may be called by the same names, but they are no longer the same jobs because they are now filled by better educated people who make something more of the job, and make a better living from it. This long 'job-upgrading' process, we hasten to add, was not, in the case of today's industrialized nations, a smooth and well-planned affair in which nobody got hurt. It was far from that. There were rough bumps along the way and no small amount of human misery. It is to be hoped that the journey will be somewhat smoother and quicker for today's developing nations. But it would be naive to expect that it will not have many serious problems and discomforts. One of the worst will be unemployment, for the uneducated and educated alike.

It is important to be clear that the development programs of the world did not *create* the unemployment problem, nor did the rapid expansion of education. What they did do was to make an ancient problem more visible, and more vocal. Vast hidden unemployment, and more particularly, vast underemployment, have been the hallmark of static, traditional societies all though history. This curse has now been brought to the center of conscious attention. Unemployment has become a matter of public concern. With the better (though still imperfect) statistics now available, it is even possible to make caliper-fine calculations on the problem. And on the behavior of these statistics, governments may stand or fall, especially if a good many of the unemployed turn out to be educated unemployed congregated in the cities. For educated unemployed are not inclined to suffer in silence, hidden in the bush. To this extent, and in a special sense, it can fairly be said that education has contributed to the noise level of the problem, but not to its quantitative level.

The problem, however, is much worse than it might have been, and the reason for this lies in three important facts. The first forces us to qualify what we have just said about development programs not creating the unemployment problem, because it was already there. Paradoxical as it may sound, the fact is that modernization tends to generate more unemployment than employment, at least in the initial stages. This is because, in the economic sense, modernization means raising human productivity – doing more work, producing more output, with fewer manhours of effort. Translated into practical terms, this means that a given increase – say of 10 per cent – in a nation's total output is accompanied by a lesser increase in employment – the more so if much of the increase in the GNP comes out of the industrial sector where labor productivity is rising most rapidly. In fact, at the early stages of the development process, the GNP may be *rising*, while paid employment may be *falling*. This is precisely what happened in Tanzania and Kenya in recent years, though it is hoped they have now turned the corner of this 'wringing out' process.

The second fact compounds the difficulty of the first. If, at the time a nation is making its painful initial adjustments to the modernization process, it is seized by an abnormally rapid population growth, its unemployment problem becomes much larger. This is because its labor force grows much more rapidly than the economy can absorb new employees. And if, on top of this, the educational system's output has expanded considerably, then many of the newcomers onto the labor market who cannot find jobs will have had an education of some sort. It then begins to look, at least on the face of things, as if the nation had somehow got itself 'overeducated'. Such a conclusion is patently absurd when one takes into consideration the probability that the bulk of the population is still illiterate and that a majority of youngsters are still not in primary school. Nonetheless, there is a strong temptation at this point for someone in high authority to push the panic button on the educational budget. From a long-range view, nothing could be more self-defeating. Yet, it can happen.

The third fact points directly at a major, ubiquitous cause of employment difficulties. It is the unhappy fact that for many historical reasons, the employment structures of many developing countries, their labor market mechanisms, wages and salary structure, and the resultant deployment of their educated manpower are all seriously at odds with what is necessary to encourage optimum economic growth. More specifically, there is a wide disparity in most developing countries between the manpower *needed* for economic growth and the manpower *actually demanded* by the market. Likewise, there is a wide disparity between how the economy should use its available supply of educated manpower in order to promote economic growth, and how it actually uses it.

The main causes of these costly disparities include: (a) inappropriate wage and salary relationships, which tend to draw scarce manpower in the wrong directions; (b) inappropriate and overly rigid relationships between particular types of jobs and the 'official' educational qualifications for them; (c) traditional prejudices and concepts of status (opposed especially to manual labor) that repel young people from the very types of work most needed for development, drawing them instead to relatively less productive jobs; (d) a traditional 'caretaker' and 'supervisory' concept of government – in contrast to the 'activist' concept needed to spur development; this leads to an inflation of the civil service establishment and chains many of the most competent people to paper work when they should be released for positive development action.

If this is a fair statement, what are the conclusions for education? One is that unemployed engineers, for example, are not necessarily a sign that the educational system has produced too many. For many countries it is more likely a sign that the economy and the government have not yet learned how to use engineers – or agriculturalists, or architects, or public health specialists – in the best interests of national development. The chances are that too many of these often well-trained specialists are behind desks, 'administering' instead of out building roads and schools, producing more food, improving public health. The chances are, also, that the pay is too high for 'administering' and too low for 'doing things'.

Should educational planners under these circumstances 'follow the market' and retrench their engineering program? Or should they follow the nation's true manpower needs and produce still more? There is no simple answer. The manpower estimates of need can sometimes be as wrong as the market, and in some cases mirror it. Still, to cut back educational output just because the economy and the system of public administration are not in harmony with national development would seem a strange way to foster development. The answer must obviously be left to those on the scene most competent to judge from all the circumstances. But one thing is clear – educational authorities have a strong interest in seeing that the noneducational bottlenecks to development get attention, even though such matters lie largely beyond their own official jurisdiction.

All this, however, does not relieve the educational system of responsibility for integrating itself, even with an imperfectly functioning economy or system of administering development. To spin off on its own and produce however much it wishes of whatever mix of students would be irresponsible and ultimately self-defeating. An educational system *can* produce too many engineers, and too many of other sorts of specialists, at a very high cost per unit – thereby greatly prejudicing other forms of education and injuring national development.

There are no general solutions to the problem of education and unemployment in developing countries, solutions can only be devised in each individual context. It will be at best a very troublesome problem for a long time to come. It is one of the inescapable difficulties of taking the passage to modernization. But the problem can be kept from being made worse than it needs to be if, by understanding its nature, those in positions of responsibility avoid the panicky decision to cut back education at the sight of some educated unemployed – a decision which, in the charity of hindsight, could prove to have been a serious error.

References

HUNTER, G. (1967), 'High level manpower for development', *Higher Education and Development in South East Asia*, vol. 3, part 1, UNESCO.

INDIAN EDUCATION COMMISSION (1966), *Report of the Education Commission 1964–6, Education and National Development*, Ministry of Education.

KERR, M. H. (1965), 'Egypt', in J. S. Coleman (ed.), *Education and Political Development*, Princeton University Press.

17 Gunnar Myrdal

The Effect of Education on Attitudes to Work

Extract from Gunnar Myrdal *Asian Drama*, vol. 2, ch. 23, pp. 1124–31, © 1968 by the Twentieth Century Fund, Penguin, 1968.

As we have seen in earlier sections, labour force participation in urban areas has been bolstered by the lack of a dole, since this obliges most persons of working age to seek out something to do, no matter how meagre a livelihood it may offer. However, members of one group – 'the educated' – have displayed a remarkable ability to sustain themselves without gainful work, largely by relying on family assistance and support. They account in fact, for a large proportion of those recorded as unemployed in the official statistics. In one respect, analysis of worklessness among the educated in terms of unemployment presents fewer conceptual difficulties than does analysis of non-participation among other groups in the labour force, as it can be assumed that the former are actively seeking jobs. Moreover, the jobs they seek are in a segment of the economy where conditions bear some resemblance to those in the West. But because members of this group impose severe restrictions on the types of work they will accept, unemployment among the educated fails to fit into the analytical scheme of the modern approach. While the educated demonstrate a high degree of geographical mobility as between urban areas, their functional mobility is negligible. They are looking for non-manual work and are not prepared to accept work that 'soils their hands'. With this restriction, statistics on the numbers of educated unemployed can be assigned a reasonably unambiguous meaning – the same cannot be said of most other statistics purporting to measure unemployment.

There is a hierarchy of educated people, beginning with those who are merely literate – mainly individuals who have finished primary school. Next come matriculates from secondary schools, those who have taken an intermediate examination, graduates of tertiary schools, and, finally, those who hold still higher degrees, having had post-graduate training. The statistics on the educated unemployed and the discussion of their problems generally refer to the four higher strata, but it should be remembered that even persons who have merely acquired some degree of literacy by going through primary school, or who have dropped out of secondary school before matriculating, often consider themselves educated and exempt from any obligation to work with their hands (Nair, 1961, p. 75).

These views about education and about the types of work appropriate for persons with some measure of schooling are solidly founded in traditional attitudes towards manual work which are bolstered by the existing social stratification. However, they have been strengthened in several ways by influences from the West. For one thing, most westerners who came to live in South Asia quickly acquired the habit of avoiding physical toil; they behaved like members of a 'super-caste'. Thus they created a false impression of contemporary conditions in western countries. Of even greater importance was the type of school system built up by the colonial governments. Western rule created openings for clerks and junior administrators; in time, higher positions in the administration also became available to the indigenous population, though to different degrees in the several colonies. At the same time a need for clerical and administrative personnel was felt in business and the professions. Schools were established so the native-born could acquire the skills they needed to fill these positions. The curriculum in the schools was literary and academic, and this emphasis also agreed with the traditional inclinations in South Asia. Parents in the upper strata were generally very eager to have their children take advantage of these new educational opportunities. Government jobs had a particularly high prestige value, but they had other recommendations as well. In colonial times a simple clerk commanded an income far above that of a common labourer.[1] Even outside government service a person with a western type of education could usually obtain a position that was extremely rewarding both financially and socially.

It is an indication of the pressure for that type of education that even in colonial times the spectre of unemployment among the educated raised its head. Complaints about this type of unemployment can be traced back to the early 1920s, not only in India, but also in Indonesia,[2] Burma, and other South Asian countries. The problem assumed more serious proportions in the 1930s as the number of school graduates rapidly increased and the number of job opportunities declined. In India several official commissions were appointed to study the problem of unemployment in the educated 'middle class' in the years between the two world wars.

Taking an overall view of the development of educational institutions in South Asia since the end of the colonial era there has been a tremendous

1. It is reported that in Indonesia shortly after the turn of the century a junior clerk could earn fifteen to thirty times as much as an ordinary laborer (Furnivall, 1957, p. 377).

2. Thus in Indonesia, 'within a little over ten years from 1914, there was a surplus of unemployed school graduates, and diehards were criticizing Western education as breeding unemployment, discontent, and political agitation' (Furnivall, p. 378).

increase in the number of schools and in school enrolment in all of the countries of the region, although enrolment in the secondary and tertiary schools has increased more rapidly than enrolment in the primary schools. Attempts to give the schools a more practical and technical character have, on the whole, been less successful. Most of the secondary schools are still 'general' schools of the type inherited from colonial times. The bulk of the students in tertiary schools study for degrees in law, arts and similar subjects. The tertiary schools, in particular, have deteriorated in quality. They accept students who are not properly prepared, have a large number of dropouts, and graduate individuals who are not of a particularly high calibre. Efforts in the field of adult education have been weak.

Under these circumstances it is not surprising that unemployment among the educated has grown. In India in 1955 the educated unemployed (matriculates, intermediates and graduates) were estimated to number considerably more than half a million. It was then forecast that almost five times this number of persons would emerge from school and enter the labour force for the first time during the period of the second Five Year Plan. At the beginning of the third Five Year Plan, five years later, the educated unemployed were estimated at nearly a million. When considering these figures, it is important to recall that there is a considerable fringe of unemployed young people who do not qualify as educated for survey purposes but consider themselves educated enough to shun manual labour.

To place this development in perspective, it is necessary to stress the fact that the educated do not want to do manual work. Much of the drive to widen the opportunities for children to acquire a secondary and tertiary school education, and much of the resistance that has frustrated the efforts to give schooling on all levels a technical and practical direction, stem from parents who want 'to save their sons from the socially degrading necessity of manual work'.[3] The parents' views are reflected in the young people's refusal to entertain the notion of taking employment outside the urban white-collar occupations.[4]

From a rational planning point of view, these attitudes towards manual work are obviously highly detrimental to development. The attempt to build up a modern industrial structure is hampered by the lack of skilled

3. See Mills (1958, p. 10). See also *Asian Drama*, ch. 33.
4. Some studies in India have thrown light on the kind of employment preferred and the salary demanded by the educated unemployed. In a sample for Indian towns, only 10 per cent of the unemployed who had matriculated (but had not received a degree) indicated that they were looking for manual – and then mostly skilled – work. On the other hand, some 59 per cent of the same group indicated their willingness to accept jobs with monthly remunerations ranging from 50 to 100 rupees, an average sum no higher than the wage of the lowest-paid workers in a factory (Government of India, 1956a, pp. 91 ff.).

workers who can calculate and work according to written instructions and work-sketches. It should be noted that ordinary workers in western (and East European Communist) countries are as a rule not less but more educated than most of those called 'educated' in South Asia. The tendency of even graduate engineers – who are too few in relation to needs, because of the bias against technical training in the school system – to expect desk jobs and recoil from the prospect of physical contact with machines aggravates this obstacle to development. Similarly, doctors and nurses cannot be deemed thoroughly qualified if the handling of a diseased human body and its excrements is repugnant to them. Nor is the acquisition of expertise in agricultural problems consistent with unsoiled hands.[5]

These attitudes have an anti-rural bias that is a serious obstacle to progress in countries where agriculture is by far the most important industry and agricultural reform is of overwhelming importance. The educated do not want to go to the villages; even those who come from rural areas see education primarily as a means of escaping the misery and dreariness of village life.[6] This is one of the factors that make it difficult to infuse life into an adult education movement.[7] Generally speaking, the rural areas, being

5. In a speech given in 1961, Prime Minister Nehru complained that Indian agricultural students went to the United States for higher studies 'without cultivating the habit of manual labour' and that this 'made them a laughing stock in that country'. He added: 'You can imagine my embarrassment when I was told by a college professor that students who had come there for advanced training in the dairy industry did not even know how to milk a cow' (the *Overseas Hindustan Times*, 20 July 1961).

6. In a study of unemployed graduates from Lucknow University, those who came originally from rural areas were asked whether they would have been willing to return to that rural area after completion of their studies, had a job been available. Only 35 per cent answered in the affirmative (Majumdar, 1957, pp. 32 ff.).

'. . . Even youngsters from the villages, brought to the cities for short courses in modern farming methods, do not want to return where they can impart and supply this knowledge. They prefer to stay in town and seek a white-collar job' Mead (ed.) 1953, p. 70) '. . . in the Netherlands Indies and Burma nurses refused to do rural work since it involved manual work which in the urban hospitals was performed by menials'. (1953, p. 273).

7. See *Asian Drama*, ch. 32, section 4. Note also the following contrast between conditions in pre-revolutionary Russia and those in modern India.

'Meeting teachers in Indian villages brought up old memories of primary education in pre-revolutionary Russia around the turn of the century. Thousands of young men and women with a university education went to the villages to teach the people. With little support from the Czarist government they did their work out of sheer idealism. By the time the Communists came to power the country was rapidly approaching universal literacy, at least among younger generations.

'We noticed nothing similar to that crusade in India. We heard complaints about mass unemployment among young graduates of the universities, but we could get no answer to the question: "Why cannot a million of them be mobilized for rural teaching?" Such a mobilization would be possible if Indian intellectuals felt the urgency of

backward, are deprived of those people who could supply the intellectual stimulation they sorely need because of their backwardness.[8]

An observation made about India towards the end of the colonial era aptly summarizes the situation that exists in most South Asian countries today: 'India is faced not so much by a problem of unemployment as of unemployables. Those who might have promoted the well-being of Indian industry and of the Indian countryside now loiter in the market-place, seeking work and finding none' (Anderson, 1946, p. 268). The waste involved in this under-utilization of manpower is tragic. But the issues involved in the status and attitudes of the educated in South Asia extend far beyond the relatively straightforward matter of economic waste. At least equally serious are the broader social consequences of the alienation of this group from the bulk of their countrymen and from the real development problems of their nations. The more successful among them are swallowed up by government bureaux and business firms; their detachment from the harsh realities of existence as they affect the mass of the population minimizes their potential contribution to the task of development. Everyone who has visited the South Asian countries can testify to the strange make believe atmosphere that prevails in the higher echelons of the educated class. In the lower strata of the employed and unemployed educated there is even less sense of identification with national interests.

The problem of how to integrate the rising number of the educated unemployed into the working community has occasioned much concern, particularly in India, Pakistan, Ceylon and the Philippines. It has received somewhat less attention in Burma and Indonesia, possibly because of the departure of most of the Indians and Dutch (including Eurasians), who had held most of the jobs coveted by the educated, and because the governments of these countries have been even freer than others in the region to increase the number employed in the lower brackets of administration. But even in these other countries the problem is increasingly coming to the fore, as the

---

primary education for the villagers as keenly as did the Russian intellectuals in the days of my youth' (Woytinsky 1957, p. 137).

8. Under the circumstances, even people with modest education almost invariably migrate out of villages, thus destroying whatever possibilities there might otherwise have existed for the evolution of an enlightened leadership. Thus, like our soil, leadership itself has been eroded over a long period and our village community left exhausted and in a state of unreplenished vitality'. (Datta, 1961, p. 148).

'One of the most serious obstacles to economic change in India lies in the prevailing patterns of social relationships. What modernization of farming can be expected when trained agricultural scientists and graduates tend to keep off the land and go in for non-agricultural work? Apart from the inhibitions of the caste system, agricultural occupations are generally stigmatized' (Rangnekar, 1958, p. 80).

schools turn out a swelling flood of graduates. Against the background we have given, we should not be surprised to find much ambivalence in the positions taken in public discussions of the problem in South Asia. The animus against manual work has so permeated not only the upper and middle strata but all walks of society that, with few exceptions, articulate persons, who, of course, are educated, are reluctant to find anything extraordinary in the restrictions the educated unemployed place on jobs they would accept.[9]

On the one hand there are individual leaders who condemn the prevalent attitude towards manual work and are frank enough to recommend that the educated unemployed seek work where it can be found and where, in addition, their services are badly needed. Nehru, for example, asserted that 'If educated young men do not accept manual work, our responsibility of providing employment to them ceases' (Government of India, 1956b, p. 35). Gandhi before him had laid great stress on the advantages of combining manual labour and training in arts and crafts with formal education. 'Basic education' along this line has, in fact, been adopted by the Indian government as the general pattern for primary education, but little has been done to put the idea into practice. And at various times schemes have been proposed that would make physical work a mandatory part of the educational system even at the tertiary level, but they have not been acted upon.[10]

Recommendations for practical reform have emphasized the creation of more jobs of the type educated persons will accept, that is, non-manual

9. At a seminar in Rangoon in 1959, presided over by Burma's Minister of Education, a young psychologist who had just returned from his doctoral studies in the United States presented a very learned paper, based on intricate statistical compilations, showing the vocational preferences of high school students in Rangoon. The long list of possible careers identified in the questionnaire used in the study included such extravagant occupations as film producer and public relations expert. Apparently no one was assumed to be interested in devoting himself to agriculture except as an official, or even to industrial enterprise except as a desk man. Nor was the omission of these sectors challenged by the audience. The Minister concluded the session by praising the study and saying that more such studies were needed in the big cities – but apparently not in the countryside.

10. In India, for example, various proposals have been made to introduce a work camp system for students, and one report (that of the Deshmukh Committee in 1959) recommended that participation in such an arrangement be made compulsory. The author of a subsequent report commissioned by the Indian government described the reaction to the work camp proposal as follows: 'Barring two or three papers which are generally favourable – but even they commend a "cautious" or "wary" approach – all the others – so far as I have been able to obtain the data – seem to be opposed to the Scheme in the form in which it has now emerged. The grounds for criticism are manifold. There is opposition to the idea of compulsion which is regarded as a "totalitarian approach" as "opposed to democratic values"' (Saiyidain, 1961, p. 73).

jobs. The inflation of jobs at the lower levels of administration in all the South Asian countries is, of course, a pragmatic application of this policy. The official study group in India whose findings we have already quoted was solicitous about the tastes of the educated. While paying lip service to the desirability of instilling a high regard for 'the dignity of labour' in the young, 'it did not wish to antagonize public opinion by setting its face against the popular craze for degrees and diplomas', as one commentator observed (Das, 1960, p. 39). The study group's major recommendation was that work of a non-manual kind be created.[11] Other official bodies have dealt with the problem of the educated unemployed in equally 'understanding' terms.[12]

As the basic attitudes towards work that are at the root of the problem of unemployment among the educated are shared by educated persons in general, the tenor of public discussion and government policy is understandable. The radical change in attitudes that would be desirable from a rational planning point of view would require an equally radical change in the whole educational system; both the attitudes towards work among the educated and the present school system are deeply rooted in the social structure of the South Asian countries. The practical reformer must concentrate his efforts on breaking down the monopoly of education held by the upper strata, by broadening and redirecting schooling.[13] Rapid progress, especially in the larger and poorer countries, cannot be expected.

11. The following observation is noteworthy: 'There are . . . certain schemes which are urgently needed in connection with economic development in general and with the socialistic pattern of society in particular [sic], though the jobs are not such as involve manual work. A typical example of this type is the development of the cooperative organizations in the country. [The] Planning Commission and the Planning Minister himself have stressed the importance of this, and though the beneficiaries from these schemes will be the educated classes, he felt that such schemes should be considered as deserving high priority' (Government of India, 1956b, p. 4).

12. Typical is the following statement in the Second Five Year Plan: 'Educated unemployment . . . assumes a special significance mainly because of the following factors: (a) rightly or wrongly there is an impression among the public that investment in education by an individual should yield for him a return in terms of a remunerative job; (b) an educated person *naturally* looks for a job suited to the particular type of education he has received with the result that there has been an abundance of supply in regard to certain occupations and professions and shortage in others, depending on the development of education in the country . . . and (c) there is a general disinclination among the educated to look for employment other than office jobs' (Government of India, 1956c, p. 120).

In a later document from the Planning Commission the dearth of educated persons in rural areas is explained in the following way: 'Educated persons come to cities simply because the rural economy is not geared up to absorb them' (*India, Outlook on Employment and Related Papers*, chapter 2, p. 4).

13. This problem is discussed in *Asian Drama*, ch. 33.

References

ANDERSON, G. (1946), 'Education', in E. Blunt (ed.), *Social Service in India*, HMSO.

DAS, N. (1960), *Unemployment, Full Employment and India*, Asia Publishing House.

DATTA, A. (1961), 'Place of the rural section', in *Problems in the Third Plan: A Critical Miscellany*, Ministry of Information and Broadcasting.

FURNIVALL J. S. (1957), *Colonial Policy and Practice*, Cambridge University Press.

GOVERNMENT of INDIA (1956a), *National Sample Survey no. 8, Report on Preliminary Survey of Urban Unemployment, September 1953*, Calcutta.

GOVERNMENT of INDIA (1956b), *Outline Report of the Study Group on Educated Unemployed*, New Delhi.

GOVERNMENT of INDIA (1956c), *Second Five Year Plan*, New Delhi.

MAJUMDAR, D. N. (1957), *Unemployment Among the University Educated, a Pilot Inquiry in India*, Center for International Studies, MIT.

MEAD, M. (ed.) (1953), *Cultural Patterns and Technical Change*, Tensions and Technology Series, UNESCO.

MILLS, L. A. (1958), *Malaya: A Political and Economic Appraisal*, University of Minnesota Press.

NAIR, K. (1961), *Blossoms in the Dust*, Duckworth.

RANGNEKAR, D. K. (1958), *Poverty and Capital Development in India*, OUP.

SAIYIDAIN, K. G. (1961), *National Service Scheme: A Report*, Ministry of Education.

WOYTINSKY, W. S. (1957), *India: The Awakening Giant*, Harper & Row.

18 Mark Blaug

The Unemployment of the Educated in India

Extract from Mark Blaug 'Applications of cost-benefit analysis', in *An Introduction to the Economics of Education*, Allen Lane, 1970, reprinted in Penguin, 1972.

[. . .] We begin with educated unemployment, taking India as a case in point, although Pakistan, Korea, the Philippines, the United Arab Republic or Argentina would have served just as well. The number of 'educated unemployed' in India in 1967 is conservatively estimated at half a million; the estimate is conservative because it counts only men who are out of work the entire week and does not allow for about an equal number doing casual or part-time work for several hours a day on two or three days in the week; it also excludes educated women who show much higher unemployment rates than men. The term 'educated' refers to all those who have at least completed secondary education, or in Indians' parlance, 'all those who are matriculates and above'. Half a million is undoubtedly a relatively large figure; it is equal to 6 to 7 per cent of the total stock of 'educated labour' in India in 1967. Expressing it in other terms, it is equivalent to nearly two thirds of the annual output of matriculates and graduates from schools and colleges. If Britain faced similar problems of unemployment among people with one or more A levels and with one or more university degrees, educated unemployment in Britain would amount to over 100,000.

That a poor country should suffer from a chronic surplus of labour is hardly surprising. But general unemployment is one thing and educated unemployment is another. The Indian economy has been growing at about 3·5 per cent per annum since Independence, a sufficient rate of growth, one would have thought, to absorb all of its best-educated people into employment. Nevertheless, educated unemployment, which was already a serious problem in 1947, has remained a more or less constant proportion of a rapidly growing stock of educated labour. And yet matriculates and graduates constitute only 4 per cent of the labour force in India. Even among this relatively small group of highly educated people, however, the unemployment rate exceeds anything normally experienced in advanced countries. Clearly, here is something of a mystery, difficult to square with popular notions of the crying manpower 'needs' of underdeveloped countries.

Why then is there educated unemployment in India? Because there are too many matriculates and graduates relative to the number of job opportunities that require these qualifications. But this answer only throws up more questions. Why do so many students rush headlong into secondary and higher education when they know that on average one out of fifteen of them will be unemployed? They may not know the precise figures for educated unemployment but they are perfectly familiar with the phenomenon. Besides, why is it that the existence of educated unemployment does not cause salary differentials to fall, so as to increase employment in the short run and to reduce the financial advantages of acquiring more education in the long run?

The standard retort to this line of questioning, so standard as to have become the stock-in-trade of foreign visitors to India, is to point to the self-defeating search for status which drives Indian students to seek education without regard to career prospects. Instead of acquiring qualifications in technical and vocational subjects, like science, engineering and medicine, they pursue traditional academic subjects like law and literature, or commercial subjects like book-keeping and accounting. In other words, the fault lies partly with the educational system for not imparting technical and vocational education, and partly with educated individuals themselves for preferring white collar to manual and industrial occupations, the implication of the argument being that educated unemployment would soon vanish if only education were vocationalized and if only educated people were willing 'to get their hands dirty'.[1]

This conclusion receives support from the fact that educated unemployment is greater among graduates in arts and commerce than among graduates in science and engineering. Even among BScs and MScs, however, high rates of unemployment are not uncommon and in the last year or two, unemployment has appeared among engineers and technicians. Besides, whose fault is it that so many more students study academic rather than vocational subjects? It is certainly not what students want. We know from attitude surveys and from application rates that every second Indian student would like to study medicine or engineering, probably because employment prospects in these fields are excellent; they end up in arts and commerce only because they cannot gain admission into medicine and engineering. The reason is quite simple: while technical education has been deliberately restricted in the light of anticipated demand for technically qualified people, secondary and general higher education have been allowed to grow at a pace determined by the pressures for admission.

In point of fact, there has been so far no real attempt in India to gear the scale of secondary and higher education to forecasts of manpower requirements, this despite the fact that two thirds of all graduates and nearly two

1. See Reading 17.

thirds of all matriculates work in the public sector. The enrolment targets that have appeared in the three Five Year Plans since 1950 have been mere extrapolations of past trends in the private demand for education and hence predictions of what is considered likely rather than what is considered desirable. By and large, Indian secondary and higher educational institutions have practised an 'open-door policy' and only medical and engineering colleges have rationed their places in accordance with admission quotas. The fact that over half of all Indian university students are enrolled in arts and commerce courses is not evidence that they are addicted to purely academic pursuits: it is simply a consequence of restrictive entry into colleges of medicine and engineering.

But why is there any demand at all for arts and commerce degrees if the incidence of unemployment among graduates with these specializations is as high as it is? The answer is that a BA can earn more than a matriculate, although much less than a BEng, even after allowing for the possibility of unemployment; the adjusted private rate of return to BAs is less than that to a matriculate qualification (see Table 1) but it still compares favourably with the rates which urban Indians could earn on their personal savings or which they would have to pay if they borrowed capital to finance education (borrowing to enable children to continue their schooling is much more common among Indian parents than among British or American ones). Thus, an arts degree is a vocational degree in Indian circumstances and this is not really surprising because a growing economy needs administrators and clerks with BA qualifications, just as much as it needs doctors and engineers.

As for educated unemployment, can we really explain it all away by the unwillingness of matriculates and graduates to take up blue collar occupations? In one sense, of course, it is tautologically true that unemployment would always disappear instantly if only the unemployed were willing to accept any job whatever at any rate of pay, however low. The question is one of degree: are the educated unemployed in India really less willing than unemployed professionals in advanced countries to accept a cut in pay and a decline in status? The first thing that must be said is that unemployment among the educated has, in fact, led to a reduction in their relative earnings, exactly as predicted by economic theory: the notorious stickiness of occupational rates of pay in underdeveloped countries has not prevented a decline in the real earnings associated with educational qualifications in India at a rate of about 2 to 3 per cent a year. There has been widespread and persistent upgrading of minimum hiring standards in India ever since Independence. In other words, jobs that used to be filled by matriculates now increasingly call for graduate qualifications, and so on for jobs lower down the occupational hierarchy; in consequence, highly educated people

Table 1 **Private and social rates of return, urban India, males, 1960**

Level of education	Private rates			Social rates		
	†Un-adjusted rate	Adjusted for *$\alpha = 0.65$	Adjusted for $\alpha = 0.5$	Un-adjusted rate	Adjusted for $\alpha = 0.65$	Adjusted for $\alpha = 0.5$
(1) Primary over illiterate	24·7	18·7	16·5	20·2	15·2	13·7
(2) Middle over primary	20·0	16·1	14·0	17·4	14·2	12·4
(3) Matriculation over middle	18·4	11·9	10·4	16·1	10·5	9·1
(4) First degree over matriculation	14·3	10·4	8·7	12·7	8·9	7·4
(5) Matriculation over illiterate	21·4	16·5	14·7	18·1	13·9	12·2
(6) First degree over illiterate	18·5	13·9	12·3	15·9	12·0	10·3
(7) Engineering degree over illiterate	21·2	17·0	15·2	17·3	13·8	12·3

Source: Blaug, Layard and Woodhall (1969, Tables 9-1, 9-2).

* α is that proportion of the differential in average earnings of persons of different levels of education assumed to be the result of education itself, and *not* of intelligence, family background or of other factors with which education might be correlated.

† The unadjusted rates of return in the first column represent a maximum, while those adjusted for $\alpha = 0.5$ in the third column represent a minimum. For the individual, the true *ex ante* rate of return is likely to fall between these values, depending on how students estimate their own chances of dropping out and of being unemployed after entering the labour market. For the Indian authorities, the true rate likewise falls in between the two extreme values, depending in this case on the particular policy that is being considered and on estimates of future demand and supply relationships. Table 1 is a summary of a much more comprehensive menu of possible alternative rates of return prepared by the authors of the Indian study (Blaug, Layard and Woodhall, 1969, ch. 9).

have constantly tended to drift down to lower-paid jobs. Nevertheless, upgrading has failed to clear the market for educated manpower. Earnings have never declined fast enough to reduce the incentives to acquire still more education. Indeed, the supply of educated people has so persistently run ahead of demand that, as we mentioned earlier, educated unemployment as a fraction of the total stock of educated manpower has remained relatively constant for at least twenty years.

The persistence of educated unemployment ever since 1947, and probably ever since the 1920s, can be explained only by certain features of Indian labour markets that slow down the process of adjustment to unemployment and, in particular, the rate at which the unemployed lower their 'reservation price' (the price at which they offer themselves for employment). Educated unemployment in India constitutes, as it were, a revolving queue: it is not that some are permanently employed and others are permanently unemployed, but rather that large numbers are made to wait years before finding a first job. The number of jobs is growing all the time and everyone will eventually find employment if they are prepared to wait long enough. The 'average waiting time' in 1967 for matriculates was just under a year and a half and, for graduates, just over six months. There are strong taboos in India about changing jobs to enhance one's prospects and this alone puts a premium on a lengthy search for work. In addition, however, searching for work can be a full-time occupation in a poorly organized labour market. Despite the rapid growth of labour exchanges around the country since 1950 and despite the increased use of newspapers as sources of information about vacancies, Indian labour markets still rely to this day to an extraordinary degree on personal contacts as a source of job offers, which again tends to lengthen the period of search. Lastly, the institution of the 'joint family', with its creed of pooling resources, reduces the incentive to cut down on the length of search: the unemployed Indian student can rely almost indefinitely on some support from his family.

When we put all these factors together, it is hardly surprising that the 'average waiting time' of the educated unemployed is much longer in India than it is in advanced countries even for school leavers. Nor is it surprising that, despite the incidence of unemployment, the supply of matriculates and graduates goes on growing faster than the demand for them; as we noted, additional education is a good investment for individuals even though they take from six to eighteen months to find employment. But it does raise the question whether it is also socially advantageous that people should continue their education in the face of so much unemployment. Surely, the implied waste of resources would be reduced if fewer educated people competed for the limited pool of jobs? To cut down on college places, however, would simply increase the number of unemployed matriculates; to cut down on secondary school places, would simply increase the number of unemployed primary school leavers, and so on. Is there no advantage in keeping people off the labour market as long as possible, particularly as the incidence of unemployment does seem to fall with every additional educational qualification after matriculation?

Unfortunately, resources are used up in producing more educated people, a social cost which is only partly borne by individuals themselves.[2]

2. This is what some authorities forget when they recommend that poor countries

Indian secondary and higher education is subsidized, inasmuch as fees are set below unit costs, and scholarship finance is made available to some students. Although four out of five arts and science colleges and two out of three secondary schools are private institutions, they receive substantial grants from state governments who are, in turn, supported by the central government. In fact, three quarters of total educational expenditure in India comes from government funds. Levels of subsidization fall below those in Great Britain but generally exceed those prevailing in the United States. Furthermore, the government recovers little of the extra earnings of the better educated by taxation; income tax in India is surprisingly light and begins to apply at levels of income that are only attained by graduates after the age of 30 or 35. The result, as we might expect, is that social rates of return on educational investment in India invariably fall below private rates. More to the point, however, is the fact that social rates of return to secondary and general higher education are considerably less than rates of return to primary and middle school education (see Table 1). This fact alone argues for a reallocation of educational expenditure towards primary education. Even if we drop the assumption of a given budget for education and compare the rates of return on education with the yield of other public investments, it is impossible to justify continued expansion of general higher education. The social opportunity cost rate of capital in India is estimated to be about 20 per cent; the social time preference rate appears to be about 5 per cent; since about half of total outlays on Indian education displace private investment, with the other half displacing private consumption, the 'composite social discount rate' for appraising investment in education is 12·5 per cent. While the argument leading to this conclusion is at best crude and ready-made, the resulting figure compares reasonably with the target rates of return of at least 11 to 12 per cent required of public sector enterprises in the Fourth Five Year Plan (1966–71) document. If this much is accepted, it follows that there is social underinvestment in primary and middle schooling and social overinvestment in secondary and general higher education (see Table 1 assuming $a = 0·65$ or $a = 0·5$).

Have we left anything out of the comparison? Social rates of return on educational investment ignore the consumption benefits and the externalities of education, but provided the magnitudes of these two effects are identical at all levels of education, our central finding is unaffected by these considerations. Although cogent arguments can be produced on both sides of this question, it is difficult to sustain the view in a largely illiterate country that higher education necessarily generates a greater sense of personal

'ought to produce more educated people than can be absorbed at current prices, because the alteration in current prices which this forces is a necessary part of the process of economic development'. See Lewis (1962, p. 38).

enrichment, as well as greater indirect benefits for the less educated, than primary education. Furthermore, the bulk of graduates are employed in the public sector which tends to disguise unemployment by overmanning, causing earnings to exceed the marginal private product of labour whereas the bulk of primary school leavers are employed in the private sector which is more likely to pay labour no more than its marginal private product. This means that even if primary school leavers and graduates generate identical spill-overs, we have, in fact, overestimated the social rate of return on college degrees. This doubles the force of our previous conclusion: higher education is badly overexpanded relative to primary education.

To be sure, education serves other ends than that of economic growth. The objectives of educational planning may include, apart from maximizing the contribution of education to the growth of national income, equality of educational opportunity, political stability and national solidarity. The social inequality that exists between an illiterate and someone with primary education, however, is much greater than the inequality between a matriculate and a graduate. If the goal were equity rather than efficiency, therefore, there is no doubt that too much of the educational budget has gone to the higher levels and too little to the lower levels of the educational system. Similarly, it is difficult to argue that political stability and the reduction of regional and religious strife in India would be better served by producing more unemployed matriculates and graduates than by increasing enrolment rates in primary education and thus producing more people with at least three or four years of schooling. In short, if equality, political stability and social cohesion in India can be secured by educational policies (which is doubtful) the optimum policy is once again to divert resources from secondary and higher education to primary education, middle schooling and perhaps adult literacy (see Myrdal, 1968, pp. 1669, 1817–18, which argues along these lines to reach identical conclusions).

It is interesting to contrast the results of rate-of-return analysis with those of manpower forecasting in India. The Indian Education Commission, which published its recommendations in 1966, made use of a manpower forecast based on the assumption of rate of growth of GNP of 6·5 per cent per annum over the years 1961–76, compared with 4·1 per cent actually realized over the decade 1951–61. It recommended that the *stock* of matriculates and graduates in employment should grow by 8 per cent per year, compared with a growth rate of slightly under 6 per cent a year experienced in the 1950s which, nevertheless, implied that the proportion of middle school leavers who went on to matriculation, as well as the proportion of matriculates who stayed on for a first degree, would have to be reduced below current levels. By way of contrast, rate-of-return calculations for 1961, had they been available to the commission, would have indicated reducing the rate of growth of the *stock* of higher educated manpower below 6 per cent with correspondingly sharper reductions in the rate of growth of the *flow* of matriculates and graduates.

The work of the Education Commission was nearly completed before the recession of 1965–8 set in but even at that stage it was doubtful whether any reasonable acceleration of the Indian growth rate could have outweighed the low observed rates of return on secondary and higher education. By 1969, however, these rates have fallen still further and by now even engineers are in oversupply. In other words, the events of the last few years have thrown into relief the folly of basing educational planning on forecasts of the manpower requirements of unrealistic targets for national income.

The case for cutting back the growth of secondary and higher education in India is overwhelming but the instruments for actually enforcing this policy are few. In Indian circumstances, it would be suicidal for a government to deny higher education to students who would have qualified for a degree if only they had been born earlier. However, there is more than one way to kill a goose. One possibility is gradually to raise the real values of fees in an effort to lower the private rate of return to secondary and higher education; another is for the public sector to adopt a policy of maximum rather than minimum educational qualifications for a job; still another is to select people for public service jobs before they go to college, making their appointment conditional on their getting a satisfactory degree; lastly, there are a number of curriculum changes that have been proposed by the Indian Education Commission, such as diversification of secondary courses, vocationally oriented education at post-primary level, and so on. Space does not allow discussion of the relative merits of these proposals. The fact is that no easy remedy is available: the causes of educated unemployment in India run deep in the functioning of Indian labour markets, the hiring practices of the government, and from there to the institution of the joint family and the attitudes of educated Indians. The basic thread, however, is the Malthusian-like tendency of higher education in India to grow faster than the ability to absorb graduates into employment. For a while, the progress of upgrading minimal hiring standards disguises the problem. By the time the labour market is saturated, however, the scramble of students for higher and higher qualifications has built up a pressure that few governments can resist. The process has probably gone further in India than anywhere else, but India is the mirror in which the rest of the underdeveloped world can see the problems they may well be facing in the decade of the 1970s.

The difficulties of eliminating educated unemployment in India are essentially those of taking policy decisions which run against the grain of private rate-of-return calculations. Whatever remedies are eventually adopted must take the form of altering the terms on which private decisions are made – or fail. This is merely one illustration of a general thesis: the private rate of return is no less a vital statistic for educational planning than the social rate of return. Indeed, educational planning in underdeveloped countries could be considerably improved merely by paying due attention to the economic benefits of education to the individual, even when private rates of return are not actually calculated.

References

BLAUG, M., LAYARD, P. R. G., and WOODHALL, H. (1969), *The Causes of Graduate Unemployment in India*, Allen Lane.

LEWIS, W. A. (1962), 'Priorities for educational expansion', OECD Policy Conference on Economic Growth and Investment in Education, vol. 2, *The Challenge of Aid to Newly Developing Countries*, OECD.

MYRDAL, G. (1968), *Asian Drama*, © Twentieth Century Fund, Penguin, 1968.

Part Five
Employment in Agriculture

Much of the economic literature on employment and unemployment has centred on the discussion of two related theoretical issues. Firstly, there has been the debate on whether zero marginal productivity of labour exists in traditional agriculture and following on from this, the extent to which labour can be withdrawn without this causing a fall in the level of agricultural output. Some of the differences of opinion stem from conceptual differences and confusions over the way such measurements should be made: in particular whether the condition of *ceteris paribus* is rigidly observed, or whether some degree of reorganization of agriculture and greater use of capital is assumed to take place. This debate is summarized in an article by Kao, Anschel and Eicher (1964), which has been excluded from the present volume only because of its ready availability elsewhere. The conclusion the authors reach, after an examination of the available empirical evidence, is that there is little reliable evidence to support the existence of more than a token 5 per cent disguised unemployment as defined by zero marginal product of labour and the condition of *ceteris paribus*.

The employment problems and poverty existing in the rural areas (as illustrated by Dandekar and Rath in Reading 10) are vastly more intricate and complex, and one might say are mis-specified by the above type of approach. Rural employment patterns need to be analysed with reference to the seasonal demand for labour and within the particular social and institutional context. Reading 19 by Hansen is taken as an example of a thorough empirical study estimating rural employment and wage levels in Egypt. When examining the actual employment situation, the survey makes clear that a distinction must be drawn between the employment patterns of men, women and children, and also that actual employment may include a much higher proportion of time spent on non-field work and non-agricultural work than was previously assumed. Readers are also referred to the important study by Sen (1966) on the nature of the Indian rural labour market.

In the literature on employment there has been a general neglect of the historical factors and of the evolution of the labour situation in traditional agriculture. Reading 20 is an extract from a book by Geertz, which traces the development over time of rural employment characteristics in Java. Geertz argues that the present highly labour-intensive agriculture based on wet-rice cultivation results from the fact that the growing population could only be absorbed within certain rural areas because plantation estates closed off access to parts of the agricultural lands and, more seriously, the export of the agricultural products in their unprocessed state to the colonial metropolis precluded the growth of non-agricultural branches of the economy. Peasant agriculture responded through a process of 'involution' in order to provide some form of employment for the rising population. Another important study is that by Arrighi (1970) which traces the impact of European colonisation and settlement on the African employment situation. Since only brief extracts of this study are included, the reader is strongly advised to refer to the detailed discussion in the book.

The policies suggested for the creation of more productive employment in agriculture are linked with the possibilities of reorganising agrarian structure through land reform (see for example Barraclough, 1970) and the possibilities of increasing the labour input as well as output per unit of land through changes in the types of inputs and methods used (see Ladjinsky, 1969, for a study on the impact of the 'Green Revolution'). Reading 21 by Pollitt illustrates the agricultural employment situation in Cuba – a country that has experienced a dramatic change in its whole institutional structure and its political economy. Cuban experience is in sharp contrast to that of other poor countries. Since the Revolution, a situation of marked underemployment of labour has been replaced by a situation of acute labour shortage. A major question posed by the Cuban experience is the following: how serious are the costs brought about by disruption during the critical changeover period from a capitalist to a socialist system and how can a country overcome these problems while continuing to work towards socialist goals including that of full and productive employment?

References

ARRIGHI, G. (1970), 'Labour supplies in historical perspective; a study of the proletarianization of the African peasantry in Rhodesia', *J. Devel. Stud.*, vol. 6. no. 3.

BARRACLOUGH, S. (1970), 'Alternate land tenure systems resulting from agrarian reform in Latin America', *Land Econ.*, vol. 46, no. 3, pp. 215–228.

KAO, C. H. C., ANSCHEL, K. R., and EICHER, C. K. (1964), 'Disguised unemployment in agriculture: a survey', in C. K. Eicher and L. Witt (eds.), *Agriculture in Economic Development*, McGraw-Hill.

LADJINSKY, W. (1969), 'The Green Revolution in Punjab: a Field Trip', *Economic and Political Weekly*, Bombay, June.

SEN, A. (1966), 'Peasants and dualism with or without surplus labour', *Journal of Political Economy*, October.

19 Bent Hansen

Employment and Wages in Rural Egypt

Extract from B. Hansen, 'Employment and wages in rural Egypt', *American Economic Review*, vol. 59, no. 3 (1969), pp. 298–313.

Egypt often appears as a classical example of overpopulation and surplus labor in development literature. Government planning has been based on the assumption that agricultural surplus labor amounts to about 25 per cent of the labor force. Yet, among those who have studied rural employment conditions in Egypt more concretely, doubts have been expressed for a long time about the realism of such assumptions, and some evidence has been presented against the hypothesis of surplus labor and zero marginal productivity of labor in agriculture. [. . .]

In 1963, the International Labor Organization (ILO), and the Institute of National Planning, Cairo, (INP), decided to undertake a joint, large-scale, rural employment survey. Its main purpose was to collect detailed and complete labor records from a sample of households during a full year. The survey took place from March 1964 to February 1965, with a supplementary interview survey made during a week in January of 1965. The results are now available in a series of mimeographed reports (INP, 1965).[1]

The rural employment survey

After some pilot studies, it was decided to work with a sample of 480 households selected from forty-eight villages in six Governerates (*mudeyerat*). The villages were selected in pairs from four districts (*markazat*) of each Governerate: a big village and a neighbouring small village. Of the ten households selected from each village, two were non-agricultural. The eight agricultural households were to be selected so as to represent eight strata with respect to household size and size of farm. Three working members became the line of demarcation between small and big households. Agricultural households were divided into four groups: landless, i.e. with less than one half feddan,[2] and farms with one half to two feddan, two to five feddan, and five feddan and more. It was decided to use rotating samples so

1. These have now been brought together in a research paper published by the ILO (1969).
2. One feddan is slightly more than one acre.

that a household was only interviewed once per four days concerning the last two days' labor; an eight-day period was chosen, therefore, as the basic unit period of tabulation. The interviewers were mainly village teachers whom the villagers might be supposed to trust and who had a good first-hand knowledge of the households and their situations. The questionnaires recorded all operations (outside household work proper) lasting more than half an hour. Household work proper was not recorded. The exclusion of small jobs implies a downward bias in the work time recorded. Another downward bias (important in particular for women and children) is related to the fact that temporary workers have not always been included.

All persons covered by the survey were classified as *men* (adult males fifteen years and above), *women* (adult females fifteen years and above), and *children* (males and females, six to fifteen). All persons six years and above were considered working members of the household where they appeared unless they were obviously incapable of doing work for reasons of health, old age, etc. or had not been recorded at all as working outside the household proper. In the sample, 72 per cent of all males and 45 per cent of all females were recorded as 'working'. For males, the participation ratio of the sample is somewhat higher than that of the population census of 1960; for females it is much higher.

Although great efforts were exerted to obtain a representative sample, the results cannot be inflated to national totals. All averages presented in the following are, therefore, simple sample means, but for the six (out of a total of eighteen) Governerates chosen, the sample is presumably representative. [. . .]

The period of the study was characterized by inflationary conditions in the country. Excess demand prevailed and the official cost of living index increased by 15 per cent during this period. This should presumably tend to imply good employment opportunities. Government expenditures expanded strongly and both defence and public works (such as the High Dam at Aswan) must have absorbed manpower from rural districts. It is difficult to gauge how much this has contributed to an increase in rural employment and the absorption of rural labor. [. . .]

The labor records: annual data

A striking and unexpected feature of the labor records is the large number of hours worked per year by all categories of rural labor. Table 1 shows the annual average number of working hours recorded for men, women, and children in three broad types of households, namely farmers (that is, cultivators, whether owners or tenants), farm laborers, and others, as well as the distribution of annual hours worked on various types of work.

For men, the annual number of hours worked is, on average, close to what

Table 1 **Average annual working hours according to sex-age groups, types of households, and types of work**

| | | | *Percent of annual work time spent on:* | | | | |
Type of household	Sex-age group	Number of hours worked annually	Field work	Animal husbandry	Processing farm products	Other agricultural work	Non-agricultural work
Farmers	Men	2280	53	21	3	13	10
	Women	869	19	63	11	3	4
	Children	1022	49	39	3	5	4
	Total	1642	48	30	4	10	8
Farm-laborers	Men	2324	58	13	3	11	15
	Women	904	31	35	4	8	22
	Children	1374	55	23	2	7	13
	Total	1716	53	18	3	10	16
Others (nonagri-cultural)	Men	2482	8	4	3	3	82
	Women	697	14	29	6	2	49
	Children	1087	25	26	2	1	46
	Total	1738	11	10	3	2	74

corresponds to a normal eight-hour day, namely 2280 to 2482 hours per year. Men from other households, i.e. service workers such as barbers and shopkeepers, seem to work longer hours than both farmers and farm laborers. It is difficult to say to what extent recorded work for these men really represents work proper; idle hours in the shop waiting for customers have been recorded as work. For this group, therefore, the figures for hours worked should be taken with a grain of salt. Women seem to work one third of an eight-hour day, and children about half that time. Women and children belonging to farm laborer households work longer than women and children in the other categories.

In the earlier attempts to estimate labor requirements (Hansen and El Tomy, 1965; Moheieddin, 1966), the authors agree that the requirements for plant production or field work correspond only to about 60 per cent of full-time work (three hundred days). Table 1 points to almost full employment for men. The distribution in Table 1 of hours worked by type of work solves this problem. For men in farm households, field work occupied only 53 per cent of the total work time. Of the time spent on agricultural work, 41 per cent went to animal husbandry, processing of agricultural products, and other agricultural work. Therefore, the findings here seem to be consistent with the earlier labor requirement estimates. These earlier estimates went wrong because it was not understood what a modest part field work is of total agricultural work. For women and children, the comparison is more difficult, although the Rural Employment Survey and the earlier labor requirement estimates seem to be fully consistent.

Another remarkable feature of Table 1 is that men in farm households work about 10 per cent in nonagricultural work, that is, as hired labor outside agriculture. This shows that a substantial amount of work must have been done outside the farmer's own enterprise. We shall look at this point in somewhat more detail in Table 2, because it contains crucial evidence against the notion of zero marginal productivity of labor in Egyptian agriculture.

Table 2 **Agricultural households: hours worked annually, totally and outside own farm, by size of farm, and family, and age-sex groups**

Strata		Men		Women		Children	
Size of farm	Number of working family members	Hours worked per year	Per cent of which outside own farm	Hours worked per year	Per cent of which outside own farm	Hours worked per year	Per cent of which outside own farm
½ to 2 feddan	3 and less	2384	18	906	4	1070	14
2 to 5 feddan	3 and less	2420	4	1112	5	1096	9
≥ 5 feddan	3 and less	2062	3	834	6	1702	2
½ to 2 feddan	more than 3	2190	33	1010	9	1122	34
2 to 5 feddan	more than 3	2230	14	794	2	1020	14
≥ 5 feddan	more than 3	2358	5	734	1	848	11
landless*	3 and less	2444	69	838	35	1374	80
landless	more than 3	2208	73	948	30	1374	65

* With less than ½ feddan or no land at all.

Note: the percentages for work outside own farm are calculated on family members with at least 30 days recorded work.

The number of working hours for men is of the same order of magnitude in all the agricultural strata. On farms it varies between 2062 (but see below) and 2420 hours per year. There is no clear dependency upon farm size or family size. Nor is there any *a priori* reason to expect any particular relationship between hours worked per year and farm and family size. On a larger farm there may be more work to do, but, on the other hand, income is higher and the owner can afford to rely on hired labor to a larger extent. With a larger family, the need for income is higher, but so is the number of children who can work. It should be expected that women work less outside the household when the income is higher and the family is larger. There is, perhaps, such a tendency in the table, but it is by no means clear. For children, similar remarks apply, although the picture is disturbed by the very high figure for hours worked by children in big families with big farms.[3]

Concerning the time worked outside the own farm, the picture is very clear. The members of the smallest farms work a substantial part of their time outside the own farm. For men the percentages are 18 and 33, respectively, in small and big families. For children the percentages are of the same order of magnitude. For women they are much smaller, 4 and 9 per cent, respectively; this could be expected on the basis of the attitudes toward women's work. Small farmers' households thus rely heavily on income from outside. Farmers, by and large, are fully occupied, taking into account the work outside their own farms. Moreover, the work outside shows a seasonal pattern similar to that of the farms' labor input. It seems clear, therefore, that farmers have a real choice between taking paid labor outside the farm or working on the farm. Under these circumstances, there is little reason to believe that the value of the marginal product of labor, even on the smallest farms, would be smaller than current rural wages.[4]

Work outside the own farm declines rapidly with increasing size of farm, as expected. Yet the households on smaller farms (two to five feddan), especially those farmers with large families, do substantial amounts of work outside their own farm. For the landless farm laborer households, the majority of work is, of course, done outside the own farm. However, this group may have up to one half feddan, and we still find a considerable amount of work done on their own farm. The argument about the marginal product of labor obviously applies to this group too.

For all men in farm households, 14·2 per cent of the work done was outside their own farm. Moreover Table 1 shows 10 per cent of the work was nonagricultural, so that about two thirds of the work outside the own farm is nonagricultural, including canal work for the government.

So far we have dealt exclusively with the labor performed by various types of households, that is, the output of labor by households, while nothing has been said about the input of labor on farms of various sizes. In order to arrive at the input for a certain farm, we have to deduct the household members' work outside the farm and add nonhousehold members' work

3. I have not been able to find the definite explanation of this high figure. Hours per year, per person, are calculated by dividing the tabulated total hours worked by number of individuals. However, the number of children in this group is remarkably low as compared with the number of men. I suspect, therefore, a classification mistake, where some children may have been classified as men. Indeed, the number of hours worked for men in this group is remarkably low.

4. Two major forms of unpaid labor outside the own farm exist – *el mosharka*, where the peasants share work, and *el zamala*, where an exchange of labor takes place. Neither form is so important, however, that it can upset the argument of the text. For agricultural households, paid labor amounted to 96 per cent of all labor outside own farms.

Table 3 **Work by nonfamily members as per cent of total labor input on farms, by farm size, family size, and sex-age groups**

Strata		Men		Women		Children	
Size of farm	Number of working family members	Permanent nonfamily	Permanent nonfamily plus all temporary	Permanent nonfamily	Permanent nonfamily plus all temporary	Permanent nonfamily	Permanent nonfamily plus all temporary
½ to 2 feddan	3 and less		7·3		9·4		26·2
2 to 5 feddan	3 and less	6·1	21·7		16·3		33·5
≥ 5 feddan	3 and less	19·3	52·9		41·1	15·4	77·8
½ to 2 feddan	more than 3		6·2		2·0		4·6
2 to 5 feddan	more than 3	2·1	10·9		13·6		16·2
≥ 5 feddan	more than 3	7·9	28·2		23·1	2·2	43·1

(permanent or temporary) on the farm. Table 3 illuminates to what extent farms of different sizes depend on labor from nonfamily members. The distinction in this table between permanent and temporary workers is based on the number of work days which has been recorded for an individual at a given farm. If more than thirty days have been recorded, the worker is considered permanent; otherwise he is temporary. Unfortunately, no breakdown of the temporary workers into family members and nonfamily members is available. The second column for men, women and children includes, therefore, some work by family members. Now, it is clear that the probability that a man belonging to the family should be recorded for less than thirty days' work during a year is very small indeed. For men, the second column must, by and large, consist of nonfamily labor. For women, the same will probably tend to be true. But for children, the chance is larger that the family's own children may have been recorded for less than thirty days work and thus appear as temporary. However, also for children, nonfamily members must dominate among the temporary workers. From the table it is seen that the percentage of child work performed by temporary workers is much larger for small families than for big families. If the family's own children dominated the temporary child work, the picture should be the opposite.

As one could expect, the use of hired labor is smaller on farms with big families than on farms with small families. Down to two feddan, farms rely heavily on hired labor and even from the very smallest farms of one half to two feddan, there is a certain demand for hired labor. This has a bearing upon the findings of Moheieddin (1966), namely, a tendency for larger farms (above ten feddan) to be concentrated in certain regions. Moheieddin (1966) and Mabro (1967) argue that for this reason household members from the small farms would not get in contact with labor demand where it actually exists. Labor demand seems to exist everywhere, even if there are no farms above ten feddan.

The percentage of total labor input performed by nonfamily members seems to be particularly high for children's work, and very high, indeed, for farms with small families. Women and children are hired mainly for cotton picking, weeding, and similar work, and to judge from the seasonal data, a typical pattern of small-farm behavior is to hire women and children for this kind of work at the same time as the men of the farm take hired labor outside the farm. The reason for this is obvious: a man can usually earn more outside the farm than he has to pay women and children for work which they can do as well or better than he can.

Finally, a distribution by regions is of interest because Upper Egypt should, *a priori*, be expected to offer fewer employment opportunities than the Delta. Substantial areas in Upper Egypt were still basin irrigated in

1964–5, with only one crop per year. Table 4 shows the average annual hours of work by Governerates and sex-age groups.

Table 4 **Average annual work time per working person by regions and sex-age groups** (hours per year)

Governerate	Men	Women	Children
Delta			
Beheira	2579	1134	1616
Gharbiya	2042	884	889
Menufiya	2531	1391	1462
Upper Egypt			
Assiout	2141	562	698
Quenna	2244	755	1180
Fayoum	2330	459	1064

The table confirms Mead's result (1967) that employment is at a lower level in Upper Egypt than in the Delta. He argued that at least in Upper Egypt there was heavy underemployment. But the lower employment in Upper Egypt is concentrated mainly among women and children. Taking simple averages of the Governerate averages for the two areas, the annual number of working hours for men in the Delta is slightly below 2400 hours, while for Upper Egypt the corresponding figure is slightly below 2250 hours. The difference is only about 6 per cent. Women however, work much less in Upper Egypt than in the Delta, slightly below 500 hours as against almost 1150 hours. For children the difference is also substantial, slightly below 1000 hours as against almost 1325 hours. Thus, it would seem that woman and child labor serves as a buffer, with the men working about full time and the women and children doing what has to be done beyond that. The low figures for women in Upper Egypt may also be related to the much more conservative attitudes and traditions in that area with respect to women's activities,[5] although it is difficult to say here what is cause and effect. Attitudes and traditions have a wonderful ability to adjust themselves to the necessities of life. Similar attitude differences do not exist for child labor. We should also point to the much hotter climate of Upper Egypt which may necessitate shorter working hours than in the Delta.

5. These attitudes should probably show themselves also in lower participation ratios for women in Upper Egypt. It is not possible from the published data to see whether this really was the case.

The labor records: seasonal fluctuations

The seasonal employment pattern revealed by the labor records confirms, by and large, the earlier labor requirement estimates in so far as there seem to be two clearly distinguishable seasonal peaks for agricultural households; one in May–June and one in September. The first peak is related to the wheat and maize harvest; the second to the cotton harvest. The slack season occurs from the middle of October to the middle of February. The difference between seasonal peaks and troughs is much smaller, however, than that found in the labor requirement studies. The reason is that types of work not included in the labor requirement studies either have little seasonality (animal husbandry) or may be counterseasonal (canal work). For adult male farmers and family farmhands the peak is around 1 June, with slightly above fifty-seven hours work per eight-day period; while during the slack period, average work time for this category remains above forty hours (disregarding January which that year coincided with the fasting month, Ramadan, and where work time drops further to 36 hours). For farm laborers, the seasonal spread is almost the same, from sixty-one hours per eight-day period in mid-September to around forty-four hours (thirty-seven during the Ramadan). The seasonality of craftsmen labor is quite similar to that of farmers and farmhands, while salespeople have quite a different seasonal pattern with work time increasing from May to September–October and thereafter falling sharply. This may be related to the pattern of cash earnings in agriculture, but may also simply reflect the fact that during the hot seasons, sales take place, to a larger extent, during the cooler nights. For men, women, and children, the seasonal employment pattern appears in Figures 1, 2, and 3. Hours worked by women and children have somewhat stronger seasonal fluctuations than men. Finally, there does not seem to be any systematic difference between the seasonal fluctuations in the Delta and Upper Egypt. Everywhere men have long working hours during the busy seasons and are, at least during these seasons, fully employed.

Unemployment

In the theoretical sense of people willing to work at going market wages, supply of labor could not be measured directly. Hypothetical questions of this type do not make sense to illiterate villagers. The true supply of labor is not measured by the labor record of working persons nor by actual employment. An attempt to measure involuntary unemployment directly was carried out in the larger interview survey. This survey was undertaken in January and thus should tend to show the maximum seasonal unemployment. To judge from this survey, unemployment proper seems to have been about 8–9 per cent of the 'labor force' at the seasonal trough.[6] Since this

6. This result is a little higher than the unemployment percentages found in rural districts by the labor force surveys of the Ministry of Labor.

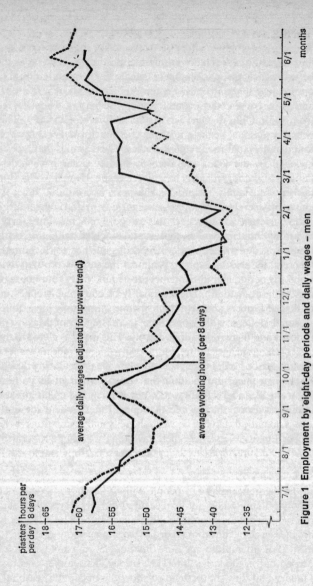

Figure 1 Employment by eight-day periods and daily wages – men

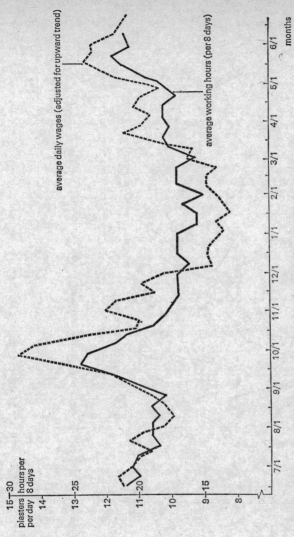

Figure 2 Employment by eight-day periods and daily wages – women

average daily wages (adjusted for upward trend)

average working hours (per 8 days)

piasters hours per
per day 8 days

15—30
14
13—25
12
11—20
10
9—15
8

7/1 8/1 9/1 10/1 11/1 12/1 1/1 2/1 3/1 4/1 5/1 6/1

months

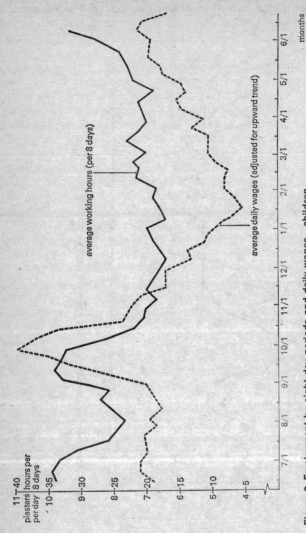

Figure 3 Employment by eight-day periods and daily wages – children

particular survey did not consider part-time employment, unemployment may have been somewhat higher.

Rural wages

Information about rural wages was collected together with the labor records. The laborers and the employers were not directly asked about wages received or paid. Rightly or wrongly, this was thought to be a delicate question which might call forth negative reactions. The village *sheikh* or *oumda* was asked weekly how much was paid per day to men, women and children for various kinds of work. The wage records were not complete. From some villages, information is missing entirely. For other villages information is missing for the slack season where, during certain weeks, there may have been no wages to record. In such cases it is somewhat difficult to talk about an annual average. This problem appears mainly for women and children whose hours have the strongest seasonality. Given these shortcomings, the wage statistics collected throw an interesting light on wage formation and behavior in rural areas. In particular they contradict the notion of subsistence or institutional wages.

If rural wages were strongly influenced by a subsistence level which acted as a floor for actual market wages, we should expect the distribution of villages with respect to average wages to be truncated and squeezed up against the subsistence minimum, as illustrated in Figure 4.

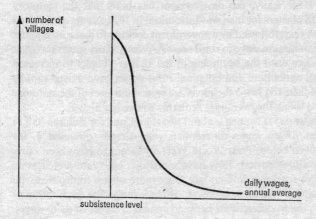

Figure 4

The distribution actually found looks fairly normal for men, women and children as shown in Table 5. The figures for all villages (with records) may be biased for women and children due to incomplete records (see below). The right-hand part of the table therefore shows the distribution for the smaller number of villages with satisfactory records (fifty weeks and more); these figures, however, may be biased in another way since they contain no villages from Upper Egypt, apart from Fayoum. The only sign of concentration at the lower end of the distributions are for men, where we find six villages at ten piasters per day.[7] These six villages are all situated in Fayoum, a kind of oasis separated from the Nile Valley by some ten miles of desert. Should this represent a subsistence level, the implication would be that the whole Nile Valley proper is substantially above the subsistence level, and that for the valley itself we have to look for other explanations of rural wages. It may be pointed out also that during the slack season daily wages in Fayoum are considerably below the average of 10 piasters.

Table 5, in addition, gives information about the average daily wages by Governerate and for all villages included in the sample. There are substantial differences between Governerates, with Menoufia (near Cairo) at the top, and Fayoum at the bottom. The average for all villages is 18·0 piasters for men, and an institutionalist might point out that this is exactly the statutory minimum wage for male rural workers. However, the distribution in the upper and lower parts of the table shows that this is a lucky statistical coincidence. Historically, the development has been that the statutory minimum of 18 piasters for men was introduced in 1952 as part of the Land Reform of that year, followed by a government decision to make no attempt to enforce the minimum wage in rural areas.[8] Average daily wages stayed at about 12 piasters until the beginning of the sixties. Thanks to increased productivity in agriculture and inflation, rural wages have moved rapidly upwards since then. In 1964–5 their average passed the level of the statutory minimum, and today the average is probably somewhat higher.

The average wage for women is about two thirds, and for children half of that paid men. These wages differentials were already observed in the thirties (and even before First World War) and seem to have been fairly constant over a long period. They have sometimes been interpreted as an institutional law for wage differentials. Once more we are confronted with deceptive statistical averages, however. Table 6 shows the distribution of villages according to differentials between annual averages of daily wages.

7. According to the official exchange rate, one piaster is equal to 2·25 US cents.

8. The minimum wages have, in principle, been applied by the government itself in rural areas. But it is difficult to say how this has worked in practice when contractors have been in charge of the works.

Table 5 **Distribution of villages by sex-age groups and size of daily wages** (annual averages)

| Piasters per day | Number of villages with annual average of daily wages | | | | | |
| | All villages with records | | | Villages with records for 50 weeks and over | | |
	Men	Women	Children	Men	Women	Children
4– 5·9		3	8			4
6– 7·9		4	4			2
8– 9·9		4	16		4	6
10–11·9	6	8	13	6	6	7
12–13·9	1	6	5	1	3	
14–15·9	4	10		2	2	
16–17·9	12	3		7	1	
18–19·9	11			7		
20–21·9	8			5		
22–23·9	3			2		
24–25·9	2			1		
26–27·9	1					
Total number of villages	48	38	46	31	16	19

Governerate	Piasters per day					
Beheira	18·5	12·5	10·0	18·3	11·8	9·2
Gharbiya	18·7	11·6	9·6	18·8	11·5	9·6
Menufiya	21·4	13·0	10·0	21·0	12·8	10·0
Assiout	17·6	11·7	9·8	17·6	10·6	
Quenna	20·4	11·9	9·0	19·8		
Fayoum	11·7	6·1	5·1	11·7		4·9
Total village average	18·0	11·7	8·7	17·3	11·9	8·6

The wage differentials vary widely between villages. For women the wages vary between 45–50 and 85–90 per cent of men's wages, and for children the variation is greater. Even if we move to the figures of the right-hand half of the table, the variation remains large. It should be added that the variations of the differentials are also sizable within Governerates. The proportions of two thirds and one half for women's and children's wages thus seem to be statistical averages without any deeper meaning.

Table 6 **Distribution of villages according to wage differentials for women and children**

| | Number of villages | | | |
| | All villages with records | | Villages with records for 50 weeks and over | |
Per cent of men's wages	Women	Children	Women	Children
35–40		1		
40–45		8		3
45–50	1	15		8
50–55	2	7		2
55–60	11	6	3	3
60–65	6	6	3	1
65–70	7	2	4	
70–75	3			
75–80	5		2	
80–85	2	1	1	
85–90	1			
Total number of villages	38	46	13	17

Table 7 shows that stable, institutional, wage differentials do not exist even within the individual villages. It shows the distribution of all weeks with wage records, according to wage differentials, for women and children, for three selected typical villages with large, medium and small variations in the differentials within the year. In Kilishan, women's and children's wages are equal to men's at the peak demand for woman and child labor (the cotton harvest), but drop to 30–39 and 20–29 per cent of men's wages in the slack season. Even the village with the most stable differentials, El Nigila, has appreciable variation during the year. There is no doubt that the variation of the differentials is related to the seasonal fluctuations of the demand for various types of labor [. . .].

With some reservations, Figures 1, 2, and 3 point to a close association between the employment and the wage series for men, women and children. If one identifies employment with demand for labor, and assumes that, from a seasonal point of view, wage and employment fluctuations are the result of a shifting demand curve and a fixed supply curve, the graphs then clearly support the hypothesis of demand and supply determined wages. The seasonal fluctuations of the daily wages are very strong. The highest daily wage

Table 7 **Distribution of weekly records according to wage differentials for women and children in three selected villages**

| Per cent of men's wages | Number of weekly records | | | | | |
| | Kilishan | | El Haddad | | El Nigila | |
	Women	Children	Women	Children	Women	Children
20– 29·9		2				
30– 39·9	4	9				
40– 49·9	11	9	4	4		29
50– 59·9	15	20	9	17		13
60– 69·9	6	6	25	17	38	10
70– 79·9	7		5	5	12	
80– 89·9	3	2				
90– 99·9					2	
100–109·9	5	5	6	6		
Total number of weekly records	51	53	49	49	52	52
Average per cent	58	49	63	61	67	48

is about 50 per cent above the lowest for men; the corresponding figures are about 100 and 175 per cent, for women and children, respectively.

The adjustments of the wage series of Figures 1, 2, and 3 for inflation were made by comparing wage averages for two corresponding two-week periods in mid-June in 1964 and 1965, and a linear inflationary increase during the year was then assumed. Another method of adjusting for the inflationary increase is to regress wages on employment and time. Here we meet the obstacle that the wage series contained fifty-two observations of weekly averages, whereas the employment series contained forty-six observations of average hours worked per eight-day period. We preferred to interpolate on the employment series (since this was the smoothest one) to obtain fifty-two observations for seven-day periods. The results were

Men $\quad W_t = \quad 5·630 + 0·219\, H_t + 0·073\, T, R = 0·88$
$\qquad\qquad\qquad (0·023) \qquad (0·008)$

Women $\quad W_t = -1·269 + 0·721\, H + 0·052\, T, R = 0·88$
$\qquad\qquad\qquad (0·058) \qquad (0·007)$

Children $\quad W_t = \quad 3·431 + 0·173\, H_t + 0·060\, T, R = 0·61$
$\qquad\qquad\qquad (0·040) \qquad (0·013)$

where W denotes average daily wages, H average number of hours worked and T (running from 0 to 52) is time. All coefficients are highly significant, and the trend corresponds to an increase of money wages by about 30 per cent during the year, which is about the same found by the simpler method underlying Figures 1, 2, and 3. The correlation coefficients for children are somewhat lower than for men and women. Examination of Figure 3 shows a lag between employment and wages. This lag is most certainly related to difference of coverage of the wage and employment series mentioned above, the wage series for children covering the Delta and Fayoum only, whereas the employment series also covers the rest of Upper Egypt. Children's employment is closely related to the cotton crop, and all major operations related to cotton are done some weeks earlier in Upper Egypt than in the Delta. We should, for that reason, expect a lag of some few weeks between our wage and employment series for children. [. . .]

Conclusions

In order to discuss rural employment in Egypt, and presumably in many other underdeveloped countries, a clear distinction has to be made between adult males, adult females and children. The level of employment for these three categories and the functions they perform differ widely. Moreover, the social and developmental implications of men's, women's and children's work are radically different.

The Rural Employment Survey of the ILO and INP, Cairo, shows, first that the level of employment in rural areas is *much* higher than had earlier been thought. By ignoring nonfield work and nonagricultural work, earlier labor requirement calculations systematically and grossly underestimated actual employment.

Male adults seem, by and large, to be fully employed with long working hours during spring and summer, and with some underemployment from October to February. The seasonal variations appear to be much smaller than those shown by earlier labor requirement calculations. There does not seem to be any great difference in the level of employment for male adults in the various sample strata and regions. The differences in the employment possibilities have consequences mainly for the employment of women and children. Small farmers are brought to a high level of employment by the substantial opportunities for obtaining employment outside their own farm, on other farms, and outside agriculture.

Female adults seem, on the average, to work one third of the time outside the household farm. Taking into account household work in a rather mechanical and arbitrary way, it appears that female adults in rural areas are slightly underemployed. The differences between sample strata and regions are much larger than for male adults. Female work outside the household is particularly low in Upper Egypt (south of Cairo). This may be due to lack of employment but may well reflect more conservative traditions. Female adults on small farms and in landless laborer families in the Delta more often than not are heavily overemployed (including household work), whereas on bigger farms and in Upper Egypt they seem to be able to live a more leisurely life.

Children of both sexes between six and fifteen work, on the average, slightly more than women outside the households. The variations between strata and regions are somewhat smaller for children than women; but Upper Egypt seems also to offer (or require) less employment for children than the Delta.

Wages generally appear to be highly flexible and react strongly and rapidly to changes in demand. There are large differences between villages and regions as well as between seasons, and for various types of work. Wage differentials reflect differences between demand and supply, and there is nothing to indicate that the wage level should be governed by a subsistence minimum, or by institutional factors.

The Rural Employment Survey pictures an active labor market in which even very small farms participate, both on the demand and the supply side. The farm household members take paid work outside their own farm (on other farms or outside agriculture) and hire laborers for the farm, sometimes simultaneously. The two phenomena can be correlated to the size of the farm, the former negatively and the latter positively. This active, pervasive labor market, which seems to exist everywhere, is difficult to reconcile with the idea of surplus labor as a general phenomenon with zero productivity of labor.

No information is available on the supply of labor (in the sense of labor offered at the current wages), but with the employment actually enjoyed by men it is inconceivable that men should want to work substantially more than they do at current wages during the busy half of the year. Apart from seasonalities, the only feature of rural employment which points in the direction of some elasticity of supply of labor is the employment of women and children which apparently adapts itself to employment opportunities. The fact that both women and children, particularly the former, do more outside work in the Delta than in Upper Egypt might be considered a proof of underemployment in Upper Egypt. There is a discernible tendency for woman and child wages to be relatively low in Upper Egypt, and this might suffice to establish an equilibrium at a lower level of employment. More likely, however, it is the conservative traditions of the South with respect to woman labor which is the decisive factor: it keeps the supply of woman labor down and thus prevents woman wages from being particularly low in spite of a relatively weak demand for such labor.[9] We are involved here in the tricky problem of woman and child supply of labor from family units where the men are already employed. Theory has little to tell us about this, and there have been few empirical studies of labor supply at very low income levels. But it is tempting to see here a (long-term) mechanism similar to the well known (short-term) adaptation of labor supply to labor demand in the United States and other developed countries.

We meet here an elasticity of labor supply very different from the unlimited supplies of labor which Lewis and others had in mind. The policy implications are radically different. Whatever the relationship between supply proper and actual employment of women and children, there can be no doubt that when we turn to social norms and development possibilities, the women and children do not represent a reserve of labor available for industrialization. Children between six and fifteen who are employed between one third and one half their time are certainly *overemployed* by any reasonable, modern, social standard. Thinking in terms of development programs, child labor is simply an obstacle which has to be abolished. A sensible development program must presumably include efforts to have children attend school regularly, and this must imply a reduction of child labor in agriculture and elsewhere. In the sample of the Rural Employment Survey, children worked about 15 per cent of the total number of hours worked; women account for another 15 per cent. If the child labor in Egyptian agriculture had to be done by the women, they would in all probabilities become heavily employed; whether this would also imply 'overemployment' in relation to 'supply' or to social standards is more difficult to say. Some child labor is naturally compatible with good educational programs (e.g. holidays), but satisfactory education for the village children would presumably, on balance and *ceteris paribus*, imply an increased demand for adult hired labor in agriculture.

9. All this may be history now. The increase in perennial irrigation in Upper Egypt which will become one of the major benefits from the High Dam at Aswan will also increase the demand for labor. Conditions of agricultural production are changing and should become, before the end of this decade, quite similar to those in the Delta. It will be interesting to see if traditions will give way with respect to woman labor as they did in the Delta, when employment and income possibilities there increased many decades ago.

References

HANSEN, B., and EL TOMY, M. (1965), 'The seasonal employment profile in Egyptian agriculture', *J. Devel. Stud.*, vol. 1, pp. 399–409.

ILO (1969), *Rural Employment Problems in the United Arab Republic*, Employment Research Papers.

INP (1965), *Employment Problems in Rural Areas*, Statistical Tables, the labour record sample survey, parts 1 and 2, Cairo.

MABRO, R. (1967), 'Industrial growth, agricultural underemployment and the Lewis model. The Egyptian case, 1937–65', *J. Devel. Stud.*, vol. 3, pp. 322–51.

MEAD, D. (1967), *Growth and Structural Change in the Egyptian Economy*, Irwin.

MOHEIEDDIN, A. (1966), *Agricultural Investment and Employment in Egypt since 1935*, unpublished Ph.D. thesis, London University.

20 C. Geertz

Agricultural Involution: the Processes of Ecological Change in Indonesia

Extract from C. Geertz, *Agricultural Involution: the Processes of Ecological Change in Indonesia* (1968), University of California Press, for the Association of Asian Studies.

At the inception of the colonial period, the overall ecological pattern was fairly well set: on Java, a wet-rice agrarian heartland [the sawah ecosystem] shading off into less developed regions to the west, east, and north; in the Outer Islands, an immense tropical forest worked only here and there by small tribes of swidden farmers. The first object of interest of the Dutch, as of the Portuguese who immediately preceded them, were the Moluccas, the fabled spice islands; but their attention soon turned toward Java, and it is upon it that they mainly superimposed their colonial economy, turning back again to the Outer Islands only toward the end of the past century.

'Superimposed' is the proper word, because what the Dutch were essentially concerned to do, from 1619 to 1942, was to pry agricultural products out of the archipelago, and particularly out of Java, which were saleable on world markets without changing fundamentally the structure of the indigenous economy. The Netherlands was never able, particularly after William I's attempt to reabsorb Belgium failed, to develop a manufacture export economy even remotely comparable to that of Britain, and so the interest of the Dutch in Indonesia remained overwhelmingly mercantilist to the end. The stimulation in Indonesia of extensive markets for industrial goods, it was feared, would lead only to increased British (or, later, Japanese) influence; the essential economic task was to maintain a decent differential between the import and re-export prices of East Indian agricultural products – a task which implied the developing of Dutch commercial institutions and the discouraging of Indonesian ones. Amid the apparent fluctuations of policy, the colonial period consists, from the economic point of view, of one long attempt to bring Indonesia's crops into the modern world, but not her people.

The means for accomplishing this effort to keep the natives native and yet get them to produce for world markets was the formation of a chronically, and in fact intrinsically, unbalanced economic structure sometimes referred to as 'dual'. In the export sector, there was administrative capitalism: a system in which the holders of capital, the Dutch, regulated selling prices and wages, controlled output, and even dictated the processes of production. In the domestic sector there was family-unit agriculture, a little home industry, and some petty internal trade. As the first expanded, stimulated by rising world commodity prices, the second contracted; land and labor were taken out of rice and other village staples and put into sugar, indigo, coffee, tobacco and other commercial crops. As the first contracted, responding to collapsing international markets, the second expanded; and a steadily growing peasant population attempted to compensate for a lost money income, to which it had become increasingly accustomed, by intensified production of subsistence crops. [. . .]

The inability of Dutch private enterprise to provide the capital necessary to exploit Java efficiently was one of the main motivating forces for the institution of the Culture System[1] in the first place. From 1816 (when the English interregnum ended) to 1830 (when van den Bosch, plan in hand, arrived in Java), the Dutch in Indonesia faced a situation similar to that faced by some newly independent nations today. A once effective mechanism for producing foreign exchange – the Dutch East India Company – had become exhausted and discredited, and had disappeared, leaving behind it an intense theoretical controversy over how to increase the island's profitability. Land and labor were available enough, but capital was in short supply, which hampered rapid expansion of private enterprise (at least by the Dutch) of the sort desired by the Liberal opponents of van den Bosch. Looked at against this background, the Culture System appears to represent the kind of government mobilization of 'redundant' labor for capital creation projects which has been often proposed and occasionally attempted in underdeveloped areas. Within the framework of the labor-tax system, itself cast in the mold of the traditional corvee powers of the indigenous aristocracy, the government built roads and bridges, expanded irrigation facilities, cleared and improved large tracts of 'waste' land, constructed buildings, and generally substituted the labor of the Javanese for the capital Holland lacked in laying the preparative foundations of a very rapidly accelerating, if distorted, process of economic growth. [. . .]

From the developmental point of view, the Culture System represented an attempt to raise an estate economy by a peasantry's bootstraps; and in this it was remarkably successful. Benefiting from the external economies created by the formation of social capital, the forced diffusion of plantation

1. *Cultuurstelsel.* Properly, this term ought to be Englished as 'Cultivation System', but the 'Culture System' mistranslation is so embedded in the literature that it seems less confusing to employ it. The System proper was the stroke of fiscal genius by Governor General van den Bosch: it involved the remission of the peasant's land taxes in favor of his undertaking to cultivate government-owned export crops on one fifth of his fields or, alternatively, to work sixty-six days of his year on government-owned estates or other projects. But this was only part of a much larger complex of politico-economic policies and institutions.

crops and attendant labor skills over the island, and a certain amount of more direct governmental assistance, private enterprises steadily multiplied; soon their returns were great enough that they could provide most of the investment required for the qualitative changes in capital stock, particularly in sugar-milling, which were becoming necessary.[2] The protracted 'fall' of the Culture System (which lasted from about 1850 to about 1915) and its gradual replacement by the Corporate Plantation System were largely self-generated, because its success in establishing a serviceable export economy infrastructure made private entrepreneurship, originally so hampered by lack of capital, progressively more feasible. [. . .]

If 'take-off' is defined as a largely self-generated, relatively sudden transition to sustained economic growth, then there is at least presumptive evidence that something of the sort occurred on the estate side of the dual economy during the Culture System period, or – if the system itself be viewed as merely establishing preconditions – just after it.[3] The fact that the estate sector became progressively more closely integrated into the modernizing Netherlands economy (and progressively segregated from the rigidifying Javanese one) does not mean, as has sometimes been asserted, that it was a simple creation of that economy; it was a creation of Javanese land and labor organized under Dutch colonial political direction. If anything, the flow of support ran the other way: 'The true measure of (van den Bosch's) greatness', Furnivall has justly written, 'is the renascence of the Netherlands' (Furnivall, 1944, p. 152).

The true measure of van den Bosch's malignancy, however, is the stultification of Indonesia. For, although the Javanese helped launch the estate sector, they were not properly part of it, nor were they permitted to become so; it was just something they did, or more exactly were obligated to do, in their spare time. On their own time, they multiplied; and 'take-off' on the peasant side was of a less remunerative sort – into rapid and sustained population growth. In 1830 there were probably about 7 million people on Java; in 1840, 8·7; 1850 (when census-taking first became reasonably systematic), 9·6; 1860, 12·7; 1870, 16·2; 1880, 19·5; 1890, 23·6; 1900, 28·4 – an average annual increase of approximately 2 per cent during seventy years (Reinsma, 1955, p. 175). And, here too, the pattern once established, persists (though the rate slows): 1920, 34·4; 1930, 41·7. What the precise causes of this 'explosion' were and, particularly, how far it was directly rather than merely indirectly detonated by Culture System policies, are,

2. In 1840, private estates accounted for 17 per cent of agricultural export volume, government forced cultivation 78 per cent. In 1850, the figures were 26 and 73; in 1860, 58 and 39; in 1870, 43 and 52; in 1873, 72 and 19 (Reinsma, 1955, p. 157).

3. The 'take-off' concept is from Rostow (1960), pp. 36–58. However, Rostow's analysis generally ignores the developmental patterns of colonial economies.

reliable data being scarce, matters of debate. But there is little doubt that it was during the Culture System period that the saying about the Dutch growing in wealth and the Javanese in numbers first hardened into a sociological reality. By the end of it, the Javanese had, as they have today, the worst of two possible worlds: a static economy and a burgeoning population.

The unreliability (as well as the scarcity) of agricultural statistics on the peasant sector during the nineteenth century, on both the extent of cultivated land and the production of food crops, makes an exact tracing of the way in which the Javanese coped with this deepening demographic dilemma difficult. But, although the stages through which their adaptation passed have to be described in speculative terms, shored up only by fragmentary and indirect evidence plus some hard reasoning, the overall nature and direction of that adaptation are clear, and comprise what I am going to call 'agricultural involution'.

Unable to attack the problem head on, let us attempt to get at it by a circuitous route. Beginning with a picture of the general situation at a later period, when statistics on peasant agriculture are more reliable, we can try, first, to figure out how the situation characteristic of this later period could have been produced and then, second, we can see whether the scattered historical evidence supports the notion that it was in fact so produced. [. . .] (Data for 1920 reveal that) whatever the causes, the tie between sugar (the export crop), wet rice (the subsistence crop) and population density is unmistakable: all three flourish, if that is the proper word, together (in particular regions). The main factor which makes this seemingly contradictory phenomenon possible is a progressively higher per hectare sawah productivity. [. . .] Evidently, sugar cultivation, through its improvement of local ecological conditions for rice, binds those three together when they are found together, and pushed all of them to higher than average levels.

But without more effective cultivation methods the Javanese could hardly have taken advantage of these better facilities. And as there was virtually no variation in capital inputs in sawah agriculture from one part of the island to another, aside from irrigation works, this greater efficiency in cultivation derived almost entirely from a great intensification of labor – an intensification made both possible and necessary by the increasing population. The practices included pre-germination, transplanting, more thorough land preparation, fastidious planting and weeding, razor-blade harvesting, double-cropping, a more exact regulation of terrace-flooding, and the addition of more fields at the edges of volcanoes. The concentrative, inflatable quality of sawah, its labor-absorbing capacity, was an almost ideal (in an ecological, not a social, sense) complement to capital-intensive sugar-growing. [. . .]

The process resembles nothing else so much as treading water. Higher-level densities are offset by greater labor inputs into the same productive system, but output per head (or per mouth) remains more or less constant from region to region. This, however, is only the synchronic picture. From the diachronic point of view, the important questions are: how long has this water-treading been going on? What set it off? What sustained it? And in this respect, two otherwise isolated facts take on significance: first, that *local* overcrowding begins to be reported from Java as early as the beginning of the nineteenth century. [. . .] Second, that, with few exceptions the distribution of sugar cultivation in 1860, and for the most part even in 1833, was about the same as it was in 1920, though only about a sixth as much acreage was involved.

These fragments suggest that the ever-more energetic, regionally uneven process of water-treading which led to the swollen population and intensely driven rice terraces of 1920 and later went on steadily during the whole of the past century. From 1850 on there are even some reasonably reliable figures to support this view: the *per-capita* production of rice between 1850 and 1900, when population was mounting as rapidly as it probably ever has in Java, is given as averaging about 106 kilograms, with no clear trend in any direction:[4] 1850, 106; 1865, 97 (the low); 1885, 119 (the high); 1895, 105; 1900, 98, and so on. After the turn of the century the 1900–1940 average declined to about 96. [. . .] Boeke (1953, p. 174) summed the whole picture up in a single, mordant phrase: 'static expansion'.

The superimposition of sugar cultivation on the already unequal distribution of sawah and population over Java left the Javanese peasantry with essentially a single choice in coping with their rising numbers: driving their terraces, and in fact all their agricultural resources, harder by working them more carefully. There was no industrial sector into which to move and, as the returns from cultivation went, in Furnivall's words, to keep the Netherlands from becoming another Portugal, none was developed (1944, p. 151). Coffee-growing was still almost wholly a forced-labor occupation and no real substitute for subsistence cultivation; and the same was true of the other Culture System crops. The Javanese could not themselves become part of the estate economy, and they could not transform their general pattern of already intensive farming in an extensive direction, for they lacked capital, had no way to shuck off excess labor, and were administratively barred from the bulk of their own frontier, the so-called 'waste lands' which were filling up with coffee trees. Slowly, steadily, relentlessly, they were forced into a more and more labor-stuffed sawah pattern of the sort the 1920 figures show: tremendous populations absorbed on minuscule rice farms,

4. Table quoted from Scheltema (1936, Table II.10).

particularly in areas where sugar cultivation led to improved irrigation; consequent rises in per-hectare productivity; and, with the assistance after about 1900 of an expansion in dry-crop cultivation, a probably largely stable, or very gradually rising, standard of living. Wet-rice cultivation, with its extraordinary ability to maintain levels of marginal labor productivity by always managing to work one more man in without a serious fall in *per-capita* income, soaked up almost the whole of the additional population that Western intrusion created,[5] at least indirectly. It is this ultimately self-defeating process that I have proposed to call 'agricultural involution'.

I take the concept of 'involution' from the American anthropologist Alexander Goldenweiser (1936), who devised it to describe those culture patterns which, after having reached what would seem to be a definitive form, nonetheless fail either to stabilize or transform themselves into a new pattern but rather continue to develop by becoming internally more complicated. [. . .]

An instance . . . is provided by what is called ornateness in art, as in the late Gothic. The basic forms of art have reached finality, the structural features are fixed beyond variation, inventive originality is exhausted. Still, development goes on. Being hemmed in on all sides by a crystallized pattern, it takes the function of elaborateness. Expansive creativeness having dried up at the source, a special kind of virtuosity takes its place, a sort of technical hairsplitting . . . Anyone familiar with primitive cultures will think of similar instances in other cultural domains (Goldenweiser, 1936).[6]

From the point of view of general theory, there is much misplaced concreteness in this formulation; but for our purposes we want only the analytic concept – that of the overdriving of an established form in such a way that it becomes rigid through an inward overelaboration of detail – not the hazy cultural vitalism in which it is here embedded.

The general earmarks of involution that Goldenweiser lists for aesthetic phenomena characterized the development of the sawah system after about the middle of the nineteenth century: increasing tenacity of basic pattern; internal elaboration and ornateness; technical hairsplitting, and unending virtuosity. And this 'late Gothic' quality of agriculture increasingly per-

5. Just what the factors producing the population rise in the nineteenth century were is not quite so clear as the usual references to the removal of Malthus' positive checks would make it seem. Improved hygiene could hardly have played a major role until fairly late. The Pax Nederlandica had perhaps more effect, but probably not so much because so many people had been killed in wars in the precolonial period but because the attendant destruction of crops ceased. Probably most important, and least discussed, was the expansion of the transport network which prevented local crop failures from turning into famines.

6. As his own reference to late Gothic art demonstrates, however, there is nothing particularly 'primitive' about this process.

vaded the whole rural economy: tenure systems grew more intricate; tenancy relationships more complicated; cooperative labor arrangements more complex – all in an effort to provide everyone with some niche, however small, in the overall system. [. . .] But what makes this development tragic rather than merely decadent is that around 1830 the Javanese (and, thus, the Indonesian) economy could have made the transition to modernism, never a painless experience, with more ease than it can do today. [. . .]

A sharper sense for these lost opportunities and possible ties is developed if one looks to another area where they were seized – not allowed to slip through the fingers like the proverbial chances of a lifetime. [. . .]

For Java, the obvious comparative case is Japan. Much differs between them: geography, history, culture, and of course, *per capita income* – Japan's being about twice Java's.[7] But much too, is similar. Both are heavily populated. Both rest agriculturally on a labor-intensive, small-farm, multi-crop cultivation regime centering on wet rice. Both have managed to maintain a significant degree of social and cultural traditionalism in the face of profound encounter with the West and extensive domestic change. In fact, in agriculture, the further back one goes toward the mid-nineteenth century the more the two resemble one another. Japanese per-hectare rice yields at the beginning of Meiji (1868) were probably about the same as those of Java at the beginning of the Corporate Plantation System (1870); today they are about two and a half times as high (Ohkawa and Rosovsky, 1960). Between 1878 and 1942 the percentage of the Japanese labor force employed in agriculture dropped from around 80 to around 40; the Javanese figure for the end of the nineteenth century is not known, but in 1930 – and probably still today – it had not fallen below 65 per cent. And, though it is even more a matter of head-long estimate, the percentage of aggregate net income contributed by agricultural production in the Japan of the 1880s was of the same general order as that in the Java of the 1950s, by which time the Japanese percentage was only a third as large. Given, then, all the admittedly important background differences, one can hardly forbear to ask when one looks at these two societies: 'What has happened in the one which did not happen in the other?'

A satisfactory answer to such a question would involve the whole economic, political and cultural history of the two civilizations; but even if we confine ourselves to predominantly ecological considerations, a number of dramatic differences leap to the eye. The most striking – and the most decisive – is the contrast between the way Japan utilized its rapid population increase and the way Java utilized hers. Between 1870 and 1940 Java

7. Estimated gross national product *per capita* (1955) for Japan is about $240, for Indonesia about $127. Ginsburg (1961, p. 18). Javanese *per capita* product, is, of course, below that of Indonesia as a whole, though by how much it is impossible to say.

absorbed the bulk of her increase in numbers – about thirty million people – into post-traditional village social systems of the sort already described but

in the first century of modernization, Japan maintained a relatively unchanging population in agriculture while the total population increased two and one half fold. Practically all the increase in the labour force was absorbed in non-agricultural activities. There was little change in the size of the rural population. Almost all the natural increase of the national population was absorbed in urban areas (Taeuber, 1960).

From 1872 to 1940, the Japanese farm population remained virtually constant around 14 million people (or $5\frac{1}{2}$ million households) at the same time as the total population grew approximately 35 million (Ohkawa and Rosovsky, 1960). Comparable statistics on the farm population of Java are not available, but that it grew at better than an average of 1 per cent a year during this entire period seems a conservative estimate.[8] Japan, in short, did not involute; which should cut the ground out from under any charges of 'paddyfield determinism' which might be brought against our Javanese analysis. But what, then, did it do?

For one thing, it increased agricultural productivity *per worker*, not just *per terrace*. 'Using the latest and best computations', Ohkawa and Rosovsky estimate that the productivity of agricultural labor (net output/labor force in agriculture) increased 2·6 per cent annually between 1878 and 1917. Thus, as I have attempted (with much less adequate computations) to demonstrate, where Java increased per-hectare yields at least to the First World War but not per worker yields, Japan increased both over roughly the same period. The contrast is all the more impressive, because, in Japan as in Java, the basic structure of proprietary control, the general form of the producing unit, and the overall pattern of rural culture seems to have been relatively unaltered. [. . .]

No move to extensify agriculture; no marked trend toward a class polarization of large landlord and rural proletarian; no radical reorganization of the family-based productive unit – characteristics of Java and Japan alike since the turn of the century. But Japan increased productivity per agricultural worker 236 per cent, Java – the estates aside for the moment – hardly increased it at all [. . .] The readiest explanation for this difference – and the one most commonly invoked – is the greater technological advance in Japanese agriculture. [. . .] But it is just this difference in technological

8. Starting around 1920, Javanese towns seem to have begun, evidently for the first time, to grow more rapidly than the general population, and this trend has accelerated since the revolution. However even today they come nowhere near absorbing the entire increase as the Japanese towns seem to have done since the last quarter of the nineteenth century.

progress that we wish to explain. There is little in the two technologies around, say, 1870 – the end alike of the Culture System and of the Tokugawa period, which could account for their divergence since that time.

More genuinely determinative of the separation into contrasting courses was the manner in which a traditional labor-intensive, Lilliputian, family-farm, wet-rice-and-second-crop type of ecosystem came to be related to a set of modern economic institutions. Specifically, where Japanese peasant agriculture came to be complementarily related to an expanding manufacturing system in indigenous hands, Javanese peasant agriculture came to be complementarily related to an expanding agro-industrial structure under foreign management. As labor productivity in the capital-intensive sector in Japan increased, it increased also in the labor-intensive sector; as it increased in the capital-intensive sector in Java it remained approximately constant in the labor-intensive one. In Japan, the peasant sector supported the industrial one during the crucial three decades of the latter's emergence largely by means of extremely heavy land taxation; in Java, the peasant sector supported the industrial one through the provision of underpriced labor and land. In Japan, the industrial sector, once underway, then re-invigorated the peasant sector through the provision of cheap commercial fertilizer, more effective farm tools, support of technical education and extension work and, eventually, after the First World War, simple mechanization, as well as by offering expanded markets for agricultural products of all sorts; in Java most of the invigorating effect of the flourishing agro-industrial sector was exercised upon Holland, and its impact upon the peasant sector was, as we have seen, enervating. The dynamic interaction between the two sectors which kept Japan moving and ultimately pushed her over the hump to sustained growth was absent in Java. Japan had and maintained, but Java had and lost, an integrated economy.

To a great extent, Japan maintained it and Java lost it in the critical four decades of the mid-nineteenth century – 1830–70. At the same time that van den Bosch was superimposing an export-crop economy upon the traditional Javanese sawah system, Japan had locked herself away from Western interference and was moving toward a more commercialized, less immobile rural economy on its own. In both societies, peasant agriculture was becoming, within a generally unchanging basic pattern, steadily more labor intensive, more skillful and more productive. But in Java the increase in output was soon swamped by the attendant spurt in population; in Japan the population remained virtually constant. In both societies, the peasant's agricultural productivity increased. But in one it was, so to speak, reserved (largely through the operation of a tributational tax system) for, as it turned out, future investment in an indigenous manufacturing system. In the other, it was immediately expended to subsidize the swelling part-time labor force (i.e. the peasant in his two fifths corvee role) of a foreign-run plantation system, and its potential for financing Indonesian take-off dissipated. [. . .]

There never really was, even in Company times, a Netherlands East Indies economy in an integral, analytic sense – there was just that, admittedly highly autonomous, branch of the Dutch economy which was situated in the Indies ('tropical Holland', as it was sometimes called), and cheek-by-jowl, the autonomous Indonesian economy also situated there. And though, indeed, the two interacted continuously in ways which fundamentally shaped their separate courses, they steadily diverged, largely as a result of this interaction, to the point where the structural contrasts between them were overwhelming. What Boeke regarded as an intrinsic and permanent characteristic of Indonesian (or 'Eastern') economic life, 'a primarily spiritual phenomenon', was really an historically created condition; it grew not from the immutable essence of the Eastern soul as it encountered the incarnate spirit of Western dynamism, but from the in no way predestined shape of colonial policy as it impressed itself upon the traditional pattern of Indonesian agriculture (Boeke, 1953, p. 14).

References

BOEKE, J. (1953), *Economics and Economic Policy of Dual Societies*, H. D. Tjeenk Willink.

FURNIVALL, J. S. (1944), *Netherlands India*, Cambridge University Press.

GINSBURG, N. (1961), *Atlas of Economic Development*, University of Chicago Press.

GOLDENWEISER, A. (1936), 'Loose ends of a theory of the individual pattern and involution in primitive society', in R. Lowie (ed.), *Essays in Anthropology*, presented to A. L. Kroeber, University of California Press.

OHKAWA, K., and ROSOVSKY, M. (1960), 'The role of agriculture in modern Japanese economic development', *econ. Devel. Cult. Change*, vol. 9, pp. 43–67.

REINSMA, R. (1955), *Het verval van het Cultuurstelsel*, S'Gravenhage, van Veulen.

ROSTOW, W. W. (1960), *The Stages of Economic Growth*, Cambridge University Press.

SCHELTEMA, A. M. P. (1936), Table II.10 in W. Hollinger (1953), *Indonesia*, *Quantitative Studies* no. 3, MIT.

TAEUBER, I. (1960), 'Urbanization and population change in the development of modern Japan', *Econ. Devel. Cult Change*, vol. 9, pp. 1–28.

21 B. H. Pollitt

Employment Plans, Performance and Future Prospects in Cuba

Extract from B. H. Pollitt, 'Employment plans, performance and future prospects in Cuba', in R. Robinson and P. Johnston (eds.), *Prospects for Employment Opportunities in the 1970s*, papers and impressions from University of Cambridge Overseas Studies Committee Conference, HMSO, 1971.

It is premature to regard Cuba as a 'centrally planned' economy in any rigorous sense for the term implies the existence of a planning system. Cuban economic experience over the 1960s in practice does not reflect the operation of such a system but suggests its tortuous, oft-disrupted and as yet partial evolution.

Analogies with the USSR in the 1920s can be pointed to in part to suggest the need for some sense of historical perspective when considering the first decade of Cuba's post-revolutionary economic performance. It was no easy matter to see in Soviet economic practice in the 1920s – one not generally corresponding to what is now understood as 'centrally planned economy' – the foundations for the decade of extraordinarily rapid growth in employment and output that was to follow. In somewhat similar fashion, Cuban economic prospects for the 1970s are not automatically perceived by reviewing her practice in the 1960s. This is not to suggest any comprehensive congruity of economic structure and strategy (for in many crucial particularities the contrasts are more illuminating than the comparisons) but it is to stress that in both cases one is treating periods of more or less continuous social, political and economic convulsion – in brief, of sustained 'crisis' – and when there are so many trees of vivid and varied hue to divert attention, it is more than usually difficult to see the wood.

It is to be suggested that any argument suggesting the 'exceptional' or 'unorthodox' nature of Cuban economic experience since the Revolution will find a receptive audience outside the socialist world. After all, few theoretical models (or empirical descriptions) of development or the lack of it in developing countries incorporate upsets in both a national and international system of political and economic relationships that can properly be described as revolutionary. Where such an upset does occur it is not surprising that the outcome fails to fit neatly within the parameters of discussions generally presupposing evolution rather than revolution in political, social and economic institutions and structures.

Even so, the 'oddity' of Cuban experience is defined with particular sharpness given the theme [of unemployment] with which this Conference is concerned. For most, if not all, economists one of the gravest problems of the 'Third World' is that the annual increment to the would-be economically active population – a substantial proportion of which is already under- or unemployed – is as great as if not greater than the annual sum of new jobs created. Consideration of employment prospects for under-developed countries thus becomes virtually synonymous with searching for those ways and means that will in specific cases most rapidly accelerate the creation of new (and preferably productive) employment opportunities. In Cuba, by contrast, while the net addition to the economically active population between 1958 and 1970 has recently been estimated at 580,000, the number of new employment opportunities created over the same period has been calculated at some 1·2 million.[1] And if one was obliged to specify the most important single problem hitherto encountered in the process of post-revolutionary economic development in Cuba it would be classified generically as an acute 'shortage of labour'. [. . .]

Since the Revolution of 1959, quite a few economists have studied the socio-economic structure that it inherited, and of all its oft-listed 'defects', one of the most formidable was the volume of 'open' and 'disguised' unemployment. Of a labour force calculated at some 2·2 million in 1957 – rather more than one third of the total population – the average rate of 'open' unemployment was estimated to exceed 16 per cent, rising to more than 20 per cent in the summer months of the 'dead season' and not falling too much below 10 per cent even in the months of peak activity of the sugar industry (generally January to May). A further 20 per cent of the labour force was reported as 'partially' or 'temporarily' employed or to be engaged as unpaid family labour.[2]

In analyses of the causes of such unemployment, stress was rightly placed on the predominance of the sugar sector in industry, agriculture and foreign trade. The production techniques and market conditions prevailing in and for that sector ensured that Cuba's sugar industry experienced both seasonal and cyclical unemployment and the 'fall-out' of sharp seasonal and cyclical fluctuations in the level of income and employment in that industry (and in the flow of foreign exchange derived from its activities) affected most other branches of the economy.

While a rapid increase in both the level and stability of employment in rural and urban Cuba was not the sole objective of the development strategy

1. Speech of Dr F. Castro, Havana, 26 July 1970.
2. These estimates (which are open to several criticisms) were based on a survey of 5000 households carried out in 1957 and embracing the period May 1956 to April 1957. They constituted a sample of about 0·4 per cent of the households enumerated in the Population Census of 1953.

pursued in the early years of the Revolution, such an increase was rightly seen to be an integral part of it. That strategy was in essence:

1. The diversification of agricultural production, with a particular emphasis on the expanded production of food and 'industrial' crops of which all, or a major part, had hitherto been imported.

2. The rapid development of much 'light' and some 'heavy' industry calculated to reduce Cuban dependence on foreign trade while conferring upon her the varied benefits of 'modern' society.

The policy of agricultural diversification was accompanied by major changes in property relations. The First Agrarian Reform, largely implemented by the second half of 1960, expropriated landholdings exceeding about 400 hectares in area and these were to be owned and controlled (in initially variable form) by the State. In October 1963, the Second Agrarian Reform expropriated almost all private landholdings exceeding some 67 hectares in size and ownership of these farms expanded the area under State control to some 65–70 per cent of the total farm area. [. . .] The State was to assume control of a farm area incorporating abundant 'reserves' of underutilized land traditionally used only for the extensive grazing of cattle.

Coexisting with such reserves of underutilized land within the pre-revolutionary agrarian structure were comparably impressive 'reserves' of underutilized labour. Wage-workers were usually estimated to comprise about two thirds of a total agricultural labour force calculated at rather more than 800,000 on the eve of the Revolution. A 1956–7 survey of 1000 rural households headed by agricultural wage-workers reported that an average of only 6 months of paid employment was secured by their sample in the course of the year. This familiar (and not socially peaceful) coexistence of idle land and idle labour was not, from the standpoint of the large-scale 'capitalist' farmer, basically irrational. National and international 'market-constraints' could justify a restricted level and composition of agricultural output; and the generally low intensity of cultivation on such lands as were sown to crops could be explained by noting that while both land and labour might be relatively 'abundant', the former was very much 'cheaper' in Cuba than the latter. Given that the Revolution had now abolished the system of property relations within which such a rationale could be offered, there was, it seemed, no obstacle to putting underutilized labour to work on underutilized land; and there was an obvious harmony between the objectives of expanding an increasingly diversified agricultural output while increasing and stabilizing the level of employment for agricultural wage-labour.

This early strategy for agricultural development was seen to complement rather than conflict with the ambitious programme for industrial growth that was simultaneously promoted. The latter was seen to require very substantial imports of capital. However, the agricultural sector, while maintaining the production of traditional export crops (primarily sugar-cane and tobacco) at relatively stable levels would progressively free for State-controlled industrial investment the substantial volume of foreign exchange previously consumed by imports of foodstuffs and of industrial raw materials of agricultural origin (cotton, sisal, etc.) that Cuba was judged to be capable of producing herself. When combined with sharp reductions in imports of 'luxury' consumer goods and (hopefully) an expanded access to foreign credits, it was envisaged that substantially the same annual inflow of foreign exchange as had been secured over the years immediately prior to the Revolution could finance a high rate of industrial growth. This in turn would absorb a high and rising proportion of the urban unemployed. Expanded activity in the building and construction industry – in spheres of housing, roads, schools and hospitals as well as factories – would mop up reserves of underutilized labour in both urban and rural Cuba.

This, at least was the theory (which, when stated in such general terms, did not conflict with too many more or less 'orthodox' contemporary notions). In practice, however, the import content of output in the new industries turned out to be unexpectedly high – not least because such industries commonly required imported raw materials, while the quantity and quality of such output was disappointingly low. Also low was the productivity of the land, labour and capital invested in the agricultural sector in the cultivation of 'new' crops; and the effort to diversify agricultural production was accompanied by a precipitate decline in the volume of cane harvested and sugar produced. (Sugar production, just below seven million tons in 1961, was below four million tons in 1963.)

The consequences for the balance of payments were spectacular. The average annual value of Cuban imports over the 1950s was estimated at $620m and that of exports at $670m. For the years 1960–63, the average annual value of imports was put at $711m and that of exports at $577m. In short, an economy which had had a total trading surplus of $550m over the decade prior to the Revolution was in four post-revolutionary years to incur a deficit of more than $530m; and a growth strategy calculated to reduce Cuban dependence upon foreign trade was in practice to prove 'a development path of increasingly powerful and anguishing dependence upon imports' and one which could lead only to 'economic stagnation via a growing strangulation of foreign trade'.[3]

3. Romeo (1965, p. 7). A trading surplus of $26m was reported for the years 1960 and 1961. A deficit of $239m was estimated for 1962, rising to $324m in 1963. Despite a $170m increase in the value of exports for 1964 (attributable primarily to a steep, if short-lived, rise in sugar-prices) the deficit for the latter year was to exceed $300m.

The deepening balance of payments crisis forced the adoption of a new growth strategy in 1963. While some claims for its originality were made at the time, it corresponded quite closely in its general outline to a development path advocated for the Soviet economy in the 1920s. Its essence was that 'in our circumstances investment capital in agriculture is more profitable than investment in industry' and the 'biggest asset' of the economy was 'the possibility of achieving a (national) upsurge . . . through agricultural exports'. Clearly, 'by cutting the relative share of the surplus-product of agriculture to be diverted at this time from agriculture to industry, in the early years we also reduce the absolute magnitude of what we pour into industry. But later, thanks to the considerably greater fruitfulness of investment in agriculture, the reduction of the relative share of the transfusion can yield in absolute figures a greater mass for injection into industry'. Thus in the short-term, 'the relative growth of industry will be smaller because agriculture will develop faster still' but 'what we lose in the rate of industrial development in the initial years will be made up with interest in the succeeding ones'.[4]

The socialist world – and most importantly the USSR – was to play a dual role in Cuba's post-1963 development programme. Hitherto it had provided material resources with which it had been hoped (vainly) to promote rapid and increasingly self-sufficient industrial growth. It was now to provide them for the primary purpose of expanding the nation's export-capacity, particularly that of the sugar industry. At the same time, it was to provide the expanding market in which the bulk of Cuban exports could be exchanged (with mutual profit given the world division of socialist labour) for both the investment- and consumption-goods acquired in the past and those to be obtained in the future.

Revolution in the marketing prospects for Cuban sugar was highlighted by a six-year Soviet-Cuban trade agreement signed in January 1964. Soviet sugar purchases were to increase from 2·1 to 5·0 million metric tons over the period 1965–8; and over the three years 1968–70, inclusive, a total of 15 million tons of Cuban sugar was to be purchased.[5] All sales were to be at a price of 6·11 cents per pound. Similar agreements with China and other socialist economies suggested stable markets for at least another 2 million tons by 1970; and annual export earnings solely from sugar and in socialist countries alone should comfortably exceed $800m by the end of the decade.

4. See Shanin (1926, pp. 65–87). A more general case for a 'Cuban Road' to development is argued in Kuczynski (1964, pp. 221–32).

5. In the latter three years, the USSR alone would be purchasing a volume of raw sugar matching Cuba's exports to the entire world in the (relatively favourable) years of 1956–8.

In the entire pre-revolutionary history of the Cuban sugar industry its world exports had in no years reached 6 million tons. By 1970, however, an undetermined but predictably substantial volume of sugar exports to the non-socialist world was to be underpinned by a stable, profitably-priced socialist market for some 7 million tons per annum. Hence the famous plan to produce 10 million tons by 1970.

No attempt is made here to enumerate fully the myriad factors explaining the failure of Cuba's first post-revolutionary growth strategy to fulfil its major economic objectives, although the very considerable benefits of hindsight facilitate such a task. Obviously stress could be placed upon the acute scarcities of skilled manpower – administrative, technical and operational – that were then (and now) felt in both agricultural and industrial sectors; and it is noteworthy that the implementation of ambitious investment programmes over the period 1960–62, all of which required substantially increased numbers of 'professionals' of all kinds, coincided with a massive exodus of many of the relatively small numbers of 'professionals' commanding the relevant skills prior to the Revolution. Emphasis could also be placed upon the profound economic and technical 'dislocative' effects of the rupture of virtually all politico-economic ties between Cuba and the United States which vastly compounded already formidable problems of an 'organizational' kind. [. . .]

The skilled and unskilled manpower needs of particular investment projects formed, in such a context, only a part of 'new' labour requirements. At least as important was the urgent need for a relatively huge number of planning and administrative cadres to cope with the avalanche of 'organizational' problems associated at all levels not so much with the construction of any distinctively new economic system as with the veritable 'explosion' of the old one.

The nature and extent of the 'explosion' of capitalist organization of human labour in Cuba, was but dimly illuminated by the (imperfect) official statistics of early post-revolutionary changes in the volume and structure of employment. Certainly they provided only a slender clue to the nature of the labour supply problems that were to obstruct the post-1963 development strategy. In Table 1 the most significant change to be noted was the increase from one quarter to one third in the proportion of the 'active' population defined as in 'Services and Others' over the period 1958–64. This sector had been considered large prior to the Revolution and, commonly the case in underdeveloped economies, a sector where 'disguised' unemployment was prevalent. Its dramatic post-revolutionary expansion hinted at the size of the bureaucratic apparatus that was swiftly to duplicate the form, if all too often not the content, of a 'centrally planned economy'; and it reflected, too, the expansion of the social services – particularly education and public health – and of the military establishment.[6]

Table 1 **Active population of fourteen years and over by productive sector in Cuba, 1958–64** (thousands)

	1958–9	1960–61	1964
Agriculture	813·0	862·0	838·0
Industry & mining	378·5	411·8	375·7
Construction	82·8	71·7	119·0
Transport	80·6	86·5	89·7
Commerce	284·3	265·5	252·9
Services and others	558·3	572·7	832·7
Total	2197·5	2270·2	2508·0

Source: *Resumen de Estadisticas de Poblacion* no. 1, JUCEPLAN, Havana, July, 1965; from Table 21, page 24.

Table 2, however, offers a more revealing image of the nature and significance of certain changes in the structure of employment that were clearly to affect the post-1963 drive to restore export capacity to pre-revolutionary levels and then to expand it. This table gives the (broadly defined) occupational structure of a sample of male workers in Cuba for the years 1957 and 1966 and shows the inflow and outflow of workers from one employment category to another. The sample is not representative of the proportional weight of various occupational groups at a national level but the main trends of *inter*-occupational movement can be held to reflect national tendencies.[7]

The first feature of the table to be noted is a fall of almost 10 per cent in the number of workers reported to have been in agriculture in 1957 and 1966 respectively. However, it can be seen that the number of 'farmers' reported actually *rose* by some 8 per cent over the period; and there was a 6 per cent increase in those classified as 'semi-proletarians'.[8] By contrast, the number

6. The figures almost certainly concealed several new forms of disguised unemployment, partly attributable to the virtual collapse of the island's international tourist industry and partly to restrictions in the supply of a variety of domestically consumed goods and services.

7. In 1966, a survey of 1061 agricultural households, located in 11 rural areas previously studied in 1945, was conducted under this writer's direction. Table 2 reports the comparative occupational structure in 1957 and 1966 of more than 98 per cent of all the *brothers* reported by the heads of households in the sample.

8. 'Semi-proletarians' were here defined as those dividing their labour more or less equally between farms that they owned or rented and wage-work on (almost invariably) larger-scale holdings.

Table 2 The occupational structure of a sample of male workers in Cuba 1957, and 1966

1957–66	Farmers	Semi-pro-letariat	Agri-cultural workers	Rural workers (non-agri.)	Urban workers	Army or police	Retired or sick	Not working	School or university	Other	Not known	Total
Small farmers	727	22	153	20	8	1		10	2	8	1	952
Semi-proletariat	19	90	24	5	10			3				141
Agricultural workers	40	11	1037	34	10	2		80	25	7	4	1250
Rural (non-agri.) workers	19	3	98	84	4	4		7	5	3		227
Urban workers	41	4	142	27	333	19	1	9	2	6	3	587
Army or police	5	1	59	6	10	1		26	7	7	1	123
Retired or sick	11		42	11	12	4	27	3		4	1	115
School or university	1		3		1			63	8	8		76
Other	18	2	22	2	4			3	2	8	3	64
Total	881	133	1580	189	382	31	28	204	46	45	16	3535

Table 3 **Occupational structure of workers engaged in cutting cane and other agricultural work, Cuba 1957 and 1966**

	1957			1966		
Occupation	Cane cutters	Others	Total	Cane cutters	Others	Total
State farmers	145	228	373	62	311	373
Agricultural workers	46	112	158	35	123	158
Semi-proletariat	21	50	71	9	62	71
Total	212	390	602	106	496	602
Per cent	35·2	64·8	100·0	17·6	82·4	100·0

reported as 'agricultural workers' – i.e. more or less 'pure' wage-labour – fell by more than 20 per cent, the principal groups recruiting such labour being the 'farmers', 'urban workers', non-agricultural 'rural workers' and the 'Army or Police'. The group classified as 'not working' in 1957 – being then predominantly below working age rather than unemployed – was the principal supplier of post-revolutionary agricultural wage-labour in this sample.

Table 3 shows yet more significant changes occurring over the same period in the *type* of agricultural labour performed by a sample of 602 workers remaining in agriculture as wage-labour or 'semi-proletarians'. Interviewed in 1966, a total of 212 workers – 35·2 per cent of the sample enumerated in the table – reported that they had cut cane in 1957. *Half* this number – 106 workers, or 17·6 per cent of the total – reported that they had cut cane at some time during the 12 months prior to their being interviewed in 1966. The table also shows the distribution of these workers in 1966 between three categories of employment: permanent State Farm workers; agricultural wage-workers with no formal affiliation to the State sector and contracting all or a major part of their employment with farms in private ownership; and 'semi-proletarians' engaged as seasonal wage-labour in either or both State and Private sectors. The proportional fall in the number of cane-cutters reported in 1966 compared with 1957 was greatest among State Farm workers and 'semi-proletarians' and smallest among 'freelance' agricultural wage workers.[9]

9. Of the 1061 agricultural households surveyed in 1966, 610 were headed by wage-workers or 'semi-proletarians' but adequate information concerning the type of work performed in either or both of the years 1957 and 1966 was not secured in eight cases. Cane-cutters of one year or the other were encountered in 10 of the 11 zones studied, a fall in their number being reported in 9 zones. It is stressed that the sample was designed neither to represent the national proportions of the agricultural wage-labour force cutting cane or performing other agricultural work; nor the national division of the wage-labour force between State Farm Workers, 'semi-proletarians', etc.

These data suggest that while the State sector in agriculture was indeed to inherit 'abundant' supplies of underutilized land, the supply of 'professional' wage-labour with which it could be productively combined was to fall both relatively swiftly and sharply by the mid-1960s. At the same time, a high (and rising) proportion of that diminished wage-labour force ceased to cut cane – i.e. ceased to perform the specific type of work which had provided the major source of employment and income for wage-labour in large-scale farms prior to the Revolution.[10] The *productivity* of the declining number of professional cane-cutters was also estimated to have fallen by at least 20 per cent,[11] with comparable falls registered in a variety of other types of agricultural work.

While the social and economic programmes promoted by the Revolutionary Government were doubtless the cause of these various trends, they were for the most part not *planned* by it. For example, initially rising investment in urban areas was calculated in part to reduce, if not eliminate, the 'reserve army' of *urban* labour and not to precipitate an accelerated movement of wage-workers from rural areas to the towns.[12] More crucially, rising investment in the diversification of agricultural production was conceived as providing employment that would *complement* rather than *compete* with that available in the cane-harvest. The latter point merits detailed consideration here not just because the dramatic 'flight from cane' – or at least from manual cane-cutting – was of signal importance for the course of Cuban economic development but because it touched upon many issues of more general interest.

Firstly, the speed with which initially 'abundant' supplies of underutilized agricultural wage-labour were apparently exhausted suggested that this 'abundance' had been exaggerated. In fact, the Revolution inherited an agricultural system, defined like many others, to possess 'abundant' or 'surplus' labour but in which *there was no great, easily-tapped 'reserve army' of unemployed workers during the months of peak labour-require-*

10. Official estimates of the number of agricultural wage-labourers in the State sector by 1966 were of uncertain reliability but generally place it at below 400,000. Almost 45 per cent of these were estimated to be in the cane-sector although a high proportion of such workers were not actually engaged in manual cane-cutting. The number of professional cane-cutters for the period 1966–7 is usually put at somewhere between 130–150,000, as compared with the 250–300,000 cane-cutters estimated for the immediate pre-revolutionary period.

11. The average labourer securing a day's work cutting cane in the 1950s was usually estimated to cut about 200 *arrobas* (1 arroba = 25 lbs). During the harvests of the mid-1960s, the figure appears to have oscillated between about 140–170 *arrobas*.

12. Pre-revolutionary migration from rural to urban Cuba had increased after the post-1952 depression in world sugar-markets but it had probably not been sufficiently great as to effect any absolute reduction in the size of the agricultural wage-labour force of that time.

ments.[13] The peak months of employment for both wage- and non-wage-labour in Cuban agriculture – generally January to May – were not simply those of seasonally high labour requirements in the sugar-sector: sowing and/or harvesting operations for many important, if secondary, crops co-incided with at least part of the cane-harvest.[14] In such circumstances, attributable in the last resort to the rainfall pattern more than to any other single factor – diversification *per se* was no magic formula to banish un-employment and increase output. Planting land hitherto devoted to a single crop with a more varied crop-mix by no means guaranteed the creation of employment that would neatly absorb labour hitherto seasonally underutil-ized; and expanding the area under specialized cultivation by sowing a variety of 'new' crops did not automatically create employment that was complementary to, rather than competitive with, the peak labour-needs of the specialized crop-area.[15] [. . .]

The symptoms of agricultural labour shortage having been manifested relatively early in Cuba's post-revolutionary economic history, theoretical discussion of labour-intensive versus capital-intensive investment in agri-culture has been for the most part out of place. However, a question of the most lively practical concern has been that of transforming the relatively abundant foreign capital made available to Cuba in the 1960s, mainly by socialist countries, into the specific technical forms that would enable labour to be saved in the production of certain key crops. In this context, a crucial problem of agricultural development has been that while Cuba could

13. The Cuban Population Census of 1953 found 51,000 male labourers 'looking for work' when they were enumerated in (predominantly) the month of February. These comprised less than 7 per cent of the total rural male labour force then enumerated. Had the Census been taken in March (when the sucrose content of the then-prevailing mix of cane varieties reached its highest point) the figure would doubtless have been lower. Two thirds of the national total of unemployed reported for the month of February by this Census were located in *urban areas* (*Censos de Poblacion 1953*, Havana 1955, Table 43, pp. 153–4.)

14. For example, of the annual national sowings of maize, plantains, coffee, malanga and cassava, the greater part fell in the months of March to May, inclusive; and between January and April, the bulk of the harvests of sweet potatoes, yams, malanga, tomatoes and potatoes were taken. The tobacco crop was harvested in January and February.

15. All this is, of course, obvious enough in 1970. However, while it would be invidious to impute to the early theorists of economic development 'with unlimited supplies of labour' any major responsibility for initial planning errors, in Cuba it is proper to note that when Fidel Castro marched into Havana in 1959, quite a few economists of repute were publishing development models in which the seasonality of agricultural production did not exist but 'surplus labour' always did; and Havana itself was to be blessed with the policy-recommendations of several high-powered globetrotters whose economic expertise did not, alas, include knowledge of the agricultural calendar for the 'new' crops that Cuba was to produce.

import (and partly manufacture or assemble) machinery and equipment enabling some cultivation processes to be mechanized, there were other processes – of which harvesting was overwhelmingly the most important – for which there was no available labour saving machinery of proven efficacy. That Cuba was predominantly dependent upon the technology developed in other socialist economies doubtless exacerbated the problem but it was by no means its prime cause. The latter was simply that in contrast to the harvesting processes for most cereals, for example, those of crops such as coffee, fruits, cigar tobacco, sugar cane, etc. present purely technical problems that are by any standards formidable if not quite intractable; and to this can be added the fact that many such crops are associated almost exclusively with tropical or semi-tropical economies in which factor-proportions and/or property relations have historically been such as to preclude any significant research effort into the development of the appropriate mechanized techniques.

This excursion into generalities in fact facilitates appreciation of the practical consequences of certain cardinal planning principles applied in the State sector of Cuban agriculture over the greater part of the 1960s. At State Farm level, planning targets were not expressed, for the most part, in terms of the yields to be secured from either land, labour or capital. Following a procedure originally established with the first Soviet Five-Year Plan, such targets were expressed in terms of the areas to be sown to specific crops. At first there was no detailed specification of the sequence of cultivation processes to be performed subsequent to soil-preparation and sowing. Nor was there instruction on the precise time-periods in which labour and means of production were to be applied in their performance. However, accumulated experience enabled both more and less accurate assessments to be made of the number of man-days, in conjunction with specific means of production, required to perform various processes of cultivation on a given area of land. At the same time, experiments in the cultivation of crops with certain variations in technique – for example, with or without irrigation – provided the basis for specification of the time-periods in which the appropriate sequence of processes should be performed. The experiments in question were generally directed by agronomists whose prime concern – as is commonly the case in the profession – was to secure high returns to land. The sowing targets set for State Farms were highly ambitious but there was no good reason for supposing that they could not be fulfilled. By 1970, Cuba disposed of some 50,000 tractors with ploughs, harrows, etc. – about four times the number of tractors in Cuban agriculture on the eve of the Revolution – and by the mid-1960s, it was perfectly possible to implement plans requiring that the total area under crops in State Farms be increased by one third in a single year. Indeed, over the first six months of 1967, for example, it was quite plausibly estimated that the sown area in State Farms increased over its level of 1966 by just such a magnitude (Aranda, 1968, p. 47). What was quite without practical foundation, however, was the expectation that dramatic increases in the areas sown to given crops would be accompanied by comparable dramatic increases in output.

In the first place, the techniques of cultivation recommended for the expanded area under 'traditional' crops for the most part involved no radical break with the prevailing 'natural' agricultural calendar for such crops as determined primarily by the pattern of rainfall.[16] Since a greater variety of crops was being produced on large-scale farms than prior to the Revolution, and since many such crops required the performance of processes (such as more or less frequent weeding) which inherited techniques of cane cultivation had required on a far more limited scale,[17] there was an increased need for labour in traditional off-peak periods. However, since the harvest-processes for a high proportion of such crops (for which little if any labour-saving capital was available) continued to overlap or coincide one with another, there was also a steep rise in labour-requirements in traditional *peak* periods. The result was predictable: for season after season, having fulfilled State sowing-plans,[18] the administrations of numerous State Farms were obliged to decide which harvests should be sacrificed entirely or, at least, which crops should be harvested outside their optimum time-periods at the cost of a decline in their volume and/or value.

The increased requirement for labour in traditional peak periods was dramatic but did not adequately account for the drastic fall in the number of professional cane-cutters experienced by 1966, and which was to continue thereafter,[19] neither did it explain the decline in their productivity in terms of

16. Where irrigation facilities existed, they were most commonly to be used to complement natural rainfall so as to maximize returns to land rather than to offset the diminishing returns associated with shifting the sowing-harvest cycle for specific crops away from that dictated by natural rainfall.

17. New cane-sowings required intensive weeding during the first season of growth. (Thus complaints of 'labour shortage' for weeding were loud during the years 1968-9 when the cane-area was being expanded by almost 50 per cent for the 1970 harvest.) With ratoon cane, after harvesting and the clearance of trash from the roots, 'the trash can be left undisturbed, when it acts as a mulch, suppresses weed growth, and rots in a few weeks of wet weather. With natural rainfall, therefore, no work need be done for ratoons other than applying fertilizer' (Barnes, 1964, pp. 228-9). In pre-revolutionary Cuba, even the application of fertilizer to the ratoons had the character of an 'optional extra' and the ratio of plant to ratoon cane had been very low by many international standards.

18. Where sowing targets exceeded even the expanded ploughing capacity of State Farms, they were often fulfilled nevertheless by staggering sowings substantially beyond their optimum time-period. Where irrigation facilities were absent, such sowings not uncommonly yielded a very small harvest.

19. In 1969, it was estimated that perhaps 10-15 per cent of the 1970 cane harvest

the quantity of cane cut. It became clear that not only did newly created employment that coincided with the cane harvest effectively compete for the labour of cane-cutters, but effective indirect competition was also provided by agricultural employment created in traditional off-peak periods. The creation of new employment opportunities in periods of the year in which unemployment had been widespread within the pre-revolutionary mode of production effectively 'exploded' the most crucial feature of capitalist labour-organization in Cuban agriculture. Prior to the Revolution, a substantial proportion of the wage-labour force had been unable, for a relatively prolonged period of the year, to secure an income that was sufficient to provide basic subsistence for themselves and their dependants. In the months when work was generally available – primarily the period of harvesting for cane and other crops – it had thus been necessary to earn not simply a subsistence income but a surplus with which to subsidize consumption over the months when it was not. The power of this 'objective' compulsion to maximize income via maximum physical exertion during this period was reflected by the high proportion of wage-labourers reporting a seven-day working week prior to the Revolution; and there was an obvious, if socially unpalatable, symmetry between such labour-supply conditions and the techniques of agricultural production then prevailing. It was precisely this primitive but effective capitalist 'stick' that was smashed by large investments creating new employment in periods in which limited wage-work had hitherto been available. To express the matter crudely, such investments can be said to have effected a massive shift of wage-labour from operation in the realm of the most basic economic necessity to operation in the realm of at least limited economic freedom. The crucial element of choice was introduced, and 'subjective' factors – for example, to work or enjoy leisure during harvest periods, to cut cane or to perform some other type of work – came abruptly to the fore.

There was no great mystery about why a significant proportion of the agricultural wage-labour force should have left agriculture when the post-revolutionary expansion of non-agricultural employment opportunities encouraged them to do so. (After all, rural labour will leave agriculture when there are no very promising alternative employment prospects.) It was to be explained primarily in terms of the poverty and chronic insecurity experienced by most of its members within the pre-revolutionary mode of production, and one could adduce as an important exacerbating factor the arduous and generally stultifying character of agricultural labour when performed with primitive instruments of production. Of all forms of agricultural labour in Cuba, manual cane-cutting was renowned as the most

would be cut by professional *macheteros*. Their number was reckoned to have fallen below 100,000 by 1969.

'*bruto*'; and given a choice between it and 'softer' (*mas suave*) work, it was not surprising that the latter should be selected by a high proportion of the wage-workers remaining in agriculture. Neither was it surprising, furthermore, that the reduced number of workers continuing to cut cane should in general decide to work five days a week during the harvest rather than seven, and work less intensively per day into the bargain, when completion of the harvest no longer meant the onset of months of but sporadically broken unemployment. [. . .].

While the extraordinarily rapid creation of alternative types of employment for wage-labour effected an enormous expansion of economic choice, the accompanying strict rationing of almost all consumer goods sharply restricted its freedom to determine the level and physical composition of the real wage to be secured as a result of exercising that newly-acquired power of choice. The wage-labourer working a five or six hour day for five days of the week throughout the year was in general thereby enabled to command a money-income sufficient to purchase the pre-determined (and hitherto little varied) 'basket' of necessities officially placed at his disposition; and, in most cases, the more highly-priced 'luxury' goods in limited availability (radios, electric irons, bicycles and the like) were within his reach as well. That this material restriction reinforces any natural tendency to eschew intensive and sustained physical labour is clear although the extent to which it may do is a matter of subjective rather than objective judgement. However, the effect of both factors – in practice strengthened by others not discussed here – was very clear. The pre-revolutionary mode of agricultural production both required and secured a supply of labour that worked relatively intensively over restricted time-periods, being unemployed (or underemployed) for the prolonged periods of the year in which its services were not required. The Revolution 'exploded' the productive relations within which this disagreeable 'equilibrium' between the demand and supply of agricultural labour had prevailed and in effect flattened out the supply-curve of labour over time. This revolution in the *social* relations of production, however, was not matched in the short-term – and in an historical context a decade *is* the short term – by a compensating revolution in the *techniques* of production, and the consequential 'disequilibrium' has been profound.

The massive utilization of 'voluntary labour' – one of the most distinctive features of post-revolutionary economic organization in Cuba – has been the primary instrument employed at least partially to plug the enormous (and recently widening) gap between peak period labour-demand and 'professional' labour-supply in the agricultural sector. Not surprisingly, the productivity of such labour has been on average significantly lower than that of the 'professional' wage-worker, even taking into account the decline in the latter's productivity in a variety of specific agricultural processes. Nevertheless, given Cuba's present development strategy – which this writer believes to be fundamentally sound in conception if not always in execution – the massive employment of such labour must be viewed as a necessity although both its direct and indirect costs have been considerable. However, it is worth pointing out a somewhat poignant contrast between the use made of labour predominantly motivated by ideology rather than by desire for immediate individual material benefit in Cuba as compared with several other socialist states. In other socialist economies, the large-scale deployment of such labour has commonly permitted the labour-intensive construction of overhead capital crucial to rapid, sustained economic growth. It has been Cuba's misfortune that the very significant proportion of the population prepared to work intensively (if not always with adequate technique or organization) in arduous voluntary labours has seen the bulk of its energies consumed by the business of maintaining current output.

Conclusion and future prospects

By intention, the story so far told has not been a balanced account of employment plans and performance in the Cuban economy of the 1960s. Rather than touch lightly upon the entire range of relevant topics, a more detailed (although nonetheless superficial) treatment has been given to a small number of themes and economic sectors selected partly with regard to their relative importance as subjectively assessed by this writer and partly for the manner in which they touch upon issues judged to be of more general interest. The overall prospects for employment in the 1970s do not emerge, therefore, with any great clarity. It should be clear enough, however, that Cuba's problem will not be one of contriving employment for idle hands but rather one of securing a greater output from hands already occupied, albeit insufficiently gainfully.

In this regard, the prospects are highly promising but whether that promise will be fully realized is very much a matter for Cuba's economic planners. The economic apprenticeship of Cuba's leaders has been, as was recently noted by Dr Fidel Castro, both a long and costly one; and this recognition is of itself a cause for optimism and perhaps a precondition for more productive planning and employment in the future. There is particular cause to expect that the end has been seen of two distinctive, interrelated and generally negative features of development 'planning' over the past decade. The first may harshly but appropriately be described as 'brainstorm investment'. This is investment undertaken, commonly on a massive scale, on the basis of an idea or a technique that has been inadequately tested in experimental projects and the productivity of which seldom approaches expectations either because of its intrinsic weakness or because of basically predictable inadequacies in prevalent material conditions or in available technical expertise. The second may be described as the 'search for the technological super-weapon' the productivity-increasing potential of which is so great as to make complex labour problems irrelevant. The effect of shooting for the technological stars has been partly relative neglect in the pursuit of more mundane but also more practicable instruments of production; and partly relative neglect of the 'subjective' factors affecting the productivity of labour. Among these latter factors is to be included the relative demoralization of such agricultural workers in State Farms as would put forth greater effort had they not seen with such regularity the labour 'stored-up' in *part* of the sequence of agricultural processes fail finally to be materialized.

The more positive basis for optimism lies in past and present investments in both human and material factors of production. The relatively enormous expenditure on education in Cuba over the past decade should yield a rising annual flow of labour with at least the minimum technical qualifications to manage a range of productive techniques either currently operative but poorly manipulated or in limited operation pending qualified personnel.[20] In terms of material investments – which run close to one third of annual GNP – particular attention might be drawn to dam-construction for both irrigation and power purposes, rural communication systems, fertilizer and cement plants, etc., all of which should eventually induce expanded agricultural production. A necessary complement to these investments is the development of labour-saving techniques in key agricultural processes, and while the total mechanization of cane-cutting is no immediate prospect, the employment of relatively simple machines in the performance of the several *separate* processes of the harvest-cutting, stripping and loading is relatively well-advanced and can be expected to increase sharply over the coming years. The sugar-cane itself is susceptible to cultivation with the most varied technique; and, with certain other crops, can be 'de-seasonalized' to a significant extent without serious loss of yield.

Given a major increase in agricultural production for both domestic and export markets, the path will be smoothed for rising investments in industry, most particularly in the wide range associated with the processing of production of agricultural origin. With this should come a significant rise in the employment and productivity of urban labour.

20. In contrast to many developing countries which succeed in producing a flow of graduates from institutions teaching professions on the periphery of economic processes, Cuba's educational programmes are more closely geared to development plans. The 1966–7 figure of 40,000 students in 'Institutes of Livestock, Soil and Fertilizer' for example, serves to make the point.

References

ARANDA, S. (1968), *La Revolución Agraria en Cuba*, Mexico.

BARNES, A. C. (1964), *The Sugar Cane*, Wiley.

KUEZYNSKI, J. (1964), 'A new way for underdeveloped countries?', in *Problems of Economic Dynamics and Planning*, PWN, Warsaw.

OFICINA NACIONAL DE LOS CENSOS DEMOGRAFICOS Y ELECTORALES HAVANA (1958), *Encuesta Sobre Empleo, Sub-Empleo y Desempelo Mayo 1956 a Abril 1967*.

ROMEO, C. (1965), 'Acerca del desarollo economico de Cuba', *Cuba Socialista*, no. 52, p. 7.

SHANIN, L. C. (1926), *Questions of the Economic Course*, Bolshevik no. 2, 30 January, pp. 65–87.

Part Six
Employment in Urban Industries and Services

Industrialization has often been considered to be the essential force in development, and also the chief engine of employment creation. In the course of economic development, it was thought, the dwindling agricultural population and the dwindling population in traditional services would be gathered into industrial employment (and related modern services), while low wage rates and exports of labour-intensive manufactures would move the underdeveloped economy into a condition of full employment. The selected readings show how far we have come from these earlier expectations – naïve expectations as we can call them now with the benefit of hindsight. As doubts about the employment potential of modern manufacturing industry arose, more and more attention was given to the potentials of services and construction which were seen as less affected by the compulsions of capital-intensive technology and which seemed to offer wider technological choices.

As Reading 22 by Baer and Hervé indicates, the question of industrial employment is closely interwoven throughout with that of labour-intensive technology (see Part Seven). It will be noted that Baer and Hervé end up with the conclusion that we must look to productive services rather than to manufacturing industry for the bulk of employment creation. This lends emphasis to the article by Bhalla (Reading 23) with its interesting case studies of the service sector in the Philippines and Taiwan.

The final reading from C. R. Frank on Urban Employment and Economic Growth in Africa (Reading 24) also – like the papers by Baer and Hervé and Bhalla – contains valuable concrete case material, this time relating to mining in Nigeria, Ghana and Zambia, and to railways in Nigeria and East Africa. Reading 24 ends with an emphasis on the need to encourage the small-scale producer. This is a subject on which we would have liked to include further reading, if space had permitted. The example of Japan is often quoted by authors dealing with this subject as a good example of the potential role of small-scale, more labour-intensive industry even in the context of sophisticated industrialization.

Finally, in terms of employment, construction cannot be disregarded and can be of as much importance as industry and services. The paper by Strassmann, included in Part Seven, throws some light on this subject, and the conclusion (from one well qualified) that appropriate technology in building combined with reasonable wage policies can well mean an increase in employment by 3 per cent of the labour force illustrates the considerable employment potential of construction.

We would also have liked to include some reading on the question of utilization of industrial capacity. Paradoxically, in developing countries desperately short of industrial capital such capital is often heavily underutilized. This is a consequence of specific weaknesses of import-substituting industrialization under a protectionist umbrella. For instance, it has been found that the degree of industrial capacity utilization was less in Pakistan than in the capital-rich U S A. This suggests one other explanation for low employment levels and a challenge (opportunity) for an employment strategy.

22 W. Baer and M. E. Hervé

Employment and Industrialization in Developing Countries

W. Baer and M. E. Hervé, 'Employment and industrialization in developing countries', *Quarterly Journal of Economics*, vol. 80, no. 1, pp. 88–107.

I

Since the Second World War a number of countries in the economically less-developed world have adopted a strategy of rapid industrialization in order to speed up their growth. Thus, for Latin America as a whole, the pace setting sector has been manufacturing, growing at a rate of 5·9 per cent in the period 1945–9 to 1956–61, while the gross domestic product grew at 4·8 per cent.[1] Although in some countries the overall growth rate was far from satisfactory, there can be no doubt that in almost all countries where substantial industrialization was attempted, manufacturing was the most dynamic sector, being responsible for the simultaneous high growth rates in complementary activities, such as construction. The policy-makers who were responsible for industrialization policies were convinced that alternative development strategies, e.g. emphasizing agriculture, would have led to extremely low growth rates, especially due to weak world market conditions for such products.[2]

In the first half of the 1960s a note of concern, often bordering on disillusionment, could be observed among the most ardent industrialization advocates. The dynamic sector of the economy was not absorbing labor at a satisfactory rate. Not only did the industrial sector's rate of labor absorption fall behind the growth rate of the urban population in many countries, but it even fell behind the general growth rate of the population. For all of Latin America the yearly growth rate of the urban population in the period 1945–60 was 4·3 per cent, the growth rate of the economically active population in the non-agricultural sector was 3·9 per cent, and the

1. This total hides the more startling cases, such as Brazil where the manufacturing growth rate for this period was 9·4 per cent and the overall growth rate was 5·7 per cent, or Colombia where the former was 7·2 per cent and the latter 4·3 per cent. The revised figures for Argentina show an overall growth rate of 3·2 per cent and a manufacturing growth rate of 4·1 per cent in the 1950–61 period.

2. There are, of course, many exceptions. Thus a number of West African countries have greatly benefited from a development policy based on the export of a number of primary commodities, often to markets in Western Europe where they had a preferential position.

growth rate of employment in manufacturing was 2·8 per cent. In Brazil, in the years 1950–60, while the urban population grew at 5·4 per cent, the employment growth rate in manufacturing was only 2·6 per cent. In other parts of the world the situation was similar. A recent analysis of employment in the modern sector of Asian countries stated that

... In India the share of the modern sector in total employment, which was over 6 per cent in 1951, increased by barely 1 percentage point over the decade 1951–61 despite, as noted, an annual growth rate of 4 per cent of modern sector employment. In the Philippines the corresponding share, which was about 22 per cent in 1956, moved up by a mere 2 percentage points by 1961 (Doctor and Gallis, 1964, p. 558).

This tendency has led the Economic Commission for Latin America to the following conclusions:

... An appreciable proportion of the increase in the active population is not properly absorbed in the production process; economic development passes it by. This is mainly true of the population that moves from the country areas to the towns ... Far from achieving integration in city life, and sharing better patterns of living, they put up their wretched shanty towns and eke out a hand-to-mouth existence in a whole wide range of ill-paid personal services, with periods of out-and-out unemployment.

Thus poverty, frustration and resentment surge in from the country to the towns, where the symptoms of the concentration of income are already so conspicuous. This is clear proof of the explosive social polarization of development, imputable to its dynamic weakness and distributional shortcomings. (United Nations, 1963a, p. 23).

It is our purpose to examine these developments, to discern how inevitable they were, and to assess their implications for future development strategies.

II

Let us examine the extent of the employment lag in the manufacturing industries which manifested itself in a number of Latin American countries, Egypt, and India, all of which relied on industrialization to generate their economic growth in the postwar period. In Table 1 we have compared the rate of growth of output in various industries with the rate of growth of employment. In most countries the rate of growth of employment in the total manufacturing sector was substantially less than half the growth rate of output. In Argentina there was actually a fall of employment and in Mexico it was practically static.

An examination of individual industries reveals an interesting pattern. One not only finds a lag in employment in more advanced industries such

Table 1 Growth of manufacturing production and employment in selected countries (yearly growth rates)

Industrial Groups	Argentina O	Argentina E	Brazil O	Brazil E	Chile O	Chile E	Peru O	Peru E	Columbia O	Columbia E	Venezuela O	Venezuela E	Mexico O	Mexico E	India O	India E	Egypt O	Egypt E
Nonmetallic minerals	2·7	−3·0	10·1	2·6	2·1	−2·7	6·6	5·6	6·4	3·0	8·5	4·2	6·8	−5·4	12·0	3·1		
Machinery (excluding electrical)			6·1	8·4														
Fabricated metal products			12·1	5·0														
Electrical machinery	12·6	0·0	38·0	13·0	0·0	2·9			17·1	3·2	19·6	3·2			15·9	6·7		
Transportation equipment			55·0	15·4														
Furniture			3·6	7·1														
Paper and paper products	4·8	2·8	8·4	4·7	7·2	2·9	18·1	3·3	12·7	3·2	32·2	6·7	6·8	5·7	11·9	3·6		
Rubber	10·2	4·0	8·4	4·9	0·0	−0·7	9·4	7·3	11·8	7·8	19·6	12·6	6·7	4·5				
Leather goods	0·1	−4·9	4·1	2·4	0·0	−3·4	2·5	0·6	3·0	2·9	13·0	3·0			7·5	2·3		
Chemicals	6·3	0·0	25·0	3·8	3·2	0·9	7·2	6·9	10·6	3·8	14·4	1·5			11·3	4·5		
Textiles	0·6	−3·9	5·9	−2·5	0·7	−1·3	4·7	3·3	7·5	3·0	17·4	7·0	9·4	1·6	3·5	·6		
Clothing and shoes	0·5	−2·9	8·9	2·9	3·4	−1·5	10·2	2·4	7·6	1·8	17·4	−1·1	2·4	neg.	6·7	5·8		
Food products	{ 1·0	{ −2·0	7·2	0·7	{ 4·0	{ 2·7	{ 5·1	{ 6·8	{ 5·0	{ 1·1	{ 11·4	{ 4·7	{ 5·5	{ 1·8	{ 1·1	{ 2·8		
Drinks			5·1	neg.														
Tobacco			10·2	9·5	0·0	2·7	6·5	0·2			14·5	6·8						
Printing and publishing	0·9	−2·1	9·4	2·7	5·0	1·1	11·3	3·7	28·6	3·2			5·3	neg.	7·8	4·4		
Basic metals	8·4	0·2																
Wood products							5·5	3·4	6·8	2·4	3·0	2·3			18·3	8·6		
Miscellaneous											29·4	16·9						
Total	4·4	2·0	9·8	2·6	5·4	1·7	6·6	4·4	7·6	2·5	13·0	2·1	6·5	0·4	6·8	3·3	5·5	3·9

Sources: United Nations, (1963b); Revista Brasileira de Economia, Mar, 1962.

Note: O = output; E = employment.

Brazil: employment rates 1949–59; production-total 1947–60; all others 1947–58, except machinery (nonelectrical), electrical machinery, transportation equipment, furniture, clothing and shoes which are 1955–8.

Argentina: 1950–60; Chile: 1950–60; Peru: 1950–60; Colombia: 1950–60; Venezuela: 1950–60.

Mexico: 1950–61; India: 1950–60; Egypt: output 1956–60; employment 1947–57.

as fabricated metal products, transportation equipment, chemicals, etc. but it is also noticeable in the more traditional industries such as textiles, clothing and shoes. In some of the countries (Argentina, Brazil) the production of the latter dates back for a few decades. These are also the industries which are often recommended in the earlier industrialization stages due to their greater simplicity and their supposed greater capacity to absorb labor. It will be observed that not only did labor absorption substantially lag behind output, but in some cases, such as in that of textiles in Argentina, Brazil and Chile, the total amount of labor employed actually declined. This can be attributed both to the expansion of capacity by the adoption of relatively capital-intensive techniques and also to the modernization of old capacity in a more capital-intensive way.

A part of the explanation of this low labor absorption rate lies in a substantial natural increase in labor efficiency. It seems, however, that most of the explanation lies in the adoption of more capital-intensive techniques of production. As rough indicators of the degree of capital intensity in various industries we have taken installed power capacity per person employed, or, when this measure was not available, *per capita* electricity consumption by industry groups. In Table 2 we first examine the increase of this datum between the most recent census years available in various countries. The tentative conclusion one could derive from these data is that mechanization has taken place across the board. Not only was there an increase in industries which by their very nature are fairly capital-intensive (such as chemicals, metal products, etc.), but the installed *per-capita* power capacity or electricity consumption *per capita* has rapidly increased in the more traditional industries, which presumably are more labor-intensive in nature.

III

Concern about the employment effects of industrialization in underdeveloped countries has been expressed in the professional literature and in planning documents ever since the early postwar years. Although it was recognized that some degree of industrialization was necessary to attain growth rates which would raise the *per capita* income in a fairly short period of time in such countries as India or the major Latin American countries, it was also thought in most professional circles that new industries should as much as possible absorb the surplus labor which was streaming into urban centers. The strategies suggested were to develop industries which were by their very nature labor-intensive or to choose the most labor-intensive techniques possible in each industry prompted. This seemed a logical thing to do, not only from the point of view of coping with the surplus labor

Table 2 Installed capacity per person employed (percentage increases)

	Argentina (1939–53)	Brazil (1950–60)	Chile (1938–53)	Colombia (1953–8)	Mexico (1937–44)	UAR* (1948–58)
Nonmetallic minerals	26 (2·82;3·55)	89 (1·52;2·88)	120 (6·1;13·4)	60 (3·55;5·69)	163	462
Fabricated metal products	101 (1·19;2·39)	6 (3·90;4·13)		1 (1·72;1·74)		
Electrical machinery		54 (1·86;2·86)				150
Transport equipment		20 (2·14;2·57)				189
Furniture		22 (3·46;4·22)				120
Paper and paper products	58 (4·92;7·78)	47 (1·30;1·91)		−8 (4·40;4·03)	287	
Rubber	10 (3·42;3·75)	17 (7·17;8·38)		17 (3·71;4·36)		
Leather goods	71 (1·74;2·97)	51 (4·89;7·40)		1 (2·78;2·82)	150	
Chemicals	99 (2·97;5·90)	28 (2·31;2·96)	18 (3·4;4·0)	152 (1·80;4·53)		
Textiles	52 (1·35;2·05)	48 (1·65;2·44)	129 (1·4;3·2)	16 (2·48;2·88)	116	
Clothing and shoes	52 (·33; ·50)	33 (·46; ·61)	33 (·3; ·4)	11 (·27; ·30)		
Food products	36 (3·00;4·09)	58 (3·05;4·83)	47 (1·9;2·8)		55	150
Drinks		62 (2·31;3·74)		33 (2·21;2·95)		
Tobacco		4 (·52; ·54)				
Printing and publishing	107 (·82;1·70)	26 (·98;1·24)		7 (·91; ·97)		
Basic metals	156 (1·98;5·07)			87 (3·50;6·56)	−32	491
Wood products	90 (1·58;3·00)	39 (2·88;3·99)	160 (·5;1·3)	43 (1·54;2·20)		
Miscellaneous	74 (1·04;1·81)	13 (1·27;1·44)		30 (·80;1·04)		
Total Manufacturing	62 (1·88;3·05)		109 (2·2;4·6)	38 (2·00;2·75)	56	167

Note: parentheses: absolute numbers – HP per worker; electricity consumed in thousand KWH.

* *Per capita* electricity consumption in industry.

Source: same as for Table 1; also for Brazil, *Recenseomento Geral do Brasil 1960, Censo Industrial*, IBGE, 1963.

problem, but also from the point of view of minimizing cost by using the relatively most abundant and cheapest factor of production.

From the very beginning Indian planners had intentions of stressing the promotion of industries which would maximize labor absorption, e.g. cottage industries (Lewis, 1962, p. 60). However, in spite of these early efforts, Indian manufacturing development has taken place along fairly capital-intensive lines. Thus, after examining the data, Fei and Ranis (1964, p. 132) concluded that '. . . from the outset India embarked on a policy of capital deepening in her industrial sector'.

The difficulties encountered in effectively absorbing labor in newer industries in many industrializing countries were at first explained principally by the existence of a rigid factor proportion problem, in which the choices of techniques were few and of a relatively capital-intensive variety (Eckaus, 1955). However, the mounting evidence accumulated in the 1950s and early 1960s suggests that even where a choice was possible, many developing countries were not adopting the most labor-intensive techniques possible or promoting only those industries which absorbed the highest amount of labor. A survey of the literature dealing with this problem reveals that gradually an explanation for these phenomena is emerging.

The situation in which developing countries find themselves has been most interestingly expressed by Singer when he said that

. . . In many respects the technology of a hundred years ago would be desirable for them (the developing countries), and would make their economic development easier. But that technology no longer exists. It has been scrapped, and rightly scrapped, in the industrialized countries – and the technology of the industrialized countries is the only existing technology (Singer, 1964, p. 59).

The argument is not that older and more labor-intensive technologies are not available for given industries. They are indeed, in the sense that second-hand equipment can be bought. However, after acquiring an older plant, it will be found that the spare parts are not produced any more and that it would be considered a questionable use of capital to establish special spare parts industries to service outmoded machinery. Furthermore, the technicians who are contracted to install new industries will usually be conversant mainly with the most up-to-date methods.

It is commonly held that countries like France and Germany benefited from advantages of being latecomers by not having to undergo the costly process of experimentation and trial and error, which Britain as the industrial leader had to undergo. The contemporary developing countries, however, find themselves at a distinct disadvantage since they are forced to use mainly the advanced technology of the industrialized countries, which supposedly does not fit in efficiently with their factor endowments. They do not have an original technology of their own to conform to the latter or the resources to experiment widely with different types of production methods (Singer, 1964, p. 60).

Even in developing countries where older technologies have been in use for some time, the tendency is to scrap them and to adopt more modern methods. The trend towards the adoption of modern labor-saving technology has been especially supported by technical missions of international organizations. For example, in the early 1960s the Economic Commission for Latin America released two studies on the textile industry in Chile and Brazil, which recommended modernization of existing equipment.[3] Some of the reasons advanced, such as low labor productivity or high cost compared with other countries or low returns to investment, are open to doubt: low labor productivity is not unexpected in a labor-intensive industry; an international comparison of costs involves one in problems of exchange rates and other international comparison problems, and high costs are not necessarily to be avoided if one produces for a highly protected domestic market; and as far as low returns on investment are concerned, returns on already existing capital stocks should be viewed as quasi-rents. But the study found that in

. . . the cotton industry, 33 per cent of the overall operational deficiency is due to the obsolescence of the machinery, the remaining 67 per cent being due to failure to make full use of the existing machinery; the latter relates to material factors such as the quality of the raw material, balanced output and plant layout, and human factors such as efficient management, the formation of a body of technicians and supervisors, and training of the workers (1963c, p. 92).

However, because of '. . . the impossibility of solving (the problem) . . . on a piecemeal basis . . .,' the report concludes that re-equipment is the only solution. In other words, it is not possible to solve the 67 per cent deficiencies which are due to nonmachine problems in isolation of the 33 per cent deficiencies due to obsolete machinery. Re-equipment is also found to be 'by its very nature a dynamic element, which is closely linked with action in the other fields and would provide an impetus that would undoubtedly be lacking if action were confined to the administrative aspects'.

3. In the case of Chile, the study concluded that 'Without doubt, there exists an excess of personnel employed in practically all factories studied'. Much of this labor has extremely low productivity as revealed by the fact that to produce 100 yds of cotton textiles necessitates 2·33 hrs of labor in the United States, 4·74 in Japan and 12·85 in Chile. The solution recommended is, among others, the installation of modern machinery, which presumably would be labor-saving and which would increase labor productivity substantially. See Naciones Unidas (1962, pp. 13–20). In the study of the Brazilian textile industry it was found that the lower wage level in Brazil as compared with that in the United States was not enough to compensate for the much lower productivity; thus, the labor cost per unit of fabric in Brazil was 31 per cent higher than in the United States. See United Nations (1963c, p. 90).

These technical commissions made their recommendations appreciating the effects they would have on the employment picture. The report on Brazil specifically admits that new equipment will '. . . necessarily (involve) more automation, however modest the level of up-to-dateness aspired to . . .' (1963c, p. 93). And further on it states that

Any programme for the replacement of obsolete low yield equipment by modern machinery with a higher output will tend to reduce manpower absorption, and although the re-equipment considered here represents a level of productivity much lower than that in the textile industry in the United States, or even in Japan, it may well result in a considerable displacement of manpower (1963c, p. 104).

For Brazil the recommendations put forward implied a reduction of manpower of about 30 per cent in spinning mills and 45 per cent in weaving mills for each work shift.

It is clear that the institutional push is in the direction of adopting modern techniques of a labor-saving type both in new industries and in the modernization of older industries. Does this trend fly in the face of a rational use of the most abundant factor of production? The dilemma that most developing countries seem to face is an abundant unskilled labor supply, on the one hand, and on the other hand, the fact that older, more labor-intensive techniques of production are of an inefficient nature, i.e. producing a low return on capital invested in them. This conflict of interest was noted by a number of writers. Already in the mid-fifties, Galenson and Leibenstein (1955, p. 348) remarked that 'One can easily visualize situations in which the maximum labor absorption criterion would not maximize the addition to total output'. Commenting on the Indian experience, Lewis says that:

Any society, if it could rid itself of enough technique and capital, could keep every one of its ambulatory members fully employed grubbing for roots and berries. But that is not what is wanted – in India or elsewhere. The desire is for rising employment *with* rising *per capita* real income (1962, p. 52).

In the same vein Galenson and Leibenstein suggested that should

. . . it be granted that the object of development is to attain a level of economic capacity which maximizes output *per capita* at a determined future time, then the correct criterion for allocating investment must be to choose for each unit of investment that alternative that will give each worker greater productive power than any other alternative (1955, p. 351).

A half a decade later, reviewing the experience of a number of countries, a group of experts from the I L O also came to the conclusion that

. . . as techniques are made less capital-intensive, more labour can, of course, be employed with any given volume of investment, but it does not appear to be the case that techniques that employ more labour per unit of capital always yield a larger output per unit of capital. Indeed, in a number of cases it has been observed that some techniques that use much labour also use much capital per unit of output (ILO, 1961, p. 67).

These claims are substantiated by studies of alternative techniques in the cotton weaving industry in India. The results are reproduced in Table 3. The rates of profit per loom per year expressed as percentages of capital cost vary depending on the daily wage rate. It can be seen that the most labor-intensive technique is never the one producing the highest return per unit of capital. At daily wages of Rs 1, Rs 2, Rs 3, and Rs 4, the semi-automatic handloom (still labor-intensive) produces the highest return per unit of capital. But at wages of Rs 5, the factory non-automatic power loom becomes the most profitable. Theoretically speaking, the fly shuttle hand loom, the most labor-intensive combination of labor and capital, would lie on the outside of the ridge line in a production function.

The basic argument then is that given capital as the scarce factor in developing countries, the problem is not to save the use of it in the production process, but rather to maximize the output which can be gotten from it. In theory, if labor is a free factor, the production process chosen would correspond to a point on the ridge line of a production function. In this section we have examined the explanations given for deviations from this expected pattern. As convincing as these explanations are, the economist is bound to look for additional reasons of a more general, and perhaps fundamental, nature to account for the relatively capital-intensive production processes used in new industries in developing countries.

IV

Another, somewhat complementary, approach to the labor-absorption problem was made by Hirschman (1958). He stressed that due to the shortage of managerial personnel and various types of skilled labor, 'machine paced' rather than 'operator paced' operations are advisable in order to prevent breakdowns, neglect of maintenance, etc., which would curtail productivity of capital (1958, p. 145). In other words, given a shortage of skilled labor and managerial personnel, a capital-intensive technology will enable industry to economize these very scarce factors of production. More concretely, Hirschman claimed that modern and up-to-date technology

... perform(s) a crucial function in aiding management in the performance of new, unfamiliar and perhaps somewhat uncongenial tasks. By predetermining to a considerable extent what is to be done where and at what point of time, the machines and the mechanical processes they perform reduce these difficulties immeasurably in comparison with a situation where work schedules depend

Table 3 India: some economic consequences of alternative techniques in the cotton-weaving industry

Technique	Capital cost per loom (Rs)	Net value added per loom per year (Rs)	Worker required per loom per day (no.)	Rates of profit per loom per year (expressed as percentage of capital cost) at daily wages of				
				Rs 1	Rs 2	Rs 3	Rs 4	Rs 5
Fly-shuttle handloom	30–50	450	1	150	—*	—*	—*	—*
'Banaras' semi-automatic handloom	200	1500	1	600	450	300	150	0
Cottage power loom	1500	2250	1	130	110	90	70	50
Factory nonautomatic power loom	4000	6000	1	143	135	128	120	113
Automatic power loom	10,000	6000	$\frac{1}{8}$	60	59	59	59	58

Source: Raj (1959, p. 276).
* Negative percentage.

exclusively on the convergence and coordination of many human wills and actions (Hirschman, 1958, p. 146–7)[4].

Myint analyses the problem in a similar vein. He states that it is an error to examine the problem of choice of technique in a two-factor world, labor and capital. He states that in the real world

... the choice depends not only on two selected factors but on a variety of other things, notably the third main factor – skilled labor. Many underdeveloped countries suffer from a greater shortage of skills than of material capital, so that they sometimes prefer more expensive machinery, which reduces repairs and maintenance, to cheaper or second-hand machinery which, although it might reduce the ratio of capital to unskilled labour, requires a larger amount of the scarcest factor, skilled labor ... (Myint, 1964, p. 137).

Is 'skilled labor' a separate factor of production? Or can it be considered as a combination of raw labor and capital? For an individual it is clear that the latter is the case. Generally, an unskilled person can be transformed into a skilled laborer after a certain amount of time, during which he is learning, though not producing and thus consuming capital. Should this reasoning be applied to the aggregate work force, one would fall into a fallacy of composition (Marshall, 1952, pp. 561, 570).

At any given period, a certain proportion of the labor force will be skilled, usually a small proportion in a developing country. In the latter, the facilities for transforming raw into skilled labor are limited (e.g. possibilities for on-the-job training, vocational schools, etc.). Thus, in the short run, the supply of an increasing amount of skilled labor will be inelastic. This is true even if the country were prepared suddenly to channel a large proportion of investments into training facilities. Therefore, in the short run, the skilled labor supply is not likely to increase rapidly. Since when talking about development problems and their solutions we are concerned about the short run, one will have to consider skilled labor as a separate production factor.

A skilled worker without either capital or unskilled labor is unproductive. However, capital and unskilled labor need to be combined with skilled labor to be productive.[5] Thus, a minimum of skilled labor is needed per unit of unskilled labor and per unit of capital.

4. This hypothesis has yet to be fully tested. Some investigations have even come up with opposite conclusions. For example, Peter Kilby, in a forthcoming monograph on the Nigerian bread industry found that capital-intensive projects actually require more highly skilled technicians for maintenance than labor-intensive alternatives require for supervision. However, it was also found that while the expatriate maintenance expert always is equal to his task, only about one half of the expatriate supervisors prove equal to their much more difficult task.

5. It is evident that labor as a whole needs a minimum amount of capital, be it shovels or baskets, etc. And capital needs a minimum amount of unskilled labor.

Let us give an example. Suppose that for 10 unskilled workers we needed 1 skilled worker. If we have 100 unskilled workers in the economy and 5 skilled workers, the effective supply of unskilled workers is not 100, but 50. On the other hand, if the number of skilled workers exceeded 10, the effective supply of unskilled workers would be 100. It follows that the effective supply of unskilled labor is determined by the amount which can be combined with the available supply of skilled labor. Should the supply of skilled labor be higher than the amount imposed by the ratio skilled/ unskilled labor, the absolute supply of unskilled labor obviously would also be the effective supply. A similar reasoning can be applied to capital.

The effective supply of unskilled labor will probably be noticeably smaller than the absolute supply because of the scarcity of skilled labor. In the case of capital, the effective supply of capital will be little or no different from the absolute supply, because capital is also a scarce factor. If capital is scarce relative to skilled labor, the absolute supply is the effective supply. If capital is abundant relative to skilled labor, it is possible to import foreign technicians,[6] and to bring the effective capital supply to the level of the absolute capital supply.

The above reasoning should give us a framework within which to understand the tendency for adopting relatively capital-intensive techniques of production in the manufacturing sector of developing countries: effective supply of labor is in fact much smaller than the absolute supply of labor.

In Figure 1 we summarize our arguments. On the vertical and horizontal axes we measure the output of the same commodity. Y represents the commodity produced in a relatively labor-intensive way and X represents the commodity produced in a more capital-intensive way. Under the assumption that there is no shortage of skilled labor, line $Y_L - X_L$ represents the combinations of X and Y which could be produced with the available supply of labor, if capital were a free factor, and $Y_K - X_K$ represents the combinations of X and Y which could be produced with the available supply of capital, if labor were a free factor. Since X and Y are perfect substitutes, one would choose the maximum output represented by $A(Oa_y + Oa_x)$.

With the shortage of skilled labor the effective supply of unskilled labor will now determine a new production possibility line $Y'_L - X'_L$. As we have seen, this will have little influence on the supply of capital and $Y_K - X_K$ remains fixed. The new maximum output point is now represented by $B(Ob_y + Ob_x)$. A greater proportion of the good will be produced using capital-intensive techniques in B rather than in A.[7] Had one neglected the

6. Foreign technicians can be brought in to handle machines. It is more difficult, however, to import foreign skilled labor which is able or willing to work with local unskilled labor.

7. Obviously the location of B will depend on the magnitude of the shift of the curve, i.e. on the required proportion of skilled to unskilled labor.

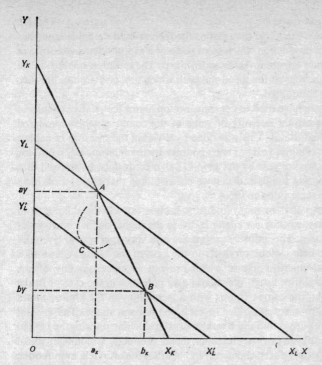

Figure 1

effects of the shortage of skilled labor, one would have expected the country to produce at A.

Moving from the choice of two processes to produce one commodity to a two-commodity choice situation, one of the latter being produced with a more labor-intensive method than the other, the result might be different if tastes of the community should be strongly biased in favor of the more labor-intensive good.[8] When X and Y are now different commodities point C will now be chosen in preference to B. However, since there is no evidence of a trend reflecting such a bias in taste, it would seem that B offers the most likely result.

8. Because of what one would expect to be the slopes of the constraint lines, this bias would indeed be very strong. Y, being the labor-intensive good, can be assumed to be a more traditional good, while X would be a good increasingly used as development proceeds. It is thus doubtful that the slope of an indifference curve would be such as drastically to favor the labor-intensive good. It is thus likely that the corner solution will be adopted.

V

So far, we have examined the reasons for the use by developing countries of methods of production which seem to be of a capital-intensive nature in relation to their apparent factor endowment. The question might now be raised about how great the speed was with which new and capital-intensive technology was adopted.

In Table 4 we have tried to get some notion about the relative change in the degree of capital intensity of some of the countries when compared with the United States. This was done by dividing the measure of capital intensity in the initial year for each country by the relevant US figure for 1939 and the second year by the 1954 US figure.[9] It must be stressed that we are comparing trends and that we are assuming that these trends have remained the same into the 1960s.

It is obvious that in many industry groups not all the difference in installed power capacity *per capita* is due to the higher capital intensity of certain processes. The industry groups are at a very aggregative level and in many instances include products in the case of the United States of a highly capital-intensive nature which are not produced in any of the developing countries listed. We should also note that in the case of Brazil and Colombia, the comparison is with a technology in the United States which is ten to six years older in each comparison made. The general impression one has is that there was no drastic catching up with the United States. In many cases (e.g. Brazilian metal products, Colombian metal products, paper products, chemicals and textiles) the ratio fell, even though the *per capita* installed capacity was rising and the labor absorption was drastically lagging behind production in those same industries (compare with Tables 1 and 2). Where the ratio rose, it should be remembered that the catching up was with the 1954 US technology (e.g. Brazilian machinery and transport equipment, Colombian food products, etc.).

This evidence would suggest that although new industries developed were of a more capital-intensive type and older industries were changing technology in a more capital-using direction, there was no drastic rush to introduce the very latest labor-saving technology of the advanced industrial countries.

VI

Granted the necessity for continued development of industries along fairly capital-intensive lines, with the result that labor is not absorbed in sufficient quantities relative to the general population growth and especially the

9. Installed power capacity *per capita* is available only up to 1954 in the United States.

Table 4 **Installed capacity per person: a comparison** (ratios comparing selected countries with the United States)

	Argentina		Brazil		Chile*		Colombia	
	1939	1953	1950	1960	1948	1953	1953	1958
	1939	1954	1939	1954	1939	1954	1939	1954†
Nonmetallic minerals	29	25			56	58	37	59
Machinery (excluding electrical)			38	46				
Fabricated metal products	32	36	101	69			46	37
Electrical machinery			52	74				
Transportation equipment			54	59				
Furniture			43	58				
Paper and paper products	39	40	62	44			34	26
Rubber	52	42	60	78			56	58
Leather goods	64	73					102	101
Chemicals	26	18			36	5	16	20
Textiles	42	38	49	50	36	27	77	65
Clothing and shoes					100	50		
Food products			43	73				
Drinks	70	64			4	34	52	66
Tobacco			46	18				
Printing and publishing	61	87	41	64			67	82
Basic metals	12	18					21	30
Wood products	34	36	49	48	37	23	33	38
Miscellaneous	63	38					48	37
Total	36	28			42	29	39	36

Per capita electricity consumption.

†These dates refer to the United States.

Source: see Table 2.

Note: these numbers represent the ratio of installed power capacity *per capita* in each country for the year indicated in the numerator to the same datum in the United States for the year indicated in the denominator.

growth of urban areas, what implications are there from the point of view of the absorption of the growing labor force in developing countries?

As a starting point, one has a tendency to look toward the historical experience of the United States and Europe. Unfortunately, the early industrialization experience was along fairly labor-intensive lines. The trend in the twentieth century has been toward greater mechanization, with a growing proportion of the labor force employed in the service sector.

If modern industry requires a substantial service sector in order to function, such a requirement would eventually provide a major source for coping with the employment problem. Of course, by definition all workers not absorbed in industry or agriculture, unless listed as openly unemployed, are presumably in the service sector. We, however, are thinking of relatively productive services, as opposed to the more parasitic services one so frequently encounters in underdeveloped countries.

Galenson is fairly optimistic along those lines. He claims that

... too little attention has been paid to those sectors of the economy in which the bulk of the new jobs are likely to be located, namely commerce and services. This does not mean that manufacturing is unimportant; on the contrary, it is, in my estimation, the key sector for economic growth. Under conditions of modern technology, however, its role is not likely to be that of a major source of new employment. Rather, it will tend to generate the effective demand leading to employment expansion in other sectors. This multiplier effect is apt to be much more significant than any direct contributions that the manufacturing sector can make to the alleviation of mass unemployment (Galenson, 1963, pp. 506–7).

Taking data from a number of developed and some underdeveloped countries he tried to establish a relationship through least squares method between employment in manufacturing and employment in tertiary activities. He found that employment in the latter was increasing a little over 1 per cent a year regardless of changes in employment in manufacturing, also that for a percentage increase in manufacturing employment there was an increase of 0·6 per cent of employment in tertiary activities (Galenson 1963, p. 510).

We have tried to summarize and interpret the relatively optimistic view of Galenson in Figure 2. In the north-east quadrant we have the relationship between new investment I and resulting changes in employment in manufacturing N_m. N_L represents this relationship if a labor-intensive technique is used; N_K if a capital-intensive technique is used. The north-west quadrant represents the relationship between changes in manufacturing employment and changes in total output. O_L represents this relationship assuming a labor-intensive technique is used; O_K assuming a capital-intensive technique is used. We are obviously assuming that the same amount of new investment will yield a larger increase in output when capital-intensive techniques are chosen. The south-west quadrant represents the relationship between changes in output and changes of employment in the service sector. It can be seen that an investment of OA can result in a creation of employment in manufacturing of AC, using labor-intensive techniques, and only AB using capital-intensive techniques. However, the labor-intensive technique results in an output of only OD and service employment creation of only OF, while the capital-intensive technique creates output of OE and service employment of OG. As drawn in this diagram, the total

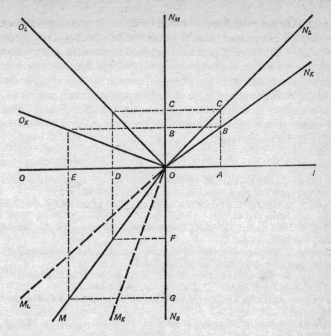

Figure 2

employment creation is greater via the labor-saving technique. Whether such a favorable relationship exists remains to be seen.

Substantially more empirical research needs to be done on employment in the service sector and its relationship to other sectors. It is quite possible that the relationship between increased employment in the service sector and output depends on the technique of production used. More capital-intensive techniques might call forth a greater amount of service employment (OM_k); whereas labor-intensive techniques might have a much weaker service employment impact (OM_L). It could also be that the slope of the OM curves, which can be drawn as straight lines in the short run, will be influenced by the degree of development which the country had attained at the starting point of our analysis. For example, a fairly developed country might have a substantially expanded service sector; thus, additional investment in the manufacturing sector will call forth relatively small amounts of increased service employment.

In this analysis we have not explored dynamic elements; capital-intensive techniques supposedly lead to distribution of incomes more favorable to the saving classes, thus there is a greater potential for further investment expansion. On the other hand, it might be asked: if more capital-intensive techniques are used, which result in an uneven distribution of income, could this lead to a situation of increased production potential in the economy without the generation of effective demand to occupy the new capacity fully?

Our purpose in this essay has been to show that the lack of labor absorption in the manufacturing sector of developing countries is not necessarily due to conscious or wrong policy choices, but has several partial explanations which should be combined with the more general explanation of effective factor endowment.

References

DOCTOR, K. C., and GALLIS, H. (1964), 'Modern sector employment in Asian countries: some empirical estimates', *Int. Lab. Rev.*, vol. 89, p. 558.

ECKAUS, R. S. (1955), 'The factor proportions problem in underdeveloped areas', *Amer. econ. Rev.*, vol. 45.

FEI, J. C. H., and RANIS, G. (1964), *Development of the Labour Surplus Economy: Theory and Policy*, Irwin.

GALENSON, W. (1963), 'Economic development and the sectoral expansion of employment', *Int. Lab. Rev.*, vol. 88, pp. 505–19.

GALENSON, W., and LEIBENSTEIN, H. (1955), Investment criteria, productivity and economic development', *Q. J. Econ.*, vol. 69, pp. 343–70.

HIRSCHMAN, A. (1958), *The Strategy of Economic Development*, Yale University Press.

ILO (1961), *Employment Objectives in Economic Development*, Geneva, ILO.

LEWIS, J. P. (1962), *Quiet Crisis in India*, Brookings Institution.

MARSHALL, A. (1952), *Principles of Economics*, eighth edn, Macmillan.

MYINT, H. (1964), *The Economics of the Developing Countries*, Hutchinson.

NACIONES UNIDAS (1962), *La industria textil de Chile*.

RAJ, K. N. (1959), 'Employment and unemployment in the Indian economy: problems of classification, measurement and policy', *Econ. Devel. Cult. Change*, vol. 7, pp. 258–85.

SINGER, H. W. (1964), *International Development: Growth and Change*, McGraw-Hill.

UNITED NATIONS (1963a), *Towards a Dynamic Development Policy for Latin America*, UN.

UNITED NATIONS (1963b), *The Growth of World Industry 1938–61*, UN.

UNITED NATIONS (1963c), *The Textile Industry in Latin America II*, UN.

23 A. S. Bhalla

The Role of Services in Employment Expansion

Extract from A. S. Bhalla, 'The role of services in employment expansion', in
W. Galenson (ed.), *Essays on Employment*, ILO Geneva, 1971.

With the exception of a few recent empirical studies (Galenson, 1963, pp.
505–19; Ofer, 1967; Sinha, 1968, pp. 53–67), economic literature has continued to neglect the growing services sectors of the less developed countries.
While writers like Kuznets (1945), Stigler (1956) and Fuchs (1968) have, it
is true, done a great deal to meet Colin Clark's (1940) complaint that 'the
economics of tertiary industry remains to be written', most work in this
field has focused on the economy of the United States or the advanced
countries of Western Europe.

Attempts to explain the relatively faster growth of employment in the
services sector (particularly in the developed economies) have usually
adopted one of the three main approaches:

1. *The income and expenditure approach*, which uses the structure of demand
as an explanatory variable. (Clark, 1940).

2. *The productivity approach*, which ascribes employment growth in services
to that sector's relatively slower growth of productivity. (Fuchs, 1968).

3. *The employment approach*, which correlates tertiary employment with
manufacturing employment (Galenson, 1963; Tulpule, 1968, pp. 207–29).

In varying degrees the above explanations of sectoral labour allocation
are relevant to the situation in the less developed countries. However, each
of them accounts for only a part of the total labour force engaged in the
services sector.[1] For instance only a small proportion of tertiary employment in the less developed labour surplus economies is a function of the
income-elasticity of demand for services. The bulk is to be found in such
traditional and unorganized services as shoe-shining and petty retail trades
bearing no observable relationship to effective labour demand. Here the

1. For the purpose of the present paper the services sector is defined to include
commerce, government and professional services, and personal and domestic services.
Basic services, such as transport and communications and gas, water and electricity,
are excluded from services since they generally bear a greater resemblance to industry
in respect of the nature of organization, scale of production and capital intensity of
technology. In the less developed countries, it is true, traditional modes of transportation may be quite labour-intensive.

supply of labour creates its own employment opportunities by sharing out a given total amount of work. Even the expansion of employment in public administration and government services – sectors commonly regarded as typifying modern development – may reflect a social need to absorb labour which would otherwise be redundant. In conditions of excess labour supply the efficient or optimum utilization of *some* manpower resources may be considered less essential than the inefficient utilization of *all* or *most* of them. Hence the overcrowding of government services when there is large-scale unemployment among the better-educated.

Modern versus traditional services

It is clear then that the entire labour force absorbed in the services sector cannot be considered as either demand-induced or a 'residual' category. For a proper economic analysis, therefore, it would be useful to disaggregate total services employment into its 'modern' (demand-determined) and 'traditional' (supply-determined) components. The 'characteristics of labour' criterion provides a tentative though not a very satisfactory answer to the problem of separating data and of analysing growth of employment in the services sector. As a rough approximation, all wage-earning and salaried employment WSW may be considered as 'modern', whereas all non-wage or self-employment SEW and unpaid family labour FW may be deemed 'traditional'.[2] This division has distinct advantages. First, it helps to identify systems of employment under which the pattern of economic organization, the nature and structure of remuneration, and the level and types of skills are very different. Second, a distinction between wage-based and family-based self-supporting labour helps to explain the existence of infinitesimal or even zero earnings in self-employment.[3] Third, it shows up the limitations of the popular interpretation of Colin Clark's thesis that, at

2. Using the criterion of numbers employed – establishments employing ten or fewer workers being considered 'traditional' and those employing more than ten 'modern' – is simple but not very satisfactory in the case of many services such as public administration and domestic and personal services. It has also been proposed to classify the economically active population according to three different levels of productivity: high, medium and low (Slawinski 1967). The productivity criterion has its limitations too, however. It is well known that output and productivity are not very meaningful concepts in the case of many services. Even apart from the conceptual problems, the difficulties of measurement are too formidable to be easily overcome.

3. The fact of zero or even negative earnings can be illustrated by the example of street fruit-sellers. The spoilage of perishables is likely to result in losses so, towards the end of the day, in an attempt to dispose of all their supplies and thus minimize losses, the fruit-sellers may often have to reduce their prices to cost or below it. It is true that it is impossible to survive at zero earnings, but under the automatic distributive mechanism that works through the extended family system, a subsidy or transfer income enables workers to survive on very low earnings.

higher levels of income per head, a redistribution of labour takes place in favour of the services sector. The fact that the services sector's share of the labour force is quite large in countries with low income levels does not necessarily invalidate Clark's proposition, which applies mainly to the 'modern', demand-induced types of services. The concept of income-elasticity of demand does not explain a large proportion of the self-supporting labour in 'traditional' services which inflates the services' share in the total labour force.

[. . .] In the pages that follow an attempt is made to disaggregate employment in the major services subsectors of China (Taiwan) and the Philippines. The choice of these countries is only partly determined by the availability of requisite data.[4] They are also interesting for purposes of comparison, since in the case of Taiwan industrial and overall economic growth has been exceptionally rapid for the past several years, whereas in the Philippines the growth rates of income and of its industrial component have both been relatively slow.[5] Irrespective of these differences, the labour absorption in the services sectors of the two countries has been quite rapid. In the case of Taiwan, during the decade 1955–65, employment grew fastest in the professions and government services. While total employment grew at a rate of about 2 per cent per annum, employment in government services grew by 5·2 per cent and in the professions by about 5·8 per cent per annum. In the Philippines, too, the heterogeneous category of 'government, community, business and recreation' recorded the most rapid growth in employment, while commerce was not far behind. The services sectors as a whole accounted for a substantial proportion of additional employment – about 46 per cent in Taiwan and 34 per cent in the Philippines.

Self-employment versus wage-employment

Urbanization and monetization of traditional subsistence sectors normally bring in their wake a shift towards tertiary employment. There is some scattered evidence that at least a part of the migrants go into 'service-type' occupations. The occupational distribution of the migrants and non-

4. For the Philippines the period 1958–64 has been chosen since the time series between May 1958 and May 1964 seem to be more regular than over a longer period. Moreover, from May 1965 onwards the sample design of households has been changed. There is also a substantial difference in the urban-rural definitions used in the new sample. Thus 'estimates from the surveys conducted under the old design are not directly comparable with those from the May 1965 survey' (Bureau of the Census and Statistics, 1966).

5. In Taiwan the gross domestic product over the period 1960–65 grew at an annual rate of 9·2 per cent and its component originating in industry at 11 per cent per annum. Over the same period the corresponding figures for the Philippines were 4·4 per cent and 6 per cent (United Nations, 1968, table 6, p. 20).

migrants revealed by a recent sample survey in a metropolitan area of Taiwan demonstrated that the largest shift of migrants was into sales and service occupations (over 30 per cent) and not into skilled or semi-skilled factory jobs.[6] However, what is less clear is whether urbanization also leads to a shift from self-employment to wage employment. In the case of 'modern' services, which with few exceptions provide greater opportunities for self-employment, responsiveness to urbanization may not necessarily show itself in the diminution of self-supporting labour. The relative importance of self-employed workers and unpaid family labour in services needs to be empirically determined. Recognizing the formidable data and conceptual limitations,[7] the ratios of self-employed to wage-employed SEW/WSW and of family labour to wage labour FW/WSW for each of the major subsectors of the services sector have been estimated. These ratios are presented in Tables 1 and 2 along with the average annual rates of change of wage and salary workers WSW, self-employed workers SEW and family labour FW over the stated periods.

In the Philippines (Table 1), the SEW/WSW ratio was quite high in manufacturing in both 1958 and 1964, coming immediately after agriculture, commerce and personal services. So also was the FW/WSW ratio. Between 1958 and 1964 both these ratios declined considerably in agriculture, manufacturing and commerce, thus suggesting a gain of wage employment over self-employment. However, in the case of 'personal services other than domestic', the ratios experienced sharp increases. Self-employment, including family labour, gained in importance when the growth rate of wage employment was negative. In construction too, self-employment

6. This survey considered a sample frame for male migrants who had moved to the city of Taichung over a two-year period. The age range of 23–42 was chosen to provide a sample of primary migrants with an age span of twenty years. A sample of non-migrants was also taken for purposes of comparison (see Speare, Jr (1969)). In an earlier survey undertaken in 1964 three types of migrants were considered, commuters, seasonal workers who worked temporarily for others, and long-term employees who left their farms and worked permanently in the cities. Most male commuters worked as public officials and teachers, whereas the largest proportion of female commuters went into factories. About 6 per cent of the seasonal workers worked as coolies and domestic servants. The long-term male workers found employment mainly as factory workers, public officials, teachers and clerks. The female workers in this category were absorbed as maidservants, factory girls and barbers (Tsui and Lin (1964)).

7. For example shifts between paid and unpaid employment seem to cause statistical difficulties. This substitution of activities, which occurs even in developed countries (witness the virtual disappearance of paid domestic servants), tends to affect the proportion of labour engaged in the services sector. In some cases the enumerators may also classify many unpaid family workers as persons not in the labour force. The concept of labour force in general has only a limited meaning in the less developed countries, where it is extremely hard to distinguish between the economically active and non-active population.

Table 1 **Philippines: self-employment and wage employment: Ratios and annual rates of change, 1958–64** (percentages)

Sector and sex	Ratio				Average annual rate of change, 1958–64		
	SEW/WSW		*FW/WSW*				
	1958	*1964*	*1958*	*1964*	*WSW*	*SEW*	*FW*
Both sexes:							
Agriculture	505·3	358·8	448·7	330·4	7·6	1·6	2·2
Manufacturing	108·5	73·6	46·6	25·2	6·8	0·2	−2·9
Construction	4·0	5·9	2·0	1·5	4·3	11·2	0·0
Commerce	248·5	206·9	81·2	67·9	9·8	4·0	6·6
Government, community, business, recreation	7·3	6·8	1·4	1·1	6·8	5·5	3·0
Domestic services	1·1	—	1·4	—	2·1	−12·2	—
Personal services other than domestic	180·3	215·6	24·2	56·2	−0·6	2·4	14·4
Males:							
Agriculture	603·8	440·3	332·9	248·8	7·2	1·7	2·1
Manufacturing	33·7	25·6	10·7	9·0	6·2	1·4	3·3
Construction	4·0	5·3	1·6	1·2	4·2	9·2	0·0
Commerce	141·1	119·2	24·1	40·2	6·5	3·6	15·9
Government, community, business, recreation	8·0	8·2	1·6	0·6	5·4	6·0	−6·9
Domestic services	—	—	6·3	—	−0·2	—	−12·2
Personal services other than domestic	153·3	128·9	16·6	26·3	3·9	1·1	12·2
Females:							
Agriculture	156·7	94·0	859·4	595·6	8·7	*	2·3
Manufacturing	230·1	144·6	105·0	50·2	7·8	*	−3·7
Construction	—	—	—	—	—	—	—
Commerce	576·2	324·2	198·3	106·6	14·9	4·3	3·6
Government, community, business, recreation	6·8	5·1	—	1·5	8·9	3·8	—
Domestic services	0·7	0·3	0·3	—	2·5	−6·9	−12·2
Personal services other than domestic	208·3	356·0	25·0	104·0	4·5	2·8	18·9

— Denotes not reported in sample households.

* Denotes negligible.

Source: Bureau of the Census and Statistics: *Philippine Statistical Survey of Households Bulletin* (Manila).

(but not unpaid family labour) increased relative to wage employment. Between sexes, while male self-employment declined and family labour gained in importance in the personal services, females showed tremendous gains in both self-supporting and wage labour. In commerce, on the other hand, both female and male self-employment declined, whereas the ratio of family labour to wage earners increased in the case of males and decreased in the case of females. This pattern of male employment in commerce seems to suggest the possibility of switching between self-employment and unpaid family work.

In Taiwan the ratio of self-employment as well as of unpaid family labour to wage employment declined in commerce generally and in the retail trade for both males and females (Table 2). However, the ratio of family labour to wage employment increased slightly for the wholesale trade. Both self-employment and unpaid family labour played a minor role in manufacturing, where between 1961 and 1966 these two categories in fact registered a rapid decline. Commerce, wholesale as well as retail, and recreational services witnessed a phenomenal growth of wage labour. The annual rate of increase of family labour was also significant (with the exception of manufacturing) although self-employment in general increased less rapidly.

The above observations can be summarized in symbols as follows (for convenience we substitute L_S for SEW and L_W for WSW and denote time by the subscript t):

$$\frac{d(L_S/L_W)}{dt} > 0 \text{ when } \frac{\triangle L_W}{L_W} < 0 \ldots \text{(Philippines)}$$

$$\frac{d(L_S/L_W)}{dt} < 0 \text{ when } \frac{\triangle L_W}{L_W} > 0 \ldots \text{(Taiwan)}$$

Thus the relative growth of self-supporting labour varies inversely with the growth of wage-earning opportunities, i.e. $dL_S/dL_W < 0$. As a special case, it may be assumed that change in self-employment need not be determined by the growth of wage employment. It may be argued that the institutional factor of a general disinclination to work for an employer, which is reinforced by the existence of the extended family system providing cheap and unpaid labour, tends to encourage self-employment. The observations relating to Taiwan and the Philippines do not seem to bear this out, however. Instead, they suggest an institutional preference for wage employment as a means of reducing risks and achieving greater stability of incomes.[8]

8. A preference for self-employment would indeed have an important implication for employment policy. If a part of the workforce preferred to work on its own account, even at low earnings, the need to create wage-earning jobs would be diminished and the level of the money wage militating against employment expansion would become irrelevant. In this context it is interesting to note that Meade (1961) proposed self-employment as one of the solutions for the unemployment problems of Mauritius.

Table 2 Taiwan: Self-employment and wage employment:
Ratios and annual rates of change, 1961–66 (percentages)

Sector and sex	Ratio				Average annual rate of change, 1961–66		
	SEW/WSW		FW/WSW		WSW	SEW	FW
	1961	1966	1961	1966			
Both sexes							
Manufacturing	13·3	7·3	8·4	3·5	8·3	−3·5	−6·6
Commerce	157·8	106·4	98·3	78·1	13·6	4·9	8·4
Wholesale trade	20·9	11·5	8·9	9·4	13·1	0·5	14·4
Retail trade	304·0	188·2	193·7	137·5	15·9	5·4	8·3
Banking and financial institutions	—	2·3	—	1·2	6·2	—	—
Personal services	69·6	59·7	40·9	37·4	4·1	1·0	2·2
Recreational services	19·8	13·7	8·4	8·3	22·4	13·8	22·3
Males							
Manufacturing	17·8	8·6	7·5	3·3	6·7	−5·8	−6·6
Commerce	139·1	98·9	48·7	40·3	12·1	4·7	8·0
Wholesale trade	21·7	12·8	6·0	6·1	10·8	0·1	10·8
Retail trade	271·2	170·6	96·5	68·9	14·9	5·3	8·0
Banking and financial institutions	—	2·5	—	0·7	5·0	—	—
Personal services	87·1	87·4	29·2	30·7	*	*	1·0
Recreational services	24·1	14·1	5·7	6·3	21·5	9·1	23·8
Females							
Manufacturing	4·4	5·1	10·3	3·8	10·9	14·3	−6·6
Commerce	242·0	131·2	322·6	203·9	19·1	5·5	8·1
Wholesale trade	16·7	7·6	23·4	19·6	22·8	5·0	18·5
Retail trade	434·2	251·5	578·8	383·7	17·9	5·6	8·5
Banking and financial institutions	—	1·8	—	2·2	8·9	—	—
Personal services	51·7	40·0	52·8	42·2	7·8	2·4	3·1
Recreation services	15·1	13·3	11·3	10·3	23·7	20·8	21·3

— Denotes that no figures were reported for owner-operators and unpaid family workers. Total persons engaged consisted of employees only.

*Denotes negligible.

Source: Second and Third Industrial and Commercial Censuses of Taiwan, 1961 and 1966.

The Philippine case, where the ratio of self-employed labour to wage labour increased in personal services when the growth of wage employment was negative, seems to suggest that the product-mix or the composition of demand in this subsector, given the total demand, changed in favour of traditional services such as barber shops, laundering, cleaning and dyeing at the expense of 'modern' commercial and wage-based services such as hotels, restaurants and lodging houses.[9] Otherwise the shift from wage employment to self-employment would have seemed unlikely. Secondly, such a shift may also occur when continued non-commercialization of traditional services is accompanied by a decline in the growth of wage employment in the commercialized services. This phenomenon of shifts between self-supporting labour and wage labour in accordance with changes in the product-mix does not seem to be peculiar to services. In the Philippines the traditional sector was quite predominant even in manufacturing. This is reflected in the large shares of self-employed workers and family labour in total manufacturing employment. Although these shares declined in 1964, they were still as high as 37 per cent and 12·8 per cent of the total respectively. It is worth noting that employment in manufacturing as a proportion of total employment also declined from 12·2 per cent in 1958 to 11·8 per cent in 1964.

Under equilibrium conditions, the allocation of total labour in the services sector into the wage (L_W) and non-wage (L_S) components (assuming perfect substitutability) will be governed by the rule that the marginal rate of substitution between L_S and L_W equals their price ratio, i.e. $dL_S/dL_W = p_S/p_W$. So will the ratio of their marginal products be equal to the ratio of their prices. If we postulate factor price equalization, which should be expected when L_S and L_W have the same skills and are freely substitutable, then $p_S = p_W$ and $p_S/p_W = 1$. In reality, however, allocative equilibrium may instead be represented by $p_S/p_W = 1 - k$, where k is a constant which denotes institutional rigidities, factor immobility and market imperfections. Thus, under conditions of equilibrium, factor price differentials may continue to exist. Various explanations have been presented for the so-called 'wage-gap' between capitalistic wage-based production and family-based activities, namely greater social costs of labour in wage employment, effects of unionization and trade union pressures which do not influence earnings in self-supporting business, and wage-efficiency relationships under a wage-based system.[10] However, little emphasis seems to be placed on the fact that it is not in the economic interest of self-employed labour to bid down the wages of their relatives working in the wage sector. Under the distributive mechanism of the extended family system income is shared by the wage

9. The indices of employment based on the data of 1289 cooperating establishments in the Philippines indicate a decline of about 4 per cent in the case of hotels and lodging houses and an increase of about 27 per cent in the case of laundering, cleaning and dyeing between 1958 and 1964 (Central Bank of the Philippines: *Statistical Bulletin*, Manila).

10. For a succinct summary of various explanations of the wage gap see Sen (1966).

earners as well as the self-employed. Those working for themselves in low-earning occupations are the beneficiaries of income transfers from their wage-earning relatives, a decline in whose wages is most likely to reduce the size of these transfer payments. It is thus uncertain that income maximization would occur if all those in precarious self-employment flooded the labour market.[11]

Changes in the relative prices of wage and non-wage labour would affect labour absorption in each category. Within the services sector, lower average earnings in self-employment than in wage-earning activities point to a relatively greater absorption of labour in self-supporting business. Secondly, if the average earnings (or their rate of increase) in services are lower than in industry or the economy as a whole, then the capacity of the services sector to absorb labour might be considered greater.

The data on income from self-employment and wage employment in China (Taiwan) are of relevance. Table 3 indicates the ratios of prices of self-supporting and wage labour and the rates of change of average earnings in service employment in relation to those in industry and commerce as a whole. In 1961 the average earnings from self-employment (excluding family labour) were higher than those from wage employment with the exception only of commerce, wholesale trade, commodity brokerage and manufacturing. In 1966, however, even in commerce as a whole, in wholesale as well as in retail trade, average earnings of self-supporting labour exceeded those of wage labour.[12] When unpaid family labour is included in the self-employed (as it should be since most of it supports family enterprise) the real income per head becomes much lower than the average earnings of the owner-operators. And in the case of retail trade and recreation services real income per head also turns out to be lower than the average real earnings of wage labour. This differential in favour of the latter may be somewhat exaggerated since under conditions of income-sharing the wage earners' real income per head is also lower than the wage rate. The real earnings gap may be attributed to differences in earner-dependants ratios.[13]

11. In the less developed countries where there is no unemployment insurance the extended family system plays an economic role by subsidizing the unemployed and the underemployed. The gains from the decline of this system may not necessarily offset the social costs involved.

12. A study of migrants from rural areas in Taiwan to an urban centre shows that the largest increase in income took place among those who changed their status from 'employees' to 'self-employed' (Speare, 1969).

13. If W is the wage per wage earner, N is the number employed at that wage level and a is the number of dependants per wage earner, then $W > WN/N(1+a)$ or $W(1/1+a)$.

If, under conditions of equilibrium, $W = aw$, where w is the average earnings per self-employed owner-operator, and a the number of dependants per owner-operator, then $W(1/1+a) > w(1/1+a')$ if $a < a'$.

In the case of family enterprises, both income-sharing and work-sharing take place in order to maintain the excess labour force, whose size roughly corresponds to that of the unpaid family labour force. In the case of wage earners, on the other hand, income is more likely to be shared without any corresponding job-sharing.

Table 3 Taiwan: relative average real earnings, 1961–6

Sector	Price ratio (Ps/Pw), 1961		Price ratio (Ps/Pw), 1966		Ratio of average earnings in each sector to earnings in 'industry' and commerce'		Ratio of rate of increase of average earnings in each sector to rate in 'industry'
	(1)	(2)	(1)	(2)	1961	1966	1961–6
Manufacturing	0·35	0·21	0·67	0·45	0·94	1·00	1·16
Commerce	0·91	0·56	1·13	0·65	0·93	0·81	0·67
Wholesale	0·96	0·67	1·23	0·68	1·48	1·11	0·31
Retail	1·16	0·71	1·28	0·74	0·80	0·73	0·79
Commodity brokerage	0·71	0·47	0·40	0·29	1·73	2·03	1·40
Recreation services	1·74	1·22	1·33	0·83	1·10	0·93	0·59
Personal services	2·23	1·17	1·97	1·21	0·91	0·69	0·34

Note: labour income from self-employment was derived from estimates of owner-disbursements by assuming that it was 85 per cent of owner-disbursements in manufacturing, 90 per cent in commerce and 95 per cent in other services. The choice of these percentages is arbitrary. There is a possibility of downward bias since in a census of survey in the less developed countries people are often reluctant to give their true income for fear that the data will be used for tax purposes.

Money earnings were deflated by a general consumer price index with 1963 = 100. Consumer prices indices were taken from *Year Book of Labour Statistics* (Geneva, ILO).

Column (1): ratio calculated by excluding family labour from the self-employed.

Column (2): ratio calculated by including family labour among the self-employed.
Source: Second and Third Industrial and Commercial Censuses of Taiwan, 1961 and 1966.

In commerce, retail trade and recreation and personal services, the average total earnings in 1966 were lower than the average for industry and commerce as a whole, whereas for wholesale trade they were higher. In terms of rates of change, only earnings in manufacturing and in commodity brokerage rose faster than the overall average. The average earnings in commerce and personal services increased relatively more slowly than those in other services and in industry and commerce.

The earnings data on Taiwan seem to bear out only partially J. S. Mill's proposition that competition in professional services and distribution 'often, instead of lowering prices, merely divides the gains of the high price among a greater number of dealers' (Mill, 1965). Mill argued that competition in retail trade is so imperfect that in every trade there are 'cheap shops and dear shops', often selling the same articles at different prices to different customers. Similarly, the fees of physicians, surgeons and barristers are fixed more by 'custom' than by competition, which only operates by 'diminishing each competitor's chances of fees, not by lowering the fees themselves'.

High price of distribution and of professional services may be only a short-run phenomenon occurring more readily in the 'modern'-type professional services than in the traditional ones such as petty retailing. Mill does not, however, make any such distinction.[14] With the influx of new competitors, particularly in the retail trade, the market share of each is likely to fall. In an effort to survive, the retail shopkeepers may raise their mark-up in order to check the reduction in their gross margins. However, continued shifts upwards in the labour supply function (as seem to have occurred in the Philippines, where the labour force displaced from the traditional handicrafts and cottage industries has apparently spilled over into retail trades and petty services) are more likely to result in the emergence of excess capacity, decline in price and closure of inefficient businesses due to high costs of distribution.

The low average earnings in retail trade and personal services in Taiwan relative to the industrial average and to the earnings in other service industries seem to point towards a certain degree of underemployment and hence greater labour absorption made possible through sharing of work and incomes. However, the measurement of underemployment is complicated by the existence of self-employment and domestic modes of production under which it is extremely difficult to distinguish between work and leisure and to determine the rate of transformation between them. There may be no underutilization of labour-time in petty trades and services, since persons engaged in them often work long hours, either in the same activity or in different casual activities, for very low earnings. In such cases it is

14. As Kuznets has pointed out, the high price of professional services may be more a reflection of monopolistic competition than of custom. 'In the early stages of development, when education was scarce and the professionally trained members of the services sector were almost in the position of monopolists, the low *per capita* income itself might have meant professional incomes that were large multiples of the country-wide average – much higher than in the later phases when education was more widespread and *per capita* income higher' (Kuznets, 1966, pp. 152–3). Under conditions of excess labour supply, competition in professional services such as law may also result in considerable idle capacity and lower prices.

better to consider underemployment as consisting of two dimensions which are related but distinct, namely:

(a) degree of labour-time (under)utilization $= (h\text{-}\bar{h}) = H$, i.e. the difference between actual and average man-hours;
(b) degree of labour (mis)allocation $= (e\text{-}\bar{e}) = E$, i.e. the difference between actual and average earnings.

At any given point of time, a composite index of the degree of labour utilization (U_L) will be given by the product of (a) and (b), so that

$$U_L = (h\text{-}\bar{h})\,(e\text{-}\bar{e}) = H \cdot E.$$

The increase in the degree of labour market imperfections reflected in an increase in underemployment will then be measured by

$$U'_L = HdE + EdH.$$

If earnings are a function of man-hours, i.e. $E = f(H)$, then

$$U'_L = \left(E + H\,\frac{dE}{dH} \right) dH.$$

The fact that the ratio of the quantity of self-employed workers to wage labour L_S/L_W declined in Taiwan when their price ratio p_S/p_W increased (see Tables 2 and 3) seems to suggest that the market mechanism has been at work in the allocation of labour. When the quantity of wage labour increased between 1961 and 1966, the real wage seems to have declined relative to earnings in self-employment. The increase in the amount of wage labour lowered the share of self-supporting labour relative to wage labour. As this happened, the price of self-supporting labour seems to have risen relative to that of wage labour. The decline of labour income from self-employment as a proportion of total earnings in the period 1961–6 (see Table 4) also seems to support this supposition.

Conclusions

No conclusive generalizations are possible on the basis of the scattered and meagre data available. There are at present significant gaps in the statistical information on real output, employment, earnings and productivity in the services sector. Besides empirical difficulties, there are also basic conceptual limitations in measuring the labour force of the less developed countries. The market mechanism does not play a significant role in allocating resources between industries and occupations. Absence of industrial and occupational specialization blurs the distinction between economically active and inactive population. The same people often devote part of their time to farming, trading, money-lending, and still other occupations. Those who are working for themselves also take on paid employment as wage labourers. Statistics fail to reflect the incidence of multiple job-holding since each member of the labour force is assigned to a specific economic activity on the basis of his principal occupation.

Table 4 **Taiwan: Share of labour income from self-employment in total earnings, 1961–6**

Sector	Self-employment income as a percentage of total earnings		Percentage change, 1961–6
	1961	*1966*	
Commerce	59·0	54·6	− 4·4
Wholesale trade	16·8	12·5	− 4·3
Retail trade	77·9	70·7	− 7·2
Commodity brokerage	13·5	1·8	−11·7
Recreation services	25·7	15·5	−10·2
Personal services	56·3	54·0	− 2·3
Manufacturing	4·5	4·7	+ 0·2

Source: Second and Third Industrial and Commercial Censuses of Taiwan, 1961 and 1966.
Note: total earnings include allowances and benefits.

In spite of these limitations, however, one can say that there is a discernible tendency, in both Taiwan and the Philippines, for the services sector to absorb a large bulk of the additional labour force. Where the two economies seem to differ is in the composition and characteristics of the labour force absorbed in services. The differential industrial and economic growth affects the distribution of labour within the services sector. It appears that there was a decline of the unorganized traditional service activities in Taiwan in the wake of rapid economic growth. In the Philippines, on the other hand, there was a shift of traditional activities from manufacturing to such services as commerce. These two different phenomena suggest (a) that the inter-sectoral flows of labour in the less developed countries need not always imply labour transfers from agriculture to industry or to services by-passing industry, and (b) that in fact labour transfers occur in two stages. In an economy such as the Philippines where the rate of growth of industrial output is relatively slow, the surplus agricultural labour shifts to traditional manufacturing and from there to traditional services when manufacturing expands under conditions of modern technology. At higher rates of growth, however, as in the case of Taiwan, the potential surplus labour in traditional services is absorbed in industry at the same time as the growth of industry generates 'modern' employment in complementary services. The net effect of these movements in opposite directions would be to raise the relative share of modern employment without necessarily raising the amount of total labour absorption in services. The rate of transformation of traditional into modern types of labour will depend on the rate at which the two contrary processes take place as a result of industrial growth.

There is also some indication that the changing proportions of the self-employed and of unpaid family labour can give a rough idea of the declining or growing importance of the 'traditional' unorganized segments in the various branches of economic activity. Nevertheless, the criterion of 'status of employment' is quite inappropriate for distinguishing between traditional and modern activities in such sectors as government services. In the less developed countries there is a developmental sector of the government in the shape of the 'public sector' services such as health, education, industry, transport and communications. There is also a traditional sector that is characterized by the unnecessary growth in the employment of clerks, messengers and watchmen who perform no well-defined economic role. Much research is required to develop suitable and systematic criteria for identifying the traditional and modern activities and for regrouping the statistical data on output and employment.

Closely related to the above question is the problem of measurement of underemployment in services. Does the expansion of employment in services, particularly in commerce, reflect conditions of underemployment? Are comparative earnings and productivity good measures of the degree of labour utilization, especially in sectors where self-employment and domestic modes of production are predominant? Does a movement from traditional self-employment to wage employment reduce 'disguised unemployment'? All these questions merit detailed investigation. The few observations made in this paper cannot provide satisfactory answers to the problem: what they do seem to suggest, however, is that at least a part of the additional employment in commerce and other services occurs through work-spreading and income-sharing.

References

BUREAU of the CENSUS and STATISTICS (1966), *Republic of the Philippines*, *special release no. 25*, Manila.

CLARK, C. (1940), *The Conditions of Economic Progress*, Macmillan.

FUCHS, V. R. (1968), *The Service Economy*, Columbia University Press.

GALENSON, W. (1963), 'Economic development and the sectoral expansion of employment', *Int. Lab. Rev.*, vol. 87, pp. 505–19.

KUZNETS, S. (1966), *Modern Economic Growth – Rate, Structure and Spread, Studies in Comparative Economics*, Yale University Press.

KUZNETS, S., and FRIEDMAN, M. (1945), *Income from Independent Professional Practice*, NBER.

MEADE, J. E. (1961), 'Mauritius – a case study in Malthusian economics', *Econ. J.*, vol. 71, pp. 521–534.

MILL, J. S. (1965), *Principles of Political Economy*, Book 2, Routledge& Kegan Paul.

OFER, G. (1967), *The Service Industries in a Developing Economy: Israel as a Case Study*, Praeger.

SEN, A. K. (1966), 'Peasants and dualism with or without surplus labour', *J. Pol. Econ.*, vol. 74, no. 5.

SINHA, J. N. (1968), 'Employment in trade – the Indian experience', *Indian Econ. J.*, vol. 16, no. 1, pp. 53–67.

SLAWINSKI, Z. (1967), 'The structure of manpower in Latin America: evolution during the past few decades and long-term prospects', in *Problems of Human Resources Planning in Latin America and in the Mediterranean Regional Project Countries*, OECD.

SPEARE, A. Jr. (1969), '*The determinants of rural-urban migration in Taiwan*', Population Association of America.

STIGLER, G. J. (1956), *Trends in Employment in the Service Industries*, Princeton University Press.

TSUI, Y. C., and LIN, T. C. (1964), *A Study on Rural Labour Mobility in Relation to Industrialization and Urbanization in Taiwan*, Chinese–American Joint Commission on Rural Reconstruction, Economic Digest Series.

TULPULE, A. H. (1968), 'Towards an integrated model of distribution of service employment in the non-central areas of Greater London', *Bull. Oxford Univ. Inst. econ. Stats.*, vol. 30, pp. 207–29.

UNITED NATIONS (1968), World Economic Survey 1967, Part One: *The Problems and Policies of Economic Development: an Appraisal of Recent experience*, UN.

24 C. R. Frank Jr

Urban Unemployment and Economic Growth in Africa

Extract from C. R. Frank Jr, 'Urban unemployment and economic growth in Africa', Yale Economic Growth Centre Paper, no. 120, New Haven, 1968.

One of the characteristics of the less-developed economies of the world is a rapidly growing urban population and urban work force combined with a much slower increase in employment opportunities in the larger-scale urban establishments. The result has been either unemployment or under-employment in small-scale, often individual or family-run, establishments. This phenomenon has been noted in economies such as Puerto Rico and India with high population densities as well as in the relatively under-populated countries of Africa. (Reynolds, 1965; Pearson, 1964; Fried-lander, 1965; Calloway, 1963; Doctor and Gallis, 1964.) Those countries which are industrializing rapidly seem to suffer from this phenomenon just as much, if not more, than those which are not industrializing quickly. (Baer and Hervé, 1966).

The growing mass of urban unemployed and underemployed is regarded by many as a great social evil and a prime source of human tragedy.[1] Others, including politicians in power, fear it as a source of political in-stability. The presence of large numbers of poverty-stricken and jobless people in the cities puts a great deal of pressure on governments, national and local, to increase current expenditures rapidly to provide civil service jobs for the unemployed. At the same time governments are faced with demands on their capital budgets to spend more for development purposes. In addition, increasing urban population creates demands for urban services: housing, sewerage, lighting, roads, police and fire protection and the like. A large mass of unemployed or underemployed do not generate the output or tax revenues which are needed to provide these services. For these and other reasons, the political consensus in most developing coun-tries is that the pressures of urban unemployment and underemployment have to be relieved.

How best can this be accomplished? One might say the solution is

1. For example, Calloway (1960, p. 60) asserts that '... no social and economic problem in Nigeria is so urgent as that of finding employment for the ever increasing number of school leavers. Nor is there any major policy issue of which the meanings and implications are so little understood'.

through high rates of investment and rapid growth. The history of fast-growing countries and their continued inability to cope with the problem of unemployment indicate that something else besides rapid growth is required for a solution. Many writers suggest that growth must occur by investing in relatively labour-intensive activities rather than those which are capital-intensive. The argument runs that not only will this result in more rapid growth because of the low opportunity cost of labour relative to capital, but will increase the rate of growth of employment for any given level of investment. Even in cases, however, when the labour-intensive investment is less than optimal from the point of view of growth, it may be justified if a high enough priority is given to growth in employment and/or reduction in unemployment.

In this paper, we will attempt to show that for the typical African country[2] neither high rates of growth in the modern urban sector nor an attempt to resort to labour-intensive techniques in that sector is likely to have much effect on the magnitude of the urban unemployment problem. The answer, if one exists, to the problem of urban unemployment must be sought through examination of urban-rural income differentials and the distribution of public goods and services to urban and rural areas.

Composition of the urban labour force

The urban labour force constitutes only a small fraction of the total working force of most African countries. In Nigeria, for example, one of the most urbanized of the African countries south of the Sahara, the urban population (in cities having a population greater than 20,000) is only about 13 per cent of the total population. In Uganda, one of the least urbanized African countries, only about 2·5 per cent of the total population lives in cities and towns of 2000 or more people, although many of those who work in the towns of Uganda live outside the urban areas and commute by foot or bicycle.

[. . .] Of that part of the total work force living in the cities, only a fraction is engaged in the modern sector. In Nigeria, for example, workers in the modern sector account for about one half of the urban work force or a little over 5 per cent of the total labour force. The rest of the urban labour force is either engaged in the traditional, low-productivity sector or is completely unemployed.

Growth in the urban labour force in Africa

Few data are available on urban labour participation rates in Africa. Growth in the urban labour force must be inferred from urban population

2. In referring to Africa in this paper, we generally mean Africa south of the Sahara exclusive of South Africa.

data. Table 1 gives the rates of growth for some major cities of Africa. These vary considerably from 1·7 per cent per annum (Addis Ababa) to more than 15 per cent (Fort Lamy). While the data on which these figures are based are very inadequate, the mean annual growth (weighted by initial size) of 6·8 per cent can be regarded as fairly typical. These differ considerably from the estimated growth of total population in the African countries which usually range between 2 and 3 per cent per annum. This means, of course, that the urban labour force is a growing percentage of the total labour force.

Table 1 **Sub-Saharan Africa: urban population growth**

City	Population		Population		Annual growth (per cent)
	Year	('000)	Year	('000)	
Salisbury	1946	69	1961	300	10·3
Dar-es-Salaam	1948	69	1957	129	7·2
Brazzaville	1955	76	1961	134	9·9
Dakar	1945	132	1960	383	7·4
Accra	1948	136	1960	491	11·3
Nairobi	1948	119	1962	315	7·2
Abidjan	1955	127	1960	180	7·2
Monrovia	1956	41	1962	81	12·0
Fort Lamy	1955	29	1963	92	15·5
Cotonou	1945	26	1960	113	10·3
Mombasa	1948	85	1962	180	5·5
Bamako	1945	37	1960	127	8·6
Bulawayo	1946	53	1964	214	8·1
Lusaka	1950	26	1964	122	11·7
Yaounde	1955	38	1962	93	13·8
Douala	1954	118	1964	187	4·7
Addis Ababa	1951	400	1964	505	1·7
Khartoum-Omdurman	1948	210	1960	315	3·4
Luanda	1950	150	1960	220	3·9
Leopoldville	1946	110	1961	420	9·3
Elisabethville	1950	103	1961	190	5·7
Kumasi	1955	75	1960	190	20·4
Lourenco-Marques	1950	94	1961	184	6·3

Source: United Nations, *Demographic Yearbook*, New York, various issues, and Hance (1964, p. 54).

Growth in demand for a modern urban labour force

These very high rates of growth of the urban labour force have not been matched by correspondingly high rates of growth of the quantity of urban labour demanded by the modern larger scale establishments. Table 2 gives some representative rates of growth of total non-agricultural employment. Note that many of these rates of growth are negative. Furthermore, the growth in the Kenya, non-agricultural labour force would be considerably more negative were it not for the extraordinary jump in employment between 1963 and 1964. This discontinuity was most likely the result of a mild export boom in 1964 and, more importantly, the signing of the so-called Tripartite Agreement by government, private employers, and the labour unions which called for employers to increase their employment by 10 per cent and the unions to hold back on wage demands.

The low rates of growth in Table 2 cannot be attributed to a low growth in output. Some representative annual rates of increase of non-agricultural output between 1954 and 1964 are:[3]

Kenya   6·5
Southern Rhodesia   6·7
Uganda   7·7

Non-agricultural output in Tanzania increased at a rate of 6·0 per cent between 1954 and 1958 and 9·1 per cent between 1960 and 1964.

The low rates of growth of employment in Table 2 are, on the whole, considerably below the rates of growth of urban population in Table 1. Thus, only a small portion of the annual increment in the urban labour force is being absorbed by the modern urban sector. The residual (those either unemployed or engaged in the traditional sector) are an increasing proportion of the urban work force. It is difficult to say how many of those in the residual are either under-employed or unemployed, but it is unlikely that the demand for the goods and services from the traditional urban sector has been growing at anywhere near the rate needed fully to absorb the growth of the residual labour force. In Nigeria, the large supply of workers to the traditional sector has kept the real wage-rate in the sector either constant or falling while real wages in the modern sector have risen considerably (Kilby, mimeo). The highly paid workers of the modern sector are becoming an increasingly smaller percentage of the urban work force while the wage differential seems to be widening.

Composition of labour demand

There are several striking aspects of the composition of labour demand in Africa. First, the role played by government is very large. Government

3. These growth rates were calculated from data in United Nations (1966, pp. 27–31).

Table 2 **Non-agricultural employment indices in selected African countries** (1958 = 100)

	Cameroons	Ghana	Kenya	Malawi	Nigeria
1955	102	82	107	88	n.a.
1956	104	91	105	95	95
1957	100	95	105	98	100
1958	100	100	100	100	100
1959	95	106	100	99	99
1960	91	111	102	96	106
1961	94	122	98	93	89
1962	72	128	97	87	113
1963	91	132	91	87	94
1964	92	n.a.†	111	n.a.	n.a.
Rate of growth* (per cent)	−1·0	6·3	−0·5	−0·7	0·1

	Southern Rhodesia	Sierra Leone	Tanzania	Uganda	Zambia
1955	86	87	97	94	92
1956	92	87	104	93	100
1957	98	92	101	99	100
1958	100	100	100	100	100
1959	100	98	96	99	95
1960	101	101	98	99	93
1961	98	108	104	98	90
1962	95	112	101	93	88
1963	91	119	91	89	86
1964	90	125	95	89	91
Rate of growth* (per cent)	0·2	3·0	−0·4	−0·1	−0·9

* Rates of growth calculated by fitting a logarithmic time trend.
† n.a. means not available.
Source: United Nations (1966, pp. 109–10).

non-agricultural employment as a percentage of total non-agricultural employment for selected countries is given in Table 3. It ranges from 37·6 to 52·1 per cent. Second, employment in trade, commerce, and miscellaneous services is the most important component of non-agricultural employment in most African countries, ranging from 45 to 65 per cent for those countries in Table 4. Finally, manufacturing and public utilities account for a relatively small portion of non-agricultural employment, roughly between 15 and 20 per cent (see Table 4). These characteristics of the composition of labour demand have very important implications for the growth in demand for labour.

Table 3 **Distribution of non-agricultural employment by type of employer**

	Year	Government (per cent)	Non-Government* (per cent)
Uganda	1964	52·1	47·9
Kenya	1964	41·4	58·6
Tanzania	1963	48·9	51·1
Nigeria	1962	37·6	62·4
Ghana	1961	45·6	54·4

Sources: *Uganda Statistical Abstract, 1965*, Entebbe, 1966, p. 93; *Kenya Statistical Abstract, 1965*, Nairobi, 1966, p. 122; *Tanzania Statistical Abstract, 1964*, Dar-es-Salaam, 1965, p. 142; *Nigeria Report on Earnings and Employment Enquiry, 1962*, Lagos, 1964, p. 12; and *Ghana Quarterly Digest of Statistics*, Accra, December, 1962, p. 2.
* Includes Government Corporations except for Uganda.

Table 4 **Distribution of non-agricultural employment by sector**

	Manufacturing and public utilities	Commerce and services	Construction	Mining	Transport and communications
Uganda (1964)	20·2	56·2	15·0	3·0	5·6
Kenya (1965)	19·2	65·0	5·6	0·6	9·4
Tanzania (1963)	15·2	50·5	16·2	4·2	13·9
Nigeria (1962)	14·4	45·0	20·7	9·8	10·2
Ghana (1964)	13·9	47·6	19·3	8·6	10·2

Sources: same as Table 3 except for Kenya and Ghana data which were obtained from ILO, 1966, p. 268, and *Ghana Economic Survey, 1964*, Accra, 1965, p. 105.

Government employment grows roughly at about the same rate as recurrent government expenditure less the rate of growth of the average wage or salary paid by government. Wages and salaries comprise a large proportion of this expenditure (typically 60 to 80 per cent) which tends to change very little through time for any given country. Government investment expenditure is a small fraction of the total government expenditure, and wages and salaries are a much smaller proportion than is the case with recurrent expenditure. In any case, much of the investment expenditure by African governments is in payments to private contractors and this does not affect government employment. Thus the growth in government employment opportunities is largely a function of the taxing and borrowing capabilities of African governments and their willingness to expand recurrent expenditures. It makes little sense to talk about greatly altering these relationships by the use of more labour-intensive techniques when government recurrent services are largely the services of labour anyway.

Value added in commerce, trade, and miscellaneous services, while including some profits and depreciation, is largely composed of wages and salaries (explicitly or implicitly). Thus, as is the case with government, employment tends to grow roughly the same as value added (in money terms) with an adjustment for increased average employee remuneration, i.e. employment tends to grow about the same as real value added. Furthermore, the commerce, trade, and miscellaneous services industries may be viewed basically as intermediate goods industries whose output tends to grow in fixed proportion to the general level of economic activity. To conclude, with regard to trade, commerce and other service industries, there is little scope for increasing labour intensity and the growth of employment in this industry above that dictated by the overall growth of the economy.

The scope for increased employment growth through more labour intensity therefore lies in other urban-based industries such as mining, manufacturing, transport, construction, and public utilities which, however, generally account for less than 50 per cent of the total modern, urban labour force.

The role of labour productivity

The growth of employment in these other urban-based industries is considerably reduced by growth in labour productivity which occurs independently of the choice of technique with regard to output expansion. This growth in productivity occurs for several reasons:[4]

1. Increasing quality of the labour force, particularly through on-the-job training and increased experience in a factory environment;

2. Disembodied labour-saving technical change resulting from better management, organization, and work procedures;

3. An increase in the share of the market for those firms which have achieved higher labour productivity because of better management or better labour quality;

4. Economies of scale;

4. Reasons (2), (3) and (4) cited here are similar to Leibenstein's notion of an increase in X-efficiency. See Leibenstein (1966).

5. Increasing capacity utilization resulting in increased productivity of maintenance and administration personnel.[5]

The first three of these factors tend to operate independently of increases in output or value added. Thus, there is a tendency for some gain in productivity even though output is falling, stagnant, or growing slowly, Productivity increases resulting from economies of large-scale operation and/or increased capacity utilization come into play as output growth increases. Increases in output which begin to put a strain on the existing capital stock capacity may, however, cause the growth in productivity to fall off for very high rates of growth of output.

The curve *ABEH* in Figure 1 shows the relationships between output

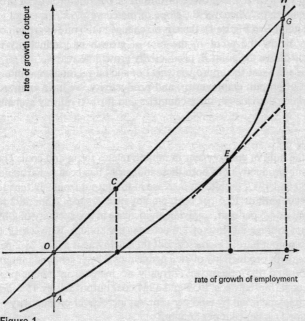

Figure 1

5. This cause of increased labour productivity is somewhat peculiar to the smaller size, less developed economies. In most African countries, there is usually only one railway company, for example. Maintenance of the right of way and administrative and clerical operations require some minimum of workers. The need for these kinds of workers does not expand nearly as rapidly as output expands. In most African countries, the railway accounts for a considerable portion of the labour force, and as the railways are used to fuller capacity, workers per unit of output falls rapidly. There is also a tendency to build certain manufacturing plants substantially ahead of demand or to build a large enough size to handle demands during export booms (e.g. cement). As the average capacity utilization increases, maintenance and administrative personnel increase their productivity.

growth, productivity growth and growth in employment.[6] The vertical axis is the rate of growth of employment, and the horizontal axis is the rate of growth of output (value added). At zero rates of growth of output the growth in employment is negative and equal to minus the distance of OA. The rate of growth of output must be greater than OB in order for there to be any positive increase in employment at all.

The growth in productivity is approximately given by the distance between the 45 degree line OCG which emanates from the origin. For example, when the rate of growth of employment is zero, the rate of growth of productivity is equal to OA (the rate of decrease of employment). When the rate of growth of output is OB, the growth in productivity is approximately given by BC. If the growth in output is OF, the growth of productivity equals zero. Whenever the slope of the curve $ABEH$ is equal to unity (at the point E in Figure 1), there is no change in the rate of growth of productivity. Below the point E, the rate of growth of productivity is increasing and above the point E, productivity growth decreases.

[. . .] In order to test the appropriateness of such a relationship among growth rates of output, employment, and productivity, we have analysed data from mining activities in three countries and for two railway systems in Africa.

Mining in Nigeria

In Nigeria, the bulk of employment in mining relates to tin and coal. The gain in labour productivity in both these industries has been remarkable. Between 1950 and 1957, despite an increase in tin output from 949 tons to 1096 tons per month or 15·6 per cent, employment *dropped* from 58·2 to 55·2 thousand or 4·6 per cent, implying an increase in productivity of 20·9 per cent or an average increase of 2·8 per cent per annum. Between 1950 and 1964, tin output hardly increased, but tin employment fell by 24·2 per cent, an increase of productivity of 36·8 per cent or 2·3 per cent per annum. Between 1950 and 1957 there was virtually no increase in labour productivity in coal, but between 1959 and 1964 coal output fell by 15·5 per cent, and employment fell by 60·5 per cent, an increase in productivity of 113 per cent or 11·4 per cent per annum.[7]

Mining in Ghana

In Ghana, most employment in the mining industry relates to gold. Between

6. A derivation of the relationship between growth in employment and growth in output assuming that there are three factors, labour, skilled labour and capital; and labour-augmenting and capital-augmenting technological change is contained in the appendix (not included here).

7. Data from Nigeria, *Quarterly Digest of Statistics*, various issues.

1948 and 1964 output increased from 672,000 fine oz. to 865,000 fine oz. while employment dropped from 32·2 thousand to 20·6 thousand. Productivity increased by about 100 per cent over 16 years, an increase of about 4·4 per cent per annum.[8]

Mining in Zambia

Copper output (electrolytic and blister combined) in Zambia more than doubled (from 309,000 to 635,000 tons) between 1950 and 1963. Employment increased by only 4·5 per cent from 37,400 thousand to 39,100. The increase in productivity was 98 per cent or 5·0 per cent per annum over the 14-year period.[9]

The East African Railways

The East African Railways is the largest non-government employer in East Africa. Employment in 1949 was 47,100, but by 1963 this had dropped to 44,700. In the meantime, ton-miles carried increased from 1·2 million to 2·1 million or 75 per cent. The implied increase in ton-mile productivity was 60 per cent or 3·4 per cent per annum.[10]

Railways in Nigeria

Between 1948 and 1963, ton-miles carried by the Nigerian Railways increased from 554,000 to 1,410,000 or nearly threefold in 15 years. Employment meanwhile increased from 22,100 to 27,400, a gain of only 24 per cent. Productivity increased at about 5 per cent per annum over the 15 years. The gain in productivity has been particularly noticeable between 1952 and 1963; ton-miles per worker more than doubled, a gain of 7 per cent per annum.

We regressed annual percentage change in employment on annual percentage increase in output for each of the above industries. In the case of East African Railways, we added a third variable, the ratio of the increase in capital expenditure to employment.[11] The results are summarized in Table 5. The constant term in each of these equations is the rate at which employment *decreases* in these industries when output is stagnant. We converted these to percentage increases in output required to prevent a drop in employment by setting $Y = 0$ and solving for X_1. The results are presented in the last column of Table 5.

8. Data from Ghana, *Quarterly Digest of Statistics*, various issues.

9. Employment data from Northern Rhodesia Chamber of Mines, *Year Book 1964*. Output data from Federation of Rhodesia and Nyasaland, *Monthly Digest of Statistics* and Zambia, *Monthly Digest of Statistics*, various issues.

10. Data are from East African *Economic and Statistical Review*, various issues.

11. This variable was added as an explanatory variable since employment figures covered workers employed on capital projects.

Table 5 Employment growth – productivity growth regressions

Industry	Regression	Data	Required growth in output to prevent employment from falling (per cent)
Nigeria Coal	$Y = -7 \cdot 1 + 1 \cdot 704 X_1$ $(R^2 = 0 \cdot 28)$	1950–64 Output in tons	4·2
Nigeria Tin	$Y = -1 \cdot 5 + 0 \cdot 875 X_1$ $(R^2 = 0 \cdot 90)$	1950–64 Output in tons	1·7
Ghana Gold	$Y = -3 \cdot 8 + 0 \cdot 720 X_1$ $(R^2 = 0 \cdot 46)$	1948–64 Output in fine oz.	5·3
Zambia Copper	$Y = -3 \cdot 7 + 0 \cdot 669 X_1$ $(R^2 = 0 \cdot 995)$	1950–63 Output in tons	5·5
East African Railways	$Y = -2 \cdot 0 + 0 \cdot 318 X_1$ $+ 1 \cdot 432 X_2$ $(R^2 = 0 \cdot 48)$	1949–63 Output in ton miles	6·7
Nigeria Railways	$Y = -1 \cdot 2 + 0 \cdot 216 X_1$ $(R^2 = 0 \cdot 70)$	1948–63 annual percentage changes in three-year moving averages of employment and output (ton miles)	4·5

Note: Y is percentage change in employment; X_1 is percentage change in output and X_2 is ratio of increase in capital expenditure to employment.

References

BAER, W., and HERVÉ, M. E. (1966), 'Employment and industrialization in developing countries', *Q. J. Econ.* vol. 80, pp. 88–107.

CALLOWAY, A. (1960), 'School leavers and the developing economy in Nigeria', *Nigerian Institute of Social and Economic Research Conference Proceedings*, Ibadan.

CALLOWAY, A. (1963), 'Unemployment among African school leavers', *J. Mod. African Stud.*, vol. 1, pp. 351–71.

DOCTOR, K. C., and GALLIS, H. (1964), 'Modern sector employment in Asian countries: some empirical estimates', *Int. Lab. Rev.*, vol. 89, p. 558.

FRIEDLANDER, S. L. (1965), *Labor Migration and Economic Growth*, MIT.

HANCE, W. A. (1964), *The Geography of Modern Africa*, Columbia University Press.

ILO (1966), *Yearbook of Statistics*, Geneva, ILO

KILBY, P. (mimeo) 'Industrial relations and wage determination in Nigeria'.

LEIBENSTEIN, H. (1966), 'Allocative efficiency *v* X-efficiency', *Amer. econ. Rev.*, vol. 56, pp. 392–415.

PEARSON, D. S. (1964), 'Employment trends in a developing economy – the case of Southern Rhodesia', *East African Econ. Rev.*, vol. 2, pp. 59–77.

REYNOLDS, L. G. (1965), 'Wages and employment in a labor surplus economy', *Amer. econ. Rev.*, vol. 55, pp. 19–39.

UNITED NATIONS (1966), *Statistical Yearbook 1965*, New York, pp. 27–31.

Part Seven
Technology and Choice of Techniques

That there is an inherent trend for modern technology to be too capital-intensive (not labour-intensive enough) for the requirements of developing countries is now universally held. It would be surprising if it were otherwise, with 98 per cent of all research and development (R and D) work concentrated in the richer countries. Where disagreement begins to arise is whether the developing countries, in the light of this situation, are free and able to choose technologies more from the labour-intensive end of the spectrum than the richer countries, and whether they would be well-advised to do so. A more labour-intensive technology could also result from a different product mix in the developing countries, with more emphasis on the more labour-intensive types of products and services. This, in turn, would require (a) an appropriate internal income distribution (generally a more equal income distribution) to produce a structure of demand with emphasis on these labour-intensive goods and services; and/or (b) an international division of labour in which the developing countries can specialize on the export of labour-intensive products to the richer countries in exchange for the capital-intensive products of the latter. Hence, the discussion in this Part of our readings should be read in conjunction with Part Three on Income Distribution.

The selection of Readings gives much of its space to the opening paper by Marsden (Reading 25). This is because it intermingles theory, survey of views, reference to actual experience and case material in a stimulating manner. His footnote references provide ample scope for further reading. The reader may like to follow up with one of the papers emerging from E. F. Schumacher or one of his colleagues of the Intermediate Technology Development Group (based in London, England), making a direct case for the concept of an 'intermediate' (as distinct from 'progressive' or 'appropriate') technology. A. K. Sen's 'Choice of Techniques' (Reading 26) also pursues some of the subjects discussed in the Marsden paper in more analytical depth. The question of choice of technology is directly connected with factor prices and factor price distortion, discussed in Part Three of this volume.

Hou (Reading 26) illustrates the issues involved from a discussion of the Chinese policy, during the 'Great Leap Forward', of 'walking on two legs' in technology. This is also known as 'technological dualism' – a combination of capital-intensive heavy industry as the spearhead of 'modernization' with the mopping-up of the unutilized labour capacity by massive labour-intensive campaigns, including the famous backyard steel furnaces. (For those who like to think in terms of Western economic thought: a combination of Galenson/Leibenstein with Nurkse.) The reader interested in following up on the Chinese experience of using technology as a method of utilizing surplus labour may find it useful to turn to Riskin (1968).

Strassmann (Reading 27) is a more detailed case study of the construction industry in Peru. It illustrates the very considerable range of technologies – with widely varying quantities of associated employment – which are available, in certain sectors, to a developing country. Strassmann goes on to show some ways in which policy might be used to maximize the employment potential of this choice of technology.

The wide-ranging reading from the 'Sussex group' (Reading 28), tries to show why science and technology have had such a limited impact on developing countries, despite their enormous potential role in the development process. Why is it that science and technology in so many ways hinder rather than help the progress of development generally, and the progress towards fuller employment specifically? This reading also leads over to the three complementary international approaches which are needed if the tremendous development and employment 'potential' of science and technology is to be converted into reality. These are:

1. The building up of indigenous scientific and technological capacity in the developing countries;

2. Higher priority in using the scientific and technological capacity of the richer countries for the problems of employment and development of the majority of mankind living in developing countries;

3. A larger and more effective transfer of science and technology between richer and poorer countries.

The Sussex group report provided the basis for the UN World Plan of Action in the field of science and technology for the UN 'Second Development Decade'. This World Plan takes up a number of priority problems on which new scientific and technological knowledge relevant to developing countries is urgently needed: from protein enrichment of rice to low-cost desalination of seawater for irrigation, studies of the bilharzia snail etc. The discussion of these concrete problems fills in the empty boxes set up by the Sussex group, and some readers may wish to go on to study the full text of this World Plan of Action (UN publication, E.71.II.A.18).

Reference

RISKIN, C. (1968), 'Local industry and choice of techniques in planning of industrial development in Mainland China', in United Nations Industrial Development Organization. *Planning for Advanced Skills and Technology*, United Nations.

25 K. Marsden

Progressive Technologies for Developing Countries

Extract from K. Marsden, 'Progressive technologies for developing countries',
in W. Galenson (ed.), *Essays on Employment*, ILO Geneva, 1971.

This paper will discuss the choice of technologies for developing countries. The word choice is used advisedly. The theme will be that technology is an important variable in development strategy, not an immutable force requiring adjustments in other factors to make way for it. Indeed, technology may have greater inherent flexibility in the short and medium terms than the human factors (skills, attitudes, behaviour, propensities and motivations) which cooperate with it in production. It will be suggested that government has a vital role to play in influencing investment decisions, directly and indirectly, so that they result in the optimum utilization of available resources [. . .].

Some reasons why the direct transfer of technologies from industrialized to developing countries may be inappropriate
Capital is dearer and labour cheaper in the developing countries

In the advanced economies labour is scarce and dear, and capital relatively plentiful and cheap. The opposite is true of most developing countries. It follows that a machine that is economic with wage rates of $2 an hour and interest charges of 4 per cent per annum may be uneconomic when interest charges are 15 per cent (or should be) and wages $0·10 an hour.

Case study illustration. The total costs of alternative methods of making wooden window frames have been compared in the two kinds of countries described above. It was found that in the labour-expensive country two special-purpose machines, one performing four-sided planing and moulding, and the other a double-ended tenoner, were the cheapest combination for output capacities in excess of 50,000 units per annum. In the cheap-labour/dear-capital country, however, they would be uneconomic unless the capacity exceeded 450,000 units per annum. Up to an output of 64,000, which encompasses the great majority of carpentry workshops, the lowest unit costs would be achieved by using single-purpose planing and thicknessing machines and single ended tenoners, with a considerably lower investment per worker (Boon, 1961, 1964).

Large-scale production may be inefficient in the conditions prevailing in some developing countries

Much modern technology has been designed for use in large-scale plants. Certain prerequisites of large-scale operations have therefore to be fulfilled before it can be employed economically. These are not always present. Large-scale capital-intensive production is not efficient if markets are small, scattered, highly seasonal or fragmented; if distribution channels are not well organized; if workers are not used to factory discipline; if management does not know the necessary managerial techniques or, though aware of them, cannot implement them because they conflict too strongly with accepted customs, beliefs, systems of authority, etc. of the employees; or if there are no service engineers who can get the complicated machinery going again when it breaks down. Scarce capital is wasted if it is invested under such circumstances. And these are factors that cannot be changed overnight by a simple planning decision.

Case study illustrations. The large public-sector shoe factory which operated at 20 per cent of capacity because it had no means of reaching the small private shoe retailers who handled 90 per cent of the shoe trade.

The battery plant which could satisfy a month's demand in five days.

The woollen-textile factory which had a 10 per cent material wastage figure (costing precious foreign exchange) because its management did not know how to set and control material usage standards.

The $2 million date-processing plant which had been out of action for two years, ever since a blow-out in the cleaning and destoning unit, because there were no service engineers who knew how to repair it.

The confectionery plant which was inactive for most of the year because 80 per cent of sales were made during the month of a religious festival.

The radio assembly factory whose production line broke down repeatedly because of the high rate of absenteeism among key workers.

Advanced technologies may reduce both employment and real incomes in certain circumstances

Even when run below capacity, advanced machinery can often make products cheaper than is possible by traditional methods. As a result a large number of indigenous craftsmen may be put out of business even when the innovation is a product not previously produced within the country. In the mass market there are very few new items which do not have their equivalents among traditional products and, where incomes are static, the traditional product will often be replaced by the new one.

The redundant workers may not be absorbed into the new factories because machinery is being employed instead of labour and the difference in productivity is so great. Some consumers may receive some benefit through lower prices, but this may be offset by a decline in average real income in the community at large. This will occur if –

1. The new substitute product has a higher proportion of imported materials and components than the old; and

2. Resources cannot be easily transferred to satisfy higher monetary demand for other products, because the surplus capital is tied up in specialized equipment and the unemployed labour lacks the educational background or the social mobility needed in the new occupations.

The fact that many countries are experiencing growing unemployment, a rising import bill and domestic inflation all at the same time would tend to confirm this explanation. In this case the persons who gain most from the technical change are the inhabitants of the already rich countries exporting the machinery, the materials and components required by the new technologies. In other words, the main benefits 'leak' abroad. So in these cases there is little opportunity to compensate the unemployed by transfer payments from those with higher real incomes elsewhere, or to wait until a long-term growth in employment opportunities absorbs them.

[. . .] In the developing countries, the innovation may take the form of an alien 'transplant' that kills off competing activities in the traditional sectors but has to be fed through external linkages established with suppliers abroad to be kept alive itself.[1] This is because the indigenous industry lacks the specific skills, materials and equipment to satisfy its immediate requirements, and time and money are too short for it to make the necessary adjustments. Decades or even centuries of development cannot be compressed into the couple of years it takes to build a plant and get it running. Thus the innovation may make little contribution to the spread of employment or to raising the skills upon which self-sustained growth depends. The backwash effects can exceed the spread effects and the technological and income gap becomes wider (Myrdal, 1957).

Case study illustration. One country imported two plastic injection-moulding machines costing $100,000 with moulds. Working three shifts and with a total labour force of forty workers they produced 1·5 million pairs of plastic sandals and shoes a year. At $2 a pair these were better value (longer life) than cheap leather footwear at the same price. Thus, 5000 artisan shoemakers lost their livelihood; this, in turn, reduced the markets for the sup-

1. Professor Hirschman introduced the concepts of backward and forward linkages to illustrate how the benefits resulting from an innovation in one area might spread to other sectors. But in the absence of existing indigenous know-how, these new linkages may be more readily established with foreign suppliers whose experience can be tapped immediately. Hirschman also underestimates the disruptive effects of new products and technologies on the existing network of interrelationships built around the substituted products. See Hirschman (1958).

pliers and makers of leather, hand tools, cotton thread, tacks, glues, wax and polish, eyelets, fabric linings, laces, wooden lasts and carton boxes, none of which was required for plastic footwear. As all the machinery and the material (PVC) for the plastic footwear had to be imported, while the leather footwear was based largely on indigenous materials and industries, the net result was a decline in both employment and real income within the country.

Policy guidelines for the selection of progressive technologies

It is clear from the above case studies that the best machinery for one country is not always the best for another. What kinds of technology would be progressive in the senses that we have defined, i.e. will induce balanced economic and social development in which all members of the community will find opportunities for increasingly productive employment and rising living standards?

This section will therefore run through some broad economic and social considerations which might be borne in mind when economic policy is being framed. It has become evident that the investment decisions of individual entrepreneurs or enterprises do not necessarily achieve maximum benefit to the society at large. There are three main reasons for this. The first is that money costs may not reflect real or social costs, so a choice which would maximize private entrepreneurial (or public-enterprise) profits will be different from the one which would achieve optimum economic efficiency or social welfare from a national point of view. The second is that non-rational factors may influence decisions unduly, e.g. prestige considerations, assiduous salesmanship on the part of machinery manufacturers, the confusion of technical efficiency with economic efficiency, the belief that the latest must be the best irrespective of circumstances, etc. The third reason is that the individual entrepreneur is often unaware of the full range of technical alternatives that exist, or may not have ready access to them.

We shall discuss the measures that can be taken to correct these biases later in the paper. Before doing so, it is necessary to indicate the broad relationships that should normally be observed if technical progress is to result in balanced economic and social development. They are expressed in the form of general guidelines. These are not precise formulae but rather rules of thumb or check-lists for planners. Again, specific case studies will be used to illustrate the principles involved.

Wide disparities in capital intensity per worker in different sectors should be avoided

Recently, more attention has been focused on the problem of the widening gap between rich and poor, both between nations and between different segments of the population in the developing countries themselves. The dual structure of many of these economies appears to be hardening. The director-general of the ILO has urged that the closing of the gap 'is a job, to which governments, workers and employers must direct their attention in the years immediately ahead' (Morse, 1966). How can this be done? Several lines of attack are necessary, including wider spread of educational and training facilities among the people. Investment policy, however, must play a central role. Recent studies have shown a close correlation between capital intensity and labour productivity.[2] The relationship between productivity and earning capacity is obvious. Thus, if the gap is to be narrowed, it would seem necessary to raise the productivity of all those in the traditional and subsistence sectors by a substantial injection of capital in these occupations. This does not mean setting up a few isolated 'model' schemes in these areas. Modernization must be seen as a continuous process, in which there is a widespread improvement in methods which use more equipment or more expensive materials than has been traditional, but far less than is currently the practice in the advanced countries. As we shall see, the few spectacular capital-intensive projects may be an essential part of development, but they cannot be the main source of progress if this gap is to be closed (Hagen, 1962).

The short-term social advantages of reducing the disparities between the modern and traditional sectors are clear. But there have been fears that the price to be paid might be a retarded rate of economic growth in the long run (Hirschman, 1958; Gerschenkron, 1962). The evidence on this is not conclusive. In theory, the rate of capital accumulation ought to be higher in large-scale, capital-intensive industry. This does not always work out in practice, perhaps because of the economic and social factors already mentioned.[3] On the other side, it can be said that the concentration of resources

2. See United Nations Centre for Industrial Development (1966). Of course, the growth of labour productivity is not simply the result of larger capital inputs. E. F. Denison (1966) has pointed out the importance of the so-called 'residual factors' (technical progress, higher skills, better management, etc.) in recent American economic growth. This fact has sometimes been taken to imply that such 'windfall gains' would accrue automatically to the developing countries if they selected the latest techniques, incorporating the full quotient of the technical progress which had occurred historically in each field. But in practice, technical change cannot be easily separated from its socio-economic environment. Technological innovations which are not accompanied by appropriate changes in the skills, education, attitudes and behaviour patterns of management, workers and consumers may result in a lowering of economic efficiency, i.e. a decline in the output/total factor input ratio.

3. Data for India and the United Arab Republic – two developing countries with long-established industrial sectors – show that small firms tend to realize a higher surplus/capital ratio than do large enterprises. See *Census of Industrial Production, 1960* (Cairo, 'Department of Statistics, 1962) and *Capital* (Calcutta), 22 June 1968. The explanations are manifold: use of cheap, second-hand equipment, greater experi-

in the modern sector, which is a feature of many development programmes, has not been conspicuously successful in achieving a satisfactory rate of growth. A stagnant agricultural sector can slow down expansion elsewhere.[4] And the lack of viable investment opportunities for small family savings may lower significantly the community's propensity to save. Perhaps even more important, this bottleneck can prevent or deter those rare individuals with a high achievement motivation to channel their entrepreneurial energies into industrial pursuits.[5] For all these reasons, a more balanced distribution of capital investment might prove to be economically as well as socially desirable [. . .].

Case study illustration. The economic and social advantages of a balanced industrial development strategy can be illustrated by the case of a typical traditional bakery in West Africa.[6] This is a family enterprise employing perhaps one or two hired hands. The premises consist of a single room with a brick-lined oven built on to the back. Firing is by charcoal. The dough is mixed and kneaded by hand in bowls and on wooden tables. Proving takes place in wicker baskets. The single-plate oven is loaded and unloaded with a wooden peel, and the loaves are left to cool on racks before being sold direct from the bakehouse or delivered to retail outlets by handcart or bicycle. Productivity per worker averages 80 14-ounce loaves per day, selling at 6d. (2½p) each; capital investment per worker is £100 and wages are 10s. (50p) per day.

Taking a shadow interest rate on capital of 15 per cent per annum, the cost breakdown per loaf (in pence) would be as follows:

Materials	3·4 (1·4p)
Labour	1·5 (0·62p)
Fuel and power	0·3 (0·12p)
Depreciation and interest	0·2 (0·1p)
Total cost	5·4 (2·25p)
Profits	0·6 (0·25p)
Selling price per loaf	6·0 (2·5p)

ence and involvement of owner-managers, achievement motivation of the entrepreneurs compared with the desire to maximize lifetime earnings of salaried managers, greater flexibility in responding to market demand, low overhead costs, etc. These factors are considered at greater length in Marsden (1969).

4. See Food and Agriculture Organization (1966, chapter 3), for a good analysis of the interdependence of agricultural and industrial development.

5. The role of achievement motivation as a driving force behind economic development is described in McClelland (1961).

6. An interesting analysis and description of the Nigerian bakery industry is given in Kilby (1965).

Consumption of bread per head is the equivalent of half a loaf a day (i.e. 49 ounces per week compared with 40·6 ounces per week in the United Kingdom in 1955 and 55·1 ounces in 1965). Thus, a town of 100,000 would consume 50,000 loaves daily, requiring a labour force of 625 spread among, say, 125 bakeries (5 workers each).

How best should such an industry be developed? One could introduce the latest processing equipment including pneumatic handling of flour, continuous mixing and dividing, proving on overhead conveyors, baking in a travelling turbo-radiant oven and feeding the loaves direct from a cooling chain to a battery of slicing, wrapping and palletizing machines. A single-plant bakery of this type would produce 50,000 loaves daily. In order to deliver the bread to the customers in time (they could no longer collect it themselves from the neighbourhood baker), a fleet of delivery vans and a chain of distribution outlets and stores would be required. The total investment in land, buildings, machinery, vehicles and working capital would be of the order of £600,000. Labour productivity would, of course, be much higher than with the traditional techniques. An estimated 60 employees would be needed. As the skills would be higher (managerial, supervision, clerical, administrative and servicing of complex equipment), an average wage of £1 per day might be necessary (in the United Kingdom, average earnings in the bread industry are nearly £4 per day). Additional materials (the wrapping paper, office records) and fuel (petrol for delivery vans) would raise the production cost, and some of them would have to be imported, requiring foreign exchange. The resulting breakdown of cost per loaf (in pence) would therefore be as follows:

Materials	4·0 (1·7p)
Labour	0·3 (0·12p)
Fuel and power	0·5 (0·2p)
Depreciation and interest	2·0 (0·8p)
Total cost	6·8 (2·8p)
Loss	0·8 (0·3p)
Selling price per loaf	6·0 (2·5p)

In other words, such a plant would not be economic in these circumstances. There are other factors which would also militate against a project of this nature:

1. The existing bakers could not accumulate the capital required. If the project were to be executed, it would probably need government finance and administration, or government financial participation. In case of a govern-

ment venture, the difficulties of finding officials with the right kind of experience and motivations to provide the standards of efficiency, hygiene, quality and spread of services demanded by the consumer in this industry are well known; such managerial experience in the private sector is scarce.

2. Five hundred and sixty-five bakers would be thrown on the labour market. Retraining would be required before they could find other jobs, imposing an additional cost on the community. The chances of finding alternative employment would be limited as the consumer would be receiving no benefits from the technical innovations through lower prices. So demand for other products would not increase.

3. The livelihood of other tradesmen would also be affected adversely, e.g. brick-makers, and producers of wicker baskets and charcoal, as their products would be replaced by imported machinery and materials (e.g. steel bread tins).

4. Advanced European bread-making plant has been designed to handle high-grade white flour, which is in general demand there. These white flours and the usual additions of vitamins, eggs, milk, etc. are more expensive than the locally milled brown wheat and maize mixtures containing a higher portion of the husks. As the choice of materials is limited by the different mixing and baking characteristics of the various flours, the use of advanced plant would, in fact, raise the material costs substantially above the figure indicated in the cost analysis above (in the United Kingdom a 14-ounce white loaf costs 11d (4·5p) today, which reflects both high material and labour costs). There is also a question whether countries which have a chronic shortage of home-grown cereals, and where the average citizen suffers from an unbalanced diet, can afford to waste some of the more nutritious parts of the grain by using white flours.

5. Technological factors would also have an impact on consumer tastes and preference in respect of the shape, colour and texture of the loaf. In these basic foodstuffs one encounters a pronounced resistance to change among consumers (still one of the principal obstacles to productivity growth in the French baking industry, for example). If such a plant were erected, there would be some risk that it would work at well below capacity because of the continued preference of most customers for their traditional loaf.

It is clear that the latest western bakery technology would not be the most rational choice in the socioeconomic climate of the country in question. If the whole package of advanced technology is not suitable, it may be that certain elements could play a part. To start with, modern technical innovations could be introduced at two levels, first in the dough-kneading operations, which are very tiring and time-consuming if performed by hand (and unhygienic), and second in the firing system for the oven. A Vienna-style, reciprocating T-arm mixer with revolving bowl would perform the work of one man in a five-man enterprise (25 per cent increase in productivity). Cheap second-hand models in good condition are readily available, as these batch mixers are being replaced in Europe by continuous mixers.

On the baking side, an oil-fired fuel system would enable more constant temperatures to be maintained, increasing fuel efficiency and reducing wastage through over-baking and burning. A reduction in the wastage rate from 6 per cent to 1 per cent would result in savings in all the cost items. Thus, the potential savings of materials, labour and fuel of the two innovations could amount to 0·7d (0·3p) per loaf, offset by an increase in 0·1d (0·04p) in capital costs. The net savings of 0·6d (0·25p) per loaf could be shared between higher wages per man (from 10s (50p) to 12s (60p) per day), lower prices to the consumer (6d (2·5p) to 5·75d (2·4p) per loaf) and higher profits for the entrepreneur (0·6d (0·25p) to 0·7d (0·3p) per loaf).

The above technical changes would be economic only for the larger baking establishments (five to ten workers). These would then expand their share of the trade, absorbing the workers from the smaller, less competitive enterprises in the process. But the rate of productivity growth in the industry as a whole need not exceed the growth of the market, which is dependent on both the price elasticity and income elasticity of demand as well as on income changes in the community as a whole. Assuming a growth of real income per head of 3 per cent per annum (which would require complementary changes in other sectors similar to what is being advocated in the bakery industry), the end result of a phased process (spread over ten years) of modernization of this type should be higher wages, lower prices (assuming no inflation), larger profits, and fewer bakery firms but a constant labour force. Higher earnings and profits in the trade would result in increased demand for the products of other industries, hence raising employment levels there ...

A technology should suit the economic and social environment in which it is employed

[. . .] Small firms using labour-intensive methods have several advantages for developing countries. They can be managed successfully by the personal supervision of the owner, without the need for sophisticated control procedures or a complex hierarchy of authority. Hence they economize scarce managerial skills which cannot be built up in a country overnight. At the same time they act as a seed-bed for management personnel for the future. They can provide immediate executive experience for indigenous entrepreneurs, and so reduce the dependence on expatriate managers and technicians, who can be a considerable drain on foreign currency reserves without passing on much of their expertise to subordinates. Direct personal contact can be maintained with suppliers and customers. The hours of work can be more flexible and the interpersonal relationships less formal. [. . .] And unlike large-scale industry, which usually needs to be in close proximity to the markets and services found only in big cities, small units can be viable in the provincial towns and villages, thus leading to the harmonious development of town and country (Singer, 1964; Staley and Morse, 1967; UN Economic Commission for Africa, 1962; Marsden, 1968).

Case study illustrations. In Japan, which has achieved the most rapid sustained economic growth of any country in this century, small and medium firms (under 300 employees) have taken the lead in many industries and as late as 1954 employed 59 per cent of the total labour force in industry. In Japan small firms make 100 per cent of the toys, 87 per cent of household utensils, 81 per cent of leather shoes, 78 per cent of printing ink, 71 per cent of farm utensils and 70 per cent of cotton textiles, for example. Much of their technology would be classed as obsolete in the United States.

In the United Arab Republic small firms (less than 100 workers) achieved a higher productivity of capital than did large firms in fifteen out of the twenty major industrial classifications in the 1960 census. Yet their capital intensity was generally much lower. A similar picture is found in data for India, Taiwan, Japan, Chile and Ecuador (Mitra, 1967; ILO, 1967; Miyazawa, 1964; Consejería Nacional de Promoción Popular, 1968; Stanford Research Institute, 1963; Marsden, 1964).

New technologies should stimulate output in indigenous industries and be capable of being reproduced locally

A technology is more likely to be progressive if it can be reproduced within the local engineering and material manufacturing industries within a short time and if it processes indigenous raw materials. The immediate benefit will be the saving of foreign currency, which is a serious limiting factor in most countries' expansion plans. Just as important in the long term is the creation of indigenous industries for machine tools, machine building and repair, and material and component manufacture. The experience of North America, West and East Europe and Japan has shown that these industries are indispensable features of a balanced industrial structure. They provide employment and incomes for large numbers of the people. They accelerate the process of technical change through their intimate contacts with the technology users. Their familiarity with the environment ensures that technical developments are practical and economical in the local setting. And developments in this sector tend to have a beneficial multiplying effect on other areas of the economy. Such indigenous industries would lessen dependence on intellectual imports.[7]

To build up such industries in the developing countries would mean starting on the ground floor and at a relatively low technical level in many cases. The technologies chosen must therefore be within their capabilities. By a combination of imaginative improvisation and adaptation, the absorption of scientific knowledge from abroad, an emphasis on technical training, tolerance of initial imperfections by the customers, and accumulated experience and confidence coming from self-achievement, each country could establish a strong and healthy technology-producing sector over a period of years. Complete technological self-sufficiency is not being proposed. Most developing countries are too small for that, and it would involve quite wasteful duplication. But if these industries are to get off the ground, some loosening of the present technological ties with the advanced nations would seem to be required.

Case study illustration. An Asian country which had formerly imported its sewing machines decided to promote its own machine-building industry. A nucleus already existed in the small workshops manufacturing replacement parts for imported models. Profiting from the temporary protection afforded by import restrictions, local entrepreneurial initiative quickly appeared to coordinate and expand the activities of these specialized workshops and to set up assembly units. In a few years the sewing machine industry, equipped with general-purpose lathes and drills (rather than multi-spindle boring machines and special jigs) was turning out models at 60 per cent of the price of previous imports. The local sewing machines had a more limited range of operations and were less accurate, but because of their lower price they had opened up a new market among small-scale clothing and footwear establishments, thus increasing their efficiency. By 1966 import restrictions could be relaxed and the industry was strong enough to have established a thriving export trade to neighbouring countries.

The productivity of capital should be maximized and the social cost of production minimized

In countries where capital is scarce and labour unemployed or underemployed (i.e. most developing countries) the emphasis should be put on

7. The director-general of UNESCO, in a speech to the United Nations Economic and Social Council in July 1966, put forward the view that the resort to foreign 'magic' was the characteristic of underdevelopment, which would persist until science and technology became part of the indigenous culture. Similarly, the director-general of the World Health Organization has pointed out: 'Technology may be international in substance, but its method of application must be adapted to the situation in which it is to be applied.' See Candau (1967, p. 508).

maximizing capital productivity rather than labour productivity. Where there are a number of alternative methods of making a given product, the one which achieves the highest output for a given *capital* cost should be selected (other things being equal). When setting up new industries, priority should be given to those products and processes which need less capital for the same value of output than would competing substitutes, e.g. cotton ginning and spinning rather than synthetic fibre production.[8]

What about price and production costs? Should not the technique be chosen which results in the lowest unit costs? This is probably the most important consideration in private investment decisions. It would also be desirable from a national point of view if money costs reflected the real costs to society of using the factors of production. Unfortunately, this is not always true. Official interest rates paid on capital made available to large enterprises (public and private) are often fixed artificially low in the developing countries. The 'usurious' rates of moneylenders may, in fact, be a truer representation of the supply price of capital, the level of risks involved and its marginal productivity in use. Similarly, current wage rates, low though they may be, can be said to overprice labour if there are large numbers of unemployed seeking work. The real cost to society of providing productive jobs for them (which would increase the size of the national 'cake') would certainly be less, if not zero (e.g. in the case of cottage industry). [9]

Another cause of distortion is the practice among some developing

8. Utilization of the other inputs – land and materials – needs to be taken into account. Advanced technologies can sometimes offer better material utilization, but this may not be realized if the requisite labour and managerial skills are lacking. It is sometimes argued that where managerial and operative skills are scarce, it would be wiser to encourage large-scale enterprises to invest heavily in automatic processes so that relatively few unskilled workers have to be controlled, rather than to foster labour-intensive factories which need many more workers and higher craft skills, thus complicating management and increasing training costs. Put like this, the argument is persuasive. But are these the only alternatives? By product and process specialization, a number of small enterprises can produce the same output as one large factory. And managerial efficiency in small enterprises depends more upon the innate entrepreneurial characteristics and motivations of the owner than upon formalized control procedures requiring higher education and institutional training. Similarly, unlike high-level mechanical and electronic engineering know-how, craft skills can be acquired on the job, so that the wage and supervisory costs of the apprentice need not exceed his marginal product, and material wastage is minimized. New techniques can be injected by machinery and material suppliers as well as by government advisory services. This is how the Japanese made full use of their labour force, at a low capital and training cost, while husbanding their managerial resources, and still gaining the advantages of a high division of labour.

9. The distortion of the price structure resulting from the use of selective government controls is discussed in Myrdal (1968, chapter 19).

countries of overvaluing their currencies and rationing foreign exchange, thus tending to underrate the real costs of projects making heavy demands on foreign exchange.

Imperfect mobility of labour between occupations and differentials in the capital market are further reasons why money costs are not always the best indicator of economic efficiency or social welfare. It has therefore been proposed that planners should use 'shadow prices', which would attempt to measure the real cost to the community of the factors of production when making investment decisions. Similarly, direct government intervention on the wage/interest rate structure may be desirable to ensure a closer identity between private economic advantage and the broader national interest than exists at present.

Case study illustrations. A tanning industry project in the Middle East envisaged building a small model tannery to act as a training centre and to demonstrate new techniques, together with a number of new buildings to rehouse existing tanneries, thus improving working conditions and separating the industry (with its obnoxious smells) from the living quarters. The total capital costs were projected as $2·5 million for an output of $15 million per annum (a high capital productivity). The buildings and some of the machinery could be made locally, so the import content was small. Demand for leather was growing at 5 per cent per annum and labour productivity was expected to rise at this rate due to improved methods and conditions; thus the total labour force in the industry of 3000 would remain the same.

This project was rejected, however, on the grounds of not being modern enough. In its place was substituted a scheme for a large government-owned tannery estate, costing $15 million, equipped with the latest imported machinery and with a total capacity 50 per cent in excess of the existing firms. Labour productivity would be doubled but the savings in wages would be more than offset by higher capital costs (interest and depreciation) if a shadow interest rate were used. The productivity of the capital employed would be only 25 per cent of the anticipated level in the first project proposed. Employment in the industry would be halved, the existing equipment made obsolete and the import bill increased by more than $8 million. The present firms would be broken up and experienced owners made redundant. Little improvement in quality could be expected because further foreign exchange to buy better hides and tanning materials (which, together with technical know-how, were the primary determinants of quality) could not be afforded. And in international terms they would not end up with the most up-to-date process but with an expensive 'white elephant', because heavy sole leather and even some upper leathers were being replaced rapidly in world markets by synthetic materials (e.g. vulcanized rubber compounds for soles, corfam poromeric material and PVC for uppers).

Thus the more modest scheme was not only more appropriate for the particular internal circumstances of this developing country but also gave it greater flexibility to take advantage of world technological developments when it had the necessary resources (i.e. a petrochemical industry).

On the other hand, there are undoubtedly examples of advanced capital-intensive technology satisfying these criteria best. A case in point is a fibre-board plant in an African country. This cost $2 million and employed only 120 workers directly, because the higher pressures and great bulk involved required very heavy machinery. However, it processed the residue of sugar-cane and maize stalks which would otherwise have gone to waste. Thus the value added during the process was high, and it provided additional incomes to the farmers. The finished product was a good, cheap substitute for certain kinds of wood for furniture and housing. This wood had previously been imported, so foreign currency was also saved. This project therefore served the national interest in several respects.

Sources of progressive technology and ways of increasing its availability
Specially designed technologies

The most effective means of overcoming economic backwardness would be to apply accumulated scientific knowledge to the solution of the particular problems of the developing countries. There is undoubtedly a great need for new technologies which will incorporate recent inventions but at the same time take account of the scarcity of capital and of certain managerial and operative skills in the developing world. Innovation is required too so that local raw material can be substituted in certain processes for the different types which are imported at present. Varying climatic conditions may demand new solutions to familiar problems. Working parties have been formed in India and Britain to undertake research into these questions and the United Nations Advisory Committee on the Application of Science and Technology to Development is keenly interested in the problems of adaptation of designs and methods. Much valuable pioneer work has been done by specialist institutes like the Tropical Products Research Institute in England.

Technological research institutes are now being set up in some countries under United Nations Special Fund auspices. But only the surface of the problem is being scratched. If just a small proportion of the ingenuity and creativity which goes into satisfying the exotic demands of an affluent society could be diverted to this end, a very real contribution to overcoming world-wide poverty could be made. Perhaps each of the advanced countries could earmark a certain percentage of its aid funds to sponsor research of this kind, preferably within the developing countries themselves so that it is based upon first-hand knowledge of the local situation.[10]

Case study illustrations. Unconventional sources of energy, such as solar heat to distil fresh water from salt water, and as an energy source for industrial purposes.

'Hover' (air-cushioned) vehicles for transport over swampy ground.

Self-maintaining machinery.

The processing of date palm fibres to replace wool and hair in upholstery stuffing.

The extraction of creosote and charcoal from the husks and shells of coconuts, and biological insecticides from coconut oil.

The derivation of food proteins from oil.

The 'spray' process, which may reduce the capital cost of making steel considerably.

Modern technologies

As emphasized previously, modern up-to-date technology from the most industrialized countries can play a part. To deprive oneself completely of these techniques would be just as wasteful as their indiscriminate application in the past. What types are likely to pass through the screen that has been proposed? One can distinguish four main groups.

The first consists of technical know-how with little or no capital element. Improved ways of making or growing things as a result of a deeper understanding of the chemical, physical and biological properties of products and materials fall into this category. The quicker this knowledge is incorporated into current practice the better, and extension services and demonstration units have vital roles in this dissemination. There would appear to be no major economic obstacles, though social resistance may be encountered.

The second group consists of technologies where the tool element can be easily separated from the labour-saving element. One particular process in a series of operations may have to be performed by a particular machine if consistent quality and precision in the final product are to be maintained. The ancillary operations, particularly materials handling, can be carried out by hand methods if labour is abundant and cheap.

The third category covers machines which replace non-existent human skills, or skills which would be more expensive to train in terms of educational facilities.

10. The United Nations Advisory Committee on the Application of Science and Technology to Development recommended, at its 13th Session in April 1970, that the targets for the Second United Nations Development Decade should include the allocation of 5 per cent of the non-military research and development expenditure of the developed countries to specific problems of developing countries.

The fourth embraces all those modern technologies that may be the only effective means of exploiting a country's physical resources, which would otherwise lie idle, and which could form the basis of other indigenous industries.

Case study illustrations. Colour charts, penetrometers and triaxial compression testing machines for measuring the properties of soil and clays – leading to improved crop selection and rotation, higher land yields, cheaper, more durable roads, and improved ceramic products.

A modern gas or oil-fired fuel system for bread ovens giving more precise temperature control, and resulting in even quality and reduced wastage.

Diagnostic machines for locating and identifying defects in automobiles.

Numerically controlled machine tools which economize on skilled labour.

Infra-red scanners and tungsten-tipped drills for discovering and tapping hidden water and oil resources.

Long-established designs

Classic designs which have proved themselves at a similar stage of development in the now advanced economies could still be relevant to the developing countries. They may not be included in the current machinery catalogues because they have been superseded in the advanced countries by more expensive, labour-saving devices. They have to be dug out of the archives of patent offices and long-established machinery manufacturers. Trade associations could carry out such sifting and collating, sponsored by multilateral or bilateral aid funds. They, in turn, would send the designs to the research institutes in the developing countries, which would disseminate technical specifications, blueprints, drawings, etc. to the engineering workshops and manufacturing firms.

The major international companies which set up subsidiaries in the developing countries could contribute considerably in this. The Philips electrical concern has given a lead by establishing a pilot radio assembly plant in Holland where simple, commonly available tools are tried out in conditions which simulate those encountered in its overseas operations.

The Intermediate Technology Development Group in the United Kingdom has published, in collaboration with the Confederation of British Industry, a buyer's guide which advertises the simple kinds of tools and equipment that might fill the gap between traditional hand methods and sophisticated technologies. Second-hand machinery is another cheap, readily available source which could be utilized more often.

The examples given below are just indications of what might be the appropriate 'new' techniques to replace the existing ones in some countries as a beginning. These should be regarded as steps and not platforms.

In each industry improved techniques need to be introduced successively over the years so that productivity is raised progressively.

Case study illustrations. Bakery industry. Steam pipe ovens which ensure an even dispersion of heat by means of coiled steam-pipes; draw-plate ovens in which loading and unloading are speeded up by putting the plate of the oven on wheels and rollers; Vienna, T-arm kneaders in which a single reciprocating arm kneads the dough in a rotating mixing bowl. This equipment is more advanced and efficient than brick-lined, open-flame ovens and hand-mixing, but is much less capital-intensive than turbo-radiant travelling ovens or continuous mixers.

Ceramic industry. Oil or coal-fired Hoffman kilns; hand-operated jiggers for forming plates, semi-automatic presses for tiles, gravity-fed extruders for pipes. These are all superior to traditional methods but less expensive than tunnel kilns and fully automatic equipment.

Shoe industry. Simple Blake sewing machines (first introduced in 1859) for stitching the sole to the upper and insole. This is quicker than hand-stitching but may be more appropriate than vulcanizing or injection-moulding equipment for soling in these countries.

Policy measures to facilitate the implementation of progressive technology

What specific measures could be taken by governments to create the economic and legal environment most conducive to optimum choice and, once selected and installed, to ensure that progressive technology is utilized efficiently? Some possible steps are listed below.

1. The formation of customs unions with other States at a similar stage of development and with complementary resources. These would encourage a new international division of labour and a competitive stimulus for efficiency, while avoiding head-on, heavily one-sided encounters between rich and poor nations in the international trade and technology fields.[11]

11. So far such agreements have been confined to small groupings of neighbouring countries, e.g. the East African and the Central American common markets. But it may be that Tanzania and Pakistan, say, are more complementary than Tanzania and Kenya, for example. The real crux is whether the developing countries are willing to accept lower-quality products from their trading partners in place of imports from the advanced countries, as the short-term price to be paid for a long-term mutual self-help programme. There is also the question of the product mix, which influences technological choice and may determine factor proportions within narrow limits. Will they be prepared to exchange cotton textiles for leather and leather products which can still be made by labour-intensive capital-saving equipment, locally produced, rather than insist upon importing capital-intensive machinery and material inputs from the advanced countries in order to manufacture the most modern versions of these products (clothing and footwear made from nylon, terylene, corfam, PVC, etc.), and

2. Higher official interest rates to raise the price of capital *vis-à-vis* labour costs. This would tend to bring more labour into productive employment as well as increase the propensity to save. It should be made clear that this is not to suggest that governments should pay a higher interest rate on what they borrow from advanced countries or international agencies.

3. Providing indigenous industries with ample scope to expand, develop and diversify over time without bumping their heads against competing industries which are technically more advanced because greater resources (uneconomically priced) have been placed at their disposal. Giving a clear run ahead to indigenous entrepreneurs is likely to be more conducive to growth and development than imposing protective subsidies and quotas in an attempt to have the best of both worlds.[12]

4. Tax concessions and political guarantees to attract foreign capital and know-how, accompanied by legislation requiring all companies to buy a certain proportion of raw materials, components and replacement machinery locally within a fixed time period (as in Mexico).

5. The setting up of documentation and information centres to keep track of past and current technological developments throughout the world. These would establish close liaison with international and other national advisory services for the selection of equipment.[13]

6. The provision of widespread primary and technical education facilities at the apprentice level, combined with night-school tuition and upgrading

---

where little technological flexibility is possible? Such alternatives are available for a wide spectrum of consumer products and services. A high proportion of the products of the latest technology did not exist at the turn of the century. Yet income per head in the United States in 1960 was well over $1000 at today's prices. High income growth could be attained by choosing the products which can be produced in ways that are most appropriate for their current resource endowment. The opportunity to make choices of this kind throws a heavy burden on the planners and political leaders of the less developed countries, particularly as they are members of the relatively high-income minority in which consumer demand is concentrated and as they have generally been most exposed to current western consumption patterns. But the key to harmonious economic and technological change probably lies here.

12. The problems encountered in India as a result of a co-existence of the most advanced and the most primitive technologies in the same industry, e.g. textiles, and from the attempts to cushion the effects of such confrontations by the use of selective controls and subsidies, are described in Ministry of Industry (1963).

13. Scientific and technological information centres have played an important part in Japanese and Soviet economic development. In 1963 about 210,000 abstracts of foreign scientific papers were made by the Japan Information Centre for Science and Technology. See Japan Council for Science and Technology (1964, p. 15). In the Soviet Union the All-Union Institute of Scientific and Technical Information has an abstracting service which digests 400,000 scientific papers a year.

courses for practising operatives, supervisors and managers. Vocational, instructor and management training institutes sponsored by the ILO already function in many countries, while UNESCO programmes cover school, college and university education.

7. Training courses for managers and planners in feasibility study and cost-benefit analysis techniques to increase the 'rationality' of investment decisions and in the use of other management tools (e.g. work study) which will increase the efficiency of existing manufacturing methods. The ILO and UNIDO are operating here.

8. The encouragement, by state subsidies, grants, etc. of trade and research associations for each industry, sponsored and run by the members themselves. Special budgets could be allocated for importing standard machines to be stripped down, adapted and eventually reproduced locally.[14]

9. The institution of incentive rewards schemes for inventions, as well as patent protection for local adaptations of foreign designs.

10. The formation of common facility cooperatives and joint production workshops to raise the productivity of artisan and handicraft industries.

11. The provision of extension services for small-scale entrepreneurs, providing advice on product and process development, technical skill

14. The need for indigenous design and development organizations is recognized in India and Tanzania. The Indian draft Fourth Five-Year Plan, 1969–74, states: 'Self-reliance in the technological sense implies the existence and effective functioning of indigenous organizations for design, construction and engineering of projects as well as capability for design and development of machinery, equipment and instruments indigenously manufactured. At present there is unwholesome dependence on foreign agencies for these services. As long as this deficiency remains, local talent will not have scope to develop, and excessive dependence on foreign help will be prolonged ... It is only by participating actively and in positions of responsibility that such skill and confidence are generated and scarce high talent human resource is developed. It is therefore of vital importance for the future development of the country that urgent attention is given to promoting and encouraging healthy development of adequate design and engineering organizations, staffed by highly qualified personnel and working under proper leadership'. Planning Commission (1969, p. 44).

In the Tanzanian Second Five-Year Plan the view is expressed that 'the tendency in the past to think of mechanization primarily in the context of tractorization has led to the neglect of opportunities to improve hand- and animal-drawn equipment, the need for simple processing equipment, water-lifting and reticulation devices, and on-farm transport such as ox carts and trailers, as well as feeder transport vehicles'. The Plan provides for the expansion of the Tanganyika Agricultural Machinery Testing Unit to engage in designing simple and inexpensive farm implements which could easily be made from available raw materials. Particular emphasis would be placed on intermediate technology, including the construction of ox carts, ox-driven water-pumps, hand-operated water-pumps for irrigation, ox-drawn earth scoops, ox-drawn tool bars and crop-driers. See United Republic of Tanzania (1969, pp. 37, 38).

formation and the selection and use of appropriate technologies. Again, the I L O is active in this work through small-industry institutes and experts on individual assignment.

12. Long-term planning of manpower and skill requirements in the various sectors of the economy, closely related to the foreseen rate and character of technical change.

13. The adoption of factory legislative and safety regulations which provide adequate working conditions and safeguards for all groups of workers but do not create dual standards (i.e. for those within and those outside the practical jurisdiction of the laws) and act as barriers to expansion for the smaller enterprises.

14. The creation of central quality-control and inspection schemes to ensure that products destined for export meet external quality standards, but without imposing unrealistically high standards on total production within the country.

15. Priority in the allocation of import licences for machinery and materials to organizations that have already demonstrated the aptitudes, skills and motivations required for success in the export markets.

16. Systematic market research surveys abroad to identify precise consumer needs (and appropriate distribution channels) which might be satisfied by the use of relatively labour-intensive techniques. UNCTAD and GATT have already sponsored and carried out such investigations on behalf of member governments.

17. The establishment of special small-business development banks to reduce the differentials in capital accessibility between the traditional and the modern sectors. The World Bank is giving technical and financial assistance in this area.

18. The planned distribution of industry to backward areas to provide more employment opportunities outside the major cities and to reduce income inequalities between regions. Processing of agricultural and other land-based products are obvious choices (the FAO has substantial interests in this field).

19. Financial incentives (e.g. tax rebates on training costs) to international companies to set up apprentice training schools, management development programmes and planned succession to management positions for indigenous staff. This would reduce the foreign exchange costs of expatriate staff, while ensuring that their essential expertise in operating, servicing and managing more advanced technology is passed on to local personnel.

20. Devaluation of currencies to ensure that the importer has to pay the real

cost of foreign machinery and materials, and that a proper evaluation is made in initial feasibility studies.

21. State-financed hire-purchase and rental schemes with lower interest rates for imported second-hand machinery and locally made equipment.

22. Subsidized factory premises in provincial towns and villages to slow down the population drift to the cities. The subsidies could be equivalent to the cost of housing and other facilities which would otherwise have to be provided in the cities.

23. 'Tax holidays' for foreign machinery and component manufacturers who set up local design and production plants to develop indigenous technologies.

24. Public information campaigns to increase the prestige and consumer acceptance of indigenous technologies and products.

Where such policies and programmes have been introduced, the results are promising. They appear to open up new avenues for a dynamic attack on poverty in the developing countries in which the progressive and widespread introduction of new methods (new, that is to say, compared with *their* traditional ones) could lead to a better use of their current resources and achieve a rapid and sustained growth shared by the whole people.

References

BOON, G. K. (1961), 'Choice of industrial technology: the case of woodworking', in *Industrialization and Productivity*, United Nations.

BOON, G. K. (1964), *Economic Choice of Human and Physical Factors in Production*, North Holland.

CANDAU, M. G. (1967), 'Knowledge, the bridge to achievement', in W H O *Chronicle*, vol. 21, p. 508.

CONSEJENRI NACIONAL DE PROMOCIÓN POPULAR (1968), *Pequeña industria y artesania en Chile*, Santiago.

DENISON, E. F. (1966), *The Sources of Economic Growth in the United States and the Alternatives Before Us*, Committee for Economic Development.

FOOD and AGRICULTURE ORGANIZATION (1966) *The State of Food and Agriculture 1966*, FAO.

GERSCHENKRON, A. (1962), *Economic Development in Historical Perspective*, Harvard University Press.

HAGEN, E. (1962), *Development of the Emerging Nations: An Agenda for Research*, Brookings Institution.

HIRSCHMAN, A. O. (1958), *The Strategy of Economic Development*, Yale University Press.

ILO (1967), *The Development of Small Enterprises in Taiwan, Republic of China*, mimeo., Geneva, ILO.

JAPAN COUNCIL for SCIENCE and TECHNOLOGY (1964), *Science and Technology in Japan*, Tokyo.

KILBY, P. (1965), *African Entrepreneurship: the case of the Nigerian Bread Industry*, Stanford University Press.

MARSDEN, K. (1964), *The Role of Small-Scale Industry in Development, with Special Reference to Egypt*, Institute of Small Industries.

MARSDEN, K. (mimeo.) (1968), 'The role of small enterprises in the industrialization of the developing countries', in ILO, *Report on the ILO Interregional Seminar on Programmes and Policies for Small-Scale Industry Within the Framework of Overall Economic Development Planning*.

MARSDEN, K. (1969) 'Towards a synthesis of economic growth and social justice', *Int. Lab. Rev.*, vol. 100 no. 5.

MCCLELLAND, D. C. (1961), *The Achieving Society*, Van Nostrand.

MINISTRY of INDUSTRY (India), (1963), *Development of Small-Scale Industry in India – Prospects, Problems and Policies,* Ford Foundation.

MITRA, L. K. (1967), *Employment and Output in Small Enterprises in India*, Bookland Private.

MIYAZAWA, K. (1964), 'The dual structure of the Japanese economy', in *Developing Economies*, Tokyo.

MORSE, D. (1966), 'Narrowing the gap', in *ILO Panorama*, Geneva, ILO.

MYRDAL, G. (1957), *Rich Lands and Poor: the Road to World Prosperity*, Harper & Row.

MYRDAL, G. (1968), *Asian Drama. An Inquiry into the Poverty of Nations*, © Twentieth Century Fund, Penguin 1968.

PLANNING COMMISSION (India) (1969), *Fourth Five-Year Plan, 1969–74*, Delhi.

SINGER, H. W. (1964), *International Development: Growth and Change*, McGraw-Hill.

STALEY, E., and MORSE, R. (1967), *Modern Small Industry for Developing Countries*, McGraw-Hill.

STANFORD RESEARCH INSTITUTE (1963), *The Artisan Community in Ecuador's Modernising Economy*.

UNITED NATIONS CENTRE for INDUSTRIAL DEVELOPMENT (1966), *Criteria for the Development of Manufacturing Industries in Developing Countries*, UN.

UN ECONOMIC COMMISSION (1962), *Economic Bulletin for Africa*, UN.

UNITED REPUBLIC of TANZANIA (1969), *Second Five-Year Plan for Economic and Social Development 1969–74*, vol. 1.

26 C. Hou

Manpower, Employment and Unemployment in Communist China

Extract from C. Hou, 'Manpower, employment and unemployment in Communist China', in A. Eckstein, W. Galenson and Ta-Chung-Liu (eds.), *Economic Trends in Communist China*, Social Science Research Council, Chicago, 1968.

Utilization and policy
Structural shift and disguised unemployment

In the years of Communist rule it has been claimed that China has undergone drastic economic changes and has experienced extraordinarily rapid economic development. Official statistics show that national income increased at an average annual rate of 9 per cent in 1952–7 and industrial production (in terms of gross value) at nearly 25 per cent in 1949–57 (*Ten Great Years*, 1959, pp. 16, 18). These claims may be questioned, but independent estimates by scholars in the West also show rather rapid development. For example, Liu and Yeh (1965, p. 87) have estimated that the national income of China increased at 6 per cent a year in 1952–7 (in 1952 prices) and that factory production increased by 21 per cent a year from 1952 to 1957. Such rapid development is usually associated with a shift in the composition of output as well as employment; that is, the share of industry (*v* agriculture) rises both in total output and in total employment.

In the Chinese case, the shift in output is clear; according to official data, the share of industrial production increased from 30 per cent of total industrial and agricultural production in 1949 to 57 per cent in 1957 (*Ten Great Years*, 1959, p. 15). Liu and Yeh's estimates show that the share of the modern nonagricultural sectors in net domestic product (in 1952 prices) increased from 28·8 per cent in 1952 to 41·2 per cent in 1957 (1965, p. 89).[1] But no significant shift in employment has taken place. What Colin Clark used to call 'Sir William Petty's Law of Economic Progress' was evidently not applicable. The proportion of nonagricultural employment in the labour force showed a modest increase during the early, largely recovery, years from 1949 to 1953, then became stable at a level somewhat lower than in 1953. It was not until the Great Leap in 1958 that the proportion rose very sharply, but also very briefly. It declined in 1959 and 1960 and probably declined even further in 1961–4, for nonagricultural employ-

1. Modern nonagricultural sectors include factories, mining, utilities, construction, modern transportation and communications, trading stores, restaurants and modern financial institutions.

ment was, at best, perhaps the same as in 1960, while the labor force continued to increase. The share of nonagricultural employment in the total labor force is given in Table 1.

Table 1 **Proportion of nonagricultural employment to total civilian labor force, 1949–60** (per cent)

	Male (ages 15–59)*	Both sexes (ages 15–59)†
1949	19·1	14·9
1950	20·7	12·9
1951	22·6	13·8
1952	23·3	14·1
1953	24·1	14·6
1954	22·9	14·1
1955	21·7	13·3
1956	22·3	13·7
1957	21·6	13·4
1958	28·5	17·5
1959	26·4	16·6
1960	25·9	16·3

* Male nonagricultural employment in total male civilian labor force, ages 15–59. The latter is obtained by deducting from total male population (15–59) the following: 3 million in armed forces, 1 per cent as disabled, and male students (age 18 and over).

† Total nonagricultural employment in total civilian labor force, ages 15–59. The latter is obtained in the same manner as above except both sexes (age 15 and over) are included.

The lack of a structural shift in manpower allocation is not difficult to explain. Although the rate of capital formation has been exceedingly high – about 20 per cent of domestic product in net terms and in 1952 prices in 1952–7 (Liu and Yeh, 1965, p. 74) – the choice of technique and scale was such that investment was put mainly into large and highly capital-intensive projects. The result was an increasing amount of investment per worker and a rising productivity of labor. But given this investment criterion, the rate of capital formation, high as it was, was not high enough to absorb even the nonagricultural labor force.

The choice of technique was probably dictated by the fact that the backbone of industrial development was the 156 projects designed and built with the help of the Russians – projects that were modern, large-scale and capital-intensive. We need not consider here why Communist China adopted such projects or whether there were other alternatives available (given the objectives of the regime). The fact remains that China did not have enough resources to build ultramodern industries, and at the same time, create enough jobs for the labor force (Yeh, 1965).

The implications of the Chinese pattern of development (that is, rapid development without a shift from agricultural to nonagricultural employment) are fairly obvious. Given fixed land area and growing population, the land–population ratio must decline; this presents serious difficulties for agricultural development, especially in an already crowded country.

It is often suggested that the land–population ratio in China was already so low in the 1930s that there was a considerable amount of disguised unemployment in the agricultural sector. (Disguised unemployment is usually defined as existing when, other things being equal, output can be maintained or even increased with a lesser amount of labor; in other words, when the marginal productivity of labor is zero or negative.) Although this assertion cannot be easily substantiated, it is safe to say that agricultural labor, at least on a year-round basis, was considerably underutilized. [. . .]

The strategy of grand substitution

The Great Leap Forward, which was launched at the end of 1957 and gained full momentum in 1958 and 1959, was, according to the Chinese expression, a large-scale attempt to 'walk on two legs' to speed up economic development at a rate of 20 to 30 per cent a year in industrial growth (Chou En-lai, 1959, p. 22). The 'two legs' were simultaneous development in industry and agriculture; in heavy and light industries; in centrally and locally managed enterprises; in large, medium and small enterprises; in modern and native technologies; in centralized leadership and mass participation (Hsu Li-chun, 1959, p. 2). Simultaneous development did not mean development at the same rate, however, for industry was still given priority over agriculture, heavy industries over light, large enterprises over medium and small ones, modern techniques over native, central enterprises over local ones.[2]

But it was pointed out the simultaneity was necessary for rapid development because of the complementary nature of different kinds of development. For instance, agriculture provides raw materials, markets and a source of capital for industry; heavy industry makes possible the mechanization of agriculture; light industry is necessary to improve living standards and hence incentives to work. Large and modern industries are essential for products that require advanced technology, high quality and large quantity; small and native industries require less capital and can be estab-

2. The share of state investment in industry in 1958–9 was larger than ever before, while that in agriculture increased only slightly. Total investment in light industry in 1958 doubled over 1957, but investment in heavy industry increased even more sharply. See Yeh (1965, pp. 33, 35).

lished in large number in a short time, satisfying many needs of the people and training skilled labor in the process (Hsu Li-chun, 1959, pp. 3–6).

How was this simultaneous development on a broad front possible in view of the scarcity of capital? The answer is that the capital was still to be used primarily for the development of heavy industry, while labor was to be the main input for other development. The strategy was one of large-scale substitution of labor for capital, a massive mobilization of the under-utilized manpower, or what Nurkse called 'hidden rural savings'. Thus, in industry the establishment of small, highly labor-intensive indigenous plants was an outstanding feature of the Great Leap, while in agriculture, intensive farming and multiple operations were the guiding principle. Intensive farming was simply intensive use of labor as required by the 'eight principles' of increasing agricultural production.[3] Multiple operations meant that the peasants were urged, especially in off seasons, to engage in fields of production other than farming, such as forestry, animal-raising, fishing, subsidiary work and rural basic construction (irrigation projects, road building, etc.). Such intensive use of labor was the very essence of the Great Leap; it was designed for the dual purpose of solving the problem of unemployment (especially seasonal) and at the same time accelerating economic development. All this had been attempted before, but the grand scale and manner in which the Great Leap was launched made it unique.

It is not necessary here to examine the details of how labor was used in the Great Leap; the following reported statistics should suffice to show the general picture:[4]

1. In 1958, there were founded some 300,000 small, indigenous industrial establishments (in manufacturing and mining); 90,000 of them were administered at the *hsien* level or above, 210,000 at the *hsiang* level (or rural communes). An estimated total of 4·4 million workers were newly recruited to staff these establishments. (This may be compared with about 6 million workers newly recruited in 1958 to staff the modern sector of industry) (Emerson, 1965a, p. 86). In addition, by the end of 1959 some 10 million peasants had participated in temporary industrial work during the off seasons (*Kuang-ming jih-pao*, July, 1960).

2. There was an increase of 3·4 million construction workers in 1958, most of whom went into local building enterprises (Emerson, 1965a, p. 88).

3. 'Street' and urban commune industry employed in 1959 and 1960 a

3. The 'eight principles' are: improve soil; increase fertilizer; irrigate; improve seeds; practice close-planting; protect plants (insecticides); provide better farm management; and improve implements and tools.
4. For a discussion of utilization of labor, see, for example, Orleans (1961) and Emerson (1961).

total of 2 million workers, of whom 85 per cent were women (Emerson, 1965b, p. 9).

4. Some 60 million persons were reportedly involved, at the end of 1958, in the movement of smelting iron and steel in backyard furnaces (Chang Fo-chien, 1958, p. 30); presumably this fantastic figure includes all persons who participated in all phases of the movement: searching for coal, iron and other material, constructing furnaces, etc.[5]

5. There was a reported total of more than 100 million persons engaged in water conservation work in the winter of 1957–8 (*JMJP*, 3 May, 1958), of whom 73 million were women. More than 67 million women reportedly worked on afforestation projects in 1958; they probably constituted more than half of all participants (Emerson, 1965b, p. 20).

6. In the winter of 1959–60, some 70 million persons were reportedly engaged in water conservation work; 30 million in forestry, animal raising, fisheries and subsidiary work; and 15 million in public welfare services (T'an Chen-lin, 1960, p. 4).

7. More than 7 million persons were mobilized in the fall of 1959 for road building and short-distance transportation (Emerson, 1965a, p. 94).

Although the accuracy of the above statistics is highly questionable, there is little doubt that in 1958 and 1959 a great number of persons, especially women, were mobilized, the primary strategy being to utilize rural labor in both agricultural and nonagricultural activities, especially those off-season. Apparently the peasants were asked to do too much non-farming work; only 50 per cent of the manpower was actually engaged in farm production (T'an Chen-lin, 1960, p. 4). As was indicated later, at least 80 per cent of rural labor was necessary for farm work in the busy seasons (Ma Wen-jui, 1961, p. 11). Thus, in the Great Leap years a severe labor shortage was widely reported. The peasants were worked so hard that it was necessary for the highest authorities to issue directives that they should work no more than 12 hours a day.

How successful was the strategy of 'walking on two legs'? Any attempt to evaluate the result of the intensive utilization of labor in the Great Leap years is complicated by the fact that many other things also happened at the same time. The people's communes which were introduced in 1958 probably facilitated the efforts to mobilize rural labor, but must also have dampened the peasants' incentive to work by the confiscation of private plots, the more or less egalitarian distribution system, and the drastic change in family life. The Great Leap years also saw the down-grading of technical expertise; the party cadres gained control of production in the name of mass participa-

5. For a description of the movement, see Academy of Sciences (1958).

tion and 'politics takes command', and pushed the campaign so ambitiously or fanatically that many basic technical constraints were neglected.

The effects of labor intensification were further blurred by the natural calamities in three consecutive years 1959–61, and by the Soviet withdrawal of technical personnel in 1960. Agricultural production in 1959 was also in part affected by a planned reduction of sown area, a mistake in planning caused by false reports of production increases in 1958.

Thus the efforts to use labor intensively were made at a time when many other events took place – events not necessarily related to labor intensification. The economic slump following the Great Leap offers no proof that the strategy of intensive utilization of labor was wrong. But the technical mistakes associated with party control over production seem to suggest that a massive mobilization of underutilized labor without the guidance of trained personnel is likely to result in a waste of resources.

A quantitative measurement of the result of the Great Leap is made particularly difficult by the poor quality of official statistics; the statistical system disintegrated as the Leap began. But if one regards the statistics for the industrial sector as reliable enough to indicate at least the rough trend of development, the basic strategy of the Great Leap did yield some positive results. The gross value of industrial production is officially reported to have increased sharply in 1958, and to a lesser degree in 1959. On the basis of the sharp increase in the incremental output-capital ratio in 1958,[6] it is reasonable to assume that the increase in production was partly brought about by intensive use of labor, although both labor productivity and the quality of output sharply declined. If net value added in industry as estimated by Liu and Yeh is used rather than the official gross value, the incremental output-capital ratio also rose in 1958, though to a much lesser degree (Liu and Yeh, 1965, p. 66).

6. To compute incremental output-capital ratio, fixed investment is used for total investment in industry (*Ten Great Years*, p. 57) after deflation by the price index for basic construction given in Liu and Yeh (1965, p. 235). The index for 1957 is used for 1958. For gross value of industrial output, see *Ten Great Years* (p. 76). Thus the incremental output-capital ratio was 8·02 for 1958, as compared with 1·64 for 1957. For previous years: 9·18 (1953); 3·11 (1954); 1·03 (1955) and 4·39 (1956). It does not make material difference if a one year lag is allowed for investment to take effect.

References

ACADEMY of SCIENCES (1958), *Kang-tieh sheng-chan ta-yao-chin lun-wen hsuan-chi* (*Essays on the Great Leap Forward of Iron and Steel Production*), Peking.
CHANG FO-CHIEN (1958), 'Some suggestions on solving the problem of labor shortage', CHCC, no. 12, 9 December.

Chou En-Lai (1959), 'Report on the adjustment of major targets in the national economic plan for 1959 and further development of the campaign for increasing production and practising economy', HHPYK, no. 17.

Emerson, J. P. (1961), 'Manpower absorption in the non-agricultural branches of the economy of communist China', *The China Q.*

Emerson, J. P. (1965a), *Nonagricultural Employment in Mainland China: 1949–58*, International Population Statistics Reports, Series P-90, no. 21, US Department of Commerce, Bureau of the Census.

Emerson, J. P. (1965b), *Sex, Age, and Level of Skill of Nonagricultural Labor Force of Mainland China*, Foreign Demographic Analysis Division, Bureau of the Census.

Hsu Li-chun (1959), 'On the policies of walking on two legs', HHPYK, no. 9.

Jen-min Jih-pao (various dates), *People's Daily*, Peking.

Jen-min Jih-pao (1959), 'A preliminary survey of the labor problem in Hung-Kuang commune', reprinted in HHPYK, no. 11, p. 105.

Liu, T. C., and Yeh, K. C. (1965), *The Economy of the Chinese Mainland: National Income and Economic Development, 1933–59*, Princeton University Press.

Ma Wen-jui (1961), 'The problem of labor in building socialism in our country', HC, no. 5.

Orleans, L. A. (1961a), 'Problems of manpower absorption in rural china', *The China Q.*

Orleans, L. A. (1961b), *Professional Manpower and Education in Communist China*, National Science Foundation.

State Statistical Bureau (1959), Wei-ta ti shih-nien, (*Ten Great Years*), Peking.

T'an Chen-lin (1960), 'Questions concerning the mechanization of agriculture of our country', HC, no. 6.

Yeh, K. C. (1965), *Soviet and Communist Chinese Industrialization Strategies*, Rand.

27 W. P. Strassmann

The Construction Sector of Peru

Extract from W. P. Strassmann, 'Construction, Productivity and Employment in
Developing Countries', in W. Galenson (ed.), *Essays on Employment*, ILO Geneva,
1971.

The effect of wage increases on choice of technique and employment can
be studied in detail only in the setting of a specific country, preferably at the
level of the firm. For my study I chose Peru, a country that has seemed on
the verge of moving into the middle income group. Between 1955 and 1967
it had a GNP growth rate of 5·6 per cent, one of the best in Latin America.
The average rate of inflation of about 9 per cent was neither among the
highest nor among the lowest. The Peruvian construction sector, as represented by the Lima-Callao area, at first grew less rapidly than gross product
and then more, as one might expect of a country entering the middle phase,
making an average growth rate of 4·3 per cent. Since the employment
growth rate appeared to be about the same, there seemed to be little or no
growth in average output per worker, however. Manufacturing productivity,
by contrast, grew. Output rose at a 7·3 per cent rate, while employment rose
only 5·8 per cent during 1955–64. Moreover, the 3·9 per cent share of
construction value added in GDP and its 2·2 per cent share of employment
were low, compared not only with middle group countries but even with
underdeveloped countries.

In 1963 Peru was, therefore, a country that seemed ripe for a great
expansion of the construction sector, a condition that was reinforced by
the coming into office of a construction-minded government. And construction output did spurt ahead.

Peruvian construction workers, however, had long been organized to an
unusual degree for an underdeveloped country. A Peruvian construction
union could be organized on any project with twenty workers or more. The
site was then covered by the annual collective agreements negotiated
between the Government, the Chamber of Construction, and the unions.
The consequence was that during 1955–67 daily earnings rose by an annual
average of 14·6 per cent. By 1960 average wages and benefits matched those
of manufacturing even though construction employed a much larger fraction of unskilled workers. During 1955–63 manufacturing wages grew at
an annual rate of only 1·7 per cent. In 1968 an unskilled construction worker
in the Lima-Callao area received a basic wage of 103·73 soles daily ($2·36),

plus an additional 42 per cent in cash for vacations, Sundays, and advance indemnification for eventual dismissal. Payments for insurance, retirement funds, and other fringe benefits brought the total of extra earnings to 69·71 per cent of the base. The total earned was 40 per cent above the earnings of unskilled manufacturing workers. Except on small sites, evasion of these rates seemed to be unusual.[1]

General evidence of Peruvian capital-labour substitution

Was the high growth rate of labour earnings in Peruvian construction associated with a trend towards capital intensity and less employment growth? The answer is, yes, there was such a trend; but, as in all such cases, association merely suggests and does not prove causation.

From 1963 to 1967, the daily earnings of a construction worker rose 69·1 per cent, but the index of construction costs rose only 39·7 per cent. Construction material prices rose 41·0 per cent. If construction materials and labour had been combined in the same real proportions in 1967 as reported in the 1963 Census of Construction, the index of construction costs thus weighted would have risen by 52·5 per cent, or 12·8 per cent more than it actually did. The growth rate of construction costs would have been 11·3 per cent annually instead of 9·3 per cent. The share of labour, including fringe benefits, in total costs would have risen from 25·3 per cent in 1963 to 29·1 per cent in 1967. In a random sample of fifteen firms in 1968, I found that the share of labour costs was only 27·4 per cent. For the nine firms that were most receptive to innovations, the share of labour costs was 26·4 per cent. The six least receptive firms reported a 29·7 per cent share that might well be explained by methods five years out of date. Willingness to adopt new techniques went with ability to hold labour costs down.

Not all labour-saving need be attributed to innovations, to techniques and materials novel to the Peruvian construction sector. One could also use known capital-intensive techniques to an increasing extent. For example, bricks compete with reinforced concrete in walls. The brick-layers' tools cost much less than the mixers, lifting equipment, formwork and supports used with reinforced concrete. In 1960 cement already made up 37·7 per cent of construction material inputs, while bricks accounted for a mere 11·5 per cent. During 1955–67 cement production plus imports (the apparent consumption) grew by 7·4 per cent per year, while construction as a whole only rose at a 4·3 per cent rate.[2] Part of this rising relative use of cement

1. Basic pay for skilled workers was 31·6 per cent higher, and fringe benefits rose in proportion. Outside of Lima-Callao, basic pay for unskilled workers ranged from a low of 67·22 soles in Ancash to 83·28 soles in Loreto. Resolución Subdirectorial, núm 39, R S E del 8.4.68, Lima, Peru.

2. The cement statistics were supplied by the Commercial Section of the United

may have been a response to growing labour costs.

The spread of labour-saving innovations

Innovations that raise the use of capital compared with labour are not necessarily due to rising labour costs (or falling capital costs). Changes in volume, speed and quality requirements may also favour more capital-intensive methods. Even in earthmoving these considerations eliminate labour-intensive options for some tasks (ILO, 1964, pp. 33–5; 1969, pp. 16–17). One cannot, therefore, claim that labour-saving innovations would have been prevented in Peru if wage levels had remained lower. A comparison of Peruvian building methods with practice in Mexico, Colombia and India, on the one hand, and with Venezuela and advanced countries, on the other, nevertheless suggests that wage levels did influence technique. An exact estimate of the wage-technique relation has not been made and may not be possible. For one thing, there are complicated problems of lags. Builders try novelties when conditions are neither too bad nor too busy. During the 1950s and early 1960s Peruvian contractors were most receptive to innovations during the two years 1957 and 1960, when wages did not increase at all.

What I attempted in the summer of 1968 was a study of Peruvian contractors and their receptivity to innovations. After discussions with contractors, architects, engineers, economists and others in Venezuela, Colombia and Peru, eleven innovations were selected as having great current practical value. There was no expectation or intention that they should all be labour-saving. But data collected later from both material suppliers and a stratified, random sample of contractors showed that each was in fact labour-saving. The proportion saved per unit of output ranged from 90 to 20 per cent, although the usual amount was about one third. Only vinyl tiles (100 per cent adoption), plastic pipes (67 per cent), and asbestos cement pipes (20 per cent) also lowered material costs. Seven other innovations raised material costs. They were, in order of increasing acceptability: prefabricated external panels (7 per cent adoption), metal wall forms (20 per cent), prestressed ceiling beams (20 per cent), sand-lime bricks (67 per cent), lightweight machine-made clay bricks (80 per cent), metal ceiling forms (93 per cent), and tubular scaffolding (93 per cent). One other innovation, integral terrazzo, was used in Venezuela but not yet in Peru. Caracas wages in 1968 were 2·6 times as high as Lima wages for skilled

States Embassy in Lima, which had obtained them directly from cement producers and from the customs authorities. In 1960 apparent consumption was 753,800 metric tons. If this amount is taken as 100, the corresponding figures for 1955 and 1967 are 74·8 and 165·7 respectively.

workers and 2·2 times as high for unskilled workers. The percentage of fringe benefits in both countries was almost exactly the same.[3]

After completing the Peruvian study, I made a brief comparison with Mexico and India, not to determine the extent and rate of spread of these innovations, but simply to find out if they were being used at all. Indian architects and builders had adopted only five of the ten changes introduced in Peru; the Mexicans had adopted seven. The two changes widely adopted in Mexico but very unusual in India were vinyl tiles and tubular scaffolding. Indians use vinyl tiles only in certain prestige buildings. In spite of government encouragement, metal scaffolding had made virtually no inroads on the use of bamboo.[4]

Since the Mexican product per head has been about 72 per cent above that of Peru, one might be surprised that fewer labour-saving changes were adopted. Mexican construction workers, however, are not as strongly organized as those in Peru, and their daily earnings were 18 per cent less than Peruvian earnings during 1955–64. By contrast, manufacturing workers earned 33 per cent more in Mexico than in Peru. The Mexican gross domestic product grew at about the same rate as the Peruvian during 1955–64, but construction output and employment grew 65 per cent faster.

Neither Mexico nor India had adopted plastic pipes, prestressed ceiling beams, or prefabricated external cement panels. Failure to use plastic pipes is likely to be due to sheer conservatism, rather than cost calculations. Such pipes reduce labour costs because they can easily be sawn, glued together, and need no painting. In addition to reducing installation costs by two thirds, their material costs in Peru were one seventh that of competing galvanized iron pipes. In other countries there are false rumours about fragility, poisoning of water, and dietary appeal for rats. In Peru plastic pipes were specified by the government housing authority and used by two thirds of my sample of contractors. In the United States in 1968, 63 per cent of building codes still prohibited them.

Prestressed ceiling beams and prefabricated external cement panels are the remaining innovations adopted with commercial success in Peru and so far rejected or only experimental in Mexico and India. Mexican ceilings most commonly are concrete blocks and cement poured on wooden forms.

3. Collective agreement between the Venezuelan Chamber of Construction and the Venezuelan Construction Workers' Federation, Caracas, February 1968. Integral terrazzo in Caracas was said to reduce floor costs by half by using marble as the aggregate for the slab and polishing the slab. Other layers are eliminated. More is spent on materials, less on labour.

4. For the Indian information I am indebted to Professor Subbiah Kannappan and to Dr Rabinder Singh of the National Building Organization, New Delhi. The Mexican data were collected by myself through personal interviews and library research in September 1968.

An attempt to adopt a European prestressed system that had been successful in Peru actually failed financially in Mexico. Prefabricated panel construction has been proposed to the Mexican Government for low-cost housing; but, perhaps because of employment implications, the reception was cool and financing not encouraged. In 1968 promotion of these two innovations had not gone beyond the experimental phase (mostly around Bombay) in India. If Mexican and Indian construction labour earnings were to rise to the Peruvian level, prefabricated and prestressed building methods would undoubtedly spread faster and reduce the rate of employment growth in construction. The fact that these methods are still novel in advanced countries themselves must not encourage complacency about construction employment projections for poor countries. The only way to avoid the radical reductions in labour requirements of ultra-modern building methods is to encourage innovation and labour productivity within more conventional building methods. According to one ILO publication, during the post-war period traditional building 'has demonstrated notable vitality and flexibility in introducing improved methods' (ILO, 1968, p. 37). These methods will have more chance of adoption in developing countries if wage and welfare policies are both moderate and predictable and keep the most capital-intensive methods unprofitable.

Conclusions

The view that construction should play a leading part in development policy was first in fashion, then out of fashion, and then in again. Eventually there will be enough data to cut out these swings of fashion. Meanwhile, however, the heterogeneity of construction output and its fluctuations make data confusing and analysis hard. One can assert with some confidence, however, that as product per head rises from under $200 per year to over $400, the construction sector will usually grow 50 per cent faster than the rest of the economy. Its share of GDP has in recent experience risen from under 4 per cent to over 6 per cent. Its share of non-agricultural employment has typically risen from under 5 per cent to over 7 per cent.

Entirely reasonable targets for the sector would be an 8 per cent share of GDP and a 10 per cent share of non-agricultural employment. In Italy, during 1955–64, a 7·4 per cent share of GDP was produced by 13·1 per cent of non-agricultural labour. However, employment possibilities are harder to judge than possible output levels since there are many ways of substituting capital or materials for labour in this sector. Japanese construction labour earnings averaged only 35 US cents per hour during 1955–1964, but they grew 29 per cent faster than manufacturing earnings. Mechanization was the result, and a 16·8 per cent output growth rate was achieved with only a 5·7 per cent employment growth rate.

In Japan the share of the non-agricultural labour force in construction (7·8 per cent) still averaged more than the sector's share of GDP (6·0 per cent). But if wages rise enough, these two fractions can be the same. Jamaican construction earnings averaged 49 US cents an hour, 40 per cent above the Japanese level, although the Jamaican income per head averaged 14 per cent below that of Japan during 1955–64. In Jamaica the construction share of non-agricultural employment was no higher than its share of GDP (12 per cent)[5]. These shares were also about equal in Peru, another country in which the bargains struck by construction workers compared very favourably with those in manufacturing.

The Peruvian case was examined in greater detail in this paper using both published statistics and data collected from a sample of contractors. The statistics showed that, in an overall way, construction firms were able to hold costs down by reducing relative labour expenses as wages rose faster than other prices. Among various capital-intensive tendencies, for example, cement construction made great inroads into the use of bricks. Moreover, all the innovations tested in a sample turned out to be labour-saving. Some of the innovations were sophisticated even by European standards and had not been adopted in countries with lower construction wages, like Mexico and India. It is nevertheless clear that certain innovations and some rise in capital intensity was and will continue to be rational even with restraint on the growth of wages. The possible range of their aggregate importance could not be measured. As in other sectors of poor countries, wise employment policy tries to promote a market for labour-intensively-made goods and to keep wages in line with other prices and productivity. It does not interfere directly in the choice of technique. If pressed for a rough order of magnitude, I would guess that in most countries on the verge of industrialization, a judicious expansion of construction finance and moderate restraint on the growth of labour earnings could raise employment by 3 per cent. The relative lowering of unemployment and unrest would, of course, be much larger.

5. Obviously, these have been percentages with different bases: totals for the economy in product have been compared with non-agricultural employment. This choice was made because output is more meaningful if agriculture is not omitted and because agricultural employment is hard to measure owing to the use of family labour.

References

ILO (1964), *Technical meeting on Productivity and Employment in Public Works in African Countries*, Lagos Management Development Series no. 1, Geneva, ILO.

ILO (1968), *Social Aspects of Prefabrication in the Construction Industry*, Geneva, ILO.

ILO (1969), *Technical Meeting on Productive Employment in Construction in Asia*, Bangkok Management Development Series no. 8, Geneva, ILO.

RESOLUCIÓN SUBDIRECTORIAL, nóm 39, RSE del 8.4.68, Lima, Peru.

28 'Sussex Group'[1]

Science and Technology in Less Developed Countries

From 'Science and technology for development – proposals for the second development decade', UN, 1970, pp. 22–37.

There is a vast gap between potentials and realization

We shall examine four main elements which between them have been highly responsible for the limited impact of science and technology in the developing countries. These are:

1. The weakness of scientific institutions in the less developed countries;

2. The 'weight' and orientation of advanced country science and technology and its impact on the developing countries;

3. The problems of access by the developing countries to world science and technology;

4. The obstacles to the application of new technologies arising from under-development itself.

There is, however, an additional factor which must be kept in mind throughout the following discussion. This is the very lop-sided nature of the present international division of labour in science and technology. We can give some rough quantitative guides to the international distribution of research and development (R and D) efforts.

Table 1 indicates that 98 per cent of the above R and D expenditure outside the socialist countries is made in the developed market economies. It is possible that the developing countries have a somewhat larger share of world scientific and technological services (STS) expenditure, since the proportionate expenditure on non-R and D STS is probably higher in the developing than in the developed countries. It is also possible that the proportion of world R and D manpower in the developing countries is greater then the proportion of expenditure, since R and D expenditures per scientist (including the salaries paid) are typically a good deal lower than in the developed countries. Finally, the R and D expenditures of centrally planned economies, which are not available to us, should be included to complete the global concept. But, we do not believe that these caveats would lead to much modification of the picture given in the table.

1. H. W. Singer (Chairman); Charles Cooper (Secretary); R. C. Desai; Christopher Freeman; Oscar Gish; Stephen Hill; Geoffrey Oldham.

Table 1 **Distribution of R and D expenditures in the world**
(excluding centrally planned economies)

Country group	United States	Other developed market economies	Developing countries
Percentage of world expenditure	70	28	2

Source: calculation based on OECD data for the developed market economies; on UNESCO and Pan American Union (PAU) data for developing economies.

The international division of labour in R and D is profoundly influenced by the national political and economic objectives of the advanced countries. Table 2 shows the distribution of R and D expenditures in the developed market economies by major objectives.

Table 2 **Percentage distribution of R and D expenditure in OECD countries by major objectives, 1964**

Atomic	Space	Defence	Sub-total	Economic	Fundamental and welfare research	Specific problems of developing countries
7	15	29	51	26	22	1

Source: OECD (1967).

Although the developed market economies make certain expenditures on R and D related to specific problems of the developing countries, these expenditures, on available evidence (from the OECD International Statistical Yearbook for R and D), are very small, amounting to less than 1 per cent of gross expenditure on research and development in all cases.

The extreme lop-sidedness of world R and D expenditure and of science and technology efforts, as well as their orientation towards certain major objectives of the advanced countries, do indeed have some beneficial 'fallout' effects upon the developing countries. But, in the main, they are responsible for the operation of the following specific factors accounting for the gaps between realization and potentials.

The weakness of scientific institutions in the developing countries

The global analysis of the international distribution of R and D expenditure shows that, in aggregate, the developing countries make very small allocations to these activities.

At the same time, there is a strong suspicion that the minimal expenditure of the developing countries is also less productive than the concentrated R and D activities of the advanced countries. They are less productive from the scientific point of view in the sense that the output of significant results seems to be small in relation to input of resources; they are less productive economically because the scientific work in question is often of little economic or social relevance to the country's own problems and also because the rate at which results are applied is low. Even the presently meagre effort of the developing countries in R and D yields less than optimal benefits to the countries concerned.

Low productivity is partly a consequence of problems in organization of science in the developing countries. University research is frequently 'squeezed out' by heavy teaching and consulting loads; applied work in government institutes suffers from lack of finance, red tape and lack of coordination between government departments or even within them. Even where there is an apparent concentration of scientific resources, say in agriculture, this hides a reality in which the total research activity consists of a large number of small projects bearing little relation to one another.

The weakness of scientific institutions in the developing countries extends to survey, testing and data-gathering activities. It is also reflected in the general shortage of scientifically and technically qualified people engaged in production activities. Finally, one immediate reason for the limited application of scientific results is generally presumed to be the weakness of the extension and service types of institutions in the developing countries.

These observations suggest that when qualitative factors are taken into account, the effective use of science and technology resources is even more lop-sided than the international resource distribution would suggest, and that the industrialized countries have a vast preponderance. But the matter does not rest there. The sheer weight of advanced country science, as well as its superior quality, has crucial effects in the developing countries.

The weight and orientation of advanced country science and technology and its impact on the developing countries

There are three main ways in which science and technology in the advanced countries affect the developing countries. We shall examine them under the headings: (a) the 'internal brain drain'; (b) the 'external brain drain', and (c) the composition of the stock of knowledge and its economic consequences.

The 'internal brain drain'. The scientific institutions in the developing countries are weak and so particularly are policymaking and planning institutions dealing with R and D and STS. In addition, as we shall state later, there is very little demand or perception of the need for science and technology in the society as a whole. In consequence, the local influence on the orientation of science and technology in the developing countries are weak.

In these circumstances, the weight and orientation of world scientific effort has a preponderant influence on the way science develops and is oriented in the developing countries. Many observers have noted how scientific and technological activities in the developing countries tend to form an 'enclave'.

Moreover, it is clear that, even in the fundamental sciences, the orientation of science in the advanced countries is strongly influenced by the major national objectives to which the scientific efforts of the advanced countries are intimately linked; objectives like defence, space exploration, the development of atomic power and so on (see Table 2). By implication, the orientation of science in the less developed countries is often influenced and determined by objectives which are external to the countries themselves and which have little enough to do with the requirements of development. Sometimes the aid activities of the advanced countries in relation to science in the less developed countries have reinforced these contradictory tendencies.

The result is a phenomenon which we shall refer to as the 'internal brain drain', whereby a substantial part of the scientific work going on in the developed countries, in addition to being under-financed and poorly organized, is irrelevant to the environment in which it is being done.

The 'external brain drain'. A more immediately noticeable consequence of the intensive development of scientific and technical activities in the advanced countries is the rapid growth in demand for scientific workers it generates: the 'external brain drain' is no doubt encouraged in considerable measure by this growth in demand. The 'external brain drain' must also be associated, however, with the incapacity of scientific institutions in the developing countries to absorb and use scientific workers.

The large-scale migration of highly qualified personnel from developing to developed countries is of recent origin. However, the volume of that movement (net) may already be approaching 40,000 per year and, as such, is larger than the movement of technical assistance personnel from developed to developing countries. Under prevailing conditions, this 'brain drain' is likely to increase over the next decade. The United States Department of Labour has estimated that 380,000 professionals (as well as about 600,000 middle-level workers) would enter that country between 1965 and 1975. A substantial proportion of those people will come from developing countries, and, in addition, further tens of thousands will be emigrating to other developed countries.

The output from third level education is increasing in the developing countries at roughly two to three times the rate of aggregate economic growth; in some countries the difference is substantially greater. Unless some way is found of bringing the employment possibilities for trained people into line with their increasing numbers, this means educated unemployment and/or international migration.

The adverse composition of the stock of knowledge. The picture that comes out of the analysis so far is of a relatively very small scientific and technical capability in the developing countries, which is undermined by organizational weakness and also by the varied responses of scientific workers in the developing countries to the mass of attraction that advanced country science constitutes. The environmental conditions in the developing countries receive scant attention. A consequence is that whilst the stock of world scientific and technical knowledge is certainly increasing at an accelerating rate, its precise composition is such that there are large gaps in scientific and technical knowledge that would be particularly relevant to the developing countries. The work of the Advisory Committee for the Application of Science and Technology to Development has been concentrated to some considerable extent on identifying these gaps. The list of priority areas where the Committee specifies that new knowledge is urgently required is in one sense a demonstration of the important technical problems which have been left neglected and unsolved by the present concentration and orientation of scientific effort to the political and economic objectives of the advanced countries. Perhaps one of the contrasts is found in the relatively vast knowledge we have of technical development in agriculture in temperate as opposed to tropical regions.

In addition, the stock of scientific and technological knowledge is proportionately less and less directly suitable for use by the developing countries. This is particularly true where the knowledge in question is about the application of scientific principles. First, the new technology is not 'appropriate' for the developing countries in that it emphasizes production methods which are suitable for capital-rich, and unskilled-labour-short countries, i.e. the richer countries of today. The developing countries by contrast are short of capital and skills, but relatively rich in labour. This discrepancy between the resource-mix for which modern technology is increasingly designed, and the actual resource-mix in the developing countries, places them at an increasing disadvantage. Secondly, the available technology emphasizes production on a large scale whereas the initial markets of developing countries (even including their realistic export markets) are usually small in economic terms. Thirdly, product design of plant, equipment and consumer goods emphasizes the needs of the richer industrialized countries. Finally, a very great deal of world scientific and technological effort is concentrated in industries which simply do not exist in the developing countries, and which will not exist there for many years to come.

But the problem is not only that the needs of the richer countries are dominant, but that the products of scientific and technological progress which result from this concentration are often such that they exert harmful 'backwash' effects on the economies of the developing countries. Apart from the 'brain drain', the development of synthetics replacing the natural raw materials produced in the developing countries is an important case in point.

Probably about $1000 million *per annum* are being devoted to R and D on synthetic materials (plastics, fibres and rubbers) in the chemical industries of the advanced countries. This is almost equivalent to the entire expenditure on research of all kinds in the developing countries and is, of course, very largely devoted to new materials of primary interest to the advanced economies.

When the advantages and benefits of further development of synthetic substitutes are considered, the harmful effect on the producers and exporters of the natural primary commodities thus displaced is not normally taken into account. The results are all too apparent: the shares of such natural commodities as rubber, cotton, tin, vegetable oils, in total world consumption and trade have declined rapidly, partly as the result of research and development devoted to the economy in the use of such materials and/or the development of synthetic substitutes for them. Work on the development and improvement of natural primary commodities of special interest to the developing countries does not receive the emphasis it deserves.

The problems of access by the developing countries to world science and technology

A further problem is that the developing countries have highly imperfect access to the body of world scientific knowledge and also to world technologies.

Easy access to sources of information, and effective 'coupling' with these sources, are essential to the efficient functioning of the science and technology system in any country. This 'coupling' function has to be done across national and cultural boundaries which present exceptionally acute problems. Thus, studies of information flows in the R and D process generally conclude that information derived from formal literature search and from formal information systems account for relatively small proportions of total information inputs. The informal communication network is of critical importance, including direct personal contact, telephone calls and correspondence. This is one of the critical advantages of the industrialized countries in the workings of their science and technology systems, and it poses special problems for the developing countries, which have to establish these informal links with the scientific community in the advanced countries.

Access to world technology on the other hand raises special problems. Much of the technology in question is in private ownership, that is, it is patented or at least secret. In general, the companies owning the technology 'release' it to the developing countries only if they are able to make direct investments there. The companies show a marked preference for direct investment as a means of exploiting the technological advantages in the developing countries, rather than entering into agreements with independent firms in the developing countries themselves. The main reason for this seems to lie in the lack of capital and skills in potential counterpart companies and also in the risks of inefficient operation of the new techniques by independent enterprises in the developing countries. The net results are that the flow of proprietary technologies to the developing countries is dependent on their capacity to bring in foreign investment (which is limited) and that the development and competition of domestic industry is hampered by lack of access to new techniques.

Even when technology is non-proprietary, there are problems of access for the developing countries. They have to obtain technology in an embodied form, that is, by importing capital goods and/or building up capital goods industries of their own. In these tasks, they are hampered by lack of domestic savings and lack of foreign exchange. The latter is, in part, the result of world science and technology effort which, as we mentioned before, has tended to reduce the earnings of the developing countries from the exports of primary products. On the other hand, the volume and costs of importing capital goods have been going up, partly reflecting the increasing sophistication of embodied technology. The capital goods which the developing countries import are not only more expensive *vis-à-vis* their exports, but, in most instances, malsuited to their resource endowments.

Underdevelopment as a basic obstacle to the application of science and technology

Whilst these various factors are important in explaining why it has been so difficult to exploit science and technology for the benefit of the developing countries and why the growth of science and technology has had adverse consequences for them, they are really only proximate causes. The real causes lie deeper, in the nature of underdevelopment itself. In brief, many of the structural and organizational characteristics of the developing economies are antithetical to the application of science and technology and, by the same token, prevent the development of what might be termed a 'realized demand' for scientific and technical knowledge. It underlies both the limited transfer of technology into local industries in the developing countries and also the weak development of local scientific institutions and their marked susceptibility to orient their activities in line with external influences. This is a particular aspect of the 'vicious circle of underdevelopment': the resolution of many of the problems of the developing economies requires the application of science and technology to production, yet the conditions of underdevelopment itself tend to limit the possibilities for their application.

Hence, whilst science and technology are certainly necessary inputs for development, their application in the developing countries nearly always requires certain important structural and developmental changes as concomitants.

Reference

OECD (1967), *The Overall Level and Structure of R and D Efforts in OECD Member Countries*, Paris, OECD.

Part Eight
Employment-Oriented Planning

The seriousness of unemployment in the Third World today and the complex range of causes underlying it will already have made clear the scale of the effort that has to be made if full employment is to be achieved in the foreseeable future. This will involve major changes in government strategy, both at the national and local levels. It will also involve major changes in the behaviour of institutions and individuals, both in the public and in the private sector. This final section includes four readings which indicate some of the issues involved and the nature of past attempts to deal with them.

It should not, however, be imagined that the changes required in strategy will be easily achieved. One difficulty is that the traditional tools of economic analysis, and even the statistics available, are often not very helpful for integrated employment planning. Central to an employment strategy is accurate knowledge of past and future changes in productivity: yet this is perhaps one of the weakest areas in terms of data, economic tools of analysis or projection techniques available. Moreover, the framework of national accounts, on which so much progress has been made in developing countries in the last two decades, is particularly inadequate as a source of data for analysing productivity and employment changes.

A second difficulty arises because of the strong interests which are threatened by the structural changes which a full employment strategy often requires. A strategy for full employment necessitates uncomfortable rethinking of many economic and social issues. It means completely changing people's attitudes to agriculture, to manual work, to modernization. It means inducing decision-makers, by regulation or incentives, to think very hard before they bring in any labour-saving machinery. It cannot but hurt some interested groups and therefore requires overcoming opposition that may, on some points, be stubborn. Important as these dimensions of the political economy of an employment strategy may be, there appears to be little serious research on which to draw for analysis or planning of these aspects.

Fundamental to preparing any plan is a clarification of national objectives and some calculation of the trade-off between them; that is, the extent to which progress towards one objective can only be achieved at the expense of less progress towards another. Stewart and Streeten in Reading 29, consider the possible conflict between output and employment objectives in planning. Their analysis reveals that the range of issues involved is much more complex than often thought. As in so many other areas of planning, the range of options open is heavily influenced by the specific context of the choice.

Although the contemporary emphasis on employment is much greater than was common a decade ago, many earlier development plans did consider employment issues in a variety of ways. Hsieh, in Reading 30, reviews the different levels with which employment-oriented planning has been and must be concerned: aggregate, sectoral, project and that of special programmes. Often the techniques used for such planning have been crude. Hsieh's descriptions of actual practice should act as a spur to other planners and critical academics to devise better approaches.

It is a mistake, however, to put sole emphasis on government policy as the condition for accelerating the growth in employment. Private industry, a whole range of non-government institutions and the individual actions of persons in every sector of the economy are also crucially involved. Their influence on employment is in part a response to the context in which their decisions and actions are made. Government has therefore a particular role in influencing this context by its own policies towards prices – particularly the crucial prices (interest rates, foreign exchange rates, wage levels and the rural/urban terms of trade) identified by Ranis (Reading 13). But in addition to such economic variables, government can influence the whole political and social climate in which other institutions operate.

Seers (Reading 31) considers the political economy of the adoption of a full employment strategy in a developing country. Building from the more technical-economic requirements of such a strategy, he explores some of the options open and the political and social implications for their adoption. Although recognizing the methodological dangers in starting with a framework of analysis of one discipline and broadening it to include others, Seers stresses that this may be the most practicable way forward given the separatist tendencies of the different social sciences as they have developed historically. Certainly the size and complexity of the employment problem is such that any discipline alone is insufficient to analyse all its parts, its major causes, or to plan for a structure of economic and social development which will eliminate it in the future.

Finally we move to an extremely important set of constraints within which national employment-oriented policies have to operate: that given by the international framework and especially by the nature of relations between rich and poor countries. In many ways, the present international framework erects barriers in the path of more labour-intensive production in developing countries, often conspiring with domestic biases in the same direction. These international barriers are often seen as part of a general syndrome of dependence by the developing countries. Many economists would name foreign exchange shortages when pressed to name the greatest single obstacle to an ambitious employment policy – interacting, of course, with other obstacles. The final reading, by Singer (Reading 32), has been selected because it offers a brief survey of all the various types of relations between rich and poor countries involved – trade, aid, private investment, transfer of technology and international liquidity.

29 F. Stewart and P. P. Streeten

Conflicts between Output and Employment Objectives

From F. Stewart and P. P. Streeten, 'Conflicts between Output and Employment Objectives', in R. Robinson and P. Johnston (eds.), *Prospects for Employment Opportunities in the 1970s*, HMSO, 1972.

Neither of the objectives, maximum output and maximum employment, are unambiguous. The output objective is ambiguous because output at any time consists of a heterogeneous collection of goods. Types of employment, in duration – daily, weekly and seasonally – in effort and by regions, etc. also differ. In addition, both output and employment occur over time. Current levels of output and employment may influence future levels. Weighting therefore both intra- and inter-temporally is crucial to the *definition* of the objectives. However, we shall begin by ignoring these ambiguities and assume that our sole concern is with current levels of output and employment, and that maximizing current levels automatically leads to achievement of future objectives, or put more formally, that maximizing current levels of output and employment is equivalent to maximizing the present value of the entire streams of output and employment over time. We shall also begin by assuming that there is a single index for output and employment.

Conflicts resulting from scarce complementary factors of production

We can then rephrase the question and ask: is maximum current production compatible with maximum employment? On the face of it, the answer seems to be an obvious 'yes'. More men must surely be able to produce more. It is hard to picture conditions in which it is impossible to find anything useful to do for extra hands.

At a given time, with a given stock of capital equipment (inherited from the past), the employment of more men on that equipment is likely to increase output, though it could be that, as a result of the reorganization of the work, of less efficient production methods used, of people standing in one another's way or of a fall in efficiency for some other reason, the extra workers do not add to, or even subtract from, production. However, the choice facing a country is not simply a question of employing additional men with the existing capital stock but of the type of new equipment to install, and in this decision about the nature of new investment there can be a conflict between output and employment. Given that the total funds available for new investment are limited, using the funds for equipment to employ people in one way will inevitably mean *not* using the same funds for some other equipment which may involve *less* employment but might also produce more output. Maximizing output involves using scarce resources as efficiently as possible. If capital is the scarce resource, it involves minimizing the capital-output ratio. The type of production this requires may be, but need not be, consistent with maximizing employment.

Suppose in the textile industry the minimum capital-output ratio is associated with fairly modern style industry. If £100,000 is available for investment in textiles, if the capital-output ratio is 2·5, and if the capital cost per work place for this type of factory is £1000 (assuming a firm degree of utilization of capacity), then investing all funds in this modern factory will involve extra employment of 100 and extra output of £40,000. An alternative way of investing the funds might be to introduce hand-spinning. Suppose for this the capital-output ratio was 5·0 and the cost per work place £100; then the extra output resulting from using the funds for hand-spinning would be £20,000 and the extra employment generated 1000. In this case there is a fairly dramatic conflict between employment and output maximization. It should be noted that this conflict (which is a fairly realistic one if one examines actual figures for costs, etc. in the textile industry)[1] arises because the more labour-intensive method in the sense of the method which uses a lower capital-labour ratio or shows lower cost per work place, actually involves *more capital per unit of output* then the capital-intensive method. Some theoretical models assume this can never happen. It would be true that it could not, if all techniques of production were invented and developed simultaneously, since the labour-intensive methods which use more capital would never be developed. But in fact methods of production are developed over an historical period with the more labour-intensive methods generally originating from an earlier period. One reason why this sort of situation develops is the existence of economies of scale; as machinery has been adapted for larger-scale production the capital costs in relation to output have tended to fall, so that for large-scale production the later and more capital-intensive methods tend to economize on capital in relation to output. For small-scale production the older machinery may remain efficient.[2] Implicit in this example is the assumption that there is a specific level of

1. Bhalla (1964), suggests that the capital-output ratio (including working capital as well as fixed capital) using factory methods in cotton spinning is about three quarters of that using the hand Ambar Charkha methods. Bhalla's analysis of rice-pounding (1965), suggests a similar conflict here; the technique which maximizes employment (or has the lowest cost per work place), the pestle and mortar, requires nearly twice the capital per unit of value added compared with the large sheller machine. The latter requires investment per work place of about 100 times as great as the former.
2. The importance of scale in determining the efficient range of production possibilities is emphasized by many empirical studies, including Boon (1964); Strassmann (1968).

employment associated with each technique, and thus that it is sensible to talk of a 'cost per work place'. In fact, the number of people employed with any given machine may vary. The variation can take the form of using the machine more hours per day, or of employing more workers on the machine, directly or indirectly, at any one time. Since greater utilization of machinery and greater employment arising from using machines more hours per day can normally occur with any type of machine, it does not affect the comparison or conflict. [. . .]

So long as output is responding positively to additional workers the level of employment associated with a given machine will depend partly on the level of wages. Even where output is invariant with respect to employment the actual employment associated with given machinery may depend partly on real wages since managerial effort may be substituted for employment as real wages rise. Thus the employment level associated with any given machine may not be independent of the wage rate. In the examples above some wage level is implicitly assumed in associating each machine with a unique output and employment level. A range to represent output and employment at different wage levels would have been a more realistic representation. If one assumes that continuous variations in output are associated with continuous variations in employment for each machine, but that there is diminishing marginal product as employment is increased, one is back in a neo-classical world where there are variable factor proportions and any amount of capital (or any machine) may be associated with any level of employment. In this neo-classical world the limit to employment is set by the real wages workers demand. There can be no conflict between output and employment because every type of machine can be associated with any amount of employment. Thus if the modern factory methods were employed in spinning, the extra 900 workers could be employed in the factory and would each add to output. At least as much employment and more output could result from choice of the factory alternative. We do not believe that this is a realistic assumption. Though some variation in employment is possible with any given machine, there comes a point at which the machine is operating at its maximum pace, when additional workers do not increase output. There is thus a limited range of employment possibilities associated with each machine, which means that there can be a conflict between output and employment. Put in another way, for any positive real wage there comes a point at which it is no longer worth while employing extra workers with a particular machine. This point may be reached at a lower employment level and a higher output level for one machine than for another. In this case there is a conflict between output and employment, which is independent of any institutional or other lower limit on the level of real wages.

Just as some economists assume that such a conflict between output and employment cannot arise, others assume not only that it has arisen in the past, but also that it necessarily must arise. The capital-intensive methods of production, it is claimed, will always involve lower capital costs per unit of output (and higher costs per work place) than the labour-intensive methods.[3]

This position is as extreme as the other. There is considerable evidence that in many industries, and in many processes, the more labour-intensive methods also save capital per unit of output.[4] In these cases maximizing employment and output are consistent. Probably of more significance is the possibility of devoting research and development (R and D) efforts to the labour-intensive methods (in the sense of low capital cost per work place) so that they become efficient as compared with capital-intensive methods. Present possibilities reflect the fact that almost all R and D is concentrated on producing methods suitable for the developed world, in which labour is scarce; the labour-intensive methods currently available are generally the products of earlier and less sophisticated science and technology. [. . .]

In the hypothetical example the hand technique involved 900 additional employees compared with the capital-intensive technique. Apart from simply maximizing output, going for the capital-intensive technique and ignoring the employment implications, three possibilities are open:

1. First, there is what we might describe as the Gandhi solution of adopting the hand technique despite halving of output.

2. Second, there is the 'Nkrumah' solution of introducing the modern factories and 'employing' the additional 900 workers in some minor and possibly completely useless capacity in the modern factory. Problems here are first that the extra workers might reduce output as a result of getting in each other's way and diverting administrative personnel (though probably output would not be reduced by as much as if the Gandhi solution were adopted and administrative difficulties might also be less). Secondly, if the modern factories also pay modern (i.e. relatively high) wages as they generally do, the wage cost may be exorbitant. This has implications for

3. See, for example, Kaldor (1965, pp. 28–9): 'There is no question *from every point of view* of the superiority of the latest and more capitalistic technologies' (our italics) Similar emphasis on the overall superiority of capital-intensive techniques is found in· Amin (1969, pp. 269–92).

4. Bhalla (1964), suggests that the capital-output ratio for traditional spinning methods, as opposed to the Ambar Charkha, may be lower than for factory methods. A. K. Sen suggests that in cotton weaving the capital-output ratio is the lowest for the most labour-intensive technique, the fly shuttle hand loom, and highest, nearly $2\frac{1}{2}$ times as big, for the automatic power loom (again including working capital). Evidence for the existence of a range of efficient techniques in a number of industries below a certain critical scale of output is also contained in Boon (1964).

savings and also for the viability of the enterprise if it is in private ownership. The Gandhi solution would probably allow lower wages per head. Thirdly, in a mixed economy it may not be possible to get employers to take on such useless labour. Voluntary agreements to increase employment by as little as 10 per cent have been notoriously short lived.

3. A third solution is to adopt the modern methods and to use some of the extra output to employ the non-employed[5] on public works, etc. The difficulty here is that if any equipment is involved in the public works, employing workers on them will again divert capital equipment from other parts of the economy where the impact on output might have been bigger – in fact we are back at the initial problem.

The dilemma arises from the existence of scarce resources (in the above case capital, but it could have been entrepreneurship, administration or some other input), which all forms of employment require. Sources of employment which do not use scarce resources will not present this dilemma. If, for example, the non-employed can make their own tools from local materials that are not scarce, and if their employment does not require the diversion of scarce administrative personnel, their employment will increase current output.[6] The same is true of employment which makes fuller use of the existing capital equipment, e.g. shift working, though inevitably some scarce resources or organization, administration, skills, etc. are always involved.

Reasons for preferring employment to output

If a conflict between maximizing current output and employment were inevitable, why should we wish to sacrifice output to employment? Four possible answers occur to us, though others might think of additional reasons. First, employment creation and the consequential wage payments may be the only mechanism by which income can be redistributed to those who would otherwise remain unemployed. With an efficient fiscal system, taxation combined with unemployment relief, free social services and other forms of assistance to the unemployed could be used as an engine of redistribution. In an underdeveloped society, loyalty to the extended family may induce the employed wage earner to share his wages with his often large extended family. But if neither fiscal system nor family provide a systematic channel of redistribution, job creation may have to be used for this purpose. Production will then be sacrificed for better distribution and, as a means to this, greater employment.

5. We use the expression '*non-employed*' to distinguish them from Keynesian 'unemployed'.

6. It was this type of employment Nurkse (1953) was considering in discussing the underemployed as a source of savings.

Second, unemployment is demoralizing. To feel unwanted, not to be able to make any contribution, lowers a man's morale and makes him lose his self-respect. The preservation of self-respect is worth sacrificing some production. As Barbara Ward has said, 'of all the evils, worklessness is the worst' – clearly not only and even not mainly because, and if, it lowers national product. It is worth sacrificing production to reduce this evil.

Third, it might be thought that work is intrinsically good, whatever its impact on morale, self-respect and other subjective feelings. The Puritan ethic may commend job creation as valuable irrespective of its contribution to production. Puritanism played a valuable part in making desirable the necessary but unpleasant sacrifices which promoted the industrial revolution in Britain. Whether this ethic, where it has been adopted in the developing world (and it is notable that most Puritan-like statements tend to come from expatriates) should be encouraged and where it has not been adopted should be promoted, if it leads to a situation which impedes rather than speeds up development by requiring the adoption of inefficient techniques to compensate for the masochistic value placed on work, is another question. Other aspects of Puritanism are certainly conducive to development; to the extent that Puritanism is a package deal, this aspect may have to be accepted along with the rest.

Fourth, there are obvious political disadvantages and dangers in widespread unemployment and non-employment. This is an important reason for valuing employment since, in so far as anyone does, it is the politicians who lay down 'the objective function' of society. Political instability may, in any case, eventually endanger output levels and growth. [. . .]

The desire for employment which is so apparent in many countries cannot be entirely divorced from the desire for higher incomes. Many of those seeking urban employment are looking for work *at the going wages* in the organized industrial sector, where wages are generally considerably higher than incomes obtainable elsewhere. Discussion of the need for rural employment opportunities to reduce the underutilization of labour normally takes place in the context of the need to create opportunities for increasing incomes through fuller labour utilization. Again the need is for incomes as much as for work. It is unlikely that the unemployed, or those scratching a living in the rural areas, would be prepared to suffer some loss in *their* incomes for the sake of more work. What is wanted is increased opportunities to work *and* earn higher incomes. Because both work and higher incomes are required it is difficult to disentangle the two. Clearly, the desire for redistribution of income is of prime importance. To achieve this redistribution, employment opportunities may be needed but the sacrifice, or trade-off involved may be of the income of the better-off for the sake of that of the worse-off, rather than of output for the sake of employment. However, it can be argued that it is not just a question of income redistribution but of providing a chance to *earn*, not simply receive, the higher incomes.

These are the only reasons we can think of as to why the employment objective might conflict with the output objective, and sacrifice of output to employment, *properly defined*, is justified. But what are the proper definitions? As argued in the first paragraph, objectives are ambiguous. Two types of ambiguity are relevant. First, national product consists of a heterogeneous collection of goods, 'of shoes, and ships and sealing wax, of cabbages' (and possibly of the services of kings) and it accrues to different people, in different regions, with varying needs. In putting all these together we must use a system of weighting the different items and different sets of weights may lead to contradictions. One set may give the impression that we are sacrificing product for employment, another may not.

Another ambiguity arises because both production and employment occur in time and stretch into the future. An infinite number of time profiles within any horizon that we care to consider can be drawn up. Any profile for either of our two objectives that lies all the way below another profile of the same objective can be dismissed as inefficient. But in order to choose between those that intersect at some moment of time, we must make additional choices in the light of our policy objectives. What if 5 per cent less employment now gives us 15 per cent more employment in two years' time? What if a rise of 10 per cent in employment now prevents us from employing an additional 5 per cent of a vastly larger labour force in 10 years and after? We must turn to the problems of *weighting* and *timing*.

Weighting: distribution

Assume a mini-community produces and consumes whisky and milk. Whisky is drunk by the few rich, milk by the many poor. In the first year national income consists of 2 pints of whisky and 5 pints of milk, in the subsequent year of 1 pint of whisky and 10 pints of milk. National income is the sum of whisky and milk, weighted not by pints, but by the appropriate prices. But the relative prices registered in the market are partly the result of income distribution. On the demand side, they depend upon the purchasing power of milk- and whisky-drinkers. The relative prices derived from an *unequal* income distribution are (let us say) 20s (100p) per pint of whisky and 2s (10p) per pint of milk. With these weights, income has *fallen* between the two years from 50s (£2·50p) (20s.2+2s.5 = 50s (£2·50p) to 40s (£2·00p) (20s+2s.10=40s). A *more equal* income distribution, putting more money into the pockets of milk drinkers relative to whisky drinkers, would give weights for whisky of 10s (50p) per pint and for milk of 4s (20p) per pint (on the assumption of increasing unit costs with increasing output). The income, weighted by these prices, would have *risen* from

40s (£2·00p) (10s.2+4s.5=40s) to 50s (£2·50p) (10s+4s.10=50s).

Let us assume that the second years' production results from employing more men because this raises the share of wages relative to profits and hence the demand for milk relative to whisky. A national income accountant, using the first set of weights, would register a fall in national income. People interpreting his statistics would say that we have sacrificed income for the sake of higher employment. But from the point of view of someone using the weights appropriate to the more equal distribution that results from greater employment, income is seen to have risen. There is a conflict between production and employment only if we use the wrong set of weights, assuming we prefer the more egalitarian income distribution.

Weighting other than by market prices should be introduced to reflect the different values of bundles of goods purchased by those at different income levels. Since the marginal utility of income is higher for a poor man than for a better-off man, greater weight should be attached to what goes to the poor than what goes to the better-off. Similar differential weighting might be attached to the expenditure of people in poorer regions within a country.

One difficulty in such an approach concerns the question of what weights to use. In the above example it was suggested that the prices emerging from the more equal income distribution should be used; these involved higher prices (and therefore weights) for the low income good – milk – and lower prices and weights for the high income good – whisky. This was only the case because of increasing costs for both goods. With elastic supply and constant unit costs the relative prices would have remained the same. With decreasing costs the relative price of the low income good would have declined as incomes became more equal. Thus to use the prices emerging from the more equal income distribution is not sufficient to deal with the problem of including the value attributed to income distribution in the measure of income. This may be so even in the case of increasing costs, when the resultant change in prices may not be enough to allow for one's judgement about the distributional implications of the change. The weights attached to the different goods need therefore have no relationship to the pattern of prices that might emerge with the desired income distribution.

Attaching different weights to different goods (e.g. milk and whisky) according to who consumes them is effective as a means of incorporating judgements about the income distribution only if the pattern of consumption differs among consumers of different income levels. At one extreme if all consumers consumed only one good, say maize, and differed only in the amount of that good they consumed, the value attributed to output would not be affected by the distribution of income whatever the weight given to the single good. In this case maize itself must be weighted or valued differently according to who consumes it. This is an unrealistic extreme. But there are many goods that are consumed at all income levels. So long as the pattern (i.e. proportion of income spent on different goods) of consumption differs according to income level a revised weighting system can, in theory, incorporate distributional judgements. Its calculation would be highly complicated, and would change over time as patterns of consumption changed.

An alternative is to attach weights to the income, according to the level of income of the recipient, rather than to goods; this is broadly the system adopted by Marglin (1967) where the value attributed to the demand for any good is weighted more heavily the poorer the consumer. For judgements about macro-income changes this approach has much to recommend it in terms of simplicity. It does not, however, rule out ambiguity in real output changes consequent upon changes in relative prices. With such a system 'income' would be increased simply by improving the distribution of income without any change in the output of goods and services. [. . .]

So long as the conventional definitions are accepted and countries placed in league tables according to them, the arbitrary nature of national income measurement tends to be forgotten and virtue gets associated with movements in this arbitrary figure. Policies as well as value judgements may be influenced by the form of measurement adopted. There is much to be said, therefore, for even a crude and arbitrary adjustment of income measurement in the direction of incorporating judgements about income distribution.

Weighting: time

Another serious ambiguity arises from the fact that sacrifices now may yield gains in the future. We must consider two opposite sets of circumstances: first, where less production and more employment now lead to more production later than would otherwise have been possible; second, where less employment and more production now lead to more employment later than would otherwise have been possible.

In order to illustrate the first case, let us return to the situation where men were demoralized by unemployment. We then regarded self-respect and high morale as ends in themselves. But we may also regard them as necessary for the continued employability of men. If men remain unemployed for long, their skills as well as their attitudes deteriorate and they are incapable of producing as much later. This situation cannot be remedied by unemployment assistance, for it is only on the job that ability to work and motivation are maintained. Just as machines sometimes have to be kept going in order to prevent attrition or rust, so workers and teams of workers have to be kept busy to prevent them from becoming rusty or apathetic. Current employment, even where there is nothing to show for it, can be regarded as a form of investment – human maintenance – which prevents future deterioration of productivity. In addition men's productive capacity, their ability to work, their initiative and organizational ability and their concentration may not merely be maintained but may actually be increased by working. This form of learning by working means that the greater current employment opportunities, the greater is future productive capacity.

The second case works in the opposite direction and is possibly the most important way in which an apparent conflict between employment and output arises. Here we maximize production in the short run, even though it means tolerating now more non-employed, because the extra production enables us to generate more jobs later than would otherwise have been possible. If there is a current conflict between output and employment, it must be remembered that output is useful not only for itself, but can be used to generate more employment.

The inter-temporal 'trade-off' between employment now and employment tomorrow arises because, by tolerating more unemployment now for the sake of producing more, we can provide the men (and their children) with more jobs later. This is only partly a matter of investment, i.e. producing now the machines, or resources with which to buy the machines, that will give jobs tomorrow. A greater volume of food which provides better nutrition for the workers and their children, of health measures and of certain forms of education can also contribute to greater employment (and fuller labour utilization) in the future. The point leads once again to income distribution, but this time not valued independently as desirable, but as instrumental to faster growth. The choice between maximum employment and maximum output reduces to one between jobs now or later, because more output can promote more, and more effective, employment in the future. To raise employment means sacrificing not only output now (and, on our assumption, the rate of growth of output) but also the rate of growth of employment. This means that at some future date the level of employment will be lower than it would otherwise have been. To go back to the example discussed earlier, suppose in each case, modern factory and hand spinning wheel, 20 per cent of income generated is saved. The factory solution will involve £8000 investment available in the next year, while the hand wheel alternative will involve £4000. The divergence will get greater in subsequent years. The factory alternative will lead to an annual growth in income (and assuming the same £1000 a work place technology is adopted, in employment) of 8 per cent per annum while the hand spinning wheel alternative will lead to 4 per cent annual growth in output and employment. (This ignores the impact of extra consumption on growth.) The diagram illustrates the possibilities [. . .].

As to the right choices, a good deal will depend upon our time horizon and on certain future developments. As far as employment is concerned, the

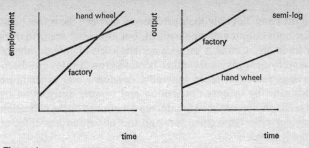

Figure 1

life span of one generation and perhaps its children will be relevant, but few
societies would be prepared to tolerate widespread unemployment over
two generations to improve the job prospects of their great-grandchildren.
This is not only because we show less concern for our great-grandchildren,
but also because we may rightly hope that their prospects will improve for
other reasons, such as the development of more appropriate technologies,
improvements in motivation, administration, education, etc. Given the
time horizon, we might say that, on the other hand, the richer society of
tomorrow can look better after its unemployed and to be unemployed then
will be a smaller hardship. On the other hand, with present trends of growth
of the labour force in less developed countries and likely opportunities for
jobs, the total number of unemployed is increasing rapidly. While the lot of
a given number of unemployed will therefore be better in the future and the
burden of maintaining them lighter, the number to be looked after will be
larger. In the more distant future, however, we may assume that population
control will have become effective or new scope for migration will have
opened up. In view of all this, it seems right to discount future jobs and to
give more weight to more jobs now and in the near future.

On balance it seems that the discount rate that we should apply to employment may be less than the one we apply to output. The main argument for
applying a discount rate to output is that the marginal utility of income is
less for a richer society. This does not apply in the same way to employment
– i.e. the value of extra employment generated does not decline as the level
increases – though increasing *incomes* per head may make employment in
the future less important as a means of income redistribution. On the other
hand, the contrasts between those employed and those not employed and
the accompanying resentment may work the other way. Poverty in the midst
of affluence is worse than plain poverty widely shared. This, and the
question of numbers, suggests that it may be correct to give greater relative
weight to future as against current employment than to future as against
current output.

Planners must know not only their preferences between the present and the future, for both output and employment, but also what opportunities there are for trade-offs. Conflicts between current levels of growth rates of output and employment may arise either because growth rates are determined by savings rates (or, more generally, developmental expenditure rates), savings rates by income distribution and income distribution by employment levels, or because growth rates are determined by the allocation of a given savings ratio between sectors and this allocation has different effects on employment.

It is common to assume in this context that a capital-intensive technique leads to a higher savings ratio for the same income level than a labour-intensive technique. On this assumption, lower employment now can give faster growth of both output and employment. Those who make this assumption (Sen, 1968; Little and Mirrlees, 1968) assume:

1. That a higher proportion of profits is saved than of wages (at its most extreme this assumption is that all profits are saved, all wages consumed); and that consumption makes no contribution to future growth;

2. That wages rates do not depend on techniques;

3. That the government is incapable of securing the savings ratio it desires by taxing wage earners and generating adequate public savings or using inflation to reduce real wages.

Since the growth rate is the product of the savings ratio and the output/capital ratio, the effect on the growth rate of raising the savings ratio by increasing the capital-intensity of technique adopted will depend on the consequences for the output/capital ratio.

Figure 2 illustrates the implications for growth of neo-classical assumptions as the capital-intensity of techniques is increased. With such a production function the most labour-intensive technique maximizes current employment, for any given output level. On the diagram, as one approaches the origin current employment levels are increased relatively to capital. But for any given capital-intensity of techniques and in the absence of technical progress (or in the presence of neutral technical progress) the growth of employment is determined by the growth of output. Assuming all wages are consumed and all profits saved, the technique which maximizes the growth of output (and also employment) will depend on the wage level. With wages per employee OW, which do not vary according to the technique adopted, the growth rate (s/v) is represented by the slope of the line from W to the production function. This is maximized when it is tangential to the production function as at g^* in the diagram. Here there is a conflict

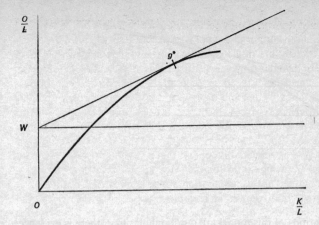

Figure 2

between maximizing current employment (which involves choosing the technique nearest to the origin for a given capital stock) and maximizing the growth of output and employment at g. However, there is no conflict between maximizing the growth of employment and output, both of which involve the same technique. The conflict between current employment and the growth of employment worsens as the wage level increases, as illustrated below.

As the wage increases from OW_1 to OW_2, the capital-intensity of the technique which maximizes the growth output and employment increases (increasing the conflict between current and future employment), while the maximum growth rate declines. If we drop the neo-classical assumption of rising capital/output ratio as the capital-intensity of techniques increases, the most capital-intensive technique available maximizes the growth rate, irrespective of the wage-level.

Additional employment of the kind discussed earlier which is costless in terms of present output since it does not require any scarce resources as additional inputs – neither capital nor administration nor skilled manpower – may impede growth on these assumptions because the extra consumption of those additionally employed will reduce society's propensity to save.

If the rate at which we discount future output is higher than that at which we discount future employment (an assumption which we argued was reasonable), we get the perverse situation that a strategy of optimum employment growth would require greater current unemployment than a strategy aiming at optimum income growth. The former would involve more capital-intensive techniques, higher savings rates and greater income growth.

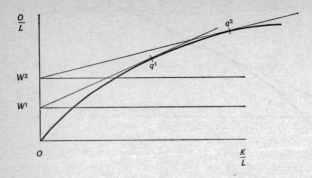

Figure 3

The assumptions of this model are questionable: first, there is evidence[7] that the level of wages is linked to labour productivity and the choice of technique, so that the more labour-intensive methods involve lower wages per man than the more capital-intensive ones. Secondly, all profits are not saved and it may not even be warranted to assume that a higher proportion of profits is saved than of other incomes. Profits remitted overseas, even if saved, will not add to the investible resources of the developing economy unless reinvested. Thirdly, there is the rather asymmetrical assumption that the government is incapable of enforcing the saving it desires by wages or taxation policy, but is capable of enforcing it through choice of technique, despite the fact that this choice, in a mixed economy, is not directly in its hands in many cases, and involves, if made effective, a lower level of employment. The sacrifice of employment, in this case, is not so much a sacrifice for the sake of future levels of output and employment, but more a sacrifice on the altar of government inability to pursue effective taxation policies.

So far, we have focused on the aggregate savings ratio. If it is determined by the distribution of income between wages and profits and if this distribution in turn is determined by the level of employment, a conflict may arise between maximizing current employment and maximizing the growth of employment and income.

[. . .] Also, so far we have been assuming that the choice made, in terms of capital-intensity of technique and division of resources between sectors, is made once and for all for the economy as a whole. In fact, of course, one starts with a particular capital-intensity of techniques and division of

7. There is considerable evidence that wages are related to the scale of the enterprise, while the smaller the enterprise the more labour-intensive (in terms of capital per worker) the technique tends to be. See for example, Dhar and Lydall (1961); Shetty (1963); Okita (1964).

resources, inherited from the past, which determine current employment opportunities and growth possibilities. Any decision one takes will have its main effect on new investment and only gradually affect the whole of the economy. This means that any change of course will take time to work its way through the economy. It also means that one must take the current situation into account in making choices about future development: the choice may be different according to the current state. For example, suppose the economy is using relatively labour-intensive techniques, much more labour-intensive than the technique which would maximize the rate of growth of output or employment. A move towards the technique which would maximize the equilibrium rate of growth of output and employment (i.e. the sustainable growth rate that would occur in the long run if a single technique were adopted and stuck to through time) might actually involve a *fall* in employment in the short run: this could occur if the new technique were used for replacement investment, so that more people were shifted from the old technique than were required to man the new technique both for replacement investment and net investment. (The situation could not occur if all investment were additional investment, not replacement investment, or if the replacement investment continued to be of the labour-intensive variety.) The process by which the shift to the new technique involved a fall in employment could last for many years. Eventually the technique which maximized the rate of growth of output would also maximize the rate of growth of employment and ultimately the level of employment would be higher. But the impact in the transitional period, during which employment fell, might outweigh the ultimate gains. Consequently, the initial situation may influence the ultimate choice. It might be argued that since the possibility of such a dilemma arises from replacement investment, the solution is to maintain replacement investment at the old capital-intensity, and confine the new choice to net investment. In practice this divorce between the nature of new investment and replacement investment is impossible to maintain – one set of relative prices and incentives affects both types of investment; the distinction between them is often more theoretical than practical.

Technical progress

Until now we have ignored technical progress and assumed that output and employment grow at the same rate if a single technique is chosen and adhered to over time. In practice technical possibilities available increase over time. Generally technical progress take a form which involves increasing labour productivity, so that the rate of growth of employment is less than the rate of growth of output. This phenomenon – output increasing faster than employment – has been observed in many developing countries. The precise form that technical progress takes will affect the terms of any conflict between output and employment.

If technical progress is disembodied, affecting existing capital equipment as much as new and therefore unrelated to the rate of investment, and if it increases the labour productivity associated with techniques of varying capital intensity to the same extent, then the technique which maximizes the rate of growth of output will be the same as the technique which maximizes the rate of growth of employment, though the latter will be lower than the former. If technical progress is embodied, affecting only new investment, the greater the rate of investment, the greater the increase in labour productivity. Hence for any increase in growth rate, resulting from an increase in the investment ratio, there will be a less than proportionate increase in the rate of growth of employment. Similarly, if labour productivity is positively related to the scale of production, measures which speed up the growth of output (whether they be investment or other means) will increase the growth of employment less than proportionately. Relationships of this type have been observed for developing countries, though the relationship appears less strong than for developed countries (Oherlihy, 1970). Since the growth in output remains bigger than the associated growth in labour productivity, the technique which increases the growth rate of output will also increase the growth of employment, but the gains in terms of growth of *employment*, will be less than the gains in terms of growth of *output*.

Technical developments are likely to affect some techniques more than others. In particular, research, development and use of techniques in the developed countries is virtually confined to techniques of high, and increasing, capital-intensity. Thus for these techniques labour productivity and often capital productivity as well, may rise over time, while the more labour-intensive techniques may be unaffected by technical progress. The labour-intensive techniques may therefore become inferior over time and their use may involve a sacrifice of output as compared with the later techniques.

However, for labour-intensive techniques various improvements are likely to result from their widespread use, including a fall in their cost simply as a result of economies of scale in their production. Labour-intensive techniques are also often easier to produce in the developing countries, because they are often of simpler design and more (in number) are required in a particular country so that some of the economies of scale may be exploited. Current relative costs and efficiency of different techniques may therefore fail to reflect potential relative costs after technical progress through use has been realized. They may also fail to take into account the differing possibilities for local production and repair of the different techniques. This means that current possibilities may understate the likely implications for output of labour-intensive techniques; the conflict between employment and output may therefore be less in reality than at first appears.

The product-mix

So far we have assumed the composition of consumption goods to be determined and have varied only the techniques of producing them and the allocation of investment between sectors. If different consumption goods require different proportions of labour and capital, we can raise the level of employment without varying the techniques of producing any product by enlarging the share of labour-intensive products at the expense of capital-intensive products. If there are opportunities for international trade on favourable terms, this is an obvious solution. If, however, a changing composition involves changing the products consumed at home, the question is whether, with a proper system of weighting, losses in consumers' welfare would arise. If the labour-intensive products are also those largely demanded by the poor, we have already seen that a fall in output may be an optical illusion and that the weights derived from a more equal income distribution might show a rise. There may also be external diseconomies of consumption or buying as a result of created wants or of habits. If a product is wanted (a) because others buy it or (b) because it was bought in the past or (c) wants are created through advertising, and if these features are peculiar to the capital-intensive products, its elimination may lead to smaller welfare losses (in cases (b) and (c) after a time) than the expenditure values would indicate or it may lead to welfare gains.

The scope for changing the consumers' product-mix in a labour-intensive direction is generally considered somewhat limited, apart from possibilities of international trade, by the need for a reasonable balance in the composition of demand. We cannot expect people to consume all food and no clothes for example, or to have more haircuts at the expense of bicycles. But the conclusions drawn from this, in terms of the narrow scope for product substitution, arise partly from a mistaken definition of product. Any given need may be fulfilled by a number of different products: nylon or cotton shirts fulfil the need for clothing, wooden houses, mud huts, reinforced concrete multi-storey buildings fulfil the need for shelter. While maintaining a reasonable balance in terms of needs (clothing, housing, shelter, etc.), there is considerable scope for substitution towards more labour-intensive products for the fulfilment of each need. The possibilities of concentrating more on labour-intensive products to fulfil each need may therefore extend the scope for using the product-mix to increase employment opportunities.

References

AMIN, S. (1969), 'Levels of remuneration, factor proportions and income differentials with special reference to developing countries', in A. Smith (ed.), *Wage Policy Issues in Economic Development*, Macmillan.

BHALLA, A. S. (1964), 'Investment allocation and technological choice – a case of cotton spinning techniques', *Econ. J.*, vol. 4, pp. 611–22

BHALLA, A. S. (1965), 'Choosing techniques: hand pounding *v.* machine-milling of rice: an Indian case, *Oxford econ. Paps.*, vol. 17, pp. 147–157.

BOON, G. K. (1964), *Economic Choice of Human and Physical Factors in Production*, North Holland.

DHAR, E. N., and LYDALL, H. F. (1961), *The Role of Small Enterprises in Indian Economic Growth*, Asia Publishing House.

KALDOR, N. (1965), in R. Robinson (ed.), *Industrialization in Developing Countries*, Cambridge University Press.

LITTLE, I. M. D., and MIRRLEES, J. (1968), in *Manual of Industrial Project Analysis in Developing Countries*, vol. 2, p. 42.

MARGLIN, S. A. (1967), *Public Investment Criteria*, Allen & Unwin.

NURKSE, R. (1953), *Problems of Capital Formation in Underdeveloped Countries*, Blackwell.

OHERLIHY, C. St. J. (1970), '*Wages and employment*', Meeting of Directors of Development Training and Research Institutes, ILO (mimeo.).

OKITA, S. (1964), 'Choice of techniques: Japan's experience and its implication', in K. Berrill (ed.), *Economic Development with Special Reference to East Asia*, Macmillan.

SEN, A. K. (1968), *Choice of Techniques*, Blackwell.

SHETTY, M. C. (1963), *Small-Scale and Household Industries in a Developing Economy*, Asia Publishing House.

STRASSMANN, W. P. (1968), *Technological Change and Economic Development*, Cornell University Press.

30 C. Hsieh

Approaches to Fixing Employment Targets in Development Plans

From C. Hsieh 'Approaches to fixing employment targets in development plans',
International Labour Review, 1968, vol. 97, no. 3, pp. 277–96.

Methods of incorporating employment targets into the plan

The fixing of employment targets may enter into the planning process at
some or all of the following levels: the aggregate level, the sectoral level, the
project level and at the level of special measures loosely linked with the main
structure of the plan.

Adjustment at the aggregate level

In some plans the employment target was broadly decided at the aggregate
level in conjunction with the total volume of investment and average capital
intensity as reflected in the weighted overall average investment per worker,
which is determined partly by the distribution of investment.

1. One approach is to fix the volume of investment and the average capital
intensity independently of employment considerations and to achieve
additional employment as a by-product. If the resulting additional employment falls short of the target special measures may be introduced to help
reach it.

This appears to be the approach used in the five-year plan of Morocco
(1960–64). Envisaging the use of modern technology the planners adopted
a figure of 1 million Moroccan francs' worth of net investment per additional
worker as the overall capital intensity. Basing their calculations on this
datum and on the planned volume of investment, independently determined,
they estimated 80,000 additional jobs a year to be the maximum that the
plan could be expected to provide. However, more detailed estimates of
additional employment by sector, according to the planned distribution
of investment and including the induced and indirect employment effects,
yielded a lower figure. Meanwhile the annual number of new entrants to
the labour force was estimated at 90,000. The conclusion was that during
the plan period unemployment would increase. To fill the gap and also to
reduce existing rural underemployment a programme of national development was instituted outside the framework of the plan. It is essentially a
rural works programme designed to promote development by improving
the rural infrastructure.

2. The total amount of planned investment and the average capital intensity of the plan, while they place considerable constraints on the fixing of aggregate employment targets, are usually capable of adjustment within certain limits: it is possible to increase the former and reduce the latter at the aggregate level in order to achieve a higher employment target, taking due account of all the objectives. To illustrate this approach two plans will now be briefly described.

When the second five-year plan of Pakistan was being drawn up the minimum employment target – that is the absorption of the additional labour force – was accorded a high priority. To achieve this target the planning authorities deliberately reduced the overall average amount of gross investment per worker from the 10,000 rupees implied in the first five-year plan to 7500 rupees, and higher priority was given to labour-intensive methods. It was estimated that the plan would then provide enough jobs for the projected 2·5 million additional workers. The release of the 1961 population census, however, made it necessary to revise the projection of the additional labour force upwards to 3·2 million. In order to create the extra new jobs required as well as to maintain the original planned growth rate of income per head the investment target was likewise revised upwards from the original figure of 19,000 million rupees to 24,600 million, or by approximately 30 per cent, the additional planned investment including a public works programme (Haq, 1963, p. 11).

The three-year plan of Brazil (1964–6) provides another instance of adjusting the overall average investment per additional worker as a way of achieving the desired aggregate employment level. The plan projected a high rate of labour force growth (3·5 per cent), which implied the creation of 1·1 million new jobs a year. To facilitate policy making the economy was divided into two sectors: the urban and the rural. As a first approximation the plan estimated that a liquid investment[1] of 1·8 million cruzeiros would be necessary to create one job in the urban sector and 600,000 cruzeiros in the rural sector. A crucial policy assumption was then made to the effect that the new jobs would have to be divided in roughly equal numbers between the urban and rural sector. On this basis the creation of 1·1 million new jobs would need a liquid investment of 1,200,000 million cruzeiros (that is an average investment per worker of about 1·2 million). This sum had to be increased by 50 per cent to provide the infrastructure needed for job creation and the capital required to increase the productivity of workers already in employment, making a total of 1,800,000 million cruzeiros or about 10 per cent of the expected gross domestic product (GDP) for 1964. Adding another 5 per cent of GDP to account for depreciation, the plan

1. It is not clear from the plan what exactly is meant by the term 'liquid investment'. It may possibly correspond to 'net investment'.

arrived at the conclusion that the rate of gross capital formation should be at least 15 per cent of GDP to absorb the 1·1 million new entrants to the labour force. The plan envisaged raising the investment ratio to some 18 per cent in order to create additional employment opportunities for the unemployed and underemployed who appeared as a result of the decline in economic activity in 1962 and 1963 as well as for the workers who would be displaced by an increase in the capital intensity of existing activities.[2] It is of interest to note that the investment ratio implied by the employment objective agrees fairly well with the planned investment ratio of about 20 per cent of GDP (including 5 per cent for depreciation) estimated on the basis of an overall incremental capital-output ratio of 2·5 and an annual income growth rate of 6 per cent (or a 2·5 per cent growth rate of income per head).

Preliminary adjustment of overall average investment per additional worker (or the capital intensity of the plan) to meet the minimum employment target at the aggregate level would, of course, need to be followed by detailed planning of the sectoral distribution of investment and of the techniques required to achieve this provisional weighted overall figure, given the limitations imposed by other objectives of the plan. As a result of this the overall figure might be further revised or the priority accorded to other objectives somewhat modified. It is not clear, however, precisely how this stage of planning was carried out in the two cases just discussed or how the final overall figure for average investment per worker was arrived at, although each plan does indicate certain special measures for achieving the final figure.

Adjustment at the sectoral level

Many plans seem to have by-passed the fixing of aggregate employment targets and to have allowed them to emerge directly from the planning of sectoral investment distribution. In several cases the objective of employment creation did play a role – along with other objectives – in sectoral planning. Examples of the various ways in which it influenced planning will now be described.

1. The original frame for the Indian second five-year plan was based on a four-sector model developed by Professor Mahalanobis (1955). The four

2. The method of fixing employment targets in terms of investment requirements, as described above, is similar to that used in the ten-year-plan of Italy. The policy implications are, however, widely different. Whereas in the Italian plan the application of this method points to the possibility of a large-scale transfer of manpower from agriculture to nonagricultural sectors, the important policy conclusion derived from the Brazilian plan is that the fulfilment of the minimum employment target requires keeping half of the additional labour force in the rural sector.

sectors were: investment goods, factory consumer goods, household enterprises (including cottage industries, construction and agriculture), and the social services (including, *inter alia*, health and education). From the available empirical data numerical values were derived for the ratio of income increment to investment and for the net investment per worker in each sector. In this model the employment target (11 million new jobs over the five-year period), the income growth target (5 per cent a year), the volume of planned total investment (56,000 million rupees) and the proportion of total planned investment allocated to the investment goods sector (33 per cent) were all given. They had been set independently with other policy considerations in mind. The problem that this planning model was designed to solve was to determine a pattern of investment allocation among the other three sectors that would result in the simultaneous fulfilment of the employment target and the income target. This was done by setting up a system of equations, and with the empirically ascertained values for the two parameters the solution of this system of equations gave the consistent values of the additional employment and the additional output in each of the four sectors including investment goods, as well as the percentage allocation of investment to the other three sectors.

The most interesting finding that emerged from the solution was the great reliance that would have to be placed on the household enterprises sector in order to achieve the 11 million new jobs in the employment target. This suggested that, with an allocation of 3·5 per cent of the total planned investment, the household enterprises sector *excluding* agriculture could be expected to make a contribution of some 28 per cent of the total planned additional employment because of the extremely low incremental capital-labour ratio in this sector. In the final version of the plan, while the investment allocation to the small-scale industry sector was the same as suggested by the theoretical solution, the expected increase in employment in this sector was greatly reduced, perhaps mainly because within the sector the emphasis in the final plan was shifted from traditional cottage industries to modern small-scale industries, which have higher capital requirements per worker. This four-sector planning model has been subjected to criticism on various grounds. For instance, apart from its neglect of inter-industry relations, the theoretical formulation embodied in the model cannot yield an optimal solution, as has been demonstrated by using the techniques of linear programming (See Komiya, 1959). Nevertheless, the model represents the first serious attempt at integrating employment planning with overall development planning and it may serve as a starting point for a formulated approach to fixing employment targets.

2. In some plans the desired employment target entered in a rough sort of

way into the policy decisions on investment allocation as between sectors and on sectoral growth of output, without going through a sophisticated planning process such as the one described above.

Ceylon's ten-year plan provides one example. It was made clear that to achieve its minimum employment objective the plan was built on a compromise between a capital-intensive and a labour-intensive approach. This policy of compromise is reflected in the balance that the plan aimed to secure between agricultural development and industrialization. It accorded a high priority to agricultural development not only as a means of achieving its balance of payments objective – through the expansion of its plantation or export crops and the substitution of domestic food production for food imports – but equally as a major element in the creation of additional employment over the plan period. In this case the two objectives are in large measure consistent. It may be mentioned that investment in tea replanting seems to serve both objectives particularly well.[3] As regards industrialization the plan made a sharp distinction in purpose between large-scale and small-scale industry. The former was intended to serve primarily the long-term development objectives and to provide a main source of savings and capital accumulation, while the latter was chiefly aimed at creating industrial employment. However, the percentage of planned investment allocated to small-scale industry was quite small (about 3 per cent); consequently its contribution to planned additional employment (12·5 per cent), though much greater than that of the large-scale industry sector (4·5 per cent), was still relatively small – only slightly more than the contribution by investment in tea replanting alone (10 per cent).

The second five-year plan of the Federation of Malaya offers a more extreme example of linking the minimum employment target (i.e. to meet the job needs of a 15 per cent increase in the population of working age, or about 340,000 new entrants, over the five years) with a high priority for agricultural and rural development. Though the sectoral distribution of planned investment (public and private investment combined) was not given, from the policy statements in the plan it seems clear that the aim was to absorb the largest possible proportion of the additional labour force in the rural sector through expanded programmes of agricultural and rural development. While part of the expected increase in rural employment

3. According to the estimates made in the plan, in tea replanting not only are the incremental capital-output ratio and investment per worker the lowest, but the expected subsequent increase in demand for labour is also relatively large because of the size of the tea crop. It is estimated that after replanting the increased yield will raise the labour requirements on tea plantations from 1·1 to 1·9 labour units per acre. As a result the additional employment provided by tea plantations alone is expected to form about 10 per cent of the total planned aggregate additional employment.

would be associated with increased rubber output resulting from the re-planting schemes started during the first plan, the main source of new jobs in this sector would come from the development of new land for cultivation, higher output of rice and other crops, and an increase in the acreage under rice. Since the man-land ratio is comparatively low, the scope for expanding rural employment by such measures is greater than in many other parts of Asia. The plan did not count on the expansion of industry to contribute much to additional employment, partly because the industrial base was very narrow and partly because of an expected trend towards more capital-intensive kinds of industrial production [. . .].

3. In certain industry-oriented plans also it would appear that ways were found to incorporate the minimum employment target into the planned structure of the industrial sector, though direct evidence of this is not as clear as in the case of plans that were oriented to agricultural or rural development. The seven-year plan of Ghana and the five-year integrated socio-economic programme for the Philippines (1963–7) may be cited as examples. In the Ghana plan the transfer of the projected additional labour force as much as possible from additional agriculture to industry was a primary objective of its declared employment policy, to be accompanied by the modernization of agriculture in order to raise its productivity. These policies are reflected in a very large contribution to planned additional employment by industry (43 per cent) and a relatively small one by agriculture (18 per cent). The Philippine integrated programme went even further. It provided for a slight absolute decline in total agricultural employment[4] and relied very heavily on the planned industrial expansion to meet its minimum employment target. Industry was counted on to provide nearly half the total number of new jobs.

The question is: How were things arranged in these two plans to enable the industrial sector to fulfil the task of employment creation assigned to it? The plans contain no clear statements in this regard. Nevertheless, from the quantitative sectoral analysis made in our earlier study some clues were obtained as to the policies implied in these two plans. First, unlike most other plans, the average investment per additional worker in the industrial sector was much less than the average per additional worker in the economy as a whole – roughly one third less in both plans. Secondly, compared with most other plans the output per additional industrial worker was low: in the Philippine five-year programme only about 14 per cent above the average for all additional workers in the economy, and in the Ghana plan even

4. In this five-year development programme the employed labour force in agriculture in the Philippines in 1967 was expected to number about 5,640,000, whereas in 1960 it was 5,800,000, according to the estimate made in IBRD (1962, supplement).

10 per cent below the average. Thirdly, of the plans examined these are the only two in which the expected percentage contribution of industry to additional output was smaller than its percentage contribution to additional employment (38 against 52 per cent in the Philippine programme and 39 against 43 per cent in the Ghana plan). These special features of the relationship between planned investment, additional output and additional employment suggest that in the programming of industrial development the planners preferred to postulate a low average level of industrial productivity in order to draw the additional labour force into the industrial sector. It would seem that small-scale industry was given a significant role in meeting the targets of industrial employment, though the plans do not contain separate estimates of the additional employment to be generated by this sector.

Adjustment at the project level

The use of more labour-intensive techniques in production in order to promote employment is favoured in a number of plans, but the way in which this is to be carried out is not always described in detail [. . .]. India's second five-year plan considers the possibilities and difficulties of their application in the production of consumer goods, and the third plan envisages their application in the construction industry, particularly in areas in which there is considerable population pressure. The second five-year plan of Pakistan likewise gives broad policy directives encouraging the use of more labour-intensive techniques. Its third five-year plan states that:

The composition of the development programme, therefore, must be geared to the employment target by making the employment effect of each project a factor in judging its acceptability. It also provides a criterion for analysing the comparative advantages of different techniques of production (Government of Pakistan, 1965).

The planners believed that if measures were adopted to enforce the maximum use of available manpower, it might be possible to exceed the target of 5·5 million new job opportunities, It is, however, emphasized in the plan that 'this would require an intensive research programme to develop non-western labour-intensive production techniques' and that it will 'require a long time before such techniques can be applied on a sufficiently large scale'.

However, of greater interest than their general policy statements regarding the use of labour-intensive production techniques are the indications as to the precise manner in which they are to be applied at the project level in various economic sectors. For example the Indian third five-year plan emphasizes that 'where mechanization does not lead to significant economies preference must be given to labour-intensive methods of construction' and that 'these considerations should be kept firmly in mind at the time of preparing project reports, and, wherever machinery is chosen in preference to men, convincing reasons should be given' (Government of India, 1961).

Again in the construction industry, the planning authorities in the Philippines, under the Emergency Employment Act of 1962, laid down the following four main criteria for the selection of projects in government-financed investment and development programmes, with a view to creating additional employment opportunities (additional, that is, to the aggregate employment target emerging from the 'normal' framework of the five-year integrated socio-economic programme):

(1) level of employment opportunity – the aim is maximum employment; (2) projects that are self-liquidating and/or revenue-producing should be given preference over those that are not; (3) economic conditions of the geographical area – preference should be given to projects in economically depressed areas; (4) side economic effects – more emphasis on projects that have greater support of the citizen or local government materially or morally (Republic of Philippines, 1962).

To facilitate proper selection of projects these criteria, in terms of five specific items, were assigned the following weights, 100 points being the maximum: employment opportunity, 40 points; revenue-producing, 30; geographical area, 10; side economic effects, 10; local support, 10. The greater the aggregate sum of points of a project, the higher its priority. For each criterion a further specific formula was given to determine the numerical value of points for the project under appraisal. Under the employment criterion, the ratio of man-days to the estimated cost of the project in thousand pesos was used as a measure in accordance with the following system of rating:

Man-days/cost ratio of 40 or above	40 points
Man-days/cost ratio of 20 to 39	30 points
Man-days/cost ratio below 20	20 points

Similar rating systems were worked out for each of the other criteria.[5]

In the first five-year plan of Turkey a system of priorities based on various criteria was likewise introduced as a means of selecting projects. Its application appears to have been extended to many different sectors. 'After careful analysis, the draft projects collected from the public sector and private

5. In an earlier development programme of the Philippines (the five-year economic and social development programme for fiscal years 1957–61) a similar priority-ordering approach was adopted for the appraisal of individual industrial projects. Employment creation was one of the four criteria to which a priority was assigned. See: Benjamin Higgins, *Economic Development* (New York, W. W. Norton, 1959), pp. 682–4.

enterprise were classified according to their order of priority within their respective sectors' (Republic of Turkey, 1964, p. 120). In determining the priority to be given to a project, employment creation was one criterion, the others being the value added by the project to the national income, its profitability and its effect on the balance of payments. The plan, however, gave no precise indication as to how the employment criterion was linked to the other criteria. It is not clear whether different weights were assigned to each or what planning techniques were used to determine the final rating of a given project after examining it according to each criterion. In another connection it was stated that priority of employment creation was given not only to projects but also to sectors. It was further stated that:

Technological developments in industry, however, are usually of a labour-saving nature. In those sectors where there is international competition, the relationship between labour intensity and costs, and the need to keep to time and quality limits in certain operations restricts the scope of the employment to be created. Priority is given in the plan to projects and sectors where labour intensity results in the desired timing and quality of production, without affecting costs (Republic of Turkey, 1964, p. 409).

The plan also gave consideration to the possibility of improving labour-intensive techniques in certain sectors, particularly construction, with a view to increasing employment.

These are some examples of ways of incorporating employment targets at the project level. In regard to the technique of embodying various criteria for project selection in a composite formula – either quantitative, as in the Philippine example, or by implication, as in the Turkish example – it is important to note that employment creation is treated as only one among several criteria and the importance attached to this criterion alone could be nullified by the combined effect of others. It would be extremely useful to ascertain to what extent additional employment has been actually created that can be traced directly to the application of this planning technique. So far, little information is available; it may also be observed that in none of the plans examined does it seem that the technique of shadow or accounting pricing of unskilled labour was applied for systematic and consistent appraisal of individual investment projects, as so frequently advocated in the literature on development planning and programming.[6]

6. In this connection, Haq (1963, pp. 42–3) suggested that 'in the case of unskilled labour, it should be legitimate to use a shadow price which is x per cent lower than the market price if unemployment is x per cent in the country', but he added that this was based on the assumption that the elasticity of demand for labour was unity, which was not necessarily correct. He pointed out that the likely increase in employment consequent on applying for planning purposes a 'shadow' wage below the actual wage level depends on the possibilities of substitution between labour and capital and on

Adjustment at the level of special programmes

In many cases, after attempts had been made to incorporate an employment target in the plan in one or other of the ways discussed above, the aggregate amount of planned additional employment that emerged still failed to reach the desired level, whether because the various possible ways were not seriously or thoroughly explored, or because of the basic constraints imposed on the plan, or because of the very high projected rates of labour force growth – or for a combination of all these reasons.

Special programmes were therefore introduced to fill the gap between the additional employment expected from the 'normal' structure of the plan and the desired employment target. In the case of Pakistan's second five-year plan the immediate aim of introducing special programmes was to achieve the minimum target of keeping pace with labour force growth; the same may be said of the programme of national development in Morocco and the works programme for fighting underdevelopment in Tunisia. In other plans the special programmes were designed to achieve a higher target: the reduction in varying degrees of existing unemployment and underemployment. This appears to be true of the special programme embodied in the Venezuelan plan, the housing programme in the Brazilian plan and, in the Philippines, the programmes established by the Emergency Employment Administration under the Emergency Employment Act of 1962, which accompanied the five-year integrated socio-economic programme.

As regards the content of the special programmes, an important difference can be discerned between those associated with the plans of the two Latin American countries and those of Asian and North African countries. In the former the special programmes appear to be primarily urban-oriented. The main component of Venezuela's special programme was the construction of housing and the improvement of the water supply system in the urban centres, coupled with a policy of withdrawing some 50,000 workers, mostly young persons, from the labour market each year for technical training. Without this special programme for urban areas the projected growth of national output resulting from the 'normal' plan alone would have been 6·7 per cent annually instead of the 8 per cent envisaged in the final enlarged plan, and at the lower rate the additional employment

---

their relative prices, and that only through the process of trial and error should the planners be able to find a satisfactory shadow price of labour. Another interesting observation he made was that, after applying a shadow price of labour, analytically it is possible to keep total profits constant by fiscal policy while increasing total wages by the full increment of output resulting from the application of the shadow price of labour without reducing the existing investible fund.

would have been just sufficient to absorb the increase in the labour force (the latter's annual rate of increase being about 3·5 per cent), owing to the high capital intensity of the 'normal' plan. In the Brazilian plan the special housing programme, designed chiefly for employment creation, was also intended for urban centres. In contrast, the special programmes associated with the plans of Asian and North African countries were mostly rurally oriented. They took the form of schemes for rural works and were designed mainly to create paid jobs for seasonally unemployed, landless agricultural labourers during the slack months and at the same time to build up the rural infrastructure essential for the expansion of agricultural and rural production. In the Indian third five-year plan and in the five-year development programme of the Philippines (1963–7) the special programmes also included rural industrialization.

[. . .] In the Indian plans the employment targets were confined to full-time new jobs, and it was probably for this reason that the targets in the third five-year plan did not include the rural works programme, which was expected to provide work for an average of only about 100 days in the year for 2·5 million persons by the final year of the plan. In the case of other plans one possible reason was that the special programmes were drawn up only after the preparation of the plan had been completed. The exclusion of the jobs generated by the emergency employment programme (estimated at 250,000 a year) from the employment figure given in the Philippines five-year integrated programme may be partly explained in this way. A more general reason, applicable to many of these plans, appears to be the reluctance of the planning authorities to announce in advance a target employment figure for the special programmes, since they represented a new venture and the anticipated results were uncertain, apart from the technical difficulties of calculation. It may have been thought preferable to take up employment target setting at a later stage when some concrete results had been achieved that could provide a basis for more precise quantitative planning. Morocco's programme of national development, for example, seems to have taken this line of approach.

It is not proposed here to discuss policy problems with respect to rural works programmes. Nevertheless, two observations may be made in this connection. First, in current thinking on employment promotion in developing countries, there is a distinct trend towards assigning a greater role to such programmes, since they not only create more direct employment – if only of a temporary nature – at a low capital cost but also contribute to the expansion of agricultural production – a laggard in economic development – and thereby provide a more permanent employment in the agricultural sector. For example, as noted earlier, Pakistan's third five-year plan intends to extend considerably the rural works programme. On the basis of this country's preliminary experience, the average capital cost for providing employment in the works programme was estimated at 600 rupees per head against an average of 5250 rupees for the second five-year plan as a whole (Government of Pakistan, June 1965). The expenditure allocated to this programme in the third plan is 2500 million rupees as compared with 800 million in the second plan (Haq, 1964, p. 124). In India the planners envisage a similar expansion of the rural works programme in the fourth plan. The main obstacle to be tackled in such schemes is lack of adequate organization (ibid. p. 123).

Secondly, in a broader perspective, rural works programmes have now come to be looked upon as only one element, however important, in the planning of integrated rural development. Meanwhile in the strategy of employment creation the emphasis is increasingly on rural development as a major intermediate solution to the employment problem especially in those developing countries where the projected rates of labour force growth are high, the initial industrial base is very low and the potential for rural development exists, as indeed it does in most of these countries. In some plans great importance is attached to community development programmes in their many variants as a means of rural development and the creation of rural employment. In the first five-year plan of Turkey, for example, it is stated that 'the effective implementation of community development programmes can prove to be one of the most important measures to help create employment outside of agriculture in rural areas and thus prevent the population from migrating to towns faster than jobs can be created for them' (Republic of Turkey, 1964, p. 96).

Inasmuch as some actual experience has already been acquired in rural works programmes and in the broader field of rural development, it may perhaps be more feasible to assess the probable increase in employment from these sources and to take this as one of the major elements in the fixing of aggregate and sectoral targets, so that a sense of proportion can be maintained over the whole range of employment planning.

Methods of estimating additional employment

In the discussion so far attention has been focused on the approaches adopted in various plans to fixing what the planners considered to be the desirable and feasible employment target. Whatever the approach, however, the numerical values of employment targets, by sector and in aggregate, depend on the methods used in making the estimates. Some plans give no indication of the methods; several contain only general or partial statements on this technical aspect of employment planning. In only a few cases is more detailed information available. However, most of the plans make it clear that the targets they give are only first approximations obtained by crude methods of calculation and based on assumptions derived from imperfect or limited empirical data.

For such meagre information as has been gathered from the plans some observations may, nevertheless, be usefully made on the methodology of estimating the employment content of a development plan.

One major variation in method concerns the treatment of additional work created by the plan for the underemployed without creating new job opportunities. Some plans (for example the Indian plans, the ten-year plan of Ceylon and the three-year plan of Brazil) limit their targets of additional employment to full-time additional jobs, wage-paid or self-employed. While the favourable effects of the plan in bringing fuller employment to the underemployed are indicated, they are not quantified.[7] In other plans (for example the Pakistan plans and the ten-year plan of the United Arab Republic) the concept of additional employment is extended to include the additional work, in terms of man-years, created for the underemployed in agriculture. This component is incorporated into the aggregate employment target. The Turkish first five-year plan treats the underemployed in agriculture slightly differently, giving a separate estimate of the total number of farmers and agricultural workers who would be provided with additional work for an assumed number of working days per year as a result of the agricultural programme. Since underemployment is a crucial element in the employment situation in most developing countries, the creation of 'additional work' for the underemployed seems as important as the creation of full-time additional jobs, when employment targets are being fixed – at least for the shorter-term plans. There appears to be great scope for improving the methods used in estimating this component.

As regards the calculation of sectoral targets of additional employment, the Italian ten-year plan (the Vanoni Plan) may be cited as an example of applying a uniform method to different sectors. In this plan, which aimed at a substantial decrease in agricultural employment, the new non-agricultural jobs were regarded as coming from three sectors: (a) industries with heavy capital requirements, (b) other industries and the handicrafts, and (c) tertiary activities. For each sector the number of new jobs to be created in the ten-year period was calculated uniformly on the basis of average capital requirements per worker and the size of planned investment in the sector. Pakistan's third five-year plan offers another example. The plan follows a uniform method for estimating the increases in both agricultural employment and non-agricultural employment over the plan period,

7. In the Indian third five-year plan, however, an estimate was made of the number of persons for whom part-time or fuller employment would be provided as a result of the development programme for the village and small-scale industries, which was included in the plan.

but it is a different method from the one used in the Italian plan: it consists in projecting additional employment on the basis of an assumed relationship between increase in output and in labour productivity.

In many other plans the quantitative targets of additional employment are arrived at by methods that differ from sector to sector. Moreover, for a given sector, the methods used often differ from plan to plan. The following illustration shows the diversity of methods used.

1. As regards the industrial sector the Indian third five-year plan used mainly capital per worker and the size of planned investment in different branches of industry as a basis for calculating additional full-time employment, whereas in the Pakistan third five-year plan and in the Turkish first five-year plan the estimates were based on the observed relations between increases in output and in labour productivity adjusted for projected changes in productivity. In the United Arab Republic's ten-year plan frame (1960–70) the volume of employment in different industries in the final year of each five-year period was calculated from the estimates of the annual wage bill and the average annual wage per worker to be paid by the industry in question in that year. The annual wage bill was obtained by dividing the estimated value added envisaged for the industry by an empirically ascertained ratio of wages to value added (adjusted for considerations of social desirability and economic feasibility), while the average annual wage was estimated after examining past trends, where data existed (ILO, 1962, p. 8). There is clearly a need for further comparative study of the advantages and limitations of these and other methods already in use and perhaps for developing more accurate methods.

2. The calculation of the additional employment to be created in the agricultural sector presents more complex problems. Apart from the question of how the fuller employment of the underemployed is treated, difficult problems arise also from such factors as the wide coverage of agricultural activities, regional differences in systems of farming and cropping, and the great variety of measures adopted for agricultural development, each with a different impact on employment. The methods used for this sector, and the degree of thoroughness with which they solve these and other problems, vary considerably from plan to plan.

The Indian third five-year plan, which limited itself to estimating full-time new jobs, used the simple method of taking a norm of four acres per person employed and multiplying this by the estimated area of land newly benefiting from irrigation, soil conservation and flood control under the plan plus land allocated to settlement schemes for landless workers. In Ceylon's ten-year plan a similar method was used for estimating the number of full-time new jobs to be created in peasant agriculture and, in addition, it provided an estimate of the additional labour force likely to be employed in plantation agriculture (tea, rubber and coconut), based on the anticipated increase in output and on the observed relationship between labour requirements and output per acre. The method used in Pakistan's third plan was based entirely on the planned increase in agricultural output and the assumed increase in labour productivity. The specific assumption was that only 35 per cent of increased agricultural production over the plan period would require additional labour input while the other 65 per cent would result from increases in labour productivity. An estimate was also made of increases in employment expected from the livestock programme based on certain assumptions regarding (a) the probable increase in demand for meat and dairy products, and (b) the amount of time devoted by farmers to the care of a given number of livestock.

A more systematic calculation of the total employment to be generated in the agricultural sector was attempted in the preparation of the United Arab Republic's ten-year plan frame. Separate estimates were made for employment in crop operations, livestock farming, fisheries and agricultural management. The method used for estimating the number of persons required for all crop operations involved the following steps (ILO, 1962, p. 6).

(a) Determination of the number of operations for each crop; (b) Assessment of the equivalent man-days required for each operation per acre for each crop; (c) Calculation of total man-days required for each area under each crop by multiplying the number of acres under each crop by the above estimates of man-days; (d) Aggregation of total man-days required for all crops; (e) Calculation of the number of persons required for all crop operations by dividing the estimated total man-days required for all crops by a norm of 195 working days per year. [. . .]

3. The methods used for estimating additional employment in the services sector appear to be the least satisfactory. In some plans employment generated in this sector was treated to a large extent as induced employment – induced, that is, by the expansion of employment in other sectors. To arrive at a quantitative target of additional employment, a ratio was applied to the total increase in employment in certain other specified sectors, as in the case of the Indian plans and the second five-year plan of Pakistan (Haq, 1963, p. 246; Government of India, 1961), the ratio used in the former being derived from a sectoral analysis of the census data. In several other plans (for example Pakistan's third five-year plan and the Turkish first five-year plan) the employment targets in services seem to have been estimated largely

from the projected output and some assumed quantitative relationship between increases in output and in labour productivity in this sector. Both magnitudes are susceptible to a wide margin of error. Such crude methods of calculation, when applied to the services sector, would tend to exaggerate the number of full-time new jobs to be created, since in most developing countries this is an overcrowded sector, in which there are considerable numbers of underemployed.

Concluding remarks

The foregoing pages have brought together, in a cursory way, some recent experience in the planning of employment objectives as reflected in the development plans. Although the actual planning processes involved are far from clear, the present survey tends to suggest that employment planning as an integral part of overall development planning is still in its infancy. One main problem is to develop effective ways and means of making the utilization of surplus labour a positive factor accelerating the pace of development. The approaches to fixing employment targets attempted in certain plans at the sectoral level, the project level or at the level of special programmes call for some kind of synthesis through more rigorous economic analysis as well as for empirical appraisal from this point of view. Another problem has to do with ways and means of improving the methods of estimating the additional employment to be created in various sectors by a development plan. As has been shown, some of the methods used are not efficient enough for planning purposes. The fixing of optimal and reliable employment targets would seem to depend much on the solution of these two problems.

References

GOVERNMENT of INDIA (1961), *Third Five-Year Plan.*
GOVERNMENT of PAKISTAN (1965), *The Third Five-Year Plan, 1965–70*, Dacca.
HAQ, M.AL (1963), *The Strategy of Economic Planning. A Case Study of Pakistan*, OUP.
HAQ, M.AL (1964), 'Problems of formulating a development strategy in Pakistan', in *Organisation for Economic Cooperation and Development: Development Plans and Programmes*, OECD.
IBRD (1962), 'Economic growth in the Philippines: a preliminary report prepared by the staff of the IBRD, 4 January 1962', in *Department of For. Affairs Rev.*, vol. 4, no. 1.
ILO (1962), *National Manpower Assessment and Planning Programmes for Economic Development: Description of Functions and Organization in Egypt*, case study no. 2, mimeo., document MED/D13, p. 8.
KOMIYA, R. (1959), 'A note on Mahalanobis' model of Indian economic planning', *Rev. Econ. Stat.*, vol. 41, no. 1.
MAHALANOBIS, P. C. (1955), 'The approach of operational research to planning in India', *Indian J. Stat.*, vol. 16, p. 26.

REPUBLIC of PHILIPPINES, (1962), 'Project appraisal', article 1, ch. 4, in *Rules and Regulations to Implement the Emergency Employment Act of 1962*, Manila.
REPUBLIC of TURKEY, (1964), *First Five-Year Development Plan, 1963–7*, Central Bank of the Republic of Turkey.

31 Dudley Seers

A Step Towards a Political Economy of Development

From D. Seers, 'A Step towards a political economy of development (illustrated by the case of Trinidad and Tobago)', *Social and Economic Studies*, vol. 18, no. 3, pp. 230–41.

[. . .] There are a number of reasons why structural unemployment tends to grow worse. One is the growth of the population of working age, which continues to rise at more than 2 per cent a year throughout the world. In the case of Trinidad this pace will slacken markedly in the late 1970s, when the fall in the birth rate in the middle of the 1960s begins to affect the numbers of school-leaving age.[1]

Secondly, the import coefficient tends to rise because of the well-known tendency for income-elasticities of demand to be high for motor cars, other consumer durables, and foreign travel, even where the income distribution is constant. This distribution may, however, well tend to become more unequal, with some incomes at the lower end rising slowly compared to the rate of increase of professional earnings, property income, salaries and modern-sector wages, if only because of the surplus population. This would reinforce the tendency of the import coefficient to rise. The expansion of television and other advertising media also creates still stronger tastes for imported consumer goods.

Thirdly, technical progress overseas, which seeps from rich to poor economies through many channels, tends to raise the productivity coefficient. Such progress can be absorbed in rich countries much more easily, because it emerges as a response to the changing pattern of the supply of the factors of production there, and 'excessively' fast labour-saving progress would be at least partially checked by the appearance of unemployment on a big scale. Modern techniques are, however, imported into *other* countries, through, for example, the subsidiaries of foreign companies, whatever the local conditions. One of the characteristics of a country which is not industrialized is that it lacks the technical and research facilities to adapt techniques to its own requirements.

It is true that imported technical progress affects only certain 'modern' sectors of an economy. But there they make possible wage increases which reduce the scope for import substitution – particularly in agriculture, where

1. The number of births declined from 34,000 in 1962 (corresponding to a birth rate of 38) to 30,000 in 1966 (a birth rate of 30).

rises in physical productivity are much slower for many institutional reasons (difficulty in obtaining capital, lower educational levels, etc.). There are, however, offsetting forces. Import substitution, despite the wage rises, can reduce the import content of certain types of expenditure. Since, however, as has been explained above, an act of import substitution requires capital goods, and since secondly it generates payments for imports of materials and for heavy outflows of profits and interest (especially if the concessions have been generous), the process of import substitution affords little net relief to the balance of payments for many decades.

Probably more important, at least in the shorter run, are two other positive influences. One is that government current spending takes a rising share of domestic expenditure; this is positive because of its rather low import content (unless there is a big or rising military component). Another is a tendency for both public and private saving to rise faster than income, making it possible for a growing share of assets to be domestically owned; this tendency could be helped by increased inequality of income distribution.

Another offsetting tendency may be for the labour participation rate to decline gradually over time, as living standards rise and a higher proportion of the population of working age is undergoing higher education or engaged solely in household management, though as yet we understand little about the forces determining this coefficient, and the reverse may well be true of more backward economies, as conventional restrictions on the employment of women are relaxed.

The other possible source of higher employment is foreign exchange receipts from exports, whether because of bigger volumes of sales, higher prices or more efficient taxation of the export sector. These receipts can also, in theory, grow quickly enough to halt the upward trend in unemployment. The experience of Trinidad, however, is evidence that this variable would have to grow at a very fast rate indeed to balance the forces which are increasing unemployment. Moreover, even if there is a fast climb in (say) the exports of petroleum, this does not solve the basic problems, but masks them, and even in certain respects aggravates them – particularly by encouraging wage increases. In any case, these mineral exports cannot rise very quickly unless the discovery of huge natural resources is at least possible, which is hardly so for most countries. In brief, therefore, employment will tend to lag behind the rise in the labour force, and chronic unemployment to grow, in a country which is economically well behind the industrial leaders, especially if it is in close enough contact to be subject to their influence in many ways. Local developments, however, such as new mineral finds, may cause this tendency to moderate at times.

The absence of a correcting mechanism

An economist naturally tends, before accepting the inevitability of increasing unemployment, to look for an *automatic* mechanism that would be called into play as unemployment rose. A neo-classical economist would expect wages to fall, as labour became surplus, attracting capital, facilitating import substitution, stimulating exports and discouraging mechanization. It is clear from the preceding section that wages did *not* fall in Trinidad; the rise in wages accelerated after unemployment reached high levels. Besides, the fall would have to be implausibly big because of negative effects via the income distribution.

There is another possible mechanism: devaluation could offset wage rises. In a mineral economy such as Trinidad (or Jamaica), currencies are not readily devalued except in response to the devaluation of an outside currency (such as sterling); this is because the rise in exports is usually fast enough to offset the effects of the wage rise on the foreign balance. It is true that in many countries, notably in the more advanced countries of Latin America, changes in wages, prices and exchange rates have been following each other in succession, checking the rise in real wages, though rarely causing a fall for any length of time. Trade unions are usually strong enough to prevent this, and, in any case, the mechanism has many inherent faults which will be considered in the next section – notably its failure to reduce unemployment.

The political constraints on employment policy in Trinidad

I have only in a very superficial sense 'explained' chronic and growing unemployment. This is like 'explaining' the spread of undernourishment in terms of declining caloric levels. The real question is why no effective policies are adopted to stop it. It would be incorrect, and in any case logically superfluous, to assume that governments are unconcerned. So the question becomes: Why did they find the elimination of unemployment so difficult? After all, in industrial countries too (as shown by the experience of the 1930s), automatic mechanisms for fully employing the labour forces are also weak; nevertheless, since the war, unemployment in these countries has been kept down, partly by deliberate policies, to levels very much lower than in Trinidad, in fact to about 3 per cent to 5 per cent of the labour force. One way of finding the real reasons for unemployment in Trinidad is first to look at the prospects that face the government, next to construct a hypothetical full employment economy, and then to ask what political restraints would prevent the government achieving it in the next few years [. . .].

Hypothetical solutions: a possible pattern of full employment

In order to probe more deeply for the reasons why solutions are not adopted or even seriously proposed, let us pose a hypothetical question: – what would happen if they *were* adopted, i.e. if the government took steps to mobilize the country's human resources within the near future, by which is meant (say) five years? The human reserves of Trinidad are considerable. Since the labour force will grow by some 16 per cent in those five years, and at most 70 per cent of it is currently being used (allowing for underemployment as well as unemployment), over 60 per cent more labour will be available in five years' time than is being used today. Actually even a 60 per cent increase in the use of labour would not entirely eliminate unemployment, because, as it dwindled, the labour participation rate would rise with, e.g. more mothers deciding to take jobs, and so also would the population of working age, with immigration from the Eastern Caribbean.[2] Moreover, there is certainly some underemployment among those 'working' for more than 32 hours a week.[3] We could assume, for the purpose of this paper, that the hypothetical full employment situation would still leave some slack. A 50 per cent rise in the use of labour over five years should nevertheless be possible; this would reduce overt unemployment very considerably.

We must now try to imagine the economy operating at (in this sense) full employment in (say) 1974. It would be a very big job to work out a full set of projections, allowing for inter-sector transactions, but the general shape of a hypothetical full employment economy is clear. The manufacturing sector would be larger, but its employment could hardly be expected to rise by 50 per cent. There would not be sufficient numbers of technicians, managers or engineers, and it is difficult to see how large enough quantities of capital could be mobilized in time. A good part would need to be attracted from abroad, and to induce foreign capital to create more labour-intensive industries at a much lower price in terms of tax concessions would require expertise in industrial policy on a scale not at present available. Indeed the very attempt to expand the economy so quickly under government initiative would discourage foreign capital. Commercial services (transport, finance and distribution) could hardly employ many more people without big rises having occurred in income in other sectors. There is certainly spare agricultural land, but the difficulties currently being experienced with the scheme for settlement on Crown Lands indicate the organizational problems which would be encountered in a big expansion of this sector. Construction – slum clearance, road-building, etc. – must therefore be the core of any policy of

2. The new Immigration Bill introduced in 1968 will, however, when enacted, reduce the possibility of such movement.
3. Because of the conventions used here, the elimination of underemployment would appear as a sharp rise in productivity.

rapid elimination of unemployment (as many governments have found in the past).

Yet this could not be sufficient. Many of the unemployed have received a good deal of education (although little or no technical instruction); among those who have completed primary education, but not reached school certificate standard, unemployment is close to 20 per cent. These expect office jobs of one kind or another and would not accept at all readily manual work, especially in the countryside, even assuming they were capable of it. (Attitudes on this question may be correlated with racial origin.) Increased output in construction, and in other sectors which produce goods, would of course create white-collar jobs, both directly and indirectly through increased use of services; but, simply in order to eliminate this type of unemployment, government services would have to rise as well. Other special measures might have to be taken to eliminate special types of unemployment.

Although it would be a somewhat fanciful description of the pattern of resource use which would emerge to call it 'optimal', we can conclude that the problem of unemployment is *physically* soluble. One is tempted by Keynes' glittering aphorism: *what is physically possible is financially possible*. But is this so? The constraint that comes immediately to mind is foreign payments. Suppose, to give us a very rough idea of the magnitude of the problem, we assume that there would be only a small rise in productivity, and that personal incomes would rise by the extent of the increase in employment, with somewhat greater increases in imports of consumer goods and in imports of materials for making such goods, and that the imports of capital goods would rise at least as fast, then the demand for imports would be more than 50 per cent higher, i.e. more than $200m above current levels. In fact it would rise more than this, because of the difficulty of expanding certain types of domestic production, especially of foodstuffs. Yet actual imports could not rise by nearly as much, on the assumptions made, and inferences drawn, above.[4]

It is not hard to visualize what would happen, especially with three decades of Latin American experience to study. The first sign of the strains involved in lowering the import coefficient would be a crisis over central bank policy. The expansion of economic activity would be halted by tighter limits on credit, especially on government borrowing, as the sinking exchange reserves approached conventional minima. It is true that the central bank could be ordered to ignore these limits. In that case, another devaluation of the exchange rate would not be long delayed. Because the supply of

4. In fact even industrial countries face more serious foreign exchange problems than Keynes realized, when they raise employment sharply.

exports is not very price-elastic,[5] the devaluation would have to be substantial, and there would be a big rise in internal prices. Purchases, especially
of imports, would rise sharply, while capital imports would fall (indeed the
export of capital would be encouraged), aggravating the foreign exchange
crisis and halting the programme of expansion.

Latin American experience shows that it is precisely in small economies
(with their greater dependence on foreign trade) that inflation can easily
become particularly violent – compare the experience of Uruguay or
Paraguay since the war with that of Brazil, for example.

Hypothetical solutions: three possible strategies

There are a number of policies which, on paper, could force down the import
coefficient sufficiently without causing an acute foreign exchange crisis.
I shall look briefly at three strategies in turn (with the diffidence due from a
British economist working well outside his own field, in terms of both
geography and discipline).

1. *Fiscal virtue.* The foreign exchange crisis and inflation might be avoided,
if tax increases were big enough. But here we begin to face the fundamental
problems of lowering the import coefficient. In the first place, taxes could
not be increased without some of the burden being borne by reduced savings
and by lowered purchases of locally produced goods and services, so the
rise in tax rates would have to be very big indeed. Unless the rise in *net*
foreign exchange receipts (allowing for the increase in profits of foreign
firms) is much greater than now seems possible, revenues would have to
rise more than $200m, i.e. almost to double. Such an increase in taxes could
hardly be achieved without hurting the wage-earner and stimulating
demands for higher wages, which would aggravate the problem of providing
employment. Moreover, it would be very hard, even if the tax increases
were designed to fall with particular severity on luxury consumption, to
avoid affecting employment, partly because domestic servants would be
dismissed, but also because the plants for making inessential consumer
goods would dismiss labour.

But, on top of these economic effects, a programme of this kind would
cause a political crisis. What would really be happening would be a reduction in the real incomes of the majority of the population in order to make
it possible to provide jobs for a minority. Would many of those affected
look on this as the necessary price to pay for political stability – indeed perhaps as the price to be paid to enjoy rising real incomes in the future?
Would they be encouraged by the press to do so? In any case, would a

5. Even the elasticity of demand for imports is lower than it would be if Trinidad
industry were less dependent on imported inputs.

foreign exchange crisis really be avoided? The political tension would hardly encourage an inflow of capital, which might well move abroad. (The 'loss of confidence' following the 1966 Finance Act is a small indication of what could happen.) For any particular government, there is not a great deal of room to manoeuvre on questions such as taxation – if it wants to continue to govern.

One variant of this theoretical route to full employment would be to raise taxes on traditional exports, which means petroleum in the case of Trinidad. It is by no means certain that the most appropriate rates of taxes have been found in countries such as Trinidad, which depend on exports of primary products (or even looked for in most of them). In some, such as Trinidad itself, the rate of taxes on company profits in general is applied, whereas it is far from obvious that the same tax rates should apply throughout all sectors.[6]

It would, however, be very rash to conclude that tax rates on exports could be raised by enough to solve this problem, without harming their expansion. For one thing, considerable expertise on the petroleum industry would be needed to judge what would be the optimal policy in this sector, and to decide what prices should be allowed for intra-company transactions in declarations of income. The result of a tax rise might well be a fall in revenue, rather than an increase. Moreover, due to the traditions of company autonomy, the government could not compel companies to maintain their output at existing levels without causing a major political crisis. Where big companies are involved, this inevitably becomes a crisis between governments too.

2. *Controlled inflation.* The Government might suppress the import co-efficient through the use of import and exchange controls instead of taxation. One difficulty is that the industrial structure that has recently emerged limits the scope of such controls: because foreign firms have been permitted, even encouraged, to establish a number of plants which do little more than assemble imported components, it is hard to check the rise in the import bill without adding to unemployment.

But the basic difficulties are more fundamental and intractable. Casting an eye on the experience of the more developed Latin American economies, one can see the consequences of the operation of a tight system of controls. The mass of excess purchasing power, which washes against the walls erected around it, places great strains on administrative capacity. Among other things, it stimulates corruption and smuggling. Could these be avoided in an

6. It is true that there are in addition royalty payments. Nevertheless, the need to keep the general rate high enough to capture a significant share of petroleum profits means rather high rates in manufacturing, and thus could be considered indirectly responsible for the generous tax exemptions.

island which is by no means geographically remote from its neighbours? In addition, the prices of domestically produced goods, especially foodstuffs, rise. Price controls could of course be used to suppress this, at the cost of burdening the administration still more, but when excess demand is very large, it is impossible to stop 'black markets' emerging. Indeed, general price rises become inevitable, leading to wage increases and further price rises. Would it be politically possible to push on towards full employment in these circumstances?

3. *The Cuban system.* The questions raised on the two former strategies point to another: could structural problems be drastically resolved by adopting central planning and comprehensive controls, including extensive nationalization, higher taxation, wage stabilization, mobilizing youth for work in the countryside, and by breaking away politically from the United States – what one can conveniently summarize as the 'Cuban solution'? The response to the word 'Cuba' is usually emotional rather than technical. Actually, however, whether such a solution is desirable is not really relevant. Although the Cuban Government did cut down heavy structural unemployment within three years of the revolution of 1959,[7] it is questionable whether this option will be open to Trinidad in the early 1970s, because a Cuban type of regime requires certain preconditions.

In the first place, a really revolutionary government needs to inherit an export industry, the sales of which can be maintained despite the loss of traditional markets. The *marketing* problem would be more severe for a petroleum exporter than for a sugar exporter (the Soviet Union absorbs the bulk of Cuba's sugar exports, but itself exports petroleum); moreover, it would be harder to *produce* (and refine) petroleum than sugar, without foreign technical personnel – and it is not easy to hire the necessary personnel, except through governments which would exact a political price of some kind.

Secondly, a regime in the western hemisphere that would be labelled 'Communist' needs to be able to rely not merely on technical support but on considerable financial (and political) help from outside to neutralize financial (and political) pressure, which could include pressures on neighbouring countries, and even those in Europe, to break off trade. Its establishment could even lead to military intervention. United States' attitudes to systems of the Cuban type are well-known, and resolutions of the Organization of American States are clear and strong, even if not precise, on this point. The smaller the country, the more essential such help would

7. By mid-1962, three and a half years after the fall of Batista, the total of wholly and partly unemployed had apparently shrunk to about 215,000 compared to over 600,000 on the eve of the revolution – respectively about 10 per cent and 30 per cent of the labour force. Official data quoted in Seers (1963).

be. Would Trinidad be able to rely on massive assistance of this type?

Finally, but most important, it is hard to imagine a Cuban system without a political organization permeating the bureaucracy, to ensure that controls are operated without corruption and to induce the public to accept the sacrifices required. An organization of this type and on this scale emerges gradually during an armed struggle with both nationalist and social objectives, involving a large section of the population, judging from historical experience (e.g. Soviet Union and China, as well as Cuba), and *only during such a struggle*. It is worth noting, parenthetically, that one country which underwent a social revolution without any of these pre-conditions being satisfied, Bolivia in 1952, lapsed into a prolonged economic, social and political crisis, which still continues. Even though the pre-conditions *were* largely fulfilled in Cuba, it has had to face considerable economic difficulties itself in the past decade.

Possible results of further increases in unemployment

The outcome of this discussion is that neither the unaided working of economic forces nor any action by the Trinidad government is likely to reduce unemployment very much in the early 1970s. Indeed, a further increase seems on balance probable. Does this mean political disaster, in some sense? One could make out a case for believing that crime and political disturbances would grow among the young men who have little hope of work, and perhaps after a while with little interest in it, especially in a country where there is evident correlation between skin colour and income. Indeed if violent crime is a signal of pre-revolutionary 'disequilibrium' (Johnson, 1966) the symptoms are already noticeable. Thus 'serious crimes reported to the police' more than doubled in the seven years between 1960 and 1967, a growth rate of more than 10 per cent a year, with 'felonious wounding' quadrupling in this period. It would be reasonable to expect that, with unemployment at the present levels, or higher, economic setbacks could easily develop into political crises.

However economists naturally tend to link political change too closely with economic trends. Many societies – Jamaica for one – are surviving much greater unemployment without disruption. It would be, moreover, possible to stimulate employment without a sharp reduction in imports (e.g. by public works), especially if petroleum revenues rose once more. There are also, of course, other social evils, and political stability depends on what is done about housing, nutrition, etc.

At some point in the growth of unemployment, however, the government might feel it had no option but to adopt 'inflationary' financial policies. The immediate result would not at first be very serious – there are all sorts of 'buffers' to stop inflation running away, such as inventories and legal or conventional limits on rises in prices, fees, etc. In fact, a moderate boost in expenditure could be for a time survived quite easily, especially if it were accompanied by higher taxation and I M F drawings, and by some tightening of controls.

In many Latin American countries, however, these developments have led to price rises which have aggravated political tensions[8] to the point where a government came to power with the objective of returning to a system which was at least partially 'open' economically, though somewhat repressive politically – what might be called the Dominican system.[9] But such a system also has preconditions, including a large and politically active military establishment, and a foreign country prepared to intervene politically and in other ways on its behalf. In any case a strategy of this type acts as a means of suppressing the symptoms, rather than of curing the disease, though it can survive for many years, even decades, where the preconditions are satisfied.

The point of this section is not, however, to predict the future state of Trinidad;[10] it is to bring out the *non-economic* factors which make a plausible economic solution hard to implement. We have seen that these include the rate of population increase, an educational system which has created a labour force difficult to mobilize, the administrative capacity of the public service, especially in mineral and industrial policy, which limits the possible range of measures, as do the power of trade unions and the position of foreign companies, the last being traceable to the influence of foreign governments. Underlying many of these obstacles is a set of tastes and attitudes, largely imported from abroad, which means that a large section of the population would rather, in the last resort, face a continuation of chronic unemployment than a reduction in their consumption of imports.

While Trinidad has been used as a case study, and the balance of emphasis might differ elsewhere (for example, in countries dependent on exports of sugar and other agricultural products), the extended framework of analysis, in political as well as economic dimensions, seems suitable for any country which exports primary products and is dependent on foreign capital. With some changes, it would be useful in other countries as well – in fact it would not be entirely inappropriate for Britain! Inadequate and irrelevant educational qualifications, and lack of interest in the jobs of social priority, are familiar everywhere. So are the administrative and political difficulties of

8. This should not be read to imply that political tensions can be contained more easily if 'orthodox' financial policies are followed in such countries (Guatemala is one object lesson which springs immediately to mind).

9. Argentina (since 1955) and Brazil (in more recent years) have formally somewhat similar politico-economic systems – as had Cuba up to 1959.

10. The above analysis would suggest in the 1970s rather frequent changes in government policies, accompanied by mild price inflation.

either raising taxes considerably or of running a policy of 'controlled inflation'. Finally, in all, apart from the United States and the Soviet Union, the development path is affected by external influences from one source or another, ranging from advice and diplomatic pressure to conditional aid and military coercion. However, each country faces a different set of political constraints, and a great deal can be learned – as is evident, perhaps, even from the brief references given above – by comparing experience with different development paths.

References

JOHNSON, C. (1966), *Revolutionary Change*, Little, Boston.
SEERS, D. (ed.) (1963), *Cuba: The Economic and Social Revolution*, Chapel Hill.

32 Hans Singer

International Policy and its Effect on Employment

From H. W. Singer, 'International policy and its effect on employment', in
R. Robinson and P. Johnston (eds.), *Prospects for Employment Opportunities in
the Nineteen Seventies*, HMSO, 1971.

[. . .] The present context of relations between richer countries and less developed countries (LDCs) has been at least consistent with a global disequilibrium in the incidence of unemployment in the two groups of countries; say 3–5 per cent in the rich countries and 20–30 per cent in the poor countries. The thesis of this paper is to suggest:

(a) That the present relations between rich and poor countries are not only *consistent with*, but also *contributory to*, this disequilibrium, with heavy persistent unemployment in the LDCs; and

(b) That reforms in the present relations of the two groups of countries are among the counter-influences which are required to improve the situation, or even to prevent it from worsening.

We shall consider the possible contribution of rich/poor countries' relations to LDC unemployment under the headings of (1) Trade; (2) Aid; (3) Private Investment; (4) Science and Technology; and (5) International Liquidity.

Trade

It is no accident that trade has been placed first. As an economist I am bound to say that the main avenue along which one would look for a major contribution to the solution of the unemployment problem in developing countries lies in trade. Traditionally, in the thinking of economists, trade has been the method by which each country exports, through the commodities produced and traded, those factors of production which it has in relative abundance, while it imports, again through commodities, those factors of which it is relatively short. For the developing countries this would mean that through trade they would find an outlet for their abundant labour, and be enabled to remedy their deficiencies in capital through imports.

Unfortunately, trade has not in fact played this major role conceptually attributed to it. But it still remains true that potentially this could be the case. The developing countries, with a good deal of support from enlightened opinion within the industrial countries as well, are putting forward in UNCTAD and elsewhere requests that their labour-intensive manufactures should be admitted to the huge markets of industrial countries on a duty-free or preferential basis. Similarly, freer access of agricultural commodities and other raw materials is also under debate. When we think of the tremendous markets involved, and the tremendous rate of expansion of international trade as a whole, in which the developing countries have so conspicuously failed to participate, one cannot help being impressed by the vast potential improvement in the employment picture of the developing countries which expanded trade could produce.

It is not easy to quantify hypothetical situations which cannot be isolated from other events and trends. However, I am going to stick my neck out and risk the guess that if the share of LDCs in world trade had been kept up since 1955 by a reduction of agricultural protectionism and trade barriers in the richer countries, the employment volume in the LDCs could be about 10 per cent higher than it is now. That would be say $82\frac{1}{2}$ per cent of the labour force instead of 75 per cent and unemployment would be $17\frac{1}{2}$ per cent instead of 25 per cent. Moreover, if this hypothetical assumption of a fully maintained share in total world trade could be projected into the future, and if world trade should continue to expand as rapidly as in the past decade, the establishment of this condition might prevent unemployment in the LDCs from rising in the next decade, even in the presence of a capital-intensive technology and a certain rapid increase in the labour force. But this is a big and extremely hopeful assumption to make. Notwithstanding favourable votes in UN bodies and acceptance of global targets which really depend upon such action, are we in the richer countries really ready for it? No doubt we could ourselves benefit in the long run by concentrating on the more sophisticated lines of production (but by the same token perpetuate global dualism and technological colonialism). But the case of aid should warn us that demonstrations of long-run advantage do not seem to be particularly compelling in eliciting from taxpayers, parliaments, civil services and politicians of richer countries any great willingness to make what looks like one-sided 'concessions' even though the sacrifice may be more readily elicited than the inconveniences of adjustment.

The trouble of course is that the burden of adjustment, if not properly handled, will tend to fall on vulnerable groups most directly in line of competition with the potential exports of the LDCs – the elderly textile worker in Lancashire, the farmer, the older more labour-intensive firms. The necessary adjustments and compensations should certainly be within the power of the richer countries, as well as being in their own interest. Nobody wants to solve the problems of the LDCs on the backs of the poorer people within the richer countries – but then we should also stop trying to solve the problems of our poorer (or simply more vocal!) sectors on the backs of the even poorer LDCs.

In this paper which deals with 'International Policies' we naturally look at the action required by the richer countries, but let us remind ourselves that the LDCs may also have to make painful and difficult adjustments in their present policies and outlook to take better advantage not only of the present, but also of any potential larger future export opportunities. This requires outward-looking policies, willingness to take risks, to study foreign markets and tastes. It takes two to export, and perhaps it takes a dash of Japanese! And the mentioning of Japan could serve as a reminder that the development of a prosperous home market base has never yet hurt a country in developing its exports as well. But there is also a counter-lesson from Latin America: the building up of a pseudo-prosperous home market under the banner of import substitution may be more of a hindrance than help in export development.

Hal B. Lary of the National Bureau of Economic Research in New York has found that the following industries stand out as particularly labour-intensive in relation both to skills ('human capital') and to physical capital: apparel and related products; leather and leather products; lumber and wood products; textile mill products; furniture and fixtures; miscellaneous manufactures; rubber and plastic products. Trade concessions in these products (which I have listed in more or less descending order of employment-intensity in terms of unskilled labour) would have particularly strong employment impact in the LDCs, and relieve wage pressures and tight labour markets in the richer countries. Is there not a ready-made agenda here for international action? If the LDCs can only provide the skills, even while lacking the physical capital, a number of other industries could be added as being employment-intensive in the LDCs: fabricated metal products; printing and publishing; electrical machinery; non-electrical machinery. This list of eleven employment-intensive industrial groups *prima facie* suited for export from the LDCs would still leave the richer countries with nine industrial classes which are both skill- and capital-intensive, and hence *prima facie* suitable for *their* exports.

The case made here for international trade concessions to the LDCs specifically directed towards employment promotion is of course additional to the more general case for trade development as a way of reducing their foreign exchange bottlenecks and speeding up their general rates of growth and investment. This more general case has been amply made in UNCTAD, the Pearson Report, and elsewhere, but by comparison perhaps not much attention has been given to how to obtain maximum employment impact through trade concessions. The scope is certainly enormous, considering that imports of labour-intensive products from the LDCs are only a small fraction of rich countries' total imports of such products, and only a fraction of that fraction when related to their total consumption of such products. Even a target of say 10 per cent of the total *increase* in the consumption of such products to be imported from the LDCs would have highly important employment impact.

But all this is 'potential', i.e. pie in the sky. Meanwhile the ugly skeleton of the scandalous international cotton 'agreement' rattles its bones to remind us of reality, and of *one* reason for 25 per cent unemployment in the LDCs! To this we should add, as equally misleading, the moderate-looking nominal tariff rates on processed and manufactured products from the LDCs which conceal the real, and much higher, effective taxes on value added by employment.

Aid

Here once again we must distinguish between the general case for additional aid, as contributing to fuller employment in the LDCs, and the specific case for adjusting the forms and methods of aid so that a given volume of aid becomes more 'employment-intensive' in its impact. The general case is no doubt valid (within certain limits and with certain qualifications): increased aid, say the achievement of the Pearson targets of 1·0 per cent and 0·7 per cent of GNP for total financial flows and public aid, would increase the rate of investment and growth, and *ceteris paribus* increase employment.[1] Improvements in the terms of aid, untying, more grants and anything that leads to more effective use of aid would have the same presumptive favourable effect on employment. The limits and qualifications mentioned include a possibility such as the following: if the additional growth and employment created by more aid are in the urban/modern sector, then the increase in the number of urban jobs created might swell the flood of migration to the cities to such an extent that unemployment, at least in its open and urban forms, could actually increase. This possibility, based on East African conditions, is inherent in Todaro's (1969, pp. 138–48) much-discussed model. Another possibility would be that the higher growth rate and investment rate in the urban/modern (and capital-intensive) sector could be accompanied by such a change in the overall *composition* of investment, by drawing complementary domestic resources out of the rural/traditional/service sector (largely labour-intensive), that overall employment is diminished rather than increased. The possibility of this applying to Colombia has been pointed out by the ILO mission under the World Employment Programme, led by Dudley Seers (ILO, 1970). However, broadly speaking, more aid, or more

1. This would be questioned by some, either on more general grounds that aid is 'bad' for LDCs, or on more specific grounds such as by Qayum (1966).

effective aid = more employment, although the conventional aid/employment ratio is almost certainly unimpressive.

How can the aid/employment ratio be improved? This is the special relationship between international aid policies and employment with which we are concerned here. Space limits us to an enumeration of changes in international aid policies which could improve the employment impact of a given volume of aid.

1. Aid is now available predominantly for the *import component* of projects, largely equipment. This puts an artificial premium, as far as the LDCs are concerned, on preferring capital-intensive projects to more labour-intensive ones, or for any given project preferring a more capital-intensive (import-intensive) to a more labour-intensive technology. Both these effects reduce (or possibly pervert) the employment effect of aid. Aid should be equally available for local expenditures on projects (including local equipment). This could be done either by giving aid as a fixed percentage of *total project costs*, whether 100 per cent or 50 per cent or 25 per cent of the total cost, or alternatively by giving aid on a programme or general budgetary basis. The Pearson Commission (1969, p. 177) has recommended that aid givers remove regulations which limit or prevent contributions to the local cost of projects, and make a greater effort to encourage local procurement wherever economically justified. This recommendation deserves full support. In particular, it is to be hoped that the multilateral aid sources will pay full attention to it; so far they have been more in the rear than in the van of the faint movement in this direction.

2. Aid is more readily available for investment in the urban/modern sector than in the rural/traditional sector. This has the dual effect of raising the overall capital/output ratios by changing the investment mix in the direction of the more capital-intensive urban/modern sector; and of intensifying rural/urban migration by increasing the rural/urban income differential and the job attractions of the towns. Both these effects tend to reduce the employment impact of aid. The aid/employment ratio could be improved (lowered) if more aid were available for the rural/traditional sector (not necessarily agricultural but inevitably much of it directly agricultural and most of it agriculture-related). Here again, we are pushing at an open door in so far as most aid programmes, especially the World Bank, have announced an intention to shift more aid into the agricultural sector, and into rural development. However, the implementation of such a policy will be more difficult than the policy-framers realize. Often the aid would have to be on a programme or budgetary basis, and channelled through local financial institutions in order to overcome the logistic difficulties of chanelling aid into a multitude of small widely dispersed projects conducted under un-

familiar and unsophisticated conditions of book-keeping, expenditure control, etc.

3. Aid is more readily available for a few large projects rather than for a variety of smaller projects. Smaller projects however are both more likely to be employment-intensive and also more likely to be found in rural or small town locations where they reduce migration to the cities and consequently urban unemployment. There is of course a certain fungibility in that external aid for large projects may release local resources for smaller-scale projects (or vice versa). This fungibility however may work in reverse if the external aid covers only a relatively small part of the total cost of the large-scale project while the rest may have to be covered from complementary local resources. The best approach would be either to channel aid through local financial institutions or to place it on a programme or budgetary basis.

It will be seen that the policy prescriptions under (a), (b), and (c) above coincide quite closely. In fact it may be said that present aid practices form an anti-employment syndrome, while the corrective measures required also form a single syndrome.

4. The employment impact of aid also suffers from a confusion within the present aid system of promoting new growth or development as distinct from promoting new development *projects*. It is a great deal easier to obtain aid for a new project rather than for the expansion of an existing project, or the repair and maintenance parts needed to keep existing projects going, or the import of raw materials required for their operation, or the additional expenditures (largely local wages) which would be needed to utilize existing plant more fully by multiple shift work. There has been some improvement particularly in the direction of providing aid for import of required raw materials, but the statement is still broadly true. As a result we have the extraordinary spectacle of scarce capital standing idle or under-utilized although no doubt deficiencies in management, income distribution, planning etc. also play a large part in this. Aid given for the more effective utilization of existing capital would nearly always be much more employment-intensive than aid given for the introduction of new capital. In fact the kind of aid here advocated would represent the best kind of intermediate technology – capital-saving yet without arousing the antagonisms conjured up by the idea of a 'different' technology.

5. Aid for the financing of public works, and especially of rural public works, is almost impossible to obtain, partly because there is no single project and partly because the expenditure involved is local. Food aid is a form of aid particularly useful for the financing of public works and labour-intensive development in general. No doubt food aid can be harmful if it depresses prices for local farmers or leads to a slackening of domestic effort

in food production. But it would be throwing out the baby with the bath water to go slow on food aid rather than administer it in such a way that it has no undesirable side effects. It is to be hoped of course that food aid, which essentially does not impose any real sacrifice on the donor of the surplus food, would be considered as additional to other aid rather than competitive with it. Perhaps for this reason it should not be counted within the 1 per cent and 0·7 per cent Pearson targets.

Private foreign investment

The present employment impact of private foreign investment is reduced by a number of factors and could be increased by changing them. A bare list must suffice here.

1. A foreign firm, particularly a multinational firm, will almost automatically fall back on the capital-intensive technology available to it internally through the research products, know-how, patents, etc. of the head office or parent company.

2. A foreign firm will not wish to be troubled with the incomprehensible and politically-charged problems of handling large masses of local labour, deciding who should be employed and who should be refused employment, etc. The employment of capital is the line of least resistance.

3. A foreign firm will be faced with a demand for wages much higher than the prevailing local labour situation and the resource endowment of the country would justify. To push up wages against foreign firms is almost a patriotic duty, and will understandably be supported by the local government as one way of keeping the money in the country and reducing the repatriation of profits.

4. Where one of the original motives of the foreign investment was to use the local subsidiary or licensing agreement as a foothold for selling equipment, spare parts, operational raw material, etc. the provision of secondary local employment by ordering locally will be absent or greatly reduced.

This is by no means a full list, and no doubt there are also countervailing factors at work – including deliberate policies of a number of foreign firms – but it will help to indicate some of the changes in foreign investment policies which might be needed if we are to increase its impact on local employment.

Science and technology

Although problems of science and technology are less discussed (at least by economists and politicians) than trade, aid or investment, in fact this is the area in which the rich countries have perhaps the most powerful impact – for better or worse – on employment in the LDCs. The dominant fact of international life is that it is the richer countries, with one third or less of the world's population, which account for 99 per cent of the world's scientific and technological innovation. Admittedly, R & D expenditures (on which the 99 per cent figure is based) is a less than satisfactory input proxy for the output of innovation, and in addition it covers only one segment of the relevant inputs; but it is the best we have. In some ways, it even understates the dominance of the richer countries: such is this dominance that even the R & D expenditures of the LDCs are largely devoted to making a marginal contribution towards 'extending the frontiers of knowledge', in ways and in directions automatically determined by the conditions and factor proportions of the richer countries.

In the Sussex Manifesto – prepared by a group of consultants to the UN Advisory Committee on Science and Technology meeting at the University of Sussex (Reading 28) we described this phenomenon as the 'internal brain drain', and as perhaps more important and dangerous to the LDCs than the external brain drain (visible geographical movement of highly qualified people) which has attracted so much more attention. It is on account of this internal brain drain as well as on account of the low efficiency of small and scattered R & D expenditures without adequate infrastructure and equipment (also discussed in the Sussex Manifesto), that one must be rather sceptical of the value of any targets of increasing the local R & D expenditures of LDCs from 0·2 per cent of their GNP to 0·5 per cent or any other figure, when such proposals are made in isolation.

It is only within the context of planned global change in the composition and direction of scientific and technological progress that such a target assumes a constructive meaning. And it is again because of the dominance of rich-country technology which not only dominates the R & D inputs and controls the R & D infrastructure, but also sets the tone and determines what is considered as 'progress' or 'modern' or 'efficient' even within the LDCs – however contrary to their true interests – that any such planned global change must include a restructuring of the R & D priorities within the richer countries. It is they who must re-define what constitutes 'progress' and where the 'frontiers of knowledge' lie. This they must do in such a way as to include more of the things which are useful to the LDCs (production on a smaller scale, simpler product design, tropical product improvement, protein foods for young children, etc.), and fewer of the things which are directly harmful to them (certain developments in synthetics, automation, machinery with extremely high repair and maintenance requirements, etc.), The target of the Pearson Report that the richer countries should shift $2\frac{1}{2}$ per cent of their R & D expenditures in this direction is an important, if modest, beginning.

For the purposes of our present discussion it should be noted that any such change in direction would be bound to give much higher priority to employment intensity, capital-saving and reduction of sophisticated skill requirements in operation, maintenance, etc. And let us not hear too much of the old *canard* that capital-intensity is good for LDCs because it economizes in skills. All the evidence is to the contrary; and the landscape of the LDCs is strewn with the evidence of this fallacy in the form of underutilized, broken down, idle, high-cost 'modern' capital equipment.

Hopefully in later years those after us will shake their heads incredulously at how we set about this business. We take technologists and other experts involved away from their familiar environment and drop them in another country (usually with insufficient briefing), leave them to find houses to live in and schools for their children, to find local counterparts, to find their ways in unfamiliar surroundings, and all too often whisk them back just when they become effective. If this reads like a parody, few with experience would deny that it contains elements of truth.

Surely, the first step in a global partnership must be to use the wonderful and dreadful machinery of science and technology where it is and where it can operate most effectively, and realize its potential blessing for world economic development. The sending of experts abroad and the building up of an indigenous scientific and technological capacity within the LDCs must take place simultaneously, and in alignment with a change of direction of progress within the dominant richer countries. The $2\frac{1}{2}$ per cent suggested by the Pearson Report is less than one twentieth of what is now spent on military, space and atomic technology, less than what the richer countries will have added to their R & D expenditures between the June day in 1970 when this is written and the end of the same year.

And once again, as with trade and aid, the thinking within the LDCs will have to change as much as the thinking in the richer countries. Feasibility studies of projects will have to be based on spectra of technology and on pricing systems which reflect the real resources and needs of the LDCs. At present, any such movement is only too easily resisted as evidence of technological colonialism, on the grounds that the LDCs are permanently to be fobbed off with an inferior second-class technology. Tragically, exactly the opposite is true: the present dominance of a technology appropriate for the rich countries, a dominance obtaining within the LDCs no less than without, ensures a continued handicap for the LDCs. The present rates of population increase, the present capital-intensive trend of technology, and productive full employment are three things which simply cannot co-exist. Something has to give – and at present it is employment.

International liquidity

Here, of course, attention should be paid to the great step forward taken by the world community by the creation of the Special Drawing Rights. A little of that progress has rubbed off on development even at present, in that the LDCs, contrary to the original intentions, at least participate in the SDRs to the extent of their IMF quotas. Perhaps more important is the widespread conviction which has emerged that now that the SDRs have been safely – and one hopes irrevocably – established, their potential for world development can be safely utilized without damage to their original and primary purpose. The technique for doing this is less important than the decision itself, although the opportunity to strengthen multilateral channels seems too good to miss – killing three birds with one stone!

The balance of payments objection to increased aid to the LDCs was never too convincing, except possibly as a question of re-distributing the overall burden of aid among the richer countries. It could always be pointed out that as long as the LDCs did not use aid to increase their foreign exchange reserves – and with exceptions the main criticism of their policies was exactly the opposite – there was never a valid balance of payments argument against increases in overall aid. Now, with the creation of the SDRs we can go a step further. The richer countries, taken together, will not only not have a balance of payments deficit, but they will in fact have a positive balance of payments surplus. The case for linking this new progress in international relations with a step forward in development assistance seems very strong – but what better direction than to link this even more specifically with the objective of providing constructive employment for the young in the LDCs?

References

ILO (1970), *Towards Full Employment*, Geneva, ILO.
PEARSON COMMISSION (1969), *Partners in Development*, Praeger.
QAYUM, A. (1966), Long-term economic criteria for foreign loans', *Econ. J.*, vol. 76, pp. 358–69.
TODARO, M. (1969), 'A model of labour migration and urban unemployment in less developed countries', *Amer. econ. Rev.*, vol. 59, pp. 138–48.

Author Index

Subject Index

Abortion, 90–92
Adjustment mechanism, 16, 21
Administration, lower levels of, 201
Adult education, 197, 198, 209
Advertising, 19
Africa, 17
  associations of unemployed in,
    129–31
  educated unemployment in, 189
  employment on railways in, 311–12
  employment trends in, 78–80, 112
  increased urban population in, 94, 106
  industrialization process in, 94–5
  social security in, 106, 110–11
  traditional social organization in, 124
  urban unemployed of, 115
Africanization, 154
Age distribution, 83–4, 87, 99
'Aggregate demand unemployment', 61
Agricultural development, 250, 389
Agricultural earnings, 96–7, 225
  growth of, 159
  opportunities for, 111
Agricultural employment, 184
Agricultural exports, 252, 414
  see also Export crop
Agricultural households, 217–18, 220
Agricultural involution, 214, 238, 241,
  243
Agriculturalists, 193
Agricultural labour force
  in Cuba, 256–7, 261–2
  employment of, 250
  income distribution in, 37
Agricultural labour households,
  120–21, 221, 250
Agricultural management, 399
Agricultural prices, 20, 110, 113
Agricultural production, output, 19,
  213, 242, 346
  diversification of, 250, 251, 257, 258
  expansion of, 264, 395, 399
  incentives, 145
  techniques of, 261, 262
Agricultural protectionism, 414
Agricultural reform, 198

Agricultural sector, 324, 398
Agricultural statistics, 241
Agricultural wage labour, 221, 235,
  256–8, 395
'Agricultural workers', 255–6
Agriculture
  average annual working hours,
    218–20, 224
  changes of attitude to, 363
  expansion of, 106
  income distribution in, 135
  labour-intensive, 214, 244, 246
  mechanization and modernization of,
    18, 19, 149, 259, 358, 390
  productive employment in, 214
  profitability of, 113
  seasonal fluctuations in, 36, 225, 232,
    258
    see also Peak period labour demand
  self-employment in, 183, 184
  state sector of, 257, 259
  technical problems in, 259
  traditional, 214
  trends in, 80–81
Aid, 416–19, 422
  employment impact of, 418
  programme or budgetary basis of,
    417–18
Aid/employment ratio, 417
Albania, birth rate in, 91
Alienation, 199
Anti-rural bias, 198
Apathy, 85
Application rates, 204
Apprentice training schools, 338
Architects, 184, 193
Argentina, 203, 271–2
Asia
  agricultural employment in, 80
  educated unemployment in, 195, 197,
    199
  employment trends in, 78–9
Association-based networks, 127–9
Attitude surveys, 204
Attitudes to work, 55, 57, 196, 197–8,
  200, 210

in West Africa, 269
see also Cuba
Diet, 34, 119
see also Food
Direct allocation process, 147
Diseases, debilitating, 11, 26, 62
Disequilibrium, 410, 413
Disguised underemployment, 34, 38,
  343
Disguised unemployment, 26, 30, 51,
  55, 146, 300
 in agriculture, 213, 343
 in Colombia, 30–32, 39
 in Cuba, 249, 254
 in India, 209
Disposable income, 143
Distribution, 297, 320
Doctors, 198
Documentation centres, 336
Dominican system, 411
Dropouts, 197
Dry-crop cultivation, 243
Dual economy, 138, 238, 240, 323
Dutch colonial economy, 238–9, 247
Dutch East India Company, 239

East Africa, 106, 112–13, 157, 164, 335
East African Common Market, 335
East African Railways, 311
East African Royal Commission, 111
East Indian agricultural products, 238
Eckaus–Blaug approach, 15–16
Economic analysis, 21, 23
Economic and social environment for
  technology, 327
Economic choice, 262
Economic Commission for Latin
  America, 270, 275
Economic development, 72, 83, 106,
  267, 270, 341
Economic growth, 303
Economic policy, 89, 116, 156, 322
Educated population, 17, 22
Educated unemployment, 27, 44, 47–8
  188–9, 358, 406
 in Asia, 57, 195, 197

and government services, 288
practical reform of, 200–201
see also Ceylon; India
Educated young, 10, 40, 94, 96
Education, 37, 57, 84, 97, 125, 300
 consumption benefits of, 208
 in Cuba, 254, 264
 expansion of, 10, 18, 73
 and unemployment, 47–8, 52, 180
 Western, 68
Educational aspirations, 186
Educational development, 186
Educational levels, 176–81
Educational objectives, 209
Educational opportunities, 132, 209
Educational planners, 193
Educational policy, 172, 210–11
Educational qualifications, 210, 411
Educational system, 193, 196, 201
Educational and training facilities, 323
Egypt *see* United Arab Republic
Elasticity of labour supply, 235–6
Elasticity of migration response, 99
Employers' Federation, 184
Employment, 22, 26, 27, 29, 100, 141
 additional, 396–400
 conditions of, 110–112
 distribution of, 79, 80
 future, 377, 379
 growth, 12, 14, 16, 22, 157, 169, 378,
  381
 level of, 369
 maximization, 367–8, 370, 376,
  379–80, 382, 420
 and productivity, 308–12
 qualifications for, 184–5, 192, 201, 210
 see also Industrial employment;
  Urban employment; Wage
  employment
Employment creation, 393, 395, 396
Employment Exchange, 129, 130
Employment growth projections, 78,
  80–81
Employment opportunities
 see Work opportunities
Employment planning, 388, 400

Employment policies, strategy, 59, 137, 142, 185, 268, 353, 363
Employment structures, 27, 192, 254
Employment targets, 385–400
 feasible, 396
 at project level, 391–3
 at sectoral level, 387–91
 at special programme level, 394–6
Engineering colleges, 205
Engineers, 173, 184, 193, 198, 204, 210
Environmental conditions, 358
Equilibrium prices, 145–6
Estate economy, 238, 240, 242
Excess purchasing power, 408
Exchange rates, 20, 144–6
Expatriates, 163, 338
Expected income, 13, 98
Export capacity, 252, 254
Export crop, 241, 246, 389
Export earnings, 157–8, 252, 360
Exports, 18, 151, 264, 403, 404, 409
Export sector, 157
Extension services, 337

Factor endowment, 144–5, 146, 148, 150, 274, 282, 286, 419
Factor price differentials, 294
Factor price disequilibrium, 12, 15, 20, 117, 148, 316
Factor prices, 16, 116, 315
Factor utilization, 145
Factory consumer goods, 388
Factory legislation, 338
Family
 extended, 109, 294, 295, 371
 joint, 207, 210
 nuclear, 10, 109
Family labour, 249, 290, 292, 294–6, 300
Family network, 125, 127
Family planning, 72, 89
family solidarity, 125
Family support, 207
 see also Relatives
Family-unit agriculture, 239, 245
Farmers, 254

Farmers Party, Nigeria, 133
Farm labourers, 225, 235
 see also Agricultural wage labour
Farm sector, 97, 154–5
Feasibility studies, 421
Fertility rates, 83–8, 91
Fieldwork, 219–20
Fiscal policies, 142, 156, 168
 see also Taxation; Tax concessions
Fisheries, 399
Flood control, 398
Food, 119, 140, 418–19
Food proteins, 333, 420
'Forced savings', 84, 380
Foreign aid policies, 64, 65, 148
Foreign capital, 65, 258, 405
Foreign companies, 402, 411
Foreign control, 18, 246
Foreign exchange, 140, 328, 331, 403, 422
 crisis, 406–8
 shortage of, 175, 365, 415
Foreign imports, 158
Foreign industrial licences, 139
Foreign inputs, 140
Foreign payments, 406
Foreign technicians, 409
Foreign travel, 141
Formal employment see Wage employment
Formal qualifications, 184, 192
Formal sector, 69, 73
France, 89, 91, 274
Fringe benefits, 156, 162, 183, 184, 349
Frustration, 12, 29
Full employment pattern, 405–7
Full employment strategy, 140, 364
Fundamental reform, 9

Gandhi, M. K., 200
Gandhi solution, 370–71
GATT, 338
Germany, 274
Ghana, 66–7, 73, 310, 390–91
Government
 concepts, 192

Income tax, 134, 156
Income transfers, 295, 297
India, 17, 85, 115, 173, 213, 323, 337
  construction in, 351–2
  cotton weaving industry, 277–8, 336
  educated unemployment in, 49, 189,
    197, 200, 203–7, 210
  educational expenditure in, 208–9
  Five-year plans, 197, 205, 208, 337,
    387, 391, 395, 397–8
  industrialization of, 270, 272, 274
  manpower forecasting in, 209–10
  population policy in, 87, 88, 91–2
  poverty in, 119–23
  rural works programme in, 396
  unemployment in, 196, 199, 302
Indian Education Commission, 189,
  209–10
Individual achievements, 124
Indonesia, 85, 196, 199
  see also Java
Industrial capacity, 268
Industrial Court, 162
Industrial development, 128, 145, 250,
  252, 264, 342
Industrial economy, 190
Industrial employment, 51, 267,
  269–70, 272, 389
  growth of, 19, 270–71
Industrial growth programmes,
  250–51, 343, 390
Industrialization, 272, 389
Industrialization strategy, 269
Industrialized countries, 22, 26,
  189–90
Industrial production, 341, 346, 390
Industrial sector, 144, 191, 242, 372,
  390
Industrial structure, 328
Industry, 18, 78–80, 296, 338, 344–5
  capital-intensive, 316, 397
  employment trends in, 80–81
  local, 36, 336
  rural, 38
Inexperienced workers, 44, 50
Inflation, 14, 145, 153, 158–9, 321, 378

controlled, 408–9, 410, 412
  in Latin America, 407
  in UAR, 218, 230, 233
Informal activity see Self-employment
Informal communication network, 359
'Informal economy', 69, 70
Informal sector, 27, 73
  see also Traditional sector
Information, role of, 73, 339
Information centres, 336
Initiation rite, 108–9
Institute of Development Studies, 23
Institute of National Planning (INP),
  Cairo, 217, 234
Institutions, 11, 17, 55, 57
Integrated economy, 246
Integrated employment planning, 363
Interest groups, 20–21
Interest rates, 64, 144–5, 146, 152, 330,
  336
Intermediate Technology
  Development Group, 315, 334
International corporations, 19, 20
International cotton agreement, 416
International Labour Organization
  (ILO), 217, 234, 276, 337–8, 352
International liquidity, 421–2
International policies, 415
Investment, 264, 381, 385–7, 389, 390
  private, 167, 208, 419
  public, 142
  in urban areas, 257
Investment decisions, 322, 331
Investment goods, 388
Investment opportunities, 324
Investment programmes, 253, 323
Investment target, 386
Ireland, 42
Irrigation, 344, 398
  in Cuba, 259, 260, 264
  in Java, 223, 236, 239, 241, 243
Italy, 88, 397

Jamaica, 353, 404, 410
Japan
  agricultural labour force of, 244, 245

and capital cost, 368, 370
and employment, 308, 378, 381, 386, 391
machine-paced, 150, 333
Labour legislation, 32, 57, 176
Labour market, 16, 21–2, 59–60
and income opportunities, 69–70
mechanisms, 192
Labour productivity, 59, 264, 275, 323, 325, 352, 380, 386
decline of, 346
growth of, 86, 191, 331, 399
and technical progress, 381–2
Labour requirements, 219, 225, 260
Labour-saving equipment, 335
Labour-saving innovations, 350, 351 353
Labour-saving techniques, 64, 264, 275, 308, 333, 393
Labour shortage, 14, 18–19, 214, 249, 345
Labour substitution, 344
Labour supply, 11, 21, 25, 161, 235, 253, 262
Labour-tax system, 239
Labour transfer, 12–13, 14, 15, 299
Labour turnover, decline in, 112
Labour-using innovations, 150
Labour utilization, 55, 59–60, 345, 405
Land, 259, 405
scarcity of, 75, 111, 120
under-utilized, 250, 257
Land development, 390
Land-intensive development, 144
Landless, 120–21, 221, 395
Land ownership or tenure, 19, 36, 40, 113
inequalities in, 11, 17, 18
Land–population ratio, 343
Land reform, 60, 214
Land taxation, 246
Land tenure systems, 244
Large-scale production or industry, 320, 368, 389
Latin America, 404, 406

educated unemployment in, 189
employment trends in, 78–80
industrialization in, 269–70, 272
Learning by working, 376
Level of Living, 56, 85
Lewis–Fei–Ranis model, 12, 14–16
Linear programming, 388
Livestock farming, 160, 399
Long-established designs, 334–5
Lower-quality products, 335
Low-productivity working, 51
Luxury consumption, 407

Machine tools, machine building, 328–9
Major national objectives, 357
Malaya, 49, 389–90
Management deficiencies, 418
Management training, 337
Managerial skills, 327
Man-days/cost ratio, 392
Man/land ratio, 85, 390
Manpower displacement, 276
Manpower requirements, 193, 204, 210, 338
Manpower utilization, 391
Manual work, 196, 197–8, 200, 204, 363, 406
Manufacturing productivity, 348
Manufacturing sector, 168, 269–70, 285–6, 405
earnings in, 296, 351
employment in, 306–7, 308
see also Modern sector
Manufacturing system, 246
Marginal income, 26, 62
Market distortions, 11
Market intervention, 19–20
Market liberalization, 146
Market mechanism, 147
Market prices, 145
Market problems, 409
Market research surveys, 338
Mass communications, 18
Mass education, 87
Material usage standards, 320, 330

in Colombia, 35–9
in Egypt *see* United Arab Republic
seasonal fluctuations in, 36, 39
Rural industrialization, 395
Rural sector, 13, 289–90
Rural security, 111, 113
Rural unemployment, 19, 21, 225
Rural–urban migration, 38, 39, 72–3,
  75, 416, 417
in Africa, 94, 96–9
models of, 96–8, 100–104
Rural wages, 229–34, 235
differentials, 230–33, 235
increase of, 234
Rural works programme, 385, 394,
  395–6

Safety regulations, 338
Salariat, 155, 165
Salaries, 164–7, 169
Salaries policy, 163–7
Salary adjustments, 173
Salary differentials, 204
Sample surveys, 32, 42–3, 51
Savings, 109, 134, 140–42, 145, 152,
  389, 403
ratio, 378–9, 380
reduction in, 407
total personal, 141
Sawah ecosystem, 238, 241–3
Scarce resources, 371
Scholarship finance, 208
School enrolment, 186–7, 197
School fees, 210
Science and technology, 354–5, 357,
  360, 419–21
Scientific institutions, 355, 361
Scientific principles, 358
'Scientific socialism', 89
Scientific and technological capacity,
  421
Scientific and technological services
  expenditure, 354
Scientific workers, demand for, 357
Seasonal employment patterns, 225–8
Secondary education, 204

Secondary school leavers, 17, 49, **171**,
  195, 203, 205
Second-hand machinery, 334
Security, 182, 183
Self-employment, 10, 32, 182–3, 184
earnings in, 298
hours of work in, 62–3
opportunities for, 25, 62, 66–7
by sectors, 291
in services, 288, 289–95, 297, 300
Semi-proletarians, 254–5, 256
Services, 78–80, 267, 308, 315, 405
demand for, 302
job trends in, 80–81, 306
modern, 288–9, 290, 294, 297, 300
traditional, 288–9, 294, 297, 300
Services sector, 18, 283–4, 285,
  399–400
in Colombia, 35
in Cuba, 253
definition of, 287
in Kenya, 157, 168
labour absorption in, 289
in Philippines *see* Philippines
in Taiwan *see* Taiwan
Settlement schemes for landless
  workers, 398
Sex structure of urban unemployed,
  45–7
'Shadow' price of labour, 100, 393
'Short time' working, 32
Simultaneous development, 343–4
Skilled manpower, 138, 163, 190
local, 163–4, 165
price of, 164
as production factor, 279–80
scarcity of, 253, 277, 279
Skill-intensive development, 65, 144
Skill requirements, 338
Skills, 11, 333
Smallholdings, 108
Small-scale enterprise or industry, 64,
  152, 327–8, 337, 344, 368, 388–90
Social benefits, 176
Social and economic reform, 90
Social insurance, 111

Unemployment crisis', 63, 64
Unemployment gap, 14
Unemployment insurance, 295
Unemployment rate, 99
Unemployment relief, 371
Unemployment statistics, 191
United Arab Republic, 397–9
  capital accumulation in, 323
  educated unemployment in, 188–9,
    203
  industrialization, 270
  Land Reform, 230
  productivity of capital in, 328
  rural employment survey, 213,
    217–36
Upper Egypt and Delta region, 223–5,
  234, 235
United Kingdom, 91, 107, 332
United Nations
  Advisory Committee on the
    Application of Science and
    Technology to Development, 332,
    358, 420
  Centre for Industrial Development,
    323
  Second Development decade, 25, 316
  Special Fund, 332
  UNCTAD, 338, 414, 415
  UNESCO programmes, 337
  World Plan of Action, 316–17
University of the Andes
  Research Centre for Economic
    Development, 32
University graduates, 17, 171, 188–9,
  195
University of Sussex, 23
Unskilled labour, 138, 151, 159, 190,
  276, 280
  wages of, 154–5
Urban drift, 146
Urban employees and rural income,
  111
Urban employment, 267
Urban growth, 106–7
Urbanization, 289–90
Urban labour force, 102

composition of, 303
demand for, 305–8
growth of, 99, 107, 302, 303–5
Urban population
  growth of, 17, 94, 302
  illiterate, 44, 47, 49
Urban–rural income differential,
  96–9, 102, 146, 184, 303
  in Kenya, 154–5, 156–7, 163
Urban–rural income stream, 100–101
Urban standards of living, 73, 111, 122
Urban unemployed, 124
Urban unemployment, 21, 26, 45–7,
  75, 95–6, 113
Urban work opportunities, 30–34, 95,
  146

Value added, 308, 309, 332, 346, 348,
  393, 398, 416
Vanoni Plan, 397
Venezuela, 394
Village artisans, 121
Village social systems, 245
Vocational guidance, 188, 337
Voluntary parenthood, 89–90

Wage bill, annual, 398
Wage control, 158, 165, 169
Wage cost, 370
Wage differentials, 73, 98, 305
Wage distortion, 146
Wage employment, 62–3, 66–7, 109,
  300
  in agriculture, 121
  growth of, 172
  probability of, 98
  reliability of, 69, 73, 113
  by sectors, 291
  in service sector, 289–95
'Wage-gap', 294
Wage levels, 73, 116, 369, 380
Wage negotiations, 161–2, 169
Wage rate increases, 145, 157–8, 160,
  162, 169, 348–9, 379, 409
Wage rates, 20, 30, 330, 378
  urban, 96, 110, 112–13
Wages, 21, 52, 112, 402–404, 419

Wage and salary differentials, 176, 178, 183–5
Wage and salary structure, 183–5, 192
Wages Council, 162
Wage-sharing, 371
Wages policy, 159–62, 168
Wage structure, 161
Wage-technique relation, 350
Water conservation work, 345
Water supply system, 394
Weather, 18
Weighting, 373, 392
  differential, 374
  distribution, 373–5
  time, 375–81
West Africa, 324
Western consumer goods economy, 64
Western-educated elite, 64
West Indies, 62
Wet-rice cultivation, 183, 214, 238, 241, 243, 244, 246
White-collar jobs, 25, 51, 197, 204, 406
  in Ceylon, 172, 181–2, 184
  in Ghana, 68, 69
William I, 238
Woman, 57, 91, 292, 345
  agricultural work of, 220, 234–5
  educated unemployment among, 180–81, 203
  participation rates of, 55, 58, 177, 218, 224, 403
  rural wages of, 229–32, 235–6
  temporary work of, 218, 223, 229
Working time rate, 56, 58
Work opportunities, 14, 16, 338, 376–7, 381, 392
  adjustments in, 176
  creation of, 249, 261–2, 387, 397
  decline in, 115, 196
  differences in, 73

for the educated, 204
formal and informal, 66–8
growth of, 18, 153, 157, 158–9, 172, 321
and income distribution, 141
in India, 120
in modern sector, 94–5
rural, 372
search for, 172
shortage of, 9, 11, 25, 29, 36–7, 115
structural imbalance of, 11, 171, 175–6, 181
Work-sharing, 19, 51, 296, 297
Work-spreading, 60
World Bank, 338, 417
World commodity prices, 239
World consumption and trade, 359
World depression 1930s, 9, 11, 26
World economic development, 421
World Employment Programme, Report on, 75, 81, 416
World food problem, 89
World labour force, 71, 76–7, 80–81
World Population Conference, Rome 1954, 90
World scientific effort, 357
World scientific knowledge, access to, 359–60
World technology, access to, 359–60
World trade, 26
World urban population, 72
Written warning of arrival, 126

Young bachelors, 110
Young unemployed, 39–40, 44, 50, 53
'Youth wings', 129

Zambia, 311
Zero marginal productivity, 213, 217, 220, 235

Acknowledgements

For permission to reproduce the Readings in this volume,
acknowledgement is made to the following:

1 International Labour Office
2 OECD Paris
3 *European Journal of Sociology*
4 Center for Developing Area Studies, McGill University
5 Institute of Development Studies, University of Sussex
6 International Labour Office
7 Twentieth Century Fund
8 International Labour Office
9 International Labour Office
10 *Economic and Political Weekly*
11 *Civilisations*; Sage Publications Inc.
12 International Labour Office
13 Vikas Publications
14 University of Dar Es Salaam and the author
15 International Labour Office
16 Oxford University Press Inc.
17 Twentieth Century Fund
18 Penguin Books Ltd
19 American Economic Association
20 University of California Press
21 HMSO
22 *Quarterly Journal of Economics*
23 International Labour Office
24 The Clarendon Press
25 International Labour Office
26 Edinburgh University Press
27 International Labour Office
28 United Nations
29 HMSO
30 International Labour Office
31 *Social and Economic Studies*
32 HMSO